Practical SharePoint Framework (SPFx) Development

Build modern, scalable, and efficient business solutions for SharePoint and Microsoft 365

Franck Cornu

Anoop T.

‹packt›

Practical SharePoint Framework (SPFx) Development

Portfolio Director: Pavan Ramchandani
Program Manager: Divij Kotian
Content Engineer: Rounak Kulkarni
Technical Editor: Vidhisha Patidar
Copy Editor: Safis Editing
Proofreader: Rounak Kulkarni
Indexer: Tejal Soni
Production Designer: Aparna Bhagat
Relationship Lead: Mohd Riyan Khan
Growth Lead: Nivedita Singh

First published: June 2025

Production reference: 3111125

Published by Packt Publishing Ltd.
Grosvenor House
11 St Paul's Square
Birmingham
B3 1RB, UK.

ISBN 978-1-83546-678-0

www.packtpub.com

I dedicate this book to my beloved wife, Anahite, and my two wonderful children, Noan and Daria, whose unwavering support and inspiration continually motivate me.

-Franck C.

To my beloved parents, Rekha and Shivarao, whose unwavering love and guidance have shaped my life and dreams. To my sister, Arpita, for her endless encouragement and belief in me. And to my wonderful wife, Daya, for being my rock and my greatest inspiration on this journey together.

– Anoop T.

Foreword

Anoop T. and Franck Cornu have been closely involved in the journey of the **SharePoint Framework** (**SPFx**) since the early dawn of this technology, which has transformed and modernized SharePoint and Microsoft 365 extensibility in recent years. This is not just about technology, but also about the power of open source and community initiatives to influence the modernization of the product.

I was personally involved with the creation of the first public version of SPFx, which was initially released to preview status back in May 2016 as part of the announcement of the so-called "Future of SharePoint." This was a fundamental shift away from the experiences and technology that SharePoint had been using on-premises.

Modern SharePoint meant a cloud-first approach focused on building out-of-the-box experiences, but more importantly, also a cloud-first approach to build extensibility for SharePoint Online, and further, across Microsoft 365. As I'm writing this, SPFx has been generally available for more than 8 years, with tens of millions of monthly active users of custom extensibility built by our customers and partners. During these years, there have been more than 25 public releases, and usage is still growing rapidly across Microsoft 365.

SPFx introduced a completely new way to build experiences to Microsoft 365, with web stack tooling, building the model on industry standards and moving away from proprietary technologies for extensibility. This also means that anyone with previous web stack development experience can easily extend SharePoint and Microsoft 365 without a need to learn product-specific programming patterns. They can simply use, for example, React as their chosen framework and build with the standard HTTP exposed API surface, as with other similar SaaS products.

This transition was not just about technology, but at Microsoft, we also focused on building an active open source community to help drive the adoption of this shift. Both Franck and Anoop have been active people as part of this amazing community for years, and they are great people to share their learnings from their day-to-day work, and from the community side, with others. It's the "best community in tech" to learn from others.

This book does a great job of explaining how to get started with SPFx, but also, more importantly, learning the recommended patterns to build your experiences within Microsoft 365 using SPFx. There are great real-world examples and code, which will help you to be successful in creating your solutions.

Whether you are a new developer familiar with the SharePoint Framework or a professional developer with previous experience, *Practical SharePoint Framework (SPFx) Development* offers something for everyone.

I'm hoping to see you involved in our open source and community efforts in sharing what you've built.

Sharing is caring!

Vesa Juvonen

Principal Product Manager, Microsoft

Contributors

About the authors

Franck Cornu is a Microsoft 365 developer, Microsoft MVP, and international speaker who has worked with Microsoft technologies for more than 15 years. He started in 2010 as a SharePoint consultant implementing solutions with MOSS 2007 and WSS 3.0. Since then, he has had the opportunity to work for several companies in many fields, especially around intranet and search topics, giving him a very good understanding of Microsoft technologies' usage.

A conference speaker since 2013 and the author of several SharePoint white papers and eBooks over the years, he is also very involved in the open source community through the Microsoft 365 & Power Platform community, formerly known as **Pattern and Practices (PnP)** initiative. He is the original author of the PnP Modern Search solution, one of the most used SharePoint Framework open source solutions in the world. He also created the "PnP Modern Search Core Components" solution, a solution focusing on bringing Microsoft Search-based experiences inside and outside the Microsoft 365 ecosystem.

I want to thank the amazing PnP community and all the dedicated individuals who generously share their expertise. The passion, creativity, and enthusiasm within this group are truly inspiring and uplifting. It's a powerful reminder that knowledge grows when shared—because sharing is caring!

Anoop T. is a Microsoft MVP in the M365 Development category and currently works at Advania Ltd, based in London, UK. He has worked across the entire lifecycle of projects, from gathering and analyzing requirements to completing the design and development of the projects. He has around 10 years of experience in Microsoft 365 development and has worked mainly on SharePoint Online, SharePoint 2013, and SharePoint 2010.

Anoop is a member of the core team of the Microsoft 365 & Power Platform community, formerly known as the **Patterns and Practices (PnP)** team, and is a regular contributor to PnP projects on GitHub. He is also a speaker at conferences and user groups and writes blog articles dedicated to his experience with M365 development, which can be found at `https://anoopt.medium.com`.

I want to thank the people who have been close to me and supported me, especially my wife, my parents, my sister, and my best friend, Rohit.

About the reviewers

Yves Habersaat is a business applications consultant and AI tech lead at Sword Group in Switzerland, specializing in building applications and solutions with Microsoft 365, Azure, Dynamics 365, and the Power Platform.

With a strong passion for modern development technologies and application lifecycles, Yves focuses on Microsoft 365 services such as Microsoft Teams, SharePoint Online, OneDrive for Business, Microsoft Viva, and Microsoft Copilot. He possesses expertise in modern development tools, including **SharePoint Framework (SPFx)**, Teams SDK, Microsoft Graph, Git, TypeScript, React, Visual Studio, and Azure DevOps.

He actively shares his knowledge and experience through speaking engagements and his blog at www.yhabersaat.ch, always ready to support and assist the community.

Denis Morielli is a Cloud Architect specializing in Azure and Microsoft 365. With over 20 years of experience, he began his career in traditional IT and has worked with SharePoint since its earliest versions. Throughout his career, he has held various roles, including business consultant, developer, trainer, and solution architect, before shifting his focus to cloud modernization.

As an independent consultant, Denis designs and implements solutions that bridge the gap between enterprise needs and modern cloud capabilities. He advises organizations on secure, scalable, and automated architectures, and leads hands-on workshops to ensure effective knowledge transfer.

Denis is passionate about productivity enhancement, automation, solution design, process management, and driving innovation.

Table of Contents

Part 1: Getting Started with the SharePoint Framework

1

Introducing Microsoft 365 and SharePoint Online for Developers   3

2

Ecosystem and Building Blocks around the SharePoint Framework   35

3

Your First Steps with the SharePoint Framework

4

Packt Product Management Solution: A Practical Use Case

Part 2: Building Web Parts with the SharePoint Framework

5

Building a SharePoint Web Part

Table of Contents

Part 1: Getting Started with the SharePoint Framework

1

2

3

Your First Steps with the SharePoint Framework 51

4

Packt Product Management Solution: A Practical Use Case 61

Part 2: Building Web Parts with the SharePoint Framework

5

Building a SharePoint Web Part 73

6

Working with the Property Pane   109

7

Connecting to Other Web Parts   131

8

Deploying a SharePoint Web Part   151

Part 3: Building Extensions with the SharePoint Framework

9

Building a Form Customizer   193

13

Building a Search Query Modifier   257

14

Building an Adaptive Card Extension   271

15

Deploying Extensions   287

Part 4: Going Further with the SharePoint Framework

16

Sharing Your Code Using Library Components   303

17

Debugging Your Solution Efficiently   315

18

Consuming APIs   339

19

Writing Tests with SPFx   359

20

Upgrading Your Solutions   373

21

Leveraging Community Tools and Libraries   383

22

Development Platforms   403

23

Unlock Your Exclusive Benefits   413

Preface

Hello fellow developers!

SharePoint usage has grown massively over the past decade, driven by the advent of the Microsoft 365 platform and SharePoint Online. More and more companies invest in the Microsoft 365 platform, either starting from scratch or migrating from SharePoint on-premises.

However, to leverage its full potential, customization and development steps are often necessary to tailor the platform to business needs. In addition to being a collaboration and document management platform, SharePoint is also a *development platform* that can be personalized to accommodate various business requirements. To this end, Microsoft offers several customization options, ranging from simple configuration in the interface, going through low-code solutions, and finally custom development. For the latter, the **SharePoint Framework** (**SPFx**) is the preferred and only option provided by Microsoft to cover this scenario.

For many years, SharePoint development has suffered from a bad reputation among developers (both frontend and backend developers). SharePoint is quite an old tool now (the first version was SharePoint 2001!), but for some reason, it still carries this reputation from its legacy on-premises development experience. This experience, we're sure you'll agree, was probably not the best development experience we've seen.

Regardless of your opinions on SharePoint development, set them aside. There is nothing comparable between on-premises SharePoint development as you knew it (or not, lucky you) and SPFx. With SPFx, SharePoint development (and beyond) is cool again, and we'll try to prove it with this book.

With this book, we'll guide you through your SPFx journey, starting with the basics and progressing to advanced development concepts. Additionally, we'll explore the underlying mechanisms of SharePoint and Microsoft 365 and discuss the vibrant community initiatives surrounding this tool to help you better understand the landscape in which SPFx fits.

This book has been written by experienced SPFx developers with several years of expertise. We've got you covered!

Who this book is for

This book is ideal for experienced web developers or existing SharePoint developers looking to build modern SharePoint solutions using the SharePoint Framework. The book covers everything from basics to advanced topics. Therefore, it is suited to the following audiences:

- *Web developers new to SPFx* with good knowledge of JavaScript/TypeScript but without any prior knowledge of SharePoint and its ecosystem and looking for guidance to get started

- *Experienced on-premises SharePoint developers* already familiar with SharePoint underlying concepts and making the transition to SPFx

- *Existing SPFx developers* wanting to enhance and refresh their skills with the latest features of the framework

What this book covers

Chapter 1, Introducing Microsoft 365 and SharePoint Online for Developers, provides an overview of SPFx, its evolution, and its role within Microsoft 365 and SharePoint. It explains SPFx's key features, the differences between cloud and on-premises versions, and the types of solutions developers can create. Additionally, it highlights valuable community resources and best practices to help developers make informed customization choices.

Chapter 2, Ecosystem and Building Blocks around the SharePoint Framework, explores the core elements of the Microsoft 365 ecosystem relevant to SPFx development, focusing on SharePoint and Teams logical structures. Developers will gain a deep understanding of key concepts, available APIs for accessing Microsoft 365 data, and how to integrate them into SPFx solutions.

Chapter 3, Your First Steps with the SharePoint Framework, outlines the essential configuration for an SPFx development environment and details the general development process for building solutions. Key topics include development tools, application lifecycle, environment setup, solution creation, and understanding the solution structure.

Chapter 4, Packt Product Management Solution: A Practical Use Case, presents a real-world example of building a product inventory management solution for Packt using SPF within Microsoft 365. It defines business requirements, plans SPFx capabilities, and sets the stage for implementing key features such as web parts and extensions, supported by a GitHub repository. Developers will gain insights into SPFx's practical applications beyond basic examples.

Chapter 5, Building a SharePoint Web Part, guides developers through the complete process of building an SPFx web part from scratch. It covers using SPFx features to meet functional requirements, integrating React lifecycle methods, accessing SharePoint data via Microsoft Graph, styling and theme support, localization, and adding top actions for quick configuration.

Chapter 6, Working with the Property Pane, explores how to configure SPFx web parts using the **Property** pane, leveraging both Microsoft-provided and custom controls. Developers will learn how to use default property controls, create custom integrations, and apply advanced techniques to manage complex configurations.

Chapter 7, Connecting to Other Web Parts, focuses on implementing a product catalog search using SPFx dynamic data to connect multiple components on a page. It covers creating a search box web part, exposing data to other components, and consuming that data in an existing web part, enabling developers to build flexible and interactive solutions.

Chapter 8, Deploying a SharePoint Web Part, covers the deployment of SPFx solutions in a Microsoft 365 environment, starting with manual steps and progressing to automation using DevOps tools such as GitHub Actions and Azure DevOps. Developers will learn about the deployment pipeline, packaging, customization, compatibility with Teams, Office, and Outlook, and automating deployment for production readiness.

Chapter 9, Building a Form Customizer, explores SPFx extensions, specifically the "Form Customizer", guiding developers through its creation and integration with SharePoint list items. It covers development using React lifecycle methods, Microsoft Graph for data interaction, and custom rendering of forms for creating, viewing, and editing list items.

Chapter 10, Building an Application Customizer, introduces the SPFx Application Customizer extension, detailing its development process using React lifecycle methods. Developers will learn how to create an Application Customizer from scratch, integrate Microsoft Graph for SharePoint list data, and understand its role in enhancing user experiences across SharePoint sites.

Chapter 11, Building a Field Customizer, focuses on the SPFx Field Customizer, enabling developers to visually highlight low-stock products by customizing the **Stock Level** field in the **Products** list. It covers creating a Field Customizer from scratch, understanding its development flow, and using custom SCSS for display control.

Chapter 12, Building a ListView Command Set, focuses on using SPFx's ListView Command Set to take action on low-stock products. Developers will learn how to create command sets that appear in list views, execute actions for specific items, and integrate external systems such as Power Automate or third-party services to enhance functionality.

Chapter 13, Building a Search Query Modifier, introduces the SPFx "Search Query Modifier"A, enabling developers to refine and customize product searches within SharePoint lists. It covers creating a Search Query Modifier from scratch, leveraging SPFx lifecycle methods, and using Microsoft Graph to filter search results effectively.

Chapter 14, Building an Adaptive Card Extension, demonstrates **Adaptive Card Extensions (ACEs)** within Viva Connections, enabling users to surface and interact with organizational data. It covers creating custom ACEs using SPFx, understanding their development flow, and integrating data with Microsoft Graph for personalized experiences.

Chapter 15, Deploying Extensions, covers packaging and deploying SPFx extensions, building on concepts from *Chapter 8*. Developers will learn about deployment scopes (tenant vs. site collection) and how to use PnP PowerShell and the CLI for Microsoft 365 for efficient extension deployment.

Chapter 16, Sharing Your Code Using Library Components, introduces library components in SPFx, explaining their purpose and usage in customization. It covers adapting code for reuse in a product catalog solution, deploying library components, and comparing them to npm packages for effective implementation.

Chapter 17, Debugging Your Solution Efficiently, provides best practices for debugging SPFx solutions efficiently. Developers will learn multiple techniques for debugging web parts and extensions, using the SPFx developer dashboard and maintenance mode, and leveraging additional tools to streamline troubleshooting.

Chapter 18, Consuming APIs, explores API usage in SPFx solutions, focusing on secure data retrieval from SharePoint and Microsoft 365 using built-in utility classes. It covers authentication complexities, integration with Microsoft Graph and SharePoint APIs, and consuming external or Entra ID-secured APIs for seamless development.

Chapter 19, Writing Tests with SPFx, explores the role of testing in SPFx development, highlighting when and why tests are necessary. It covers different testing approaches, focusing on web parts, and introduces Jest as a framework for writing efficient tests in SPFx solutions.

Chapter 20, Upgrading Your Solutions, emphasizes the importance of upgrading SPFx solutions to maintain security, performance, and access to new features. It covers staying informed about updates, as well as upgrading manually or using the CLI for Microsoft 365 for efficient maintenance.

Chapter 21, Leveraging Community Tools and Libraries, highlights key open source tools and libraries that can enhance SPFx development within Microsoft 365 and SharePoint. It introduces PnP.js, PnP React controls, PnP Modern Search, Microsoft Dev Proxy, and SPFx Fast Serve, while emphasizing the broader contributions of the active developer community.

Chapter 22, Development Platforms, explores alternative platforms for developing SPFx solutions beyond a local machine, including **Docker**, **GitHub Codespaces**, **Windows Subsystem for Linux (WSL)**, and **Azure Virtual Machines**. It covers the benefits of virtualization and compares different options for efficient SPFx development.

To get the most out of this book

Before reading this book, experience with web development is strongly recommended. Also, having a basic understanding of Microsoft 365 and especially SharePoint is also nice to have (but not required).

Software/hardware covered in the book	Operating system requirements
Visual Studio Code (recommended code editor for SPFx development)	Windows 10 or higher, macOS, or Linux

Software/hardware covered in the book	Operating system requirements
Yeoman	
Gulp	
Node.js **long-term support** (**LTS**) version, preferably Node.js 18.x	
Microsoft 365 developer tenant	

To run the samples from the GitHub repository, you will also need the following:

- Visual Studio Code installed on your machine.

- A Git client to clone the GitHub repository and run the samples locally. You can use the built-in Git feature of Visual Studio or a tool such as Sourcetree or GitHub Desktop.

- A Microsoft 365 tenant to test and deploy samples. You can get one for free by joining the Microsoft 365 developer program: `https://developer.microsoft.com/en-us/microsoft-365/dev-program`.

If you are using the digital version of this book, we advise you to type the code yourself or access the code from the book's GitHub repository (a link is available in the next section). Doing so will help you avoid any potential errors related to the copying and pasting of code.

Download the example code files

You can download the example code files for this book from GitHub at `https://github.com/PacktPublishing/Mastering-SharePoint-Development-with-the-SharePoint-Framework-`. If there's an update to the code, it will be updated in the GitHub repository.

We also have other code bundles from our rich catalog of books and videos available at `https://github.com/PacktPublishing/`. Check them out!

Conventions used

There are a number of text conventions used throughout this book.

`Code in text`: Indicates code words in text, database table names, folder names, filenames, file extensions, pathnames, dummy URLs, user input, and X/Twitter handles. Here is an example: "We first create a `models` folder under the `src` folder and create a new `IProductCatalogItem.ts` file with the following content."

A block of code is set as follows:

```
export interface IProductCatalogItem {
  modelName: string;
  retailPrice: number;
  stockLevel: number;
  lastOrderDate: Date;
  itemPicture: string;
  itemColour: string;
  size: ProductSizes;
  productReference: string;
}
```

When we wish to draw your attention to a particular part of a code block, the relevant lines or items are set in bold:

```
public async getProducts(
  siteId: string,
  listName: string,
  itemsCount?: number,
  searchQuery?: string,
  filterClause?: string
): Promise<IProductCatalogItem[]> {
```

Any command-line input or output is written as follows:

```
gulp serve --config=packtProductApplicationCustomizer
```

Bold: Indicates a new term, an important word, or words that you see onscreen. For instance, words in menus or dialog boxes appear in **bold**. Here is an example: "A **ListView Command Set** extension allows you to provide custom buttons to the default list or library experience."

> **Tips or important notes**
> Appear like this.

Get in touch

Feedback from our readers is always welcome.

General feedback: If you have questions about any aspect of this book, email us at customercare@packtpub.com and mention the book title in the subject of your message.

Errata: Although we have taken every care to ensure the accuracy of our content, mistakes do happen. If you have found a mistake in this book, we would be grateful if you would report this to us. Please visit www.packtpub.com/support/errata and fill in the form.

Piracy: If you come across any illegal copies of our works in any form on the internet, we would be grateful if you would provide us with the location address or website name. Please contact us at copyright@packt.com with a link to the material.

If you are interested in becoming an author: If there is a topic that you have expertise in and you are interested in either writing or contributing to a book, please visit authors.packtpub.com.

Share Your Thoughts

Once you've read *Practical SharePoint Framework (SPFx) Development*, we'd love to hear your thoughts! Scan the QR code below to go straight to the Amazon review page for this book and share your feedback.

https://packt.link/r/1-835-46678-8

Your review is important to us and the tech community and will help us make sure we're delivering excellent quality content.

Free Benefits with Your Book

This book comes with free benefits to support your learning. Activate them now for instant access (see the "*How to Unlock*" section for instructions).

Here's a quick overview of what you can instantly unlock with your purchase:

PDF and ePub Copies   **Next-Gen Web-Based Reader**

   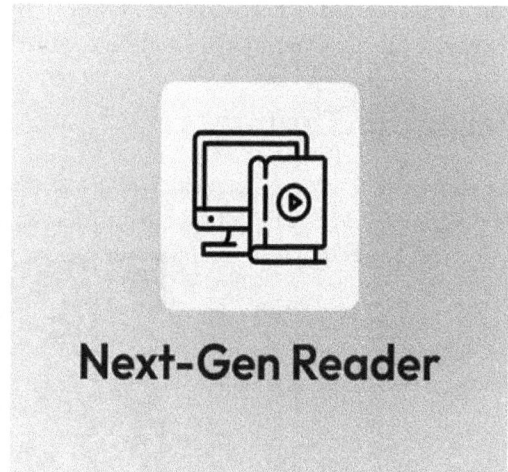

Access a DRM-free PDF copy of this book to read anywhere, on any device.

Use a DRM-free ePub version with your favorite e-reader.

Multi-device progress sync: Pick up where you left off, on any device.

Highlighting and notetaking: Capture ideas and turn reading into lasting knowledge.

Bookmarking: Save and revisit key sections whenever you need them.

Dark mode: Reduce eye strain by switching to dark or sepia themes

How to Unlock

UNLOCK NOW

Scan the QR code (or go to `packtpub.com/unlock`). Search for this book by name, confirm the edition, and then follow the steps on the page.

Note: Keep your invoice handy. Purchases made directly from Packt don't require an invoice.

Part 1: Getting Started with the SharePoint Framework

Part 1 starts with explaining the history of SPFx, its capabilities, and the core building blocks around it, including SharePoint, Microsoft 365, Teams, and so on. It also details how to set SPFx up on your local machine to begin the development. In this part, we also outline a technical solution based on fictitious requirements, which will enable us to demonstrate a specific functionality in each subsequent chapter offered by SPFx through practical business examples.

This part has the following chapters:

- *Chapter 1, Introducing Microsoft 365 and SharePoint Online for Developers*
- *Chapter 2, Ecosystem and Building Blocks around the SharePoint Framework*
- *Chapter 3, Your First Steps with the SharePoint Framework*
- *Chapter 4, Packt Product Management Solution: A Practical Use Case*

1

Introducing Microsoft 365 and SharePoint Online for Developers

Microsoft released the first version of the **SharePoint Framework** (**SPFx**) back in 2016. A lot of updates have been made since then (spoiler, this is not only about SharePoint anymore!) and it can be overwhelming to get started due to the amount of information available out there.

In this book, we try to give you the essential information you need as a professional developer to get started with this framework. Being SPFx developers ourselves, we try to focus on practical aspects of the framework, keeping in mind that we all need to deliver quality and valuable solutions to users.

This first chapter gives you the overall picture of SPFx, how it evolved, what it is now, and what type of solutions you can deliver with it. We introduce you to SPFx and its ecosystem, going from on-premises versions of SharePoint to the Microsoft 365 suite, and detail its evolution through the years and key features delivered.

At the end of this chapter, you will have a clear understanding of what the SPFx is, what its philosophy is, and what type of solutions you can create with it. You will also understand the key differences and limitations between cloud and on-premises SharePoint versions regarding SPFx capabilities.

This will give you the big picture of the environment where the SPFx takes place and all the possibilities it offers across many different tools in the Microsoft 365 ecosystem and SharePoint On-Premises. As a developer, this will help you to wisely choose between customization types according to your business requirements.

For those wanting to go beyond the traditional Microsoft documentation, we also provide useful resources leveraging the vivid community around SPFx, a must-know for every SPFx developer.

To summarize, we will be covering the following main topics in this chapter:

- Understanding the Microsoft 365 ecosystem
- Capabilities overview per extensibility platforms
- The Microsoft 365 & Power Platform Community [formerly Pattern and Practices (PnP)]

> **Free Benefits with Your Book**
>
> Your purchase includes a free PDF copy of this book along with other exclusive benefits. Check the *Free Benefits with Your Book* section in the Preface to unlock them instantly and maximize your learning experience.

Understanding the Microsoft 365 ecosystem

Before digging into SPFx development, it is important to understand the ecosystem it applies to. **Microsoft 365** is a cloud platform dedicated to productivity offered by Microsoft and regrouping several workloads (aka applications), such as the following:

- Office applications (Word, Excel, and PowerPoint)
- Specialized tools, like:

  - Exchange (Outlook for emails and calendars)
  - SharePoint (organizational document storage, intranet portals, collaboration and sharing, and so on)
  - Teams (real-time communications, meetings)
  - OneDrive (personal storage)

Microsoft 365 is accessible through several subscription plans suitable for both individuals and companies (`https://www.microsoft.com/en-us/microsoft-365/buy/compare-all-microsoft-365-products`), determining the available applications and features for users.

Being a **software-as-a-service (SaaS)** platform, the platform itself is cloud-based only and most of the offered applications are accessible through a web browser (although, you can install the Word, Excel, and Teams clients on your desktop). It means Microsoft handles updates and patches, ensuring these won't break existing features. It also means new features and capabilities are pushed automatically, whether you want/use it or not. As a developer, it implies staying up to date about the latest features and capabilities of the platform as this is a platform that moves quickly. To help you in this process, you can follow the public Microsoft 365 roadmap (`https://www.microsoft.com/en-us/microsoft-365/roadmap`).

Last but not least, a key aspect of the Microsoft 365 ecosystem is its identity platform relying on Microsoft Azure and Entra ID (formerly **Azure Active Directory**). For an SPFx developer, identity is a key topic, especially authentication flows available to you (OAuth). As long as you need to get data from the Microsoft 365 workload, identity and authentication will be involved so basic knowledge is recommended. We will get the chance to cover this part later in this book.

In the next section, we detail a little bit more about the primary target of SPFx within Microsoft 365: SharePoint Online.

SharePoint Online

SharePoint Online is a cloud-based service provided by Microsoft that allows you to create intranet sites, share documents, and collaborate with colleagues, partners, and customers. It offers a centralized, secure space for document sharing, editing, and downloading. It's part of the Microsoft 365 suite and integrates with other services, such as Teams and OneDrive, for a comprehensive collaboration experience.

SharePoint is historically an on-premises product (i.e., with physical server infrastructure) and the first version was released in 2001 followed by several on-premises versions up to the SharePoint Server 2019 and SharePoint Server Subscription editions we have today in 2025.

The *online* version (or SharePoint in Microsoft 365) is the *cloud-only* version of SharePoint offered either as a standalone subscription (i.e., SharePoint + OneDrive + Microsoft Lists) or through Microsoft 365 plans alongside other tools.

SharePoint Online is deeply integrated with other Microsoft 365 tools, such as Teams and OneDrive, as it is the storage platform behind these tools.

Over the years and versions, the core concepts of SharePoint information architecture haven't changed that much (site collection, sites, lists and libraries, columns, and content types). The main difference with on-premises versions is the abstraction of infrastructure-oriented concepts such as farms, web applications, and services as all of these are managed now by Microsoft.

SharePoint Online evolves quickly and contains the latest features deployed by Microsoft. It means many of these aren't and won't be available in on-premises versions, impacting the possibilities offered through SPFx as well.

> **What about SharePoint On-Premises?**
>
> For SharePoint, there is still an option to get it on-premises through the 2019 version or the Server Subscription Edition (`https://learn.microsoft.com/en-ca/sharepoint/what-s-new/new-and-improved-features-in-sharepoint-server-subscription-edition`). However, the Microsoft focus is clearly set on Microsoft 365 and cloud-based products. On-premises versions are likely used by companies with high technical constraints preventing them from moving to the cloud.
>
> With on-premises versions, you usually have fewer features than the cloud-based application counterpart and this applies to SPFx as well.

In this first section, we introduced the ecosystem of Microsoft 365 and its applications, including SharePoint Online. We learned about the differences between cloud-based and on-premises versions of SharePoint and the importance of understanding the ecosystem for SPFx development. Moving on to the second section, we will delve deeper into SharePoint Online, its history, and its integration with other Microsoft 365 tools.

Unveiling SPFx

SPFx is the preferred development model when it comes to customizing or extending the SharePoint experience and beyond. It was initially introduced for SharePoint as part of the *modern* SharePoint experiences introduced in Microsoft 365 (at the time called Office 365) and is the evolution of the traditional add-in development model that appeared with SharePoint 2013.

SharePoint Add-ins

With SharePoint add-ins, applications were hosted either directly on SharePoint (SharePoint-hosted solutions) or in your own server (provider-hosted solutions) and integrated into the user experience through an *iframe*. The main goals were mainly to do the following:

- Reduce the risk involved by historical SharePoint farm solutions (developed server-side with .NET), hosted, and executed directly on SharePoint servers that could harm the entire farm

- Control customizations by providing "placeholders" on sites where add-ins can be integrated safely without interfering with the rest of the **user interface** (**UI**) or breaking the experience (full page application, app parts, custom actions)

This development model had major limitations due to the *iframe* model causing issues with performances and UI integration (e.g., an *iframe* can't interact with its parent **Document Object Model** (**DOM**) and inherit the same styles easily, etc.).

> **Note**
> The SharePoint Add-in model in SharePoint Online will be fully retired as of April 2nd, 2026, and stopped working for new tenants as of November 1st, 2024.

SPFx is also an answer to another widely used approach to customize SharePoint: the Script Editor web part, which we will see next.

Script Editor web part

SPFx is a way for Microsoft to propose a more robust and future-proof extensibility model for SharePoint development. In previous versions of SharePoint, developers were used to using the *Script Editor web part* to inject their JavaScript snippets/entire applications into SharePoint pages (for instance to bypass some add-in model limitations). However, this approach had also several drawbacks:

- It was hard to package solutions and configurations

- It exposed the code directly to any user having edit permissions on the page with the possibility of breaking the application

- It required enabling the *NoScript* flag on sites and potentially introducing security risk by loading untrusted scripts and files

> **Note**
> Despite an open source version of the *Script Editor web part* existing, Microsoft does not provide such a web part by default for all the reasons mentioned previously and SPFx should always be used instead.

With SPFx, all code is *client-side*, or, in other terms, developed in **JavaScript** and executed in the browser running in the context of the currently connected user. SPFx solutions can be completed with backend solutions written in other languages (for instance, within Azure via HTTP APIs) but that is not the subject of this book.

However, don't be mistaken by the "SharePoint" word in the name; SPFx is no longer only about SharePoint. Over the years, SPFx has been extended to integrate with other applications within the Microsoft 365 ecosystem, such as Teams, Viva Connections, Outlook, and Office.

Is SPFx only for developers with a SharePoint background? No. Any web developer can develop with SPFx as it uses the modern web stack development tooling. However, depending on the customization you make and the data you retrieve, SharePoint knowledge and its concepts are clearly an advantage.

Evolution of SPFx

The first generally available version of SPFx (1.0.0) was released back on the 22nd of February 2017. Since then, several versions have been released. At the time of writing, the current version is 1.21.1 (see all releases).

We list here all the major evolutions and new features delivered over the years (excluding fixes, previews, and so on):

- **1.0.0 (February 2017):**
  - Only client-side web parts support.
  - 3 project templates supported:
    - Knockout.js
    - React
    - No JavaScript framework
- **1.3.0 (September 2017):**
  - Introduction of SharePoint Application Customizer, Field Customizer, and ListView extensions.
- **1.5.0 (June 2018):**
  - SharePoint On-Premises is no longer compatible. From this point, SPFx versions become for cloud products only.

- **1.6.0 (September 2018)**:

  - Web API feature. Now, SPFx comes with a prebuilt set of classes to connect to secured APIs (e.g., `GraphHttpClient`, `SPHttpClient`, `HttpClient`).

  - Support of tenant-wide deployment for extensions.

- **1.7.0 (November 2018)**:

  - Dynamic data (ability to connect components together).

- **1.8.0 (March 2019)**:

  - Microsoft Teams tabs support (integrates web parts in Teams).

  - App pages (a full-page application integrated into the SharePoint experience)

  - Domain-isolated web parts (run components in an iframe with isolated permissions).

- **1.9.1 (August 2019)**:

  - Library components support.

- **1.10.0 (January 2020)**:

  - Microsoft Teams personal apps support.

  - List subscription.

  - Application Customizer top/bottom placeholders.

- **1.11.0 (July 2020)**:

  - AppSource support (ability to publish to the marketplace).

  - Removed support of the `Knockout.js` template.

  - Teams tasks modules support (expose web part as Teams messaging extension).

- **1.13.0 (October 2021)**:

  - Viva Connection **Adaptive Card Extension** (**ACE**) support.

- **1.15.0 (June 2022)**:

  - Form Customizer extension support.

- **1.16.0 (November 2022)**:

  - Publish Teams solutions build with SPFx to Outlook and Office.

  - Search query extension support.

- **1.17.0 (April 2023)**:

  - Top actions for custom web parts in SharePoint.

- **1.19.0 (April 2024)**:

  - Webpack 5 support.

Let's look at the timeline:

- The focus was initially set on SharePoint only and slowly evolved to integrate with other popular Microsoft 365 products, such as Teams and Viva Connections. You can now build SPFx-built solutions with no relationship with SharePoint whatsoever (e.g., Viva Connections ACE). The name "SharePoint Framework" may evolve in the future to something else to be more meaningful.

- `React.js` is by far the preferred JavaScript UI library to use if you want to benefit from the many examples and resources available. Microsoft tried to support other frameworks in the first versions, but it wasn't very popular (e.g., `Knockout.js`). You still have the option to use plain JavaScript, but we don't recommend it.

> **Note**
> You can build SPFx solutions using other technologies such as `Angular.js` or `Vue.js` but there won't be any scaffolding or templates provided by default to get you started easily and you won't benefit from many examples.

It's important to note that SPFx IS *NOT* state-of-the-art web development and will never be.

From a technical point of view, the tools and libraries used in SPFx greatly evolved over the years. For instance, the `Node.js` version has been upgraded from version 6 with SPFx 1.1.0 to version 18 with SPFx 1.19.0. Therefore, it is important to regularly upgrade your development environment accordingly.

You can refer to the table in the official Microsoft documentation (`https://learn.microsoft.com/en-us/sharepoint/dev/spfx/compatibility`) to see all the `Node.js`/TypeScript/React versions per version (mark it as a bookmark).

Also, SPFx is and will always be behind the latest trends and libraries you will encounter in the web development area. As an example, the support of Webpack 5, (a version released in 2020 and widely used in web development) is only supported in SPFx in 2024! For experienced web developers used to working with the latest tools, yes, working with SPFx can be frustrating sometimes and we get that.

This is easily understandable as Microsoft needs to support all versions of the framework used in its platform (from v1.0.0 to 1.19.0) and needs to be very careful with any introduced breaking changes that could impact millions of users and third-party products.

While, yes, you can still build and deploy SPFx v1.0.0 solutions in 2025 – it will be supported – please don't.

As we've seen in this chapter, SPFx was initially created to solve security and usability issues regarding custom JavaScript development inside SharePoint pages and evolved over the years to go progressively beyond SharePoint, supporting customizations for other tools within the Microsoft platform, such as Teams or Viva Connections.

In the next section, we will see an overview of all the possibilities offered by the framework per extensibility platform.

Exploring SPFx capabilities

SPFx is not only about SharePoint anymore and offers a lot of capabilities beyond it, for instance, for other tools in the Microsoft 365 suite.

Depending on whether you work with the cloud or on-premises, possibilities won't be the same due to technical limitations.

Enumerating differences between SharePoint Online and SharePoint On-Premises

SPFx lets you customize parts or integrate within the default SharePoint UI experience. It can be used both with SharePoint Online and SharePoint On-Premises. However, with the on-premises products, the maximum version of SPFx you can use is 1.4.1 for SharePoint Server 2019 and 1.5.0 for SharePoint Server Subscription Edition. For SharePoint Server 2016 SP2, the maximum version is 1.1.0. It means you are limited to the following solution types with on-premises products:

- Web parts for modern or classic pages
- Application Customizer
- Field Customizer
- ListView extension

All other features are only compatible with SharePoint Online.

In the rest of this book, we mainly focus on SharePoint Online capabilities as it is the most widely used application.

SPFx offers two types of solutions that can be created: *web parts* and *extensions*. Each type of solution has its own specificities that we detail in the following subsection.

Web parts

The web part customization was the very first capability of SPFx to be released back in 2017. It allows you to create visual components that can be inserted into SharePoint pages (modern and classic), Teams (as tab, personal app meeting apps, and even messaging extensions), Outlook, and Microsoft 365 apps (thanks to Microsoft Teams compatibility).

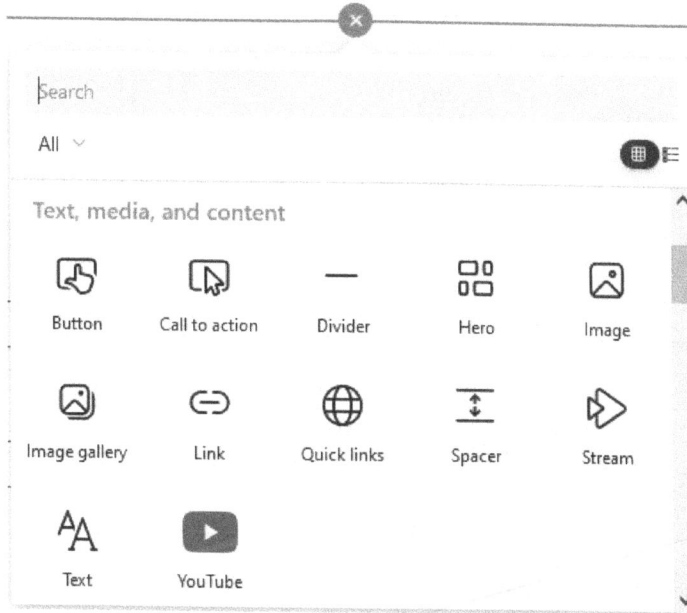

Figure 1.1 – The native web parts offered in SharePoint Online

A web part is composed of the following elements:

- **A UI canvas**: This is where the content is displayed to the user. It can be literally anything as you get total control of it using JavaScript, HTML, and CSS. This canvas adapts dynamically to the dimensions of its parent container (such as a section/column or the full-page width) and the layout of the page (e.g., it will be stacked automatically on mobile view, and so on).

> **Note**
>
> The canvas is by itself "responsive" in its layout, but it does mean your content will be by default. It is up to you to implement your visuals to adapt the dimensions of the web part canvas container itself.

- **A property pane**: A visual panel only available in *edit mode* and used to configure web part options. Options are persisted into the web part property bag depending on the integration context (see the following figure).

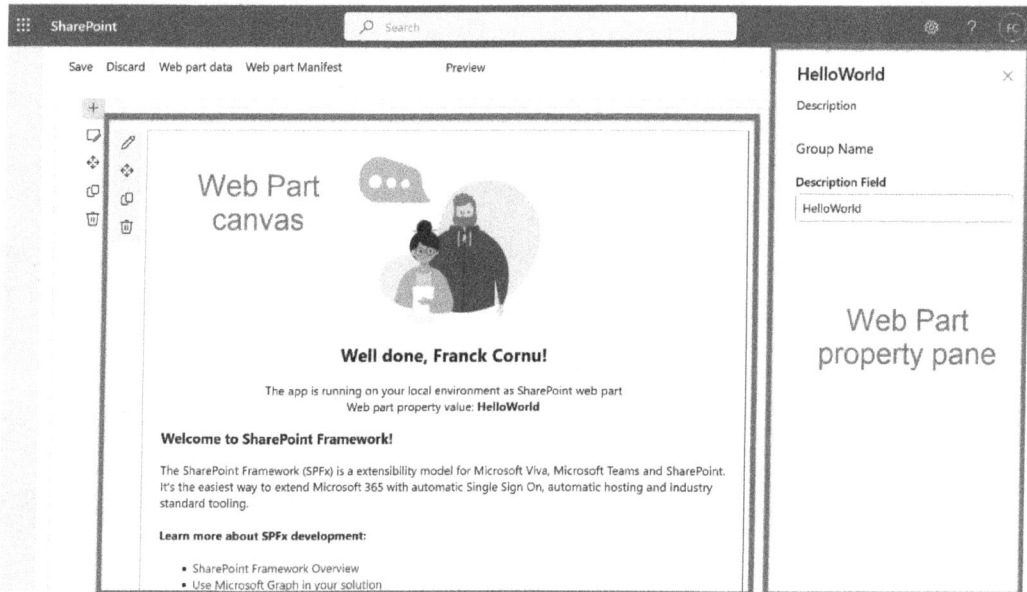

Figure 1.2 – The structure of a SharePoint web part

Web parts can be used in different ways:

- As *components* in modern or classic SharePoint pages and inserted inside sections and columns along other web parts:

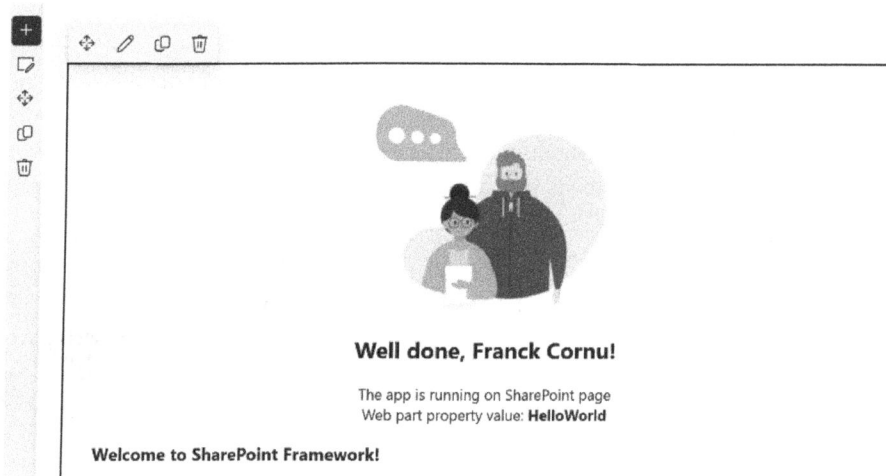

Figure 1.3 – The web part used as a component on a modern SharePoint page

- As *full-page applications* in SharePoint (such as single-page applications), through a special **App page** SharePoint page. In this case, a *single* web part is presented containing the entire application. In such pages, there are no sections or columns to configure:

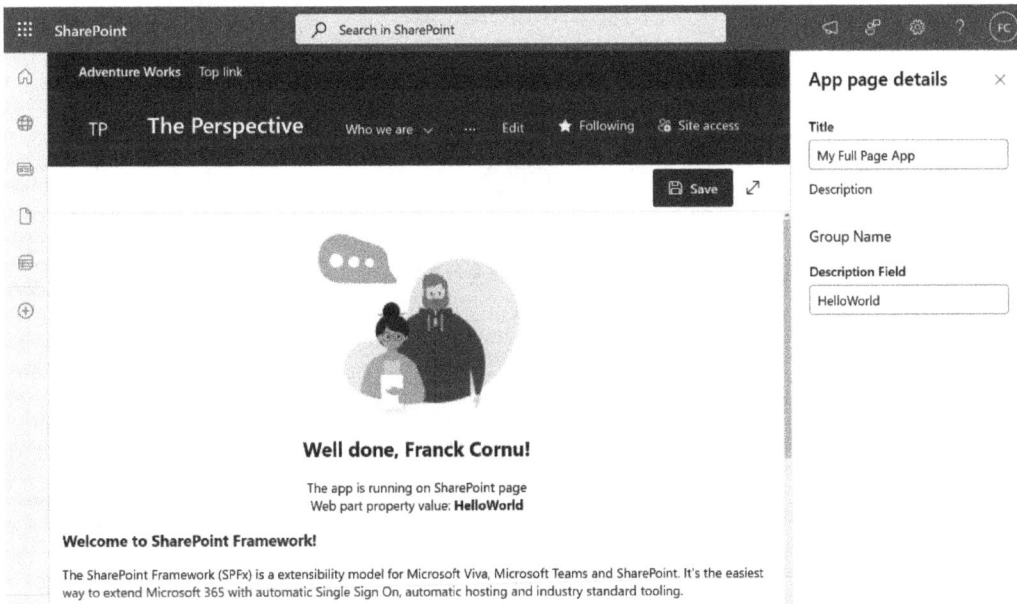

Figure 1.4 – A web part used as a full-page app on a modern SharePoint page

- As a *channel tab*, *personal app*, *meeting app*, or *messaging extension in Microsoft Teams*. Just like the full-page scenario, a *single* web part acting as the application is presented with this mode.

Here is an example of integration as a channel tab:

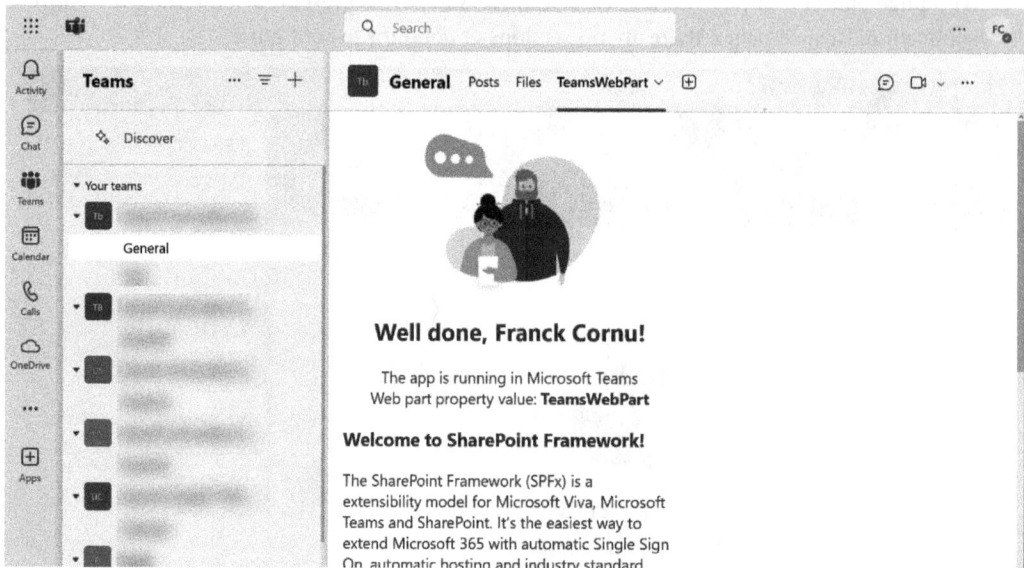

Figure 1.5 – A web part used as a Teams channel tab

Teams meeting app

SPFx web parts can be integrated in multiple ways for a Teams meeting, such as a side panel during the meeting itself, a tab inside the meeting details, or directly in the meeting chat (in this case, it behaves the same as a messaging extension).

Here is an example of an SPFx web part integrated as a meeting application:

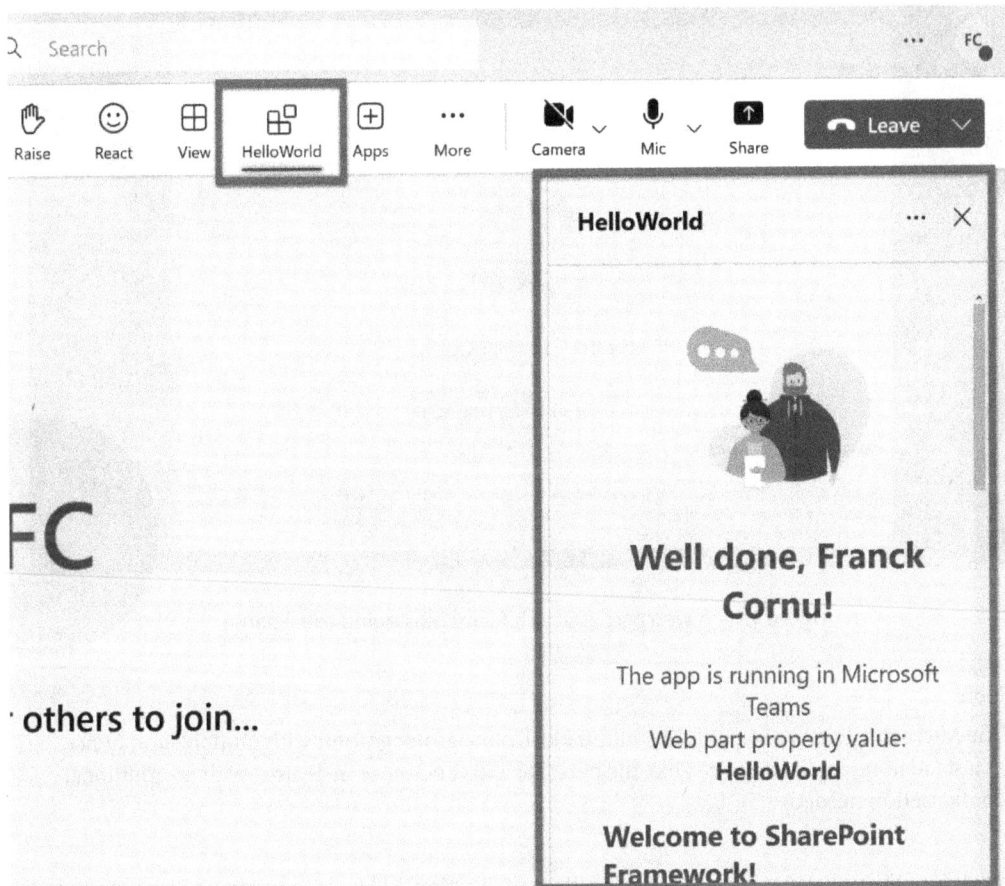

Figure 1.6 – A web part used as a Teams meeting application (side panel)

Lastly, here is an SPFx web part integrated as a messaging extension:

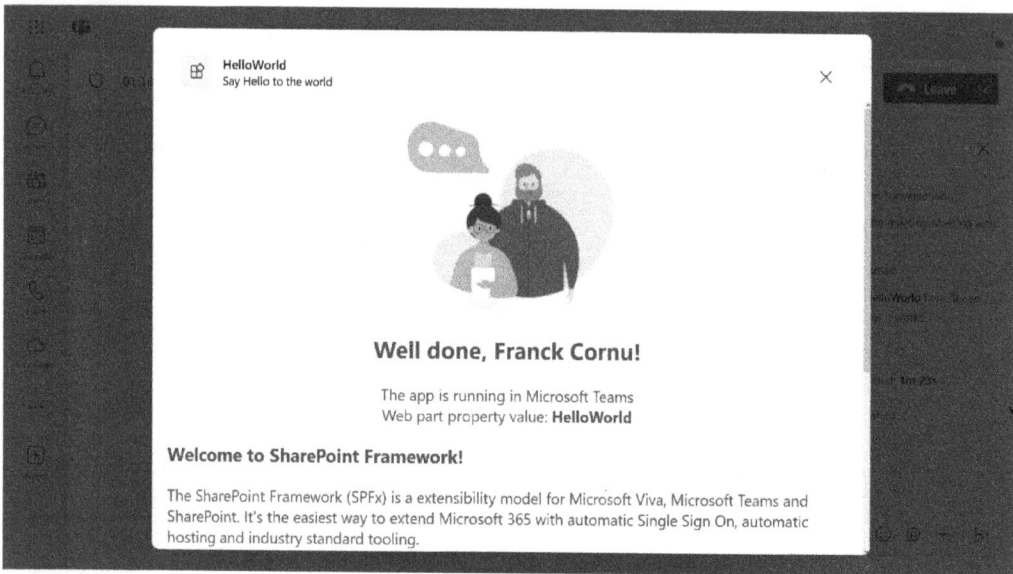

Figure 1.7 – A web part used as a Teams messaging extension

> **Note**
>
> The Microsoft Teams compatibility automatically brings integration with Outlook and Office as a standalone application (just like the personal app experience in Teams) with no additional configuration needed.

Regardless of the way you will use a web part, its configuration will have to be stored somewhere and surfaced for users to be modified through the web part *property pane.*

Property pane

The property pane is a convenient way to edit and store web part settings and let users customize the experience easily. It is usually displayed when the experience is in edit mode. For example, in SharePoint pages (regular pages and full pages), it only appears when you edit the page. However, when integrated into Teams, Outlook, or Office, the property pane may not be available as the *edit mode* concept simply does not exist. In such case, it means you cannot leverage property pane capabilities to store web part configuration. Let's look at these differences briefly. Depending on the integration context, settings are persisted differently in the web part Property bag (i.e., a JSON structure containing all setting values):

- When inserted as a component or as a full page into a SharePoint modern page, web part settings are persisted alongside the page HTML content in the `CanvasContent1` ("authoring canvas content") property.

- When inserted as a Teams tab, settings are persisted in the underlying SharePoint site behind the specific team containing the channel where the tab is configured. It uses a hidden list behind the scenes called **Hosted App Configs** (with a URL of `https://<tenant>.sharepoint.com/sites/<site>/Lists/HostedAppConfigs/AllItems.aspx`).

For other integrations, such as Teams personal apps, Outlook, and Office applications, the property pane can't be used to configure settings as these types of integrations don't provide a persistence layer. For such cases, it will be up to you to implement web part configuration strategies.

Custom property pane controls

By default, SPFx provides default controls to be used with the property pane (text fields, dropdowns, and so on). However, it also provides an extensibility model to create your own.

Now that we have covered the main capability of SPFx web parts, in the next section, we will see the other type of customizations you can build: extensions.

Extensions

SPFx extensions are used to extend the default UI. It applies to modern pages and libraries. We will cover the multiple types of extensions next.

Application Customizer

Application Customizer provides well-known placeholders in the SharePoint interface where extensions can be loaded depending on a registered scope (*site*, *web*, and *list*). A **scope** simply shows that the extension is loaded when the current user is in a particular context, for instance, when browsing into the entire site collection, only on a specific website, or only lists or libraries. We'll detail them in the next chapter.

The default provided placeholders for an Application Customizer are *top* and *bottom*:

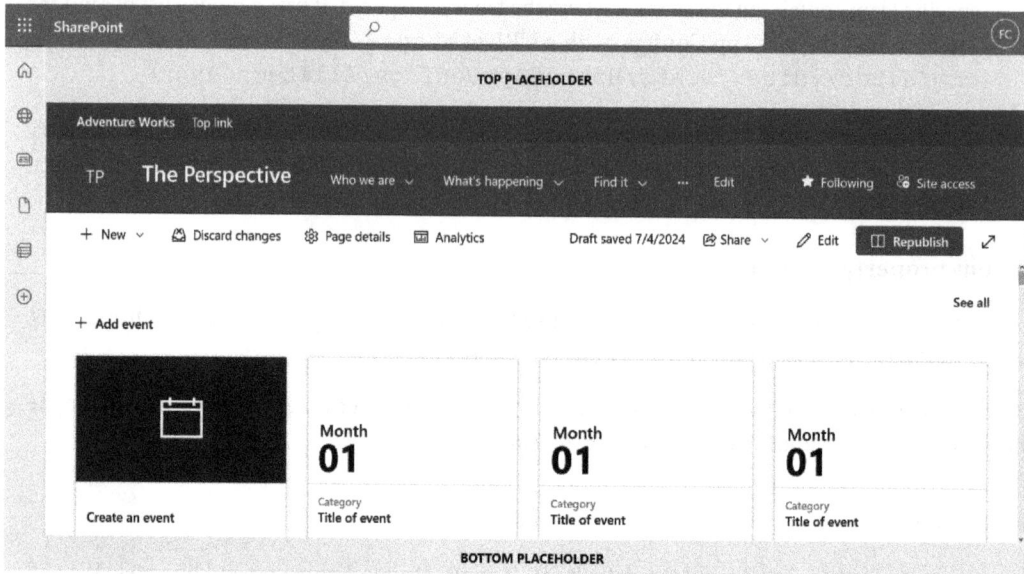

Figure 1.8 – Application Customizer default placeholders

Typical use cases for Application Customizer are banners and footers, for instance, to build custom navigation menus. However, Application Customizer isn't necessarily a visual component or forced to use placeholders. It can also be used to load customizations not tied to a specific element on the page, for instance, an extension loaded in the context of the current page checking information about the currently connected user and displaying a welcome popup on the page for a first visit.

Field Customizer

Field Customizer is used to modify the rendering of a specific list column in a SharePoint list or a library. It applies to every row on the list or library for that specific column (that is, field):

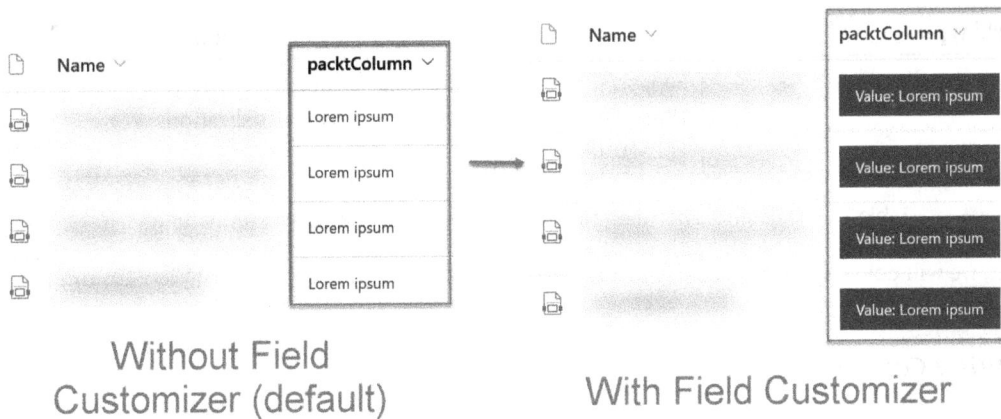

Figure 1.9 – Field Customizer attached on a list column

> **Note**
>
> Field Customizer can't be used with Microsoft Lists (https://www.microsoft.com/en-us/microsoft-365/microsoft-lists).

In Field Customizer, you can write custom JavaScript code and implement your own logic based on the context of the field value, item, list, page, and so on. It is a powerful feature to build a rich experience for field values.

Typical use cases for Field Customizer are advanced visuals such as progress bars, charts, and more. Also, because you have full control over the field canvas, customizers can be used to implement calls to actions and manipulate data dynamically (for the current field value or even fields in the current row item).

How does it compare to SharePoint column formatting?

Both options let you customize field rendering in a SharePoint list or library. Usually, Field Customizer is used for advanced scenarios when logic can be only achieved using custom code. Column formatting is used for light customizations and simple visuals via a declarative JSON schema and requires less setup than a full SPFx solution. This table from Microsoft summarizes well the possibilities:

Field type	Column formatting	Field Customizer
Conditional formatting based on item values and value ranges	Supported	Supported
Action links	Support for static hyperlinks that don't launch script	Support for any hyperlink including those invoking custom script

Field type	Column formatting	Field Customizer
Data visualizations	Support for simple visualizations that can be expressed using HTML and CSS	Support for arbitrary data visualizations

Table 1.1 – Differences between Field Customizer and JSON column formatting

Next, we will cover the way to customize the list contextual actions with the ListView Command Set extension.

ListView Command Set

A **ListView Command Set** extension allows you to provide custom buttons to the default list or library experience. They can be integrated into the top command bar, the item contextual menu, or both.

Unlike Application Customizer and Field Customizer, *you do not have control over the rendering*. The only visual information you can customize is the button labels and icons (only for the command bar for the latter).

Here is an example with the extension in the command bar:

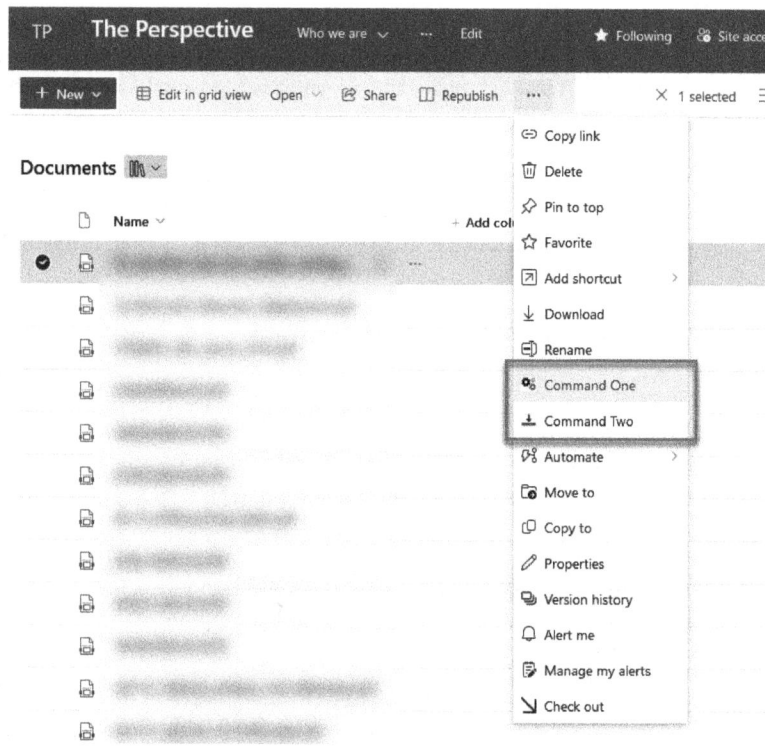

Figure 1.10 – An example of a ListView extension in the list command bar

Here is an example with an extension in the item contextual menu:

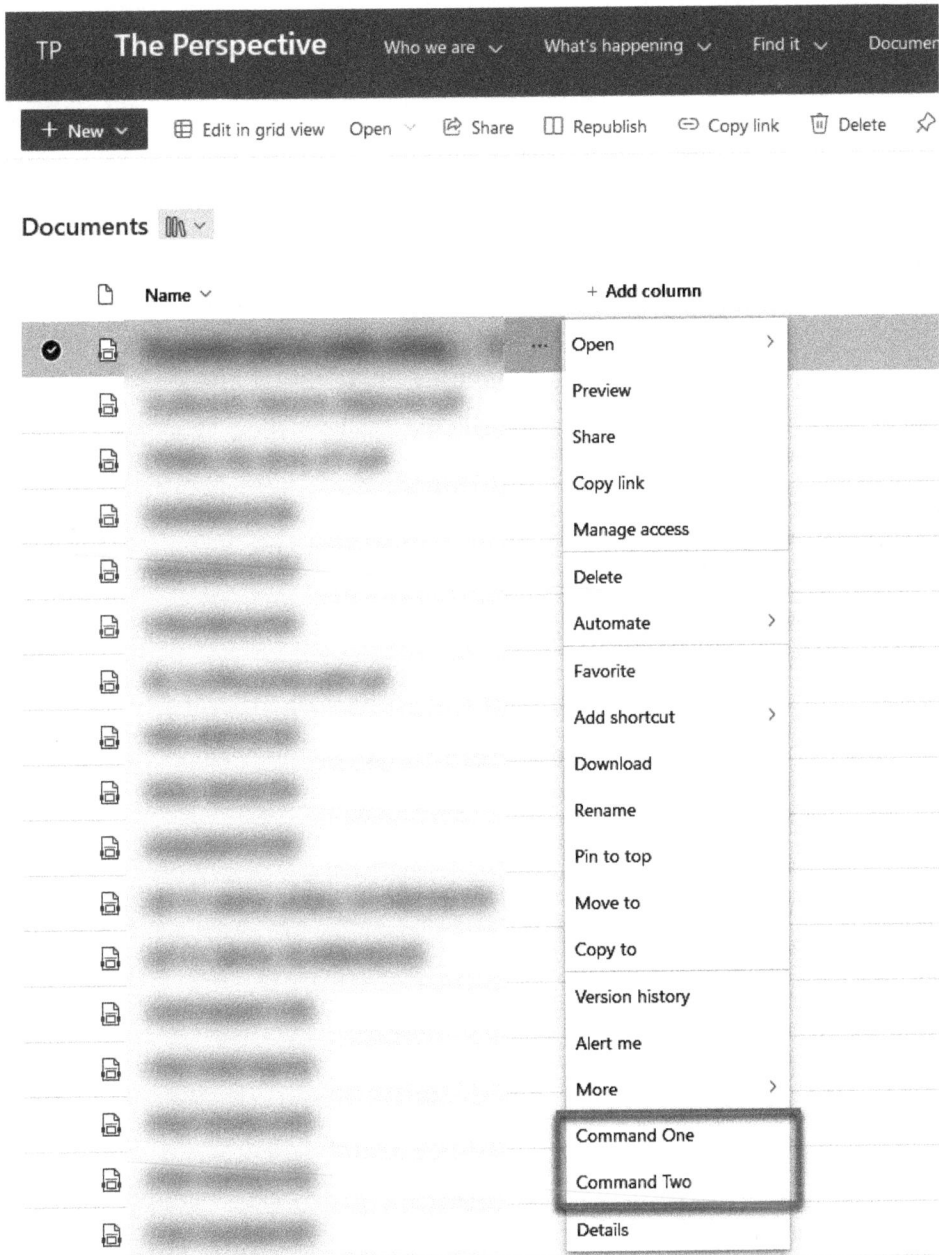

Figure 1.11 – An example of a ListView extension in the item contextual menu

ListView extensions are likely used to trigger workflows, process API calls, and so on based on the selected item information. The main challenge with such extensions is feedback notifications when actions are done. By default, if a button is clicked, there is no visual indication of any kind regarding the underlying operation, for instance, if it succeeded, failed, or is in progress. This will be up to you, as a developer, to implement your own notification system. That is why, usually, the ListView extension is coupled with UI controls, such as popup dialogs and message bars, to visually see what's going on.

Search Query Modifier

The **Search Query Modifier** extension is invoked just before the search query is executed, to be potentially modified before being submitted. A query extension can be registered in a *site* or *site collection* scope, meaning it will be executed when searching from a specific site or all sites in a site collection.

It only works with a custom search results page in the context of SharePoint that is, a SharePoint page to redirect to when submitting a search query from the top search bar. It means it won't work within the default SharePoint or Office search experiences:

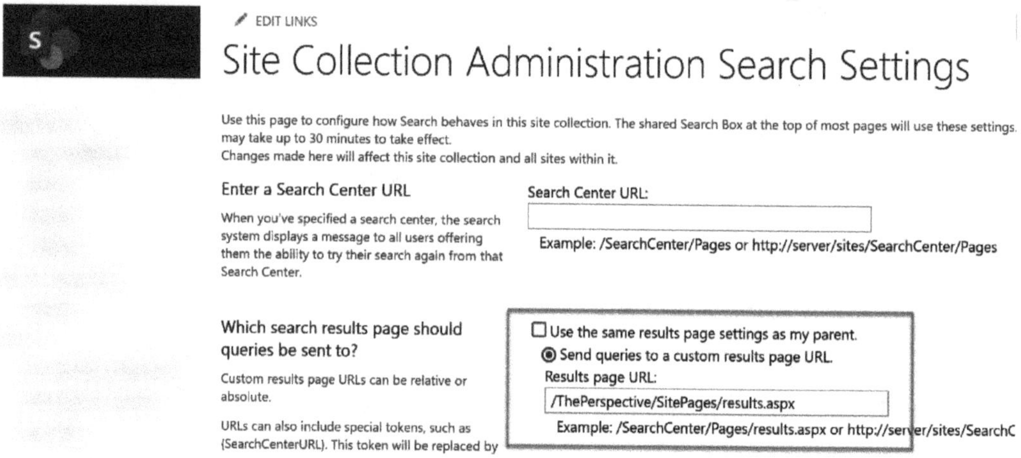

Site Collection Administration Search Settings

Use this page to configure how Search behaves in this site collection. The shared Search Box at the top of most pages will use these settings. may take up to 30 minutes to take effect.
Changes made here will affect this site collection and all sites within it.

Enter a Search Center URL

When you've specified a search center, the search system displays a message to all users offering them the ability to try their search again from that Search Center.

Search Center URL:

Example: /SearchCenter/Pages or http://server/sites/SearchCenter/Pages

Which search results page should queries be sent to?

Custom results page URLs can be relative or absolute.

URLs can also include special tokens, such as {SearchCenterURL}. This token will be replaced by

☐ Use the same results page settings as my parent.
◉ Send queries to a custom results page URL.
Results page URL:

/ThePerspective/SitePages/results.aspx

Example: /SearchCenter/Pages/results.aspx or http://server/sites/SearchC

Figure 1.12 – Configuring a custom search page for a SharePoint site

Search query extensions are usually coupled with the PnP Modern Search open source solution where the modified search query can be used as an input of these web parts:

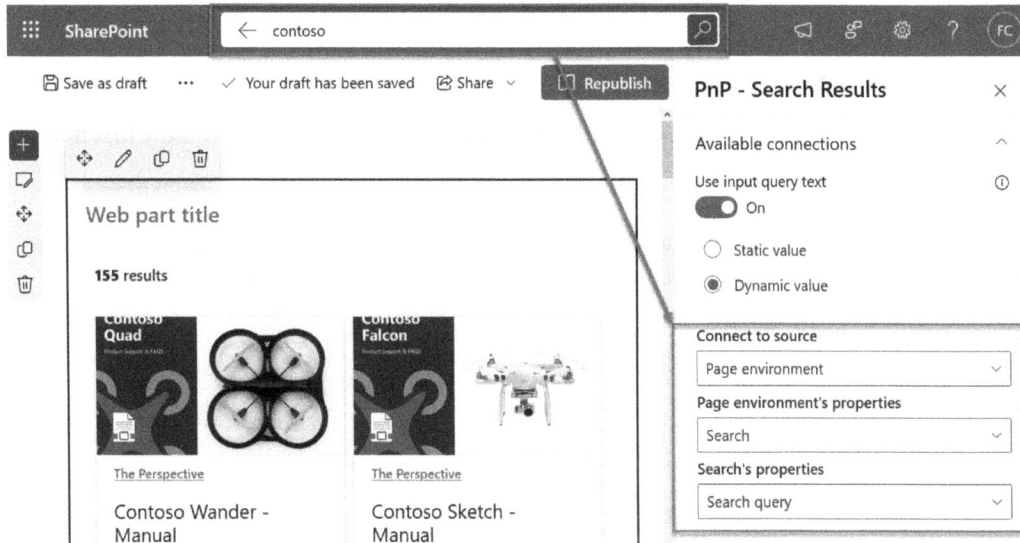

Figure 1.13 – Using search query from the top bar as query text for
the PnP Modern Search – search results web part

Search query as a dynamic data source

The search query (modified or not) can be accessed as a source by any SPFx components via the SPFx dynamic data capability.

As it has no visual considerations, query extensions are used for data manipulations only, transparent for the current user. Typical use cases are as follows:

- Dynamically fetching information about the current context to enrich the query, for instance, specific user properties (such as language, department, etc.) or current page properties

- "Cleaning" the user query by removing noise words and isolating important keywords to get more accurate results

---

Note

There is usually no need to use a search query extension to perform grammar or spelling corrections/modifications as this feature is likely handled directly by the Microsoft Search/ SharePoint Search engine.

Form Customizer

Historically, content types in a SharePoint list are associated with multiple forms corresponding to item life cycles:

- A **view** or **display** form when item properties are simply displayed
- A **new** form when a new item is created, and properties need to be filled in for the first time
- An **edit** form when item properties need to be updated

SharePoint provides default forms that automatically generate UI controls according to the item content type fields (that is, SharePoint columns) and take care of data loading/saving operations.

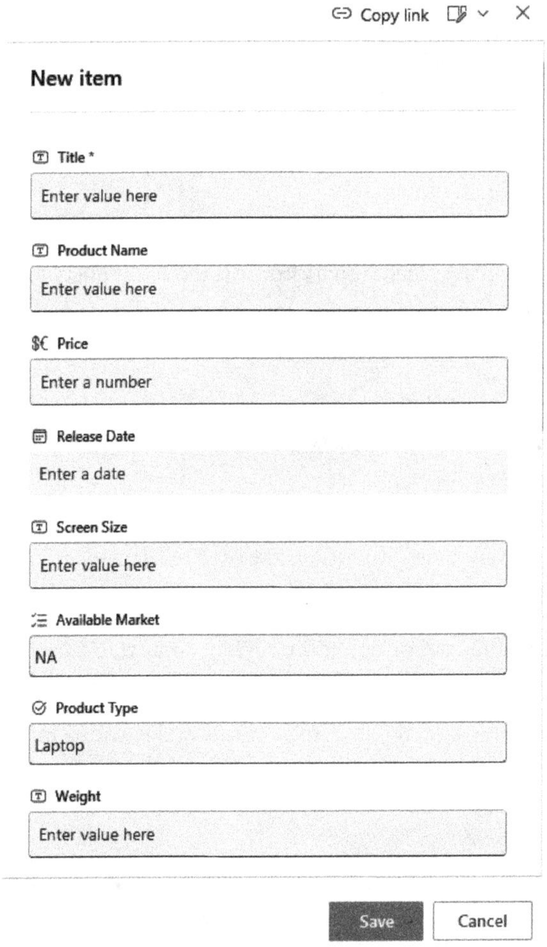

Figure 1.14 – An example of a default New item form in a SharePoint list

When complex field logic or custom visuals are required, default forms are quite limited.

An SPFx Form Customizer extension allows you to completely override one or all the default forms (display, new, and edit) to build your own form experience. In such an extension, you get total control over the form canvas, which is *blank* by default. As a developer, this is up to you to do the following:

- Implement UI controls that correspond to the underlying fields from the list you want to customize (for example, a text field control for a single line of text field type, a date picker control for dates, and so on). For instance, you can use **Fluent UI React controls** (formerly Office UI Fabric) for that purpose.
- Implement item field values load and save operations using REST APIs (SharePoint or Microsoft Graph) and provide save and cancel buttons.
- Validate these field values to comply with the underlying data format expected.

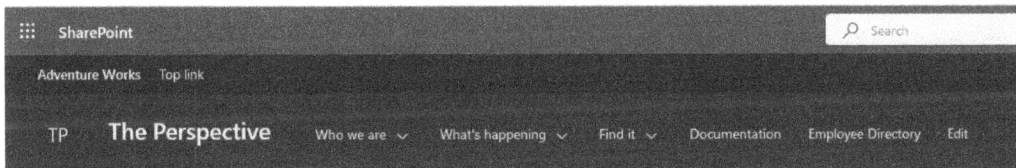

Figure 1.15 – The default experience of a Form Customizer

As you can see, this requires a fair amount of work to build a proper form. Luckily, the Form Customizer is often coupled with the DynamicForm React control (https://pnp.github.io/sp-dev-fx-controls-react/controls/DynamicForm/) created by the community and already handling these operations for you.

Once deployed, a Form Customizer needs to be associated with targeted content types using the specific (NewForm|DispForm|EditForm) ClientSideComponentId property.

Form Customizers work for both SharePoint lists and SharePoint libraries. *How does it compare to Power Apps customizations or JSON formatting?*

JSON formatting allows you to apply light customizations regarding the default form layout. With this option, you can change field control styles or behavior.

On the other side, a Form Customizer is the way to go if the form requires complex logic or visuals, such as specific business rules for conditional rendering or even custom controls. It is a more powerful option than Power Apps as you have full control over the canvas to use HTML and JavaScript to meet your requirements.

In the end, it all depends on the requirements you have for your form.

Adaptive Card Extension (ACE)

ACE is a customization type used to provide custom visuals for the Viva Connections dashboards. It uses Microsoft's Adaptive Card framework, a platform-agnostic declarative JSON schema to generate UIs.

What is Viva Connections?

Viva Connections is a component of the broader Microsoft Viva suite, which serves as an integrated employee experience platform. It consolidates various tools and resources such as communications, knowledge, learning, and insights. Viva Connections provides a mobile-first, personalized dashboard for users to access relevant news, conversations, and other resources, integrating with Microsoft Teams and other Microsoft 365 apps to enhance productivity and engagement within the workplace.

It's designed to help employees stay engaged and informed, offering a central hub for company news, important sites, and resources, all tailored to the individual user.

Administrators can create multiple Viva Connections experiences, for instance for different audiences inside a company. For each one, they can decide to use the default Viva Connections experience or use an existing SharePoint site:

Create a new Viva Connections experience

Select the type of experience you want to create. Get started quickly by creating a new Connections experience or build off an existing intranet portal. Experiences can be accessed on desktop, tablet, and mobile devices.

Learn more about how Viva Connections and intranet portals work together

ⓘ The ability to offer 2 or more Connections experiences requires a Microsoft Viva suite or Viva Communications & Communities license for all users of Connections. In the future, end users may not be able to access Connections without the required licensing. Learn more about Viva licensing

○ **Create a Connections experience**

Create and customize a brand-new employee experience for your organization.

- Minimal setup is needed
- Intranet portal is not required and can be added after setup
- Dashboard card templates and other resources allow easy access to other Viva apps

○ **Build from an existing portal to set a home site**

Use the same global navigation, branding, and theme as an existing site.

- Includes Connections dashboard, feed, resources, and an intranet portal
- Easily extend to the web using a SharePoint site
- Built-in navigation to help switch between Connections and SharePoint

Figure 1.16 – The Viva Connections experience setup from the admin portal

In the latter, this site will be set as a home site in the tenant. A **home site** can be any SharePoint site and will serve basically as the top landing page for your organization, the one users will see when clicking on the **SharePoint** tile from the Microsoft 365 app launcher.

> **Notice**
>
> You can only have one site declared as a home site in a tenant.

What is an Adaptive Card?

The main goal of Adaptive Cards is to provide UI consistency across applications meaning regardless of where the card is displayed, it will behave and look the same everywhere.

An Adaptive Card is a simple JSON file following a specific schema. You can't add JavaScript or HTML in cards, just configure properties and use ACEs. Adaptive Cards are used in a few places in the Microsoft 365 ecosystem (bot messages using different channels, such as Teams, Slack, and Outlook, Microsoft Search results, etc.).

ACEs are designed to be integrated in Viva Connections dashboards:

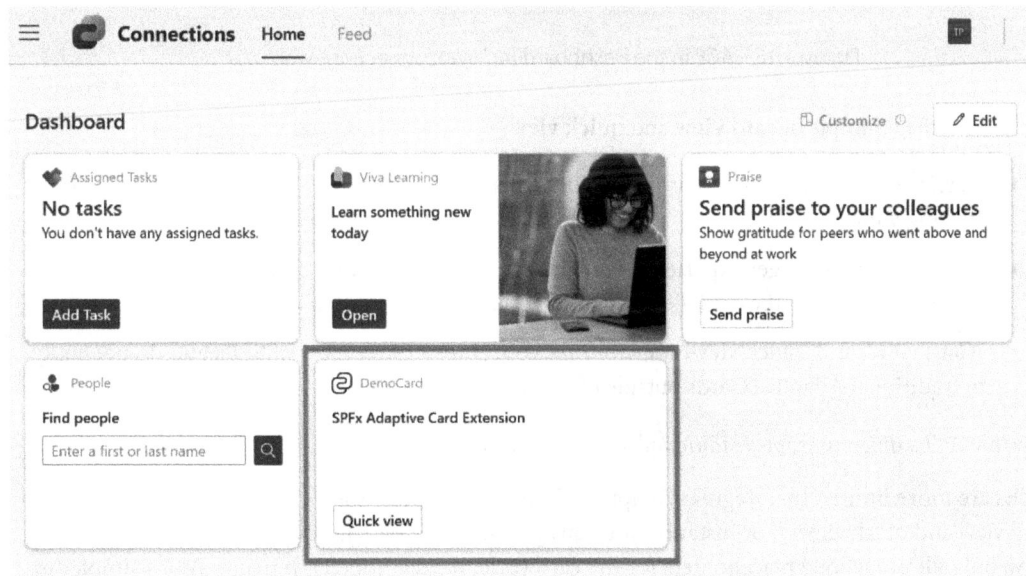

Figure 1.17 – ACE in the Viva Connections portal

They can also be used in SharePoint pages, using the "Dashboard for Viva Connections" web part:

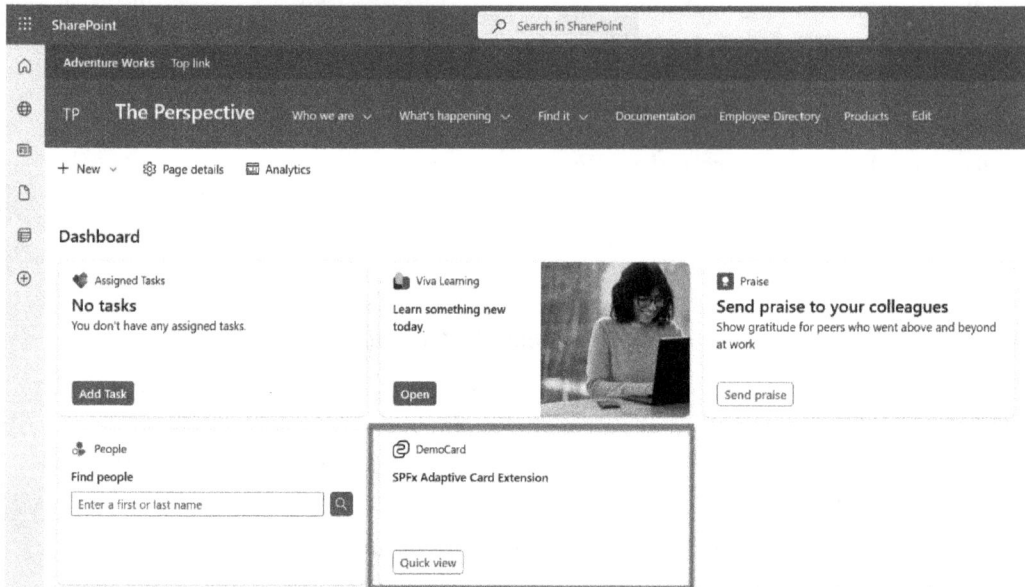

Figure 1.18 – ACE in the Dashboard for Viva Connections web part

ACEs have the concepts of **card view** and **quick view**:

- **Card view**: This is displayed as the default experience when a user opens the dashboard (i.e., starting view).

- **Quick view**: The larger experience launched from custom action on the card. You can't have multiple actions on the card view triggering multiple quick views.

- "Card view" and "quick view" are arbitrary concepts in the context of SPFx and do not apply to traditional Adaptive Cards outside of SPFx.

How are ACEs different from "traditional" Adaptive Cards?

ACEs are more limited than regular Adaptive Cards as Microsoft forces you to use the concept of card view and quick views. For instance, you can't provide your own JSON card payload for the card view, only fill predefined placeholders for the card (title, header, footer). It makes ACEs simpler to implement as the process is very streamlined and straightforward to serve its purpose: integrate into Viva Connections dashboards.

Technically speaking, you could achieve the same results using a web part solution and the Microsoft Adaptive Card JavaScript library. However, ACEs are designed for a specific purpose: integrating into the Viva Connections dashboard, which is the only way to do so.

> **Note**
> The Viva Connections dashboard web part is only available on the SharePoint site declared as a home site.

Microsoft Teams, Outlook, and the Microsoft 365 app

As we've seen in the capabilities overview, SPFx web parts can be integrated into Microsoft Teams through channel tabs, meeting apps, personal apps, and messaging extensions. This compatibility also enables integration with Outlook and the Microsoft 365 app without any required code modification:

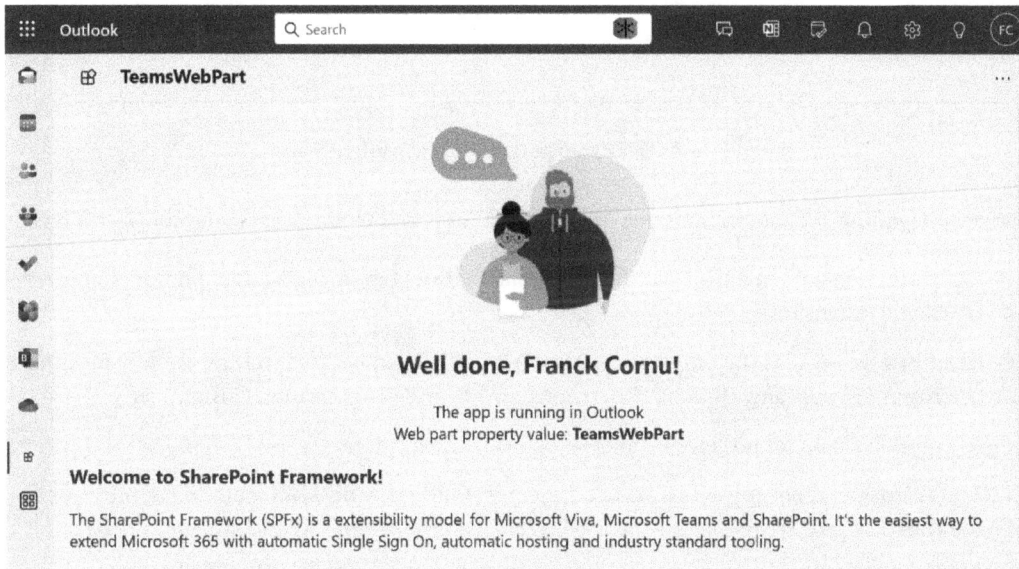

Figure 1.19 – An SPFx web part in Outlook

The experience is similar in the Microsoft 365 app:

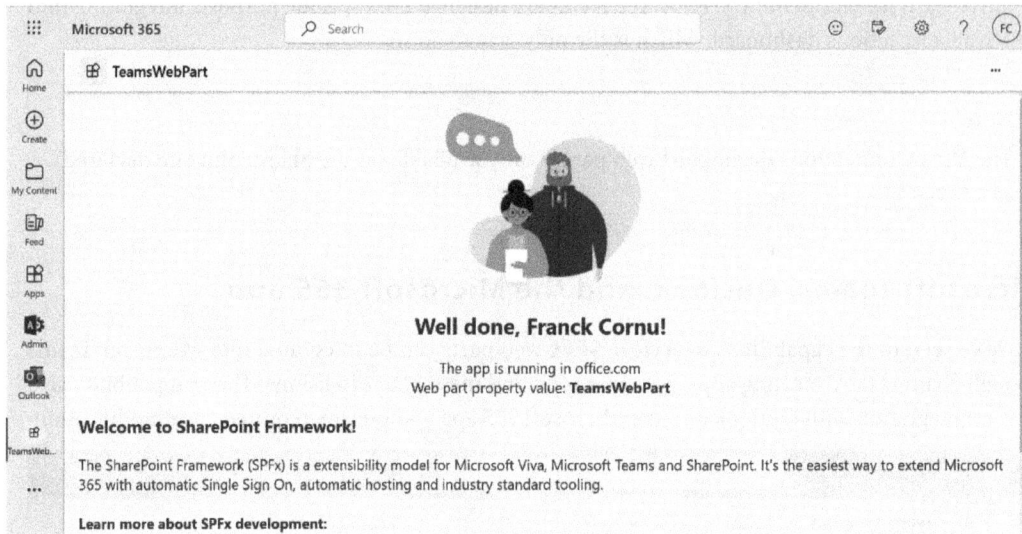

Figure 1.20 – An SPFx web part in the Microsoft 365 app

However, integrating SPFx into Teams, the Microsoft 365 app, and Outlook has some considerations:

- Only *one* web part at a time can be used as a channel tab, meeting app, personal app, or messaging extension.

- The SPFx web part is the only customization type that can be used in Microsoft Teams, the Microsoft 365 app, and Outlook. Extensions can't be used (Application Customizer, etc.).

- Integration works for both web and desktop client applications.

- For Teams personal apps, Teams meeting apps, Outlook, and Microsoft 365 applications, the web part property pane can't be used to persist user settings. Other strategies need to be implemented by the developer (e.g., store settings in the current user profile or OneDrive).

- No matter what the host application is, you are responsible for the content inside the web part canvas to be responsive and adapt to mobile or lower-resolution experiences.

- Microsoft 365 app and Outlook support is a consequence of the Microsoft Teams SPFx solutions support and does not require configuring any specific settings in the web part for these applications.

- SPFx is context "aware," meaning it allows you to conditionally execute code depending on the host application (Teams, Outlook, or the Microsoft 365 app) leveraging host capabilities (for instance, accessing the Teams JavaScript **Software Development Kit** (**SDK**) library directly from the SPFx code when running in Teams).

Should I use SPFx instead of the Microsoft Teams Toolkit to build Teams customizations?

From a strict Microsoft Teams point of view, the traditional way of building Teams customizations (tab, personal app, and so on) is to use the Microsoft Teams Toolkit. However, in some cases, SPFx presents some advantages and is a preferred option:

- For tabs, it can leverage the property pane and save you a lot of time regarding the app configuration experience implementation as you don't have to worry about storage and controls.

> **Side note**
> Microsoft Teams Toolkit provides SPFx templates to get started, but only for tabs.

- SPFx automatically handles the single sign-on authentication process. With Teams Toolkit, you will have to handle this part on your own.
- Web parts exposed in Microsoft Teams can be also used in SharePoint as regular web parts in addition to Teams.
- The development process is easier with SPFx as it does not involve deploying backend infrastructure to host the application and lets you use the SPFx tooling and project structure like any other SPFx solutions (e.g., having multiple SPFx components inside the same project solution).

In this section, we've covered the two main solution types you can create with SPFx (web parts and extensions) and how they can be integrated into Microsoft 365 tools, such as SharePoint, Teams, and Viva Connections. We roughly detailed their behavior and specificities and gave some real use case integration examples for each.

We also covered the technical limitations for SharePoint On-Premises environments.

In the next section, we give you an overview of all available resources you can leverage from the very active Microsoft 365 community to help you during your SPFx journey.

The Microsoft 365 & Power Platform Community

The **Microsoft 365 & Power Platform Community [formerly Pattern and Practices (PnP)]** (https://pnp.github.io/) is a community around Microsoft 365 and Power Platform that regroups articles, videos, samples, tools, solutions, and so on to help you get the most out of the platform, focusing on value without reinventing the wheel. It is driven by Microsoft and people from the community and is one of the widest and most active technical communities in the world.

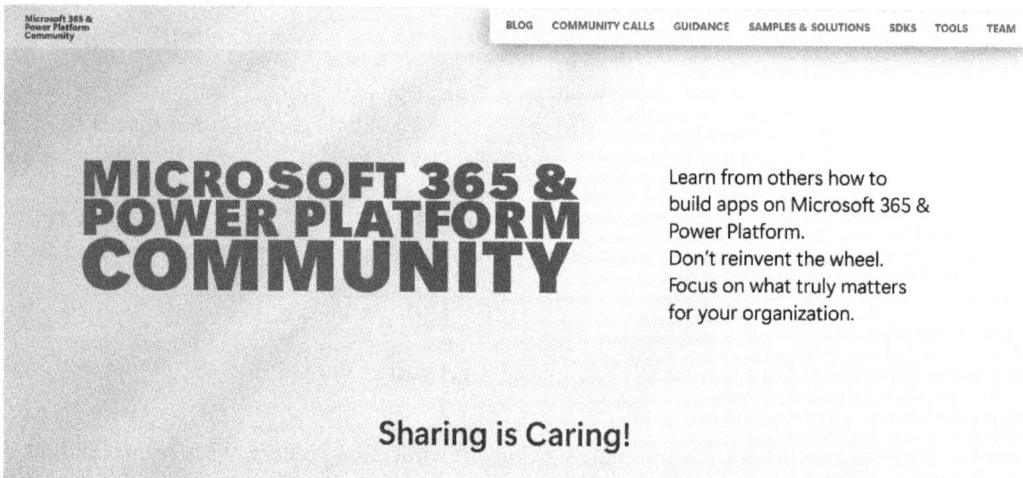

Figure 1.21 – The Microsoft 365 & Power Platform community website

This initiative is mainly technically oriented but not only; many topics around Microsoft 365, such as document management, governance, adoption, and best practices can also be found. As it is driven by Microsoft, this is also the preferred channel to stay up to date about the latest features and updates through regular community calls, especially on the SPFx side.

As an SPFx developer, it is clearly a must-see and something you should regularly check to stay up to date.

Among the most renowned PnP initiatives, we can mention the following:

- **PnP Core SDK** (`https://pnp.github.io/pnpcore/`): A .NET library to cover the needs of developers working with either SharePoint Online or Teams.

- **PnP PowerShell** (`https://learn.microsoft.com/en-ca/powershell/sharepoint/sharepoint-pnp/sharepoint-pnp-cmdlets`): A set of PowerShell cmdlets (based on PnP Core) to interact with SharePoint Online and Teams. Used by admins and developers to automate deployments and configurations across the entire platform .

- **PnP CLI for Microsoft 365** (`https://pnp.github.io/cli-microsoft365/`): This helps manage your Microsoft 365 tenant and SPFx projects on any platform (Windows, macOS, Linux).

- **PnP JS** (`https://pnp.github.io/pnpjs/`): A collection of fluent JavaScript libraries for consuming SharePoint, Graph, and Office 365 REST APIs in a type-safe way that can be used in SPFx solutions.

- **SPFx reusable controls and SPFx property pane controls** (`https://pnp.github.io/sp-dev-fx-controls-react/`): A set of reusable React controls that can be used in SPFx solutions.

- **PnP Modern Search** (`https://microsoft-search.github.io/pnp-modern-search/`): A solution providing SharePoint Online modern web parts to create custom search experiences.

The community around SPFx and, broadly, Microsoft 365 is very active and offers many resources you can use to help you get started. Don't reinvent the wheel and benefit from various samples and tools. This will give more time to focus on business value.

Summary

In this chapter, we started introducing the ecosystem surrounding SPFx, especially Microsoft 365, and we enumerated the differences between SharePoint Online and On-Premises versions. We detailed SPFx philosophy and history, highlighting key features released over the years and what it means for developers.

Then, we covered all the capabilities of the framework, listing the two types of solutions that can be created with it: web parts and extensions. We went through all possible customizations, explaining how they integrate with SharePoint, Teams, or Viva Connections, and giving usage examples for each.

We finished by listing key community resources around SPFx and Microsoft 365 to help developers speed up their developments.

In the next chapter, we'll detail the technical and functional architecture for both Microsoft 365 and SharePoint. We'll also discuss how to access data from these platforms with SPFx solutions.

Get This Book's PDF Version and Exclusive Extras

UNLOCK NOW

Scan the QR code (or go to `packtpub.com/unlock`). Search for this book by name, confirm the edition, and then follow the steps on the page.

Note: Keep your invoice handy. Purchases made directly from Packt don't require an invoice.

Ecosystem and Building Blocks around the SharePoint Framework

In the previous chapter, we introduced you to SPFx and presented all its capabilities in relation to extensibility platforms (SharePoint, Teams, Outlook, and Microsoft 365).

In this chapter, we will go in-depth into the core building blocks of the Microsoft 365 ecosystem involved in the SharePoint Framework development, especially SharePoint and Teams logical structures.

As a developer, it will give you a clear understanding of concepts you will likely have to manipulate in SPFx and use correctly to build your solutions.

We will also detail what APIs are available to access data from Microsoft 365 in your solutions and how to use them in SPFx. We will be covering the following main topics in this chapter:

- Understanding the SharePoint logical architecture
- Understanding the Teams logical architecture
- Accessing data within Microsoft 365

Overview of the Microsoft 365 architecture

As mentioned in the previous chapter, Microsoft 365 is a complete suite composed of many different tools under the same roof, and it provides many building blocks. As an SPFx developer, it is important to understand this structure as there is a high probability you'll have to manipulate these building blocks programmatically in your SPFx solutions. This can be done by either using the Microsoft Graph API, the unified endpoint to access Microsoft 365 data, or the SharePoint REST API, a legacy API used to manipulate SharePoint data only.

In the next sections, we will discuss the architecture of the two main tools commonly used with SPFx: SharePoint Online and Teams.

Understanding the SharePoint logical architecture

Since the very beginning of SharePoint, the logical information architecture hasn't changed much in SharePoint Online. The same core building blocks still apply (except those managed directly by Microsoft in SharePoint Online, such as web applications and managed services such as search and taxonomy). We will discuss each of them and provide details about the associated APIs and ways to manipulate them programmatically.

Site collection

By definition, a site collection represents a collection of…sites (what a surprise). This is the highest-level building block you will encounter in SharePoint Online. The term **site collection** is actually a *logical* concept as it does not have a *physical* counterpart. A site collection always contains at least one root site (the one you can physically see) but can contain many sites. A site collection contains settings that apply to all sites, such as security, columns, content types, and search schema.

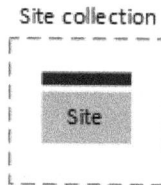

Figure 2.1 – The most basic site collection structure

Historically, SharePoint used a sub-sites architecture. However, with the new modern UI experience, this architecture has been *deprecated* due to its lack of flexibility and has been replaced by the hub architecture (multiple flat site collections (i.e., only one site) grouped together as a hub).

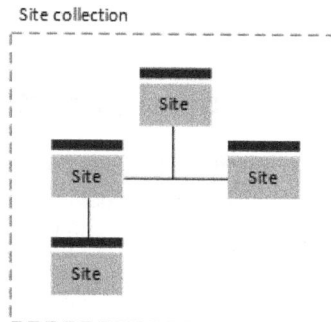

Figure 2.2 – Site collection with the sub-sites architecture (deprecated)

Programmatically speaking, a site collection is represented by the term *site* whether or not you are using the SharePoint REST API of Microsoft Graph (we'll cover the details of these two APIs later in this chapter). The following table shows you how to access a site collection using both APIs:

API	URL format
SharePoint REST API	`https://{site_url}/_api/site`
Microsoft Graph	`https://graph.microsoft.com/v1.0/sites/{site-id}`

Table 2.1 – Accessing a SharePoint site collection using SharePoint REST API and Microsoft Graph

Note

In SharePoint Online, *site* often refers implicitly to *site collection* (for instance, in the administration center) due to the new recommended modern flat structure.

In a modern information architecture site collections can be logically regrouped together as a hub.

Hub

A hub is a group of site collections. Unlike the sub-sites architecture, the main advantage of a hub is its flexibility: sites can be added and removed very easily. Once a site joins a hub, it inherits automatically from hub settings such as security, common hub navigation, theme, and search scopes. Like a site collection, a hub is a *logical* concept and always has at least one site collection acting as the root hub site, defining common parameters shared by other sites. You can register any SharePoint site collection as a hub.

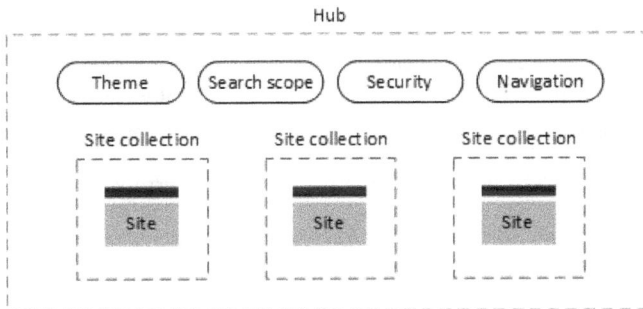

Figure 2.3 – The hub architecture

> **Hub-to-hub association**
>
> There is also a concept of hub-to-hub association, where child hubs can join a parent hub in a multi-level structure (i.e., a child hub can also be a parent hub for lower-level hubs). This gives you even more flexibility for your site architecture. Like site collections, hubs can be registered/unregistered at any time. However, unlike site collections in a single hub, multiple associated hubs only aggregate their search scope. Theme or navigation are not shared automatically.

Programmatically speaking, working with hub sites can be tricky because, unlike site collections or sites, they don't have a specific endpoint. They can only be manipulated through SharePoint REST-specific actions, living under different endpoints depending on what you are trying to achieve:

API	URL format

SharePoint REST API
 	
(not exhaustive)
	Ex: join a hub site:
	
	`https://{site_url}/_api/site/JoinHubSite(hubSiteId)`
	
	Ex: List hub sites for current user:
	
	`https://{site_url}/_api/HubSites`

Microsoft Graph	No equivalent

Table 2.2 - Access a SharePoint hub using SharePoint REST API and Microsoft Graph

Because site collections and hubs are logical concepts, they both rely on SharePoint sites in the end.

Site

A site is a physical representation of what users see. It can't exist without a site collection. It contains, among other features, navigation, lists, libraries, columns, content types, and so on. While "site collection" and "site" are confusingly similar terms, programmatically speaking, a site has different properties than a site collection and is represented by different terms depending on the API you use.

When using the SharePoint REST API, a site is represented by the term *web*.

When using the Microsoft Graph API, a site is represented by *site*. There is no distinction between site collections and sites. To access a site using both APIs, you can use the followings calls:

API	URL format
SharePoint REST API	`https://{site_url}/_api/web`
Microsoft Graph	`https://graph.microsoft.com/v1.0/sites/{site-id}`

Table 2.3 – Access a SharePoint site using SharePoint REST API and Microsoft Graph

Within a site, the data is stored in lists and libraries.

Lists and libraries

Lists and libraries are where the data lives. Libraries are used to store physical documents such as PDF or Word files, and lists contain structured raw information not stored as documents. Lists and libraries are defined in a site:

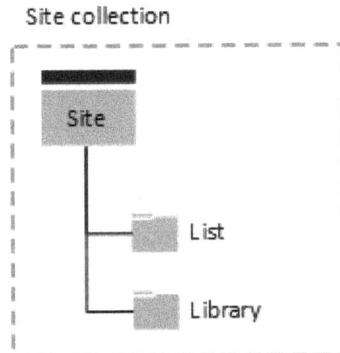

Figure 2.4 – Lists and libraries structure

Programmatically speaking, lists and libraries have different references depending on the API. Using SharePoint REST API, a list or a library is the same concept. With Microsoft Graph, a library is called a `drive` (and a document a `driveItem`) and a list a `list` (and a list item a `listItem`) and can be accessed from different endpoints (i.e., `/me` for OneDrive and `/sites` for SharePoint) despite the fact that they represent the same concept behind the scenes: a library in a SharePoint site. These are examples of how you can retrieve a list or a library using the SharePoint REST API or the Microsoft Graph API:

SharePoint REST API	`https://{site_url}/_api/web/lists` (for both lists and libraries)

Microsoft Graph	**Lists**
	`https://graph.microsoft.com/v1.0/sites/{site-id}/lists/{list-id}`
	Libraries
	`https://graph.microsoft.com/v1.0/drives/{driveId}`

Table 2.4 – Retrieving a list or library

To better classify and describe the information, lists and libraries can use columns and content types.

Columns, fields, and content types

A *column* represents metadata associated with documents or an item in a list. By default, SharePoint provides different column types (single line of text, dates, choices, taxonomy, and so on). The intersection between a column and an item in a list is called an item *field*. It is where the actual value resides for that column.

A *content type* is an aggregation of multiple columns defined by the user and used to represent a business entity type in a list or a library (for example, a *Contract* document content type includes metadata, that is columns, such as the client's name, signed date, duration, and so on). It means users will be able to create *Contract* documents using that content type, having these metadata to fill by default.

> **Content types are optional**
>
> Columns can be used outside of a content type and directly added to a list or a library. However, using content types is considered a best practice when designing an information architecture.

Here is the schema representing the relationships between lists, columns, items, fields, and content types:

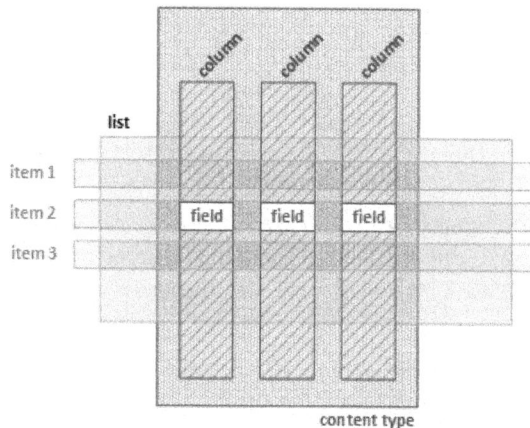

Figure 2.5 – Relationship between list, items, column, fields, and content types

Columns and content types can be defined at multiple scopes (site collection, site, lists, and libraries), making them available for child elements (for example, a column defined at the site collection level is usable at the site and list levels, and a content type defined at the site level is usable by all lists and libraries in that site).

> **Note**
>
> In SharePoint Online, there is also the notion of a content type hub, which allows you to define content types in a site collection and publish them to be consumed and synced to other site collections.

Understanding Teams' logical architecture

Microsoft Teams is a good example of a Microsoft 365 service built over many other tools that provides dedicated functions:

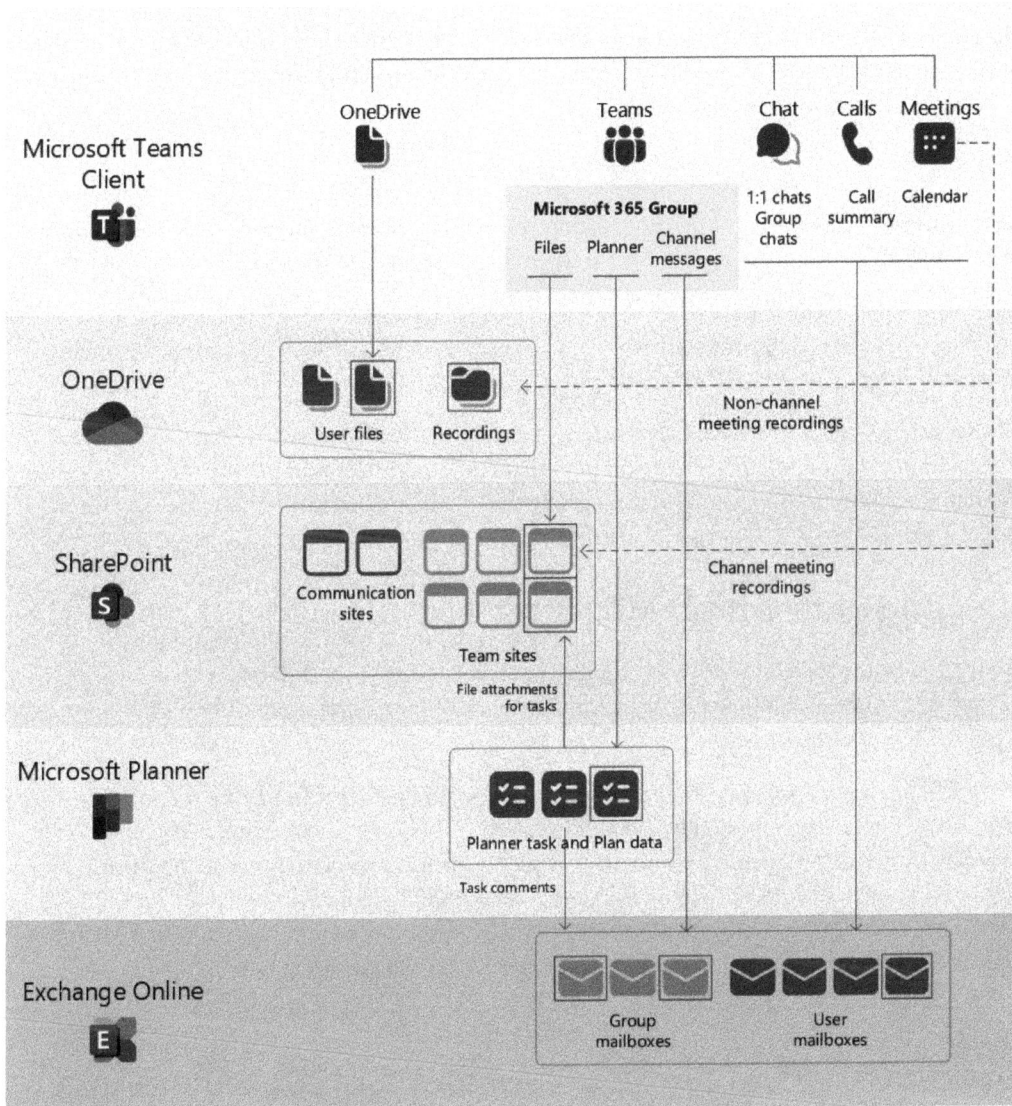

Figure 2.6 – Microsoft Teams' logical architecture

Programmatically speaking, the Microsoft Graph API is the only way to integrate with Microsoft Teams data. Being a group in Entra ID behind the scenes, a team can be accessed either by targeting the `https://graph.microsoft.com/v1.0/groups/{id}/team` endpoint or directly using the request `https://graph.microsoft.com/v1.0/teams/{id}`.

As you can see, Microsoft Teams' architecture is heavily based on the Entra ID concept of groups, allowing you to control memberships and link together multiple communications services, such as messages, calls, and meetings.

Groups

When you create a new team in Microsoft Teams, you actually create a Microsoft 365 group in Entra ID associated with a group mailbox in Exchange Online. Also, behind the scenes, a SharePoint site is also created to store all files from channels.

Depending on your development scenario, you will need to target specific APIs' endpoints to achieve parts of your solution (ex via Microsoft Graph).

In this section, we've covered the basic structure of Teams and SharePoint. Now that you have a basic understanding of the building blocks involved in these tools' architecture, in the next section, we dig down into the API side and see how to manipulate these building blocks programmatically through different APIs.

Accessing data within Microsoft 365

In your SPFx solutions, you will likely manipulate data coming from different sources within the Microsoft 365 platform (SharePoint, Teams, and so on) and it is important to know what APIs you can use and how to access them.

Microsoft 365 is a platform that groups many tools under the same roof and, as a result, provides a unified API to interact with them: the *Microsoft Graph API*. This is the recommended API for accessing data within a Microsoft 365 tenant. However, because the platform also groups tools originally coming from the on-premises world, such as SharePoint, it also contains dedicated and legacy APIs that you can still use as well. In the context of SPFx, we will focus on the SharePoint REST APs and Microsoft Graph as they are the two main APIs you will commonly have to use when building solutions.

> **Note**
>
> As long as you need to get data from Microsoft 365 workloads using APIs, identity and authentication will be involved. They rely on the Microsoft identity platform in Microsoft Azure and Entra ID (formerly Azure Active Directory). For SPFx developers, identity is a key topic, especially authentication flows available to you (OAuth).

Overview of SharePoint REST API

The SharePoint REST API is the dedicated API for accessing and manipulating SharePoint data. It is available in two API versions *v1* and *v2*:

- The *v1* version is the historical and legacy API inherited from SharePoint on-premises but is also available in SharePoint Online. The URL format is `https://{site_url}/_api/{site|web|etc.}`.

  This API offers similar operations that are available with the SharePoint **Client Side Object Model (CSOM)** and uses the **Open Data Protocol (OData)** syntax.

- The *v2* version is a new API integrated into in the broader global Microsoft Graph API and, therefore, benefits from its common features set (authentication, batching, and so on). This API can be accessed in two ways producing *the exact same output*:

  - Through the Microsoft Graph endpoint (/v1.0 or /beta): `https://graph.microsoft.com/v1.0/{sites|drives|etc.}`

  - Through SharePoint relatively to the tenant URL: `https://{tenant-name}.sharepoint.com/_api/v2.0/{sites|drives|etc.}`

> **Tip**
> To know if a Microsoft Graph REST API call is backed by the SharePoint Online v2 API, add the `$whatif` parameter to the end of the query to see the underlying SharePoint URL call (for example, `https://graph.microsoft.com/v1.0/sites?$whatif`).

Both the *v1* and *v2* APIs provide different endpoints to *create*, *read*, *update*, or *delete* data within SharePoint according to its logical structure (sites, lists, list items, and so on).

Depending on your requirements, you can use one or both endpoints in your SPFx solutions. For instance, some operations are still only available in the *v1* endpoint (such as manipulating SharePoint hub sites).

Also, most of the time, the same operation can be achieved with both APIs. For example, reading items in a SharePoint list can be achieved in multiple ways:

Using *V1* endpoint	`https://{site_url}/_api/web/lists(guid'{list_guid}')/Items`

Using *V2* endpoint	`https://graph.microsoft.com/v1.0/sites/{site-id}/lists/{list-id}/items`
	
	OR
	
	`https://{tenant-name}.sharepoint.com/_api/v2.0/sites/{site-id}/lists/{list-id}/items`

Table 2.5 – Using both endpoints to read items in a SharePoint list

The output payload between the two API versions will be different, but the content itself (i.e., the items) will be the same. In general, if an operation is available in both APIs, we recommend always using the Microsoft Graph/v2 endpoint.

> **What about the SharePoint JavaScript Object Model (JSOM)?**
>
> On-premises SharePoint developers may have used the **SharePoint JavaScript Object Model (JSOM)** in the past to access data in their solutions. JSOM consists of a bunch of well-known JavaScript files to include and load in your files to access SharePoint data (ex: `/_layouts/15/init.js`, `/_layouts/15/SP.Runtime.js`, `/_layouts/15/SP.js`) similar to the CSOM syntax. You can still use them in an SPFx solution; however, this approach is now deprecated, and we don't recommend it. All the operations you could do in the past with JSOM can be achieved using REST APIs with v1 or v2 endpoints. Unless you have a very good reason (or a legacy project to migrate), you shouldn't use this approach.

Overview of Microsoft Graph API

Microsoft Graph is an API that provides a unified endpoint for accessing Microsoft cloud services such as Entra ID and Microsoft 365 (SharePoint, OneDrive, Exchange, or Teams). It simplifies the process of integrating various Microsoft services and allows developers to access data and insights from Microsoft 365 through a single endpoint instead of using a dedicated API for each tool with different behaviors. The API is accessible through the base URL (`https://graph.microsoft.com`) and proposes two different endpoints:

- */v1.0* endpoint: A stable API designed for production usage.
- */beta* endpoint: Used to test and evaluate new upcoming features. This should be used only for testing purposes, not production, because behavior could be changed without notice by Microsoft.

The Microsoft Graph API is the recommended API when it comes to creating, reading, updating, or deleting data within the Microsoft 365 platform. The API is not organized directly by tools or services silos within the Microsoft 365 platform (such as SharePoint, Teams, Outlook, and so on) but rather by *entities* (people, files, sites, emails, calendars, and more) linked together (i.e., a graph structure). These entities are accessible through different endpoint paths according to their logical relationships. For example, files can be accessed from multiple places.

To get a specific file from the default document library associated with a Microsoft 365 group (i.e., a team in Microsoft Teams), use the following request:

```
https://graph.microsoft.com/v1.0/groups/{groupId}/drive/items/
{item-id}
```

To get a specific file in the current user's OneDrive, use the following:

```
https://graph.microsoft.com/v1.0/me/drive/items/{item-id}
```

To get a file from the default document library in a SharePoint site, use the following:

```
https://graph.microsoft.com/v1.0/sites/{site-id}/drive/items/
{item-id})
```

Depending on the entity type, a different cloud service will be used behind the scenes. For instance, to get a list of sites, the SharePoint service is used. For mail or calendars, this is the Outlook service. To see the complete list of features and services, refer to the official documentation: `https://learn.microsoft.com/en-us/graph/overview-major-services?view=graph-rest-1.0`.

Being a unified API, Microsoft Graph comes with general capabilities applicable to all entities, among them:

- **Batching**: The ability to send multiple requests at a time to the server (for example, updating multiple items in a SharePoint list in parallel) reducing the server load and improving performances for client applications. Each batch can contain up to 20 requests.

- **Throttling**: A mechanism that automatically blocks the client applications from sending too many requests in a short amount of time by returning HTTP 429 errors. In such cases, client applications are responsible for implementing the logic to wait before sending subsequent requests to the endpoint.

- **Change notification (webhook)**: The ability to subscribe to changes for some entities using a webhook (i.e., an endpoint in your application that will be called when the change occurs), for example, being notified when a file is updated in a SharePoint library or a group has been modified. As a developer, it is up to you to figure out what changed when the event is raised, for example, using delta queries.

- **Delta queries**: Delta queries are often paired with the change notification feature to identify what changed in the monitored entity (creation, update, or deletion). It avoids polling the server constantly to get the current status and filters out all the data every time.

- **Query parameters**: The ability to use common OData parameters to control request output, for instance, limit the information to retrieve using `$select`, filter out the retrieved data using `$filter`, or browsing data by pages using `$top` and `$skip`. The supported parameters depend on the entity.

> **Using the Microsoft Graph explorer**
>
> To be able to quickly test the Microsoft Graph API, Microsoft provides an online tool called **Microsoft Graph Explorer**, accessible at `https://aka.ms/ge`. It allows you to craft and test your HTTP requests live using your real data. As a developer, this is a useful tool for debugging or testing your requests before implementing them in your SPFx solutions.

Regardless of the API you are using (SharePoint v1/v2 or Microsoft Graph), all requests must be authenticated first. In the Microsoft 365 architecture, both APIs rely on the Microsoft Identity platform, Entra ID, and use OAuth 2.0 flows for authentication. The goal of this book is not to detail every single OAuth 2.0 flow as this would take up an entire book on its own. However, we will give you an overview of how authentication works and what you need to know.

Authentication and permissions

The authentication process in Microsoft cloud environments is always performed through an Entra ID application, created in an Azure tenant (for instance, one that is behind a Microsoft 365 tenant). An Entra ID application first defines APIs that can be used. By default, it provides the common APIs encountered in the Microsoft cloud ecosystem (such as the SharePoint REST API and the Microsoft Graph API), but you can also provide custom ones, for example, for connecting to custom or third-party APIs. These APIs expose a set of usable permissions (also known as scopes) that consumer applications can use (such as `Files.Read.All`).

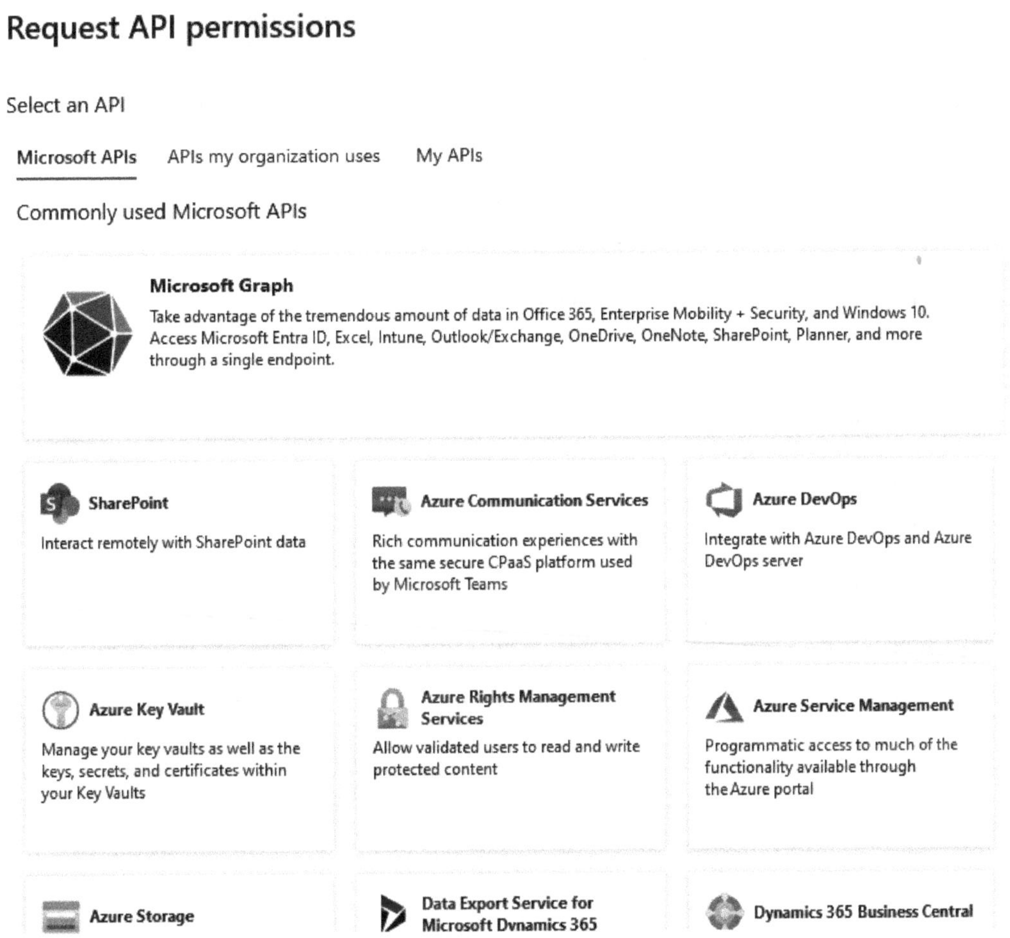

Request API permissions

Select an API

Microsoft APIs   APIs my organization uses   My APIs

Commonly used Microsoft APIs

Microsoft Graph

Take advantage of the tremendous amount of data in Office 365, Enterprise Mobility + Security, and Windows 10. Access Microsoft Entra ID, Excel, Intune, Outlook/Exchange, OneDrive, OneNote, SharePoint, Planner, and more through a single endpoint.

SharePoint

Interact remotely with SharePoint data

Azure Communication Services

Rich communication experiences with the same secure CPaaS platform used by Microsoft Teams

Azure DevOps

Integrate with Azure DevOps and Azure DevOps server

Azure Key Vault

Manage your key vaults as well as the keys, secrets, and certificates within your Key Vaults

Azure Rights Management Services

Allow validated users to read and write protected content

Azure Service Management

Programmatic access to much of the functionality available through the Azure portal

Azure Storage

Data Export Service for Microsoft Dynamics 365

Dynamics 365 Business Central

Figure 2.7 – Definition of usable APIs in an Entra ID app

In the Entra ID app, the next step is to choose the allowed *API permissions* (such as `Files.Read.All`) from the list that the API provides.

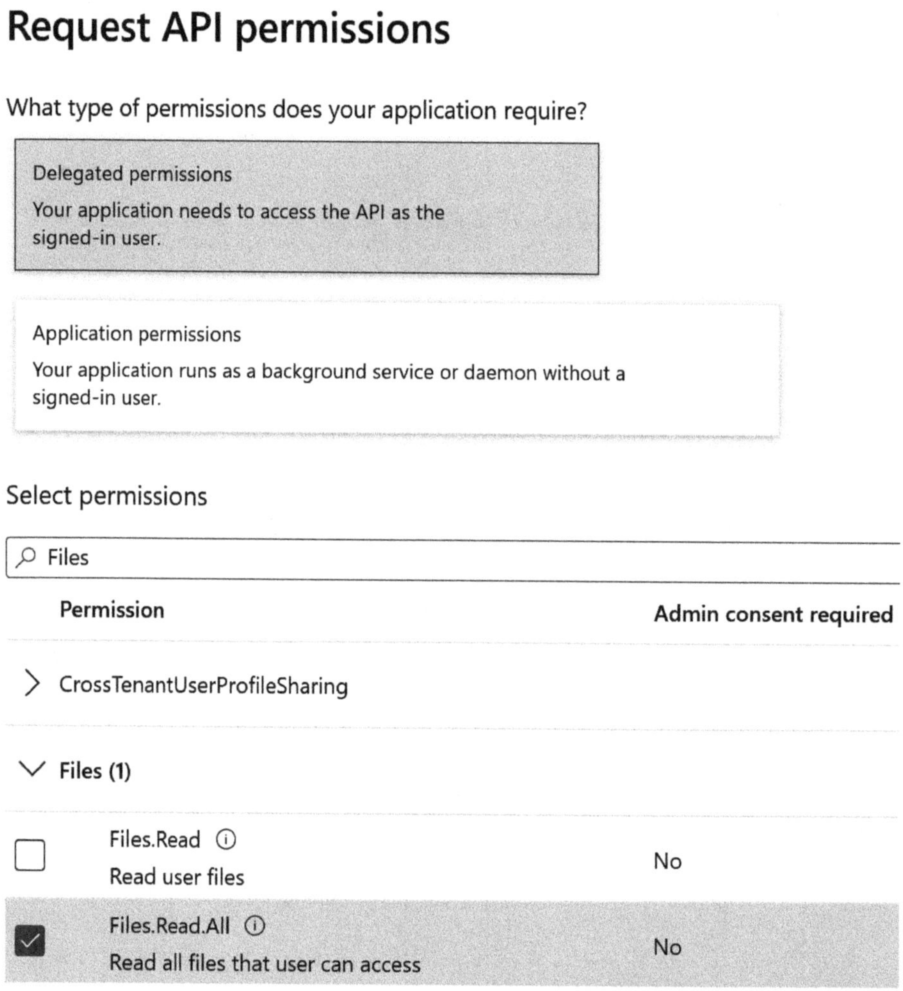

Request API permissions

What type of permissions does your application require?

Delegated permissions

Your application needs to access the API as the signed-in user.

Application permissions

Your application runs as a background service or daemon without a signed-in user.

Select permissions

🔎 Files

Permission	Admin consent required
⟩ CrossTenantUserProfileSharing	
⌄ Files (1)	
☐ Files.Read ⓘ Read user files	No
☑ Files.Read.All ⓘ Read all files that user can access	No

Figure 2.8 – Definition of API permissions per API endpoint

These permissions tell what authenticated users or applications can do when making HTTP requests to these specific API endpoints through this app and can be of two types:

- **Delegated**: Operations are done by impersonating the current user identity to perform operations, meaning users will only see what they have permission to see and do what they are allowed to do according to configurations made in the Microsoft 365 tools (such as configuring explicit SharePoint permissions or add users to an Entra ID security group). Giving a highly privileged API permission won't give a similar access level to users. It just represents the highest level of possible actions users are allowed to perform if they have the actual permission to do so for real. On the contrary, for a specific operation such as reading files on a SharePoint site, if the corresponding API permission is not defined at the Entra ID app level but the user is actually allowed to do this in the SharePoint UI, the request won't work as the minimum required permissions need to be set.

- **Application**: Operations are done under an application identity. In this scenario, no user interface or interaction is involved and not all entities support these types of permissions. Unlike delegated access, the client application can do *everything* the Entra ID application allows through its defined API permissions *without having to configure any permissions in the tools (like a group membership)*. This is highly privileged access and should be used with caution. For instance, giving the `Sites.ReadWrite.All` permission to an app will allow anyone with credentials to have total control over your SharePoint sites.

As a best practice, we recommend using the principle of least privilege when defining API permissions. The minimum required permission to call a specific endpoint entity is usually mentioned in the API reference documentation.

In SharePoint Framework, all requests are (and must be) *delegated*.

> **Warning**
> Never ever use application permissions in an SPFx solution, nor store credentials anywhere in your code or in the tenant itself, as it represents a severe security risk. If you need to use application permissions in your application, consider deploying a backend service and performing the authentication and operation process here, storing the credentials in a secure location that is not accessible by end users (such as a function hosted in Azure, protected by Entra ID, and using Azure Key Vault).

We'll see later in this book that SPFx provides utility classes to handle the authentication process automatically. As a developer, this means you do not need to know every single OAuth 2.0 authentication flow, but it is definitely valuable as it will give you a good understanding of how authentication works in the Microsoft cloud environment, even beyond Microsoft 365.

Summary

In this chapter, we've detailed the basic SharePoint and Teams logical architecture and identified the key elements you need to know before building SPFx solutions. We also covered the APIs available in the Microsoft 365 ecosystem to manipulate these elements, including the legacy SharePoint REST API (v1) and the new v2/Microsoft Graph counterpart. For both APIs, we gave examples of requests to demonstrate their usage.

We also gave you an overview of the authentication process involved for Microsoft cloud solutions through Entra ID and explained the concept of API permissions and the difference between delegated and application access.

In the next chapter, we'll guide you on your first steps with SPFx by configuring your environment and creating your first solution.

Get This Book's PDF Version and Exclusive Extras

UNLOCK NOW

Scan the QR code (or go to packtpub.com/unlock). Search for this book by name, confirm the edition, and then follow the steps on the page.

Note: Keep your invoice handy. Purchases made directly from Packt don't require an invoice.

3

Your First Steps with the SharePoint Framework

In the previous chapter, we went into the details of the core building blocks of the Microsoft 365 ecosystem involved in SharePoint Framework development and how to leverage them in solutions.

In this chapter, we will go through how to get started with the SharePoint Framework as a developer.

This chapter will provide a concise understanding of the configuration needed for a SharePoint Framework development environment. It will also provide details on the general development process that can be applied to solution development.

The main topics that will be covered as part of this chapter are as follows:

- Understanding the development tools and ecosystem
- Understanding the development process and application life cycle
- Setting up the development environment
- Create a solution
- Understanding the structure of the solution

Understanding the development tools and ecosystem

To effectively develop solutions with the **SharePoint Framework** (**SPFx**), it is crucial to have a comprehensive understanding of the development tools and ecosystem that support this environment. This includes several key tools and technologies that facilitate the development process, from writing code to building and deploying solutions. Let's explore a few such technologies.

Visual Studio Code

Visual Studio Code (**VS Code**) is a highly versatile and widely used code editor that provides powerful features for SPFx development. It supports a range of extensions that enhance productivity, such as ESLint for JavaScript linting, Prettier for code formatting, and dedicated extensions for SharePoint development. Its integrated terminal allows developers to manage their projects without leaving the editor, making it an indispensable tool for SPFx development.

Node Package Manager (npm)

npm is the default package manager for Node.js, and it plays a critical role in SPFx development by managing dependencies and packages. Through npm, developers can install, update, and manage the libraries and tools required for their projects. It also enables the use of scripts to automate tasks, streamlining the development workflow.

Yeoman

Yeoman is a scaffolding tool that simplifies the creation of new SPFx projects. It provides generators that set up the project structure and configuration files, allowing developers to focus on writing code rather than setting up the environment. The SPFx Yeoman generator is particularly useful for initializing projects with a predefined structure and best practices.

Gulp

Gulp is a task runner used in SPFx projects to automate repetitive tasks such as building, bundling, and testing. It uses JavaScript code to define tasks and workflows, which can significantly improve efficiency and ensure consistency across the development process. Common Gulp tasks in SPFx projects include compiling TypeScript, processing CSS, and packaging solutions for deployment.

Webpack

Webpack is a tool that bundles modules with their dependencies and creates static files that represent those modules. In SPFx projects, Webpack is used to bundle JavaScript, CSS, and other assets into a single package that can be deployed to a SharePoint site. It offers features such as code splitting and minification, which optimize the performance and loading times of SPFx solutions.

Other tools and libraries

In addition to the primary tools mentioned previously, SPFx development often involves other libraries and utilities. For instance, **React** and **Angular** can be used for building user interfaces, while tools such as **Jest** and **Mocha** facilitate testing. The choice of tools depends on the project's requirements and the developer's preferences.

By understanding and effectively utilizing these tools, developers can streamline their workflows, improve their code quality, and deliver robust and efficient SharePoint solutions. The integration of these tools within the SPFx ecosystem supports a seamless development experience, enabling developers to leverage the full potential of SPFx.

With this, we have explored various tools and libraries that are integral to SPFx development, such as Webpack, Gulp, and Yeoman, and how they streamline the development process.

Understanding the development process and application life cycle

In this section, we will look at an overview of the SPFx development process. Developing with SPFx involves several stages that ensure robust and efficient solutions. The process typically starts with project setup, where tools such as Yeoman scaffold the basic structure. Developers then move on to coding, leveraging libraries such as React or Angular to build user interfaces. Webpack is used to bundle and optimize assets, ensuring smooth deployment and performance. Testing is another crucial phase, often facilitated by tools such as Jest or Mocha, which help maintain code quality and functionality.

After coding and testing, the next step is packaging the solution. Gulp comes into play here, automating tasks such as compiling TypeScript, processing SCSS, and creating deployment packages. Finally, the solution is deployed to SharePoint, where it undergoes further testing and validation before going live.

This seamless integration of tools within the SPFx ecosystem not only enhances the development experience but also ensures that developers can fully leverage the capabilities of SPFx. In the next section, we will discuss setting up the development environment to facilitate this process.

We now have an overview of various tools and libraries integral to SPFx development, such as Webpack, Gulp, and Yeoman, and discussed the importance of understanding the development process and application life cycle.

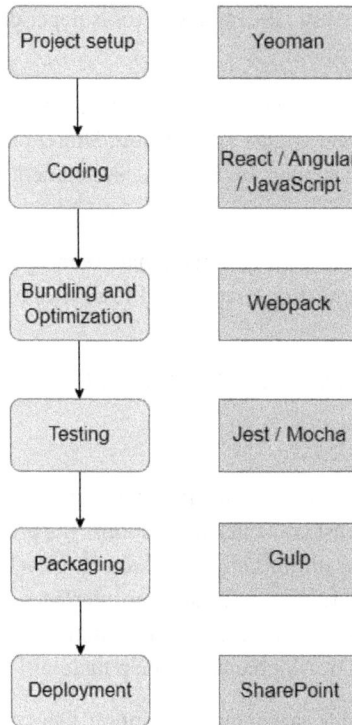

Figure 3.1 – SPFx development process and application life cycle

Setting up the development environment

In this section, we will look at setting up the development environment for SPFx. Setting up the environment is crucial for ensuring a seamless development experience. This section will guide you through the necessary steps to configure your machine and set up a Microsoft 365 developer tenant.

> **System requirements**
> As mentioned in the *Preface*, please make sure that the system requirements are met.

Installing the required tools

We are using SPFx version 1.19.0 in this book, hence, the instructions mentioned in this chapter are specific to that version. Microsoft's official documentation (`https://learn.microsoft.com/en-us/sharepoint/dev/spfx/set-up-your-development-environment`) on the setup for SPFx has similar instructions too; however, those instructions are related to the latest version of SPFx, which is 1.20.0 at the time of authoring this book.

First, you need to install **Node.js** and **npm**. Visit the official Node.js website (`https://nodejs.org/en/blog/release/v18.12.0`) and download the **Long Term Support** (**LTS**) version 18.x. Follow the installation instructions provided on the website. Different versions of SPFx support different versions of Node.js. This can be seen in Microsoft's documentation (`https://learn.microsoft.com/en-us/sharepoint/dev/spfx/compatibility#spfx-development-environment-compatibility`), which will always be kept up to date by Microsoft.

Once they have been installed, you need to verify the installation. You will use a terminal or command prompt for this. If you're on Windows, you can open **Command Prompt** by typing cmd in the Start menu search bar and pressing *Enter*. On macOS, you can open the **Terminal** application from the `Applications` folder. For Linux, the terminal is usually accessible from the main menu.

Type the following commands in your terminal or Command Prompt to verify the installation:

- `node -v`
- `npm -v`

Next, you need to install Yeoman and Gulp globally. To do this, type the following command in your terminal or Command Prompt and press *Enter*:

- `npm install -g yo gulp`

Finally, install the Yeoman SharePoint generator with the following command:

- `npm install -g @microsoft/generator-sharepoint@1.19.0`

Setting up a Microsoft 365 developer tenant

To fully utilize the SPFx, you need access to a Microsoft 365 environment. Setting up a Microsoft 365 developer tenant will allow you to experiment and test your SPFx solutions:

1. Go to the Microsoft 365 Developer Program website - `https://developer.microsoft.com/en-us/microsoft-365/dev-program`.
2. Sign up for a free account or log in if you already have one.

3. Follow the prompts to set up your tenant, including creating a new domain and admin account.

4. Once your tenant is set up, you will have access to the full suite of Microsoft 365 services, including SharePoint.

By setting up your machine and developer tenant, you are now ready to dive into SPFx development. In the next section, we will discuss creating your first SPFx solution and guiding you through the initial steps of building and deploying your solution.

Creating your first SPFx solution (step by step)

Having set up your machine and developer tenant, you are now prepared to embark on developing with the SPFx.

Configuring your development environment

With the necessary tools and tenant in place, you can now configure your development environment:

- Create a new directory for your SPFx projects. This can be done by right-clicking on your desktop or within a folder, selecting **New** and then **Folder**, and naming it appropriately.

- Open VS Code and navigate to your project directory. You can do this by opening VS Code, clicking on **File** in the top menu, selecting **Open Folder**, and then navigating to the folder you created.

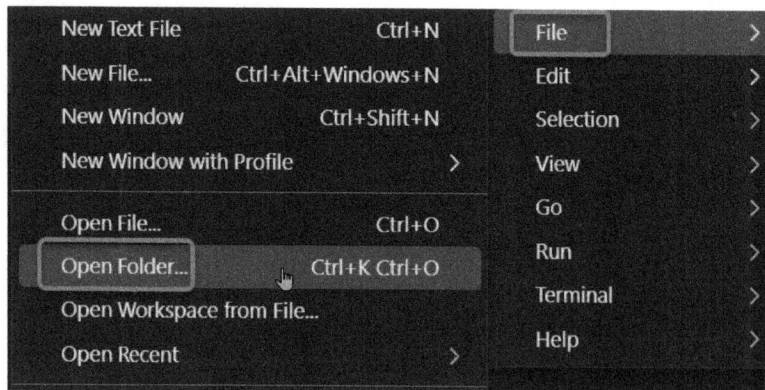

Figure 3.2 - Opening a folder from VS Code

Once you are in your project directory, open the terminal within VS Code. You can do this by clicking on **Terminal** in the top menu and selecting **New Terminal**. This will open a terminal window at the bottom of VS Code.

Create a new SPFx project

In the terminal, type `yo @microsoft/sharepoint` and press *Enter*.

Yeoman SharePoint Generator will guide you through a series of prompts. For most questions, you can accept the default choices, but for these specific questions, use the following answers:

- Which type of client-side component to create? – `WebPart`

- What is your web part name? – `HelloWorld`

- Which template would you like to use? – `No framework`

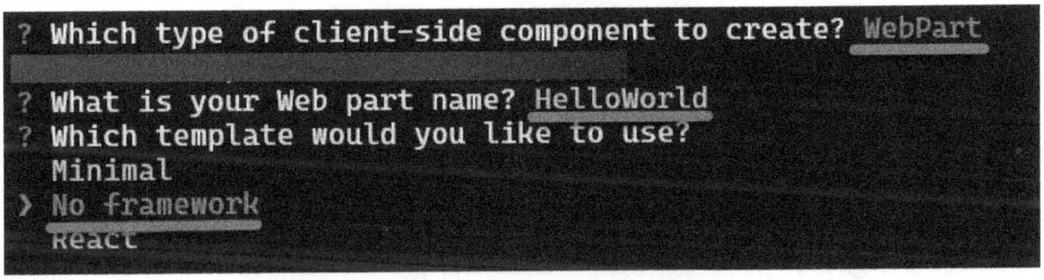

Figure 3.3 – Basic SPFx web part creation options

> **Note**
> Yeoman now sets up the project structure (folders and files) and installs necessary dependencies with `npm install`. This process typically takes a few minutes, depending on the network connection.

After the project scaffolding and dependency installation processes are finished, Yeoman will show a message confirming success.

When you create an SPFx solution, several folders and files are generated. In the next section, we will delve into the structure of these folders and files, explaining their purposes and how they fit into the development workflow.

SPFx solution structure overview

The previous section guided you through the initial setup of the SPFx project using the Yeoman generator, which resulted in the creation of a basic project scaffold for a web part named `HelloWorld`. Now, we will explore the structure of the folders and files that were generated and delve into their purposes and how they fit into the SPFx development workflow.

Upon creating an SPFx solution, several key folders and files are generated to organize your project.

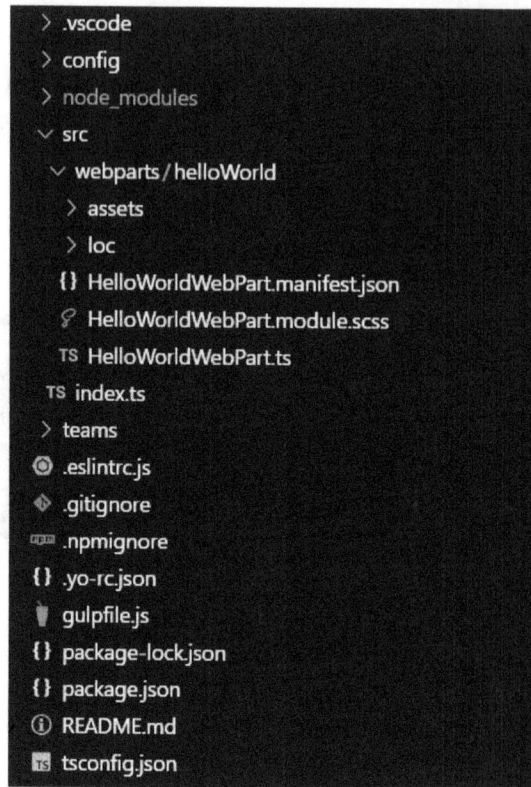

```
> .vscode
> config
> node_modules
∨ src
  ∨ webparts / helloWorld
    > assets
    > loc
    {} HelloWorldWebPart.manifest.json
    🍥 HelloWorldWebPart.module.scss
    TS HelloWorldWebPart.ts
  TS index.ts
  > teams
◎ .eslintrc.js
◆ .gitignore
🔳 .npmignore
{} .yo-rc.json
🥤 gulpfile.js
{} package-lock.json
{} package.json
ⓘ README.md
🔳 tsconfig.json
```

Figure 3.4 – SPFx web part project folder structure

Here is an overview of the primary elements:

- .vscode: This folder contains specific VS Code settings and configurations.
- Config: This folder contains configuration files for the build process. Key files include the following:
  - config.json: Configuration for the SPFx build process
  - deploy-azure-storage.json: Configuration for deploying the project to Azure Storage
  - package-solution.json: Configuration for packaging the SPFx solution
  - sass.json: Configuration for SASS compilation
  - serve.json: Configuration for serving the project locally during development
  - write-manifests.json: Configuration for writing the web part manifests

- `Src`: The `src` folder is where the source code resides. It includes the following:

  - `index.ts`: The entry point for your web part required by the Typescript compiler

  - `webparts/helloWorld`: Contains the main web part files, including the following:

    - `HelloWorldWebPart.ts`: The main TypeScript file for your web part logic

    - `HelloWorldWebPart.module.scss`: SCSS module for styling the web part

    - `HelloWorldWebPart.manifest.json`: Describes the web part's properties and configuration

    - `assets`: Directory for storing assets such as images

    - `loc`: Directory that contains files related to localization

- `node_modules`: This folder holds all the npm packages and dependencies required by your project. It is automatically generated when you run `npm install`.

This is the folder structure for SPFx web parts. The structure will vary for other SPFx elements (such as extensions or cards).

Folders generated post build and package

The following folders are generated once the code is built and the package is created:

- `dist`: This folder is where the build output is placed. It contains the compiled files that will be used for packaging the solution.

- `lib`: The `lib` folder contains the compiled output of your TypeScript files. The files in this folder are generated from the source files in the src folder.

- `SharePoint`: This folder contains the solution package for the SPFx project. Specifically, it includes the following subfolder:

- `solution`: This subfolder contains the `.sppkg` file, which is the SharePoint package file generated during the build process. This package file is used to deploy the SPFx solution to a SharePoint site.

> **Note**
> The steps to build and create a package will be explained in *Chapter 9* and *Chapter 16*.

Understanding the purpose and structure of these folders and files is crucial for effective SPFx development. Each element plays a specific role in the overall workflow, ensuring that your project is well organized and follows best practices.

Summary

In this chapter, we discussed the requirements for starting SharePoint framework projects. The chapter began by detailing the development tools needed for SPFx development, which include VS Code, npm, webpack, and Yeoman. It then explained the development process and application life cycle of an SPFx project, covering various stages such as project setup, development, and testing. We also covered how to set up the development environment by installing **Node.js**, **npm**, **gulp**, **Yeoman**, and the **SharePoint generator**, and how to set up a Microsoft 365 Developer tenant. We then looked at how to create a simple `HelloWorld` SPFx web part by executing the necessary commands. The chapter concluded with an overview of the folder structure and files contained in the SPFx web part solution. With this information, you should now be capable of creating basic SharePoint Framework web parts.

In the next chapter, we will set the business context and functional requirements (hypothetical) of a company, Packt. This context will be used to support examples that we will implement with SPFx, to demonstrate its main capabilities.

Packt Product Management Solution: A Practical Use Case

Like any other software solution, SPFx solutions are designed to solve business problems, in this case by leveraging and extending Microsoft 365 tools and services.

In previous chapters, you learned about SPFx's capabilities and how it integrates with different Microsoft 365 tools, such as SharePoint and Teams. It is now time to learn how to identify the right SPFx capability according to business requirements, just like you'll have to do in real life.

In this chapter, we will take the example of the company **Packt**, who wants us to build their new product inventory management solution in Microsoft 365. We will list and define all the requirements the company has and plan and implement SPFx capabilities accordingly by building a global solution. This will set up the context for the upcoming chapters to demonstrate the implementation of major SPFx features such as web parts and extensions. This solution will be supported by a GitHub repository illustrating the SPFx concepts used in this scenario.

As a developer, this will help you to understand the capabilities of SPFx's features and how they complement others, as well as illustrating their implementation beyond a simple "Hello World" example.

To summarize, we will be covering the following main topics in this chapter:

- Planning a business solution with SPFx
- Requirements and solutions overview

Planning a business solution with SPFx

Packt is a company selling apparel and they've contacted you to implement a *product inventory management solution* inside their Microsoft 365 tenant. They've provided a list of requirements describing all the features the solution should contain.

The company has already created a dedicated SharePoint site and stored all the products within a list using a dedicated content type. The following metadata (i.e., SharePoint columns) is defined for a product:

- **Model name**: The name of the model (e.g., Funky Teeshirt)
- **Retail price**: The price of the item (e.g., $50)
- **Stock level**: The current level of stock for this product (e.g., between 0 and 100)
- **Last order date**: The last date when a new order was made to refill stocks
- **Item picture**: A picture of the item to be shown in the catalog
- **Item color**: The color of the item from a predefined list of colors
- **Size**: The size of the item from a known list (e.g., XS, S, M, L, XL, or XXL)
- **Product reference**: A unique ID representing the reference for that product line (e.g., T311. T65 or D89)

> **Note**
>
> As a developer, when designing SPFx solutions, you will also likely have to design the underlying information architecture supporting the solution, using the building blocks, such as lists, content types, and columns, we covered in the previous chapter.

In the next section, we will go through all these requirements and identify the correct SPFx capabilities to meet them.

> **Note**
>
> When presenting a requirement, we take the point of view of the "Packt" customer providing a solution for its internal users.

Requirement 1 – viewing products as a catalog

In this first requirement, the customer wants to view the products from the list directly inside SharePoint pages as a widget. The products should be presented as tiles supporting the site and page section's theme dynamically with light/dark mode. A product tile should look like this:

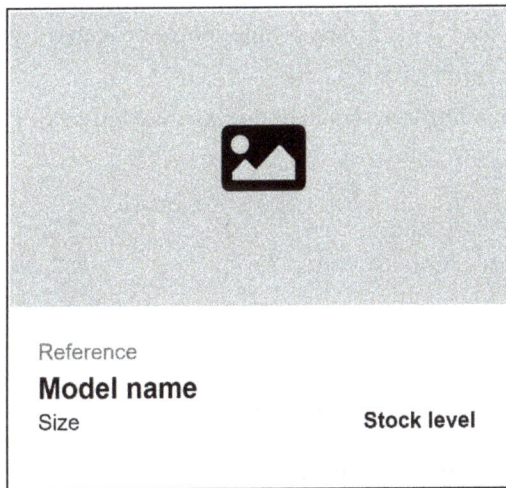

Figure 4.1 – Wireframe for a product tile

The solution should also provide a setting to configure the number of items to show in the catalog easily.

Solution – "product catalog" web part

This requirement will involve the creation of an **SPFx web part** as it is intended to be integrated into SharePoint pages. We also need to implement the property pane settings to be able to configure the number of tiles to show. To quickly configure the number of tiles, we can also use web part top actions.

Lastly, to get the data about products, we will use Microsoft Graph targeting the SharePoint list where the information is stored.

The implementation will be detailed later in this book.

Requirement 2 – selecting the color and size for a product item

When creating or updating a product from the list, the customer wants the ability to visually select a color and size from a list of predefined values:

- For the color, it should be presented in a color picker such as this:

Figure 4.2 – Appearance of the color field

Also, when changing the color, the item picture should be updated automatically according to the selected color.

- For the size, a corresponding icon should be displayed alongside the item size:

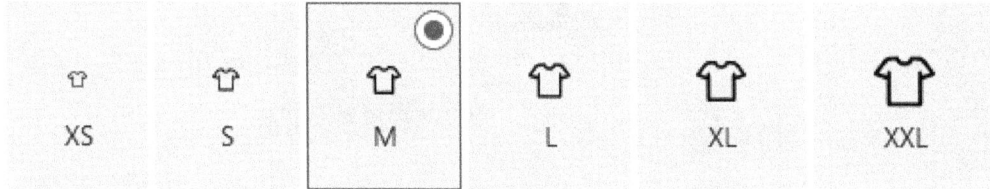

Figure 4.3 – Appearance of the size field

These icons should be present in the creation form of an item.

Solution – form customizer

As there are no such field types by default in SharePoint that allow this kind of appearance, the solution is to use a **form customizer** in SPFx. Unlike the field customizer, the form customizer allows customizations during the item creation step (the field customizer only applies to existing elements in the list). We will be able to implement the provided visuals.

Requirement 3 – getting a visual notification when a product is low in stock

When a product is low in stock, that is, below the value of 10 units, Packt customers should be notified in two ways:

- Visually while navigating the products list to easily see the low-stock items
- Globally on the site without having to go to the list of products

Solution – field customizer and application customizer

For the first requirement, we can use a **field customizer** applied on the **Stock level** column in the list and visually change the background color according to the field value. This will give a visual notification of faulty items directly from the list view experience.

For the second part of the requirement, an application customizer registered at the site collection level is a good choice as it will be executed when users are browsing the site, without the need to browse the products list. We can implement a visual banner using the "top" placeholder and implement logic, using Microsoft Graph, to fetch the information dynamically on the list for items with a **Stock level** value below 10. In that case, we redirect to the list directly.

Requirement 4 – placing a new order when a product is low in stock

The counterpart of the preceding requirement is to be able to place a new order for items that are low in stock. This action should call an external system that will be in charge of updating the item in the list with the new value.

Solution – list view command set

To fill this requirement, we can typically use a **list view command set** to create a custom **action** both in the item contextual menu and in the top command bar of the list. When the action is clicked, a call to Power Automate or any other system is made.

Requirement 5 – searching for products by model, size, or color using free-text keywords

In this requirement, the customer wants to be able to let its users search for a product in the catalog using free-text keywords. These keywords can match either the color, size, or model information in the products list.

Solution – search box web part and dynamic data

Instead of updating the first web part to include this feature, the solution leverages the **SPFx dynamic data** capability by creating a new web part search component and connecting it with the previous one. This way, the first one can be used with or without a search box, minimizing the code updates and providing more flexibility.

Requirement 6 – searching for a product from the site

Differing from the previous requirement, the customer wants to be able to search for products but using the top bar search box from a SharePoint site. They also want to let users search by product references as users often use this value to look up products.

Also, the results should be "live" and retrieve information with no delay, including the latest modifications.

Solution – search query modifier

For this requirement, we need to create a custom search page on the SharePoint site, including the product catalog web part.

To be able to detect product references from user keywords, we use a **search query modifier** that transforms and extracts the value to be passed to the product catalog web part.

Requirement 7 – visualizing the products dashboard in Viva Connections

The customer wants to quickly get product insights directly from the Viva Connections portal. To do that, they request a dashboard showing stock levels per color:

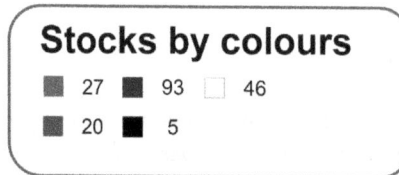

Stocks by colours

27   93   46

20   5

Figure 4.4 – Visual for the Viva Connections dashboard

Solution – adaptive card extensions for Viva Connections

We plan to create **adaptive card extensions** (**ACEs**) to implement dashboards and fetch the data directly from the product list. ACEs are the only option here to integrate with Viva Connections.

Requirement 8 – visualizing the product catalog in Teams, Outlook, and Office

In addition to SharePoint pages, the customer wants to be able to see the product catalog directly within Teams, Outlook, and Office as an application.

Solution – host applications configuration in the product catalog web part

Within Teams, Outlook, or Office, only one SPFx web part can be leveraged as an application, so we can't use the dynamic data feature and separate search box web part. It means we need to detect when the web part is running in a different context and hide the search box connection capability inside the web part property pane to avoid any confusion.

Requirements and solutions overview

In the previous sections, we detailed all the requirements to be implemented in our SPFx solution. It is now time to do a quick recap specifying for each requirement the SPFx feature we plan to leverage in the global architecture. The following schema will give you a better overview of the solution when all features are put together, with the SPFx feature in green and the requirement number that it covers in red:

SharePoint page

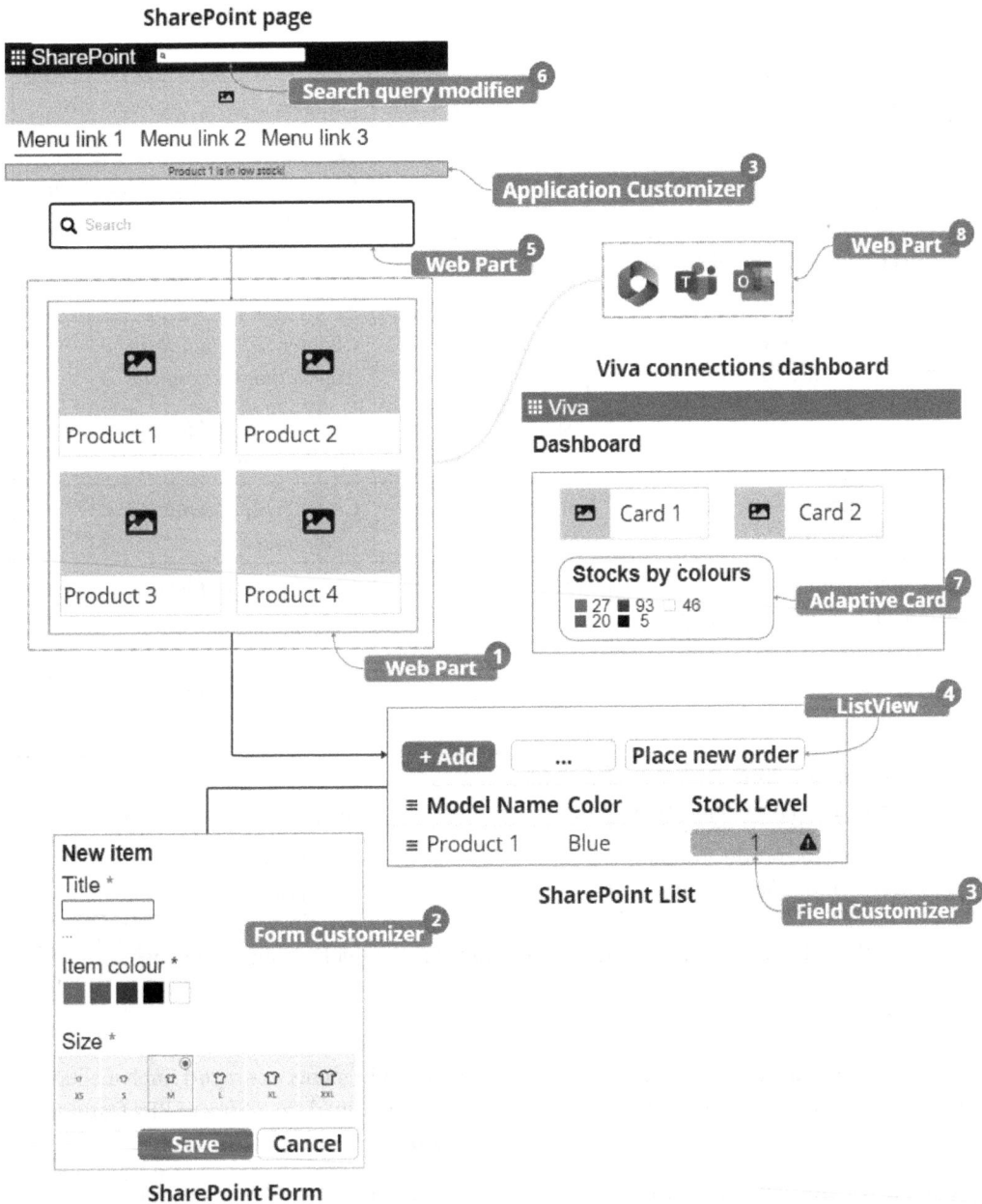

Figure 4.5 – Architecture overview for the product management solution

Also, we provide the following table listing all the requirements and the associated chapters in this book that will go in depth into the implementation:

#	Requirement	SPFx customization type	Chapter
1	Viewing products as a catalog	Web part	*Chapter 5, Building a SharePoint Web Part*
2	Selecting the color and size for an item	Form customizer	*Chapter 9, Building a Form Customizer*
3	Getting a visual notification when a product is low in stock	Field customizer Application customizer	*Chapter 10, Building an Application Customizer* *Chapter 11, Building a Field Customizer*
4	Placing a new order when a product is low in stock	List view command set	*Chapter 12, Building a ListView Command Set*
5	Searching for products by model, size, or color using free-text keywords	Web part	*Chapter 5, Building a SharePoint Web Part*
6	Searching for a product from the site	Search query modifier	*Chapter 13, Building a Search Query Modifier*
7	Visualizing the products dashboard in Viva Connections	Adaptive card extension	*Chapter 14, Building an Adaptive Card Extension*
8	Visualizing the product catalog in Teams, Outlook, and Office	Web part	*Chapter 8, Deploying a SharePoint Web Part*

Table 4.1 – Product management solution requirements with planned solutions

Summary

In this chapter, we defined a fictitious business scenario and requirements to support implementation examples used to demonstrate SPFx's capabilities. We also identified the correct SPFx features to address each requirement, explaining the envisaged solution.

In the solution architecture, we identified each feature and how they complement each other.

This process illustrates what an SPFx developer will have to do in real life to build business value solutions.

In the next part of this book, we dig down into SPFx web part implementation, taking the examples of the product catalog and search box web parts defined in our scenario.

Get This Book's PDF Version and Exclusive Extras

UNLOCK NOW

Scan the QR code (or go to `packtpub.com/unlock`). Search for this book by name, confirm the edition, and then follow the steps on the page.

Note: Keep your invoice handy. Purchases made directly from Packt don't require an invoice.

Part 2: Building Web Parts with the SharePoint Framework

Part 2 dives deep into web part development, modular and reusable components for SharePoint pages, and the primary component type available with SPFx. Through our fictitious solution, we demonstrate the key features of web parts, from their initial creation to deployment in a SharePoint environment.

This part has the following chapters:

- *Chapter 5, Building a SharePoint Web Part*
- *Chapter 6, Working with the Property Pane*
- *Chapter 7, Connecting to Other Web Parts*
- *Chapter 8, Deploying a SharePoint Web Part*

5

Building a SharePoint Web Part

In the previous chapter, we detailed the requirements of a company called Packt, requesting you to build their product management solution within Microsoft 365. It is now time to implement the solution, leveraging all the SPFx features available to you. We start with the first requirement: "Viewing products as a catalog."

In this chapter, we will review all the steps you need to create an SPFx web part from scratch. You will do the following:

- Learn how to build a web part from scratch and use the correct SPFx features to meet functional requirements
- Understand the web part development flow using React and SPFx-provided lifecycle methods
- Use Microsoft Graph to get real data from SharePoint lists
- Learn how to handle styles and support themes for your web part
- Learn how to localize your web part in accordance with users' preferred language
- Create web part top actions to provide quick configuration for users

Technical requirements

This chapter relies on the GitHub solution accessible here: `https://github.com/PacktPublishing/Mastering-SharePoint-Development-with-the-SharePoint-Framework-/tree/chapter5/building-a-webpart`. You need to first clone the repository locally on your machine to be able to follow the steps. As the solution is built step by step, for each section in this chapter, a dedicated Git branch has been created representing the solution at a specific state corresponding to a section.

Before reading the section, you must check out the corresponding branch before using either the Git command line or a Git client such as GitHub Desktop, Sourcetree, and so on.

> **Code snippets**
>
> For brevity and readability considerations, only the relevant parts of the code are detailed in the provided snippets in this chapter. For these reasons, ad hoc code such as dependencies, imports, and updates to certain files may be omitted. We recommend having the GitHub solution open alongside to get the full working version of the code and review the provided steps.

The branch name to refer to and additional instructions are indicated at the beginning of each section. Here is a summary of the Git branches to check per section:

Section in this chapter	Git branch to check out
Building a web part	`https://github.com/PacktPublishing/Mastering-SharePoint-Development-with-the-SharePoint-Framework-/tree/chapter5/building-a-webpart`
Using Microsoft Graph to get items	`https://github.com/PacktPublishing/Mastering-SharePoint-Development-with-the-SharePoint-Framework-/tree/chapter5/using-ms-graph-api-to-get-items`
Handling styles, themes, and dark mode	`https://github.com/PacktPublishing/Mastering-SharePoint-Development-with-the-SharePoint-Framework-/tree/chapter5/handling-styles-and-theme`
Localizing a web part	`https://github.com/PacktPublishing/Mastering-SharePoint-Development-with-the-SharePoint-Framework-/tree/chapter5/localize-webpart`
Using web part top actions	`https://github.com/PacktPublishing/Mastering-SharePoint-Development-with-the-SharePoint-Framework-/tree/chapter5/webpart-top-actions`

Building a web part

> **Git branch**
>
> This section uses the `https://github.com/PacktPublishing/Mastering-SharePoint-Development-with-the-SharePoint-Framework-/tree/chapter5/building-a-webpart` Git branch from the repository.

As we saw in *Chapter 1*, an SPFx web part can be consumed in many ways, such as inside a SharePoint page, as a Teams tab application, or even a Teams message extension. For the rest of this section, we'll focus on the scenario where the web part needs only to be displayed on SharePoint pages.

At this point, we assume your developer environment is set up correctly and you are ready to begin. The solution is made using SPFx v1.19.0.

Creating the solution

Because the web part is the first component we create, the very first step is to create the SPFx solution at the same time using the Yeoman generator. From a new `Packt.Solutions.ProductManagement` folder, run the following command:

```
yo @microsoft/sharepoint --component-type "webpart" --component-name
"PacktProductCatalog" --framework "react" --solution-name "Packt.
Solutions.ProductManagement" --environment "spo" --package-manager
"npm" --skip-feature-deployment
```

We use the following parameters. If omitted in the command, you'll be prompted by the generator to provide values:

- `--component-type "webpart"`: This indicates that we will create a web part.

- `--component-name "PacktProductCatalog"`: This is the base name of the component that will be used to create files.

- `--component-description`: This is the description of the web part. This description is displayed as the tooltip when users hover over the web part in a SharePoint page section callout box.

- `--framework "react"`: This is the JavaScript framework we use as a starter. We use React here, as this is the framework that has the most examples and resources available related to SPFx.

- `--solution-name "Packt.Solutions.ProductManagement"`: This is the name of the folder that will be created.

- `--environment "spo"`: This indicates that we target SharePoint Online only.

- `--package-manager "npm"`: This indicates that we use npm as a package manager to install dependencies.

- `--skip-feature-deployment`: This indicates that users won't have to install the app manually on sites. As long as the solution is uploaded to the application catalog, it will be available without any other required steps.

> **Component naming convention**
>
> As a best practice, and if you don't already have a naming convention, it is a good idea to prefix your solution/component name using the company or project name, followed by the component name base.
>
> **DOs**
>
> Do prefix with the company name – for instance, `PacktProductCatalog`.
>
> **DON'Ts**
>
> Don't use the suffix `WebPart` as it will be added automatically by the SPFx generator (e.g., `PacktProductCatalogWebPart`).
>
> - Don't use dots in names (e.g., `Packt.ProductCatalog`).
> - Don't repeat the solution name (e.g., `PacktProductManagement`).
> - Don't use long names (e.g., `PacktProductManagementProductCatalog`).
>
> Although changing names afterward is still possible, the process can be complicated and error-prone, so you should choose them carefully!

Updating the solution configuration

At this point, the base solution structure is created, and dependencies are installed. However, we still need to configure some settings to properly set up the solution.

The first setting is about the hosted workbench configuration.

Configure the workbench URL

Open the `config/serve.json` file and update the `initialPage` property, replacing the `{tenantDomain}` placeholder with the SharePoint Online site you want to use (e.g., `https://mytenant.sharepoint.com/sites/test-site/_layouts/workbench.aspx`).

This URL is used to test your web part against the hosted workbench page and will be launched when using the `gulp serve` command.

> **Use a dedicated SharePoint site to test your solutions**
>
> If you only use the root domain (e.g., `https://mytenant.sharepoint.com/_layouts/workbench.aspx`) for the workbench page, your solution will be run against the SharePoint root site. The root site has particular importance in the SharePoint Online infrastructure and should only be used for well-determined use cases. As a best practice and to avoid any conflicts, you should always create a dedicated SharePoint site to test your solution.

The next step is to configure some information about the solution itself.

Update solution descriptions and package name

When creating the solution for the first time, some information, such as the description or package name can't be set (either using a command parameter or answering generator questions). To update them, open `package-solution.json` and update the following information:

- `solution.metadata.shortDescription` and `solution.metadata.longDescription`: The solution's short and long descriptions. This information is particularly useful because it will be used by admins to quickly understand what the solution does and take appropriate actions, such as approving (or not) the deployment of your app.

- `paths.zippedPackage`: The name of the package files to be uploaded to the app catalog. It generally follows the solution name. You can also use dots in the filename (e.g., `packt.solutions.product-management.sppkg`).

Update the web part name, description, and icon

Naming your web part is important as it will be easier for users to find it and quickly understand its purpose. This information can be specified in the `<your_webpart_name>.manifest.json` file in the `preconfiguredEntries.title` and `preconfiguredEntries.description` properties.

You can also set an icon for your web part. You can use either a Fluent UI icon with the `officeFabricIconFontName` property and pick an icon from the list available at `https://developer.microsoft.com/en-us/fluentui#/styles/web/icons`, or you can use the `iconImageUrl` property.

For the `iconImageUrl` property, despite it pointing to a URL, most of the time, it is better to use a Base64 image instead of an actual file to avoid handling the provisioning part (i.e., uploading this file to a location accessible by everyone). To use a Base64 image, you can use the format `data:image/png;base64,<base64_value>`. The web part properties will be displayed in the callout picker in SharePoint pages:

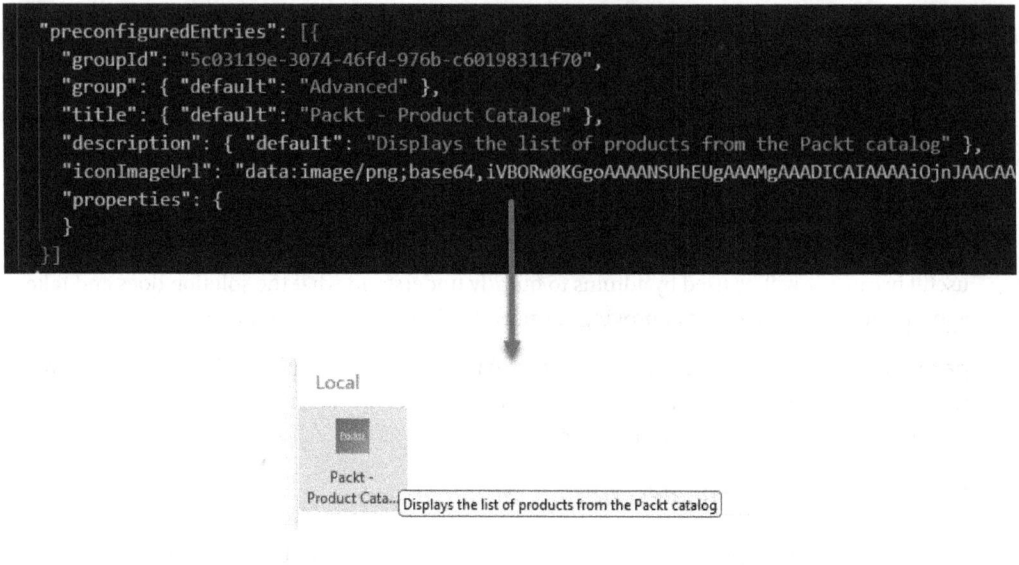

```
"preconfiguredEntries": [{
  "groupId": "5c03119e-3074-46fd-976b-c60198311f70",
  "group": { "default": "Advanced" },
  "title": { "default": "Packt - Product Catalog" },
  "description": { "default": "Displays the list of products from the Packt catalog" },
  "iconImageUrl": "data:image/png;base64,iVBORw0KGgoAAAANSUhEUgAAAMgAAADICAIAAAAiOjnJAACAA
  "properties": {
  }
}]
```

Local

Packt -
Product Cata... Displays the list of products from the Packt catalog

Figure 5.1 – Web part information displayed in the picker

Now that we have set up our web part information, it is time to start the implementation.

Defining business entities and services

Working with data means manipulating different underlying business entities. In our case, the objective of the solution is to build a product catalog. This means we need to define product item objects mapping the metadata coming from the real data store.

We first create a models folder under the src folder and create a new IProductCatalogItem. ts file. The interface attributes directly map the column and its types in the SharePoint list:

```
export interface IProductCatalogItem {
  modelName: string;
  retailPrice: number;
  stockLevel: number;
  lastOrderDate: Date;
  itemPicture: string;
  itemColour: string;
  size: ProductSizes;
  productReference: string;
}

export enum ProductSizes {
    XS,
    S,
```

```
    M,
    L,
    XL,
    XXL
}
```

Then, from the same `src` folder, we create a `services` folder that will contain the interface and class of the service used to retrieve the product information. We create a new `IProductCatalogService` interface in a dedicated `.ts` file defining a `getProducts` method:

```
import { IProductCatalogItem } from "../models/IProductCatalogItem";

export interface IProductCatalogService {
    getProducts(): Promise<IProductCatalogItem[]>;
}
```

This method is used to get data from the product list. However, for now, we simply implement it with static data to test the complete flow. We create a `ProductCatalogService` class that implements our interface like this:

```
import { IProductCatalogItem, ProductSizes } from "../models/
IProductCatalogItem";
import { IProductCatalogService } from "./IProductCatalogService";

export class ProductCatalogService implements IProductCatalogService {

    public async getProducts(): Promise<IProductCatalogItem[]> {
        const productItems: IProductCatalogItem[] = [
            {
                modelName: "UltraBoost Running Shoes",
                retailPrice: 180,
                stockLevel: 25,
                lastOrderDate: new Date("2023-04-01"),
                itemPicture: "ultraboost.jpg",
                itemColour: "Black",
                size: ProductSizes.M,
                productReference: "UB-001",
            },
            {
                modelName: "Tech Fleece Hoodie",
                retailPrice: 100,
                stockLevel: 40,
                lastOrderDate: new Date("2023-03-28"),
                itemPicture: "techfleece.jpg",
```

```
                    itemColour: "Grey",
                    size: ProductSizes.L,
                    productReference: "TF-002",
                },
                {
                    modelName: "Water Bottle",
                    retailPrice: 25,
                    stockLevel: 100,
                    lastOrderDate: new Date("2023-03-15"),
                    itemPicture: "waterbottle.jpg",
                    itemColour: "Blue",
                    size: ProductSizes.S,
                    productReference: "WB-003",
                }
            ];

            return productItems
        }
    }
```

> **Why not create the models and services folders under the webparts folder?**
>
> When planning a solution containing multiple component types (such as web parts and extensions), it is common to define models, services, and, at a higher scope, to get better readability and share them across the different components.

Initializing services and wiring up sub-components

The next step is to implement the rendering flow to display our products to users. We first create a class property, `productCatalogService`, in the `PacktProductCatalogWebPart` file that will be used to create an instance of `ProductCatalogService`:

```
export default class PacktProductCatalogWebPart extends
BaseClientSideWebPart<IPacktProductCatalogWebPartProps> {
  private _productCatalogService: IProductCatalogService;
...
```

We use the built-in `onInit()` method of the `WebPart` class to build the instance by replacing the default code. This method is the very first one that will be called in an SPFx web part. It is a good place to initialize the `services` class instances:

```
protected onInit(): Promise<void> {
    this._productCatalogService = new ProductCatalogService();
```

```
        return super.onInit();
    }
```

Use default methods to handle the web part lifecycle

SPFx provides several methods to handle the lifecycle and events occurring on a web part, from its initialization with `onInit()` (when the web part is mounted on the page) to its deletion with `onDispose()` (when the user closes the window or the web part is removed from the page). These methods are usually prefixed by the keyword `on`. Using Visual Studio Code, you can see them using IntelliSense:

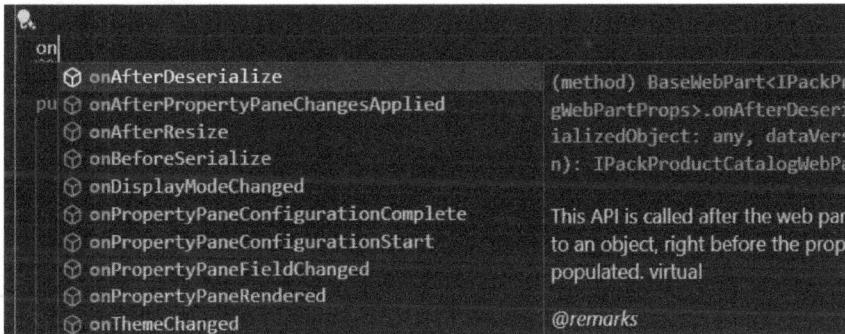

Figure 5.2 – Lifecycle methods for an SPFx web part

In most cases, you only need to implement a few methods, such as the initialization and the property pane configuration methods. In addition to lifecycle methods, the framework also provides state variables that can be used in your application (a `renderedOnce` property indicating whether the web part has already rendered once on the page).

Even though the instance is declared in the top web part class, products won't be retrieved here but rather in the `PacktProductCatalog.tsx` React sub-component in the `components` folder.

As a best practice, data shouldn't be retrieved directly in the root Web Part class as it is meant to initialize services and configurations and let sub-specialized components handle data and display.

To wire these components, we first update `IPacktProductCatalogProps` to define a `productCatalogService` property:

```
export interface IPacktProductCatalogProps {
  productCatalogService: IProductCatalogService;
}
```

We also create a dedicated interface, `IPacktProductCatalogState`, to define the state of our "products" React component:

```
export interface IPacktProductCatalogState {
    productItems: IProductCatalogItem[]
}
```

The last step is to pass the instance defined in the top web part class to the React components in the `render()` method by updating the default code:

```
public render(): void {
    const element: React.ReactElement<IPacktProductCatalogProps> =
React.createElement(
        PacktProductCatalog,
        {
          productCatalogService: this._productCatalogService
        }
    );
    ReactDom.render(element, this.domElement);
}
```

Having the "products" service instance initialized and defined as an input property for our React component, the last step is to get the product data and render it in the UI for users.

Rendering the products

By default, the SPFx Yeoman template for web parts uses the React class component (in comparison to function components). A class component uses props and state properties to manage its data. Props are basically data passed by higher-order components (in our case, the "products" service instance), and state properties are data manipulated directly by the component determining the rendering (in our case, the list of products to render). The key concept of the React framework is when the state is updated, it triggers a re-render of the entire component. Behind the scenes, React compares the previous and new states and updates only the needed elements in the DOM, resulting in a very dynamic interface.

A React class component also defines several lifecycle methods you need to implement, the more important one being the `render()` function. Let's look at these methods in detail:

- `render`: The main function to render. Uses the JSX syntax by default in SPFx.

- `componentDidMount`: Called immediately after a component is mounted on the page. This is usually a good place to fetch the data the component will use.

- `componentDidUpdate`: Called to determine whether the change in props and state should trigger a re-render. For instance, a setting in the web part used as a prop is updated.

- `componentWillUnmount`: Called immediately before a component is destroyed. Used for cleanup (DOM elements, canceled requests, etc.).

- `shouldComponentUpdate`: Called to determine whether the change in props and state should trigger a re-render.

- `componentDidCatch`: Catches exceptions generated in descendant components. Unhandled exceptions will cause the entire component tree to unmount.

> **Coding tip**
>
> A property that does not have an impact on the rendering (i.e., modifying the UI according to its value, such as a Boolean property showing/hiding something) shouldn't be defined in the state of a React component. You can use a regular class property instead.

To complete the product rendering, we initialize our state in the component constructor, replacing the default implementation with this one:

```
constructor(props: IPacktProductCatalogProps) {
    super(props);
    this.state = {
        productItems: [],
    };
}
```

Never fetch your data in the constructor!

Then, we initialize our data in the `componentDidMount` method using the products service instance passed as props:

```
public async componentDidMount(): Promise<void> {
    const productItems: IProductCatalogItem[] = await this.props.
productCatalogService.getProducts();

    this.setState({
        productItems: productItems,
    });
}
```

Finally, we implement the render function to display the list of products retrieved:

```
public render(): React.ReactElement<IPacktProductCatalogProps> {
    return (
        <>
            {this.state.productItems.map((productItem:
IProductCatalogItem) => {
```

```
        return (
            <div key={productItem.productReference}>{productItem.
modelName}</div>
        );
    })}
    </>
    );
}
```

At the end of this step, running the `gulp serve` command should produce the following output (don't forget to run the `gulp trust-dev-cert` command before if not already done; otherwise, your web part won't show up):

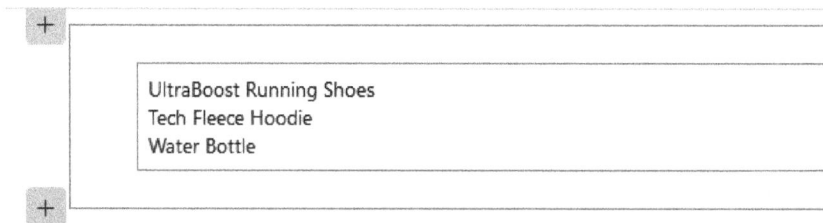

Figure 5.3 – Output after setting up components together

In this section, we saw the very first steps to build a SharePoint web part implementing the requirement to view products as a catalog. We set up the project and created folders, classes, and interfaces needed to get started. We used static data to simulate the product information and wired up all the components together to handle the complete flow. The next step will be to replace our static data by fetching the data from the SharePoint list using the Microsoft Graph API.

Using the Microsoft Graph API to get items

> **Git branch**
>
> This section uses the `https://github.com/PacktPublishing/Mastering-SharePoint-Development-with-the-SharePoint-Framework-/tree/chapter5/using-ms-graph-api-to-get-items` Git branch from the repository. Additionally, you need to set up prerequisites following the instructions provided in the `https://github.com/PacktPublishing/Mastering-SharePoint-Development-with-the-SharePoint-Framework-/blob/chapter5/using-ms-graph-api-to-get-items/README.md` file and run the deployment script: `Prerequisites/deploy.ps1`.

In the previous section, we used static data to simulate our product information and set up the render flow. Now that it is working, it is time to fetch real data coming from the SharePoint list.

As we saw in *Chapter 2* regarding SharePoint building blocks, we have multiple ways to get data from a list. We could use either the SharePoint REST API or Microsoft Graph. In our case, we will use the latter to fetch the product information.

> **SharePoint REST API versus Microsoft Graph API**
>
> In the case that you can achieve the same operation using both APIs, always prefer the Microsoft Graph API option. This API is more future-proof, and actively maintained and improved by Microsoft. Think of the SharePoint REST API as a legacy API, only useful when things can't be done with the Graph API.

Updating the packages

The first step we need to do is to add the `@microsoft/sp-http` package in `package.json` (under `dependencies`) and run the `npm i` command. By default, this module is not installed and contains all the utility classes to consume APIs such as Microsoft Graph.

Getting a Microsoft Graph client instance

Then, we need to instantiate a new Microsoft Graph `Client` object to be able to call the API and retrieve data. As mentioned in the *Initializing services and wiring up sub-components* section, service instances should be defined in the `onInit()` method of the web part root class and passed to services or sub-components whenever needed:

```
protected async onInit(): Promise<void> {

    const msGraphClient = await this.context.msGraphClientFactory.
getClient("3");
    this._productCatalogService = new
ProductCatalogService(msGraphClient);

    ...
}
```

> **Why use version 3 of the Microsoft Graph client?**
>
> Don't be mistaken here: there is a "regular" `MSGraphClient` utility class in the `@microsoft/sp-http` package. This class was used in the previous versions of SPFx to access the Microsoft Graph API. However, in the latest versions of SPFx (such as 1.19.0), a new client version, `MSGraphClientV3`, should now be used.

Defining and retrieving information from the context

According to the Microsoft Graph API reference (`https://learn.microsoft.com/en-us/graph/api/listitem-list`), to get SharePoint list item data, we need to use the `/sites/{site-id}/lists/{list-id}/items` endpoint, where `site-id` is the SharePoint site's unique ID where the products list is located, and `list-id` is the unique ID of the list itself.

To get this information, we have two solutions: either relying on the web part context object or storing this information in the web part property bag.

SPFx context object

In every SPFx customization (web part or extension), a context object (accessible through `this.context`) is available in the root class providing services, providers, and useful information about the environment. For instance, with the `this.context.pageContext` property, you can get data from the current site, list, user, and so on and use it in your code. The values are dynamic and will change according to where the customization is used (such as on a different site or list). Depending on the customization type, the available information can differ.

Here is an example of context information available for a web part:

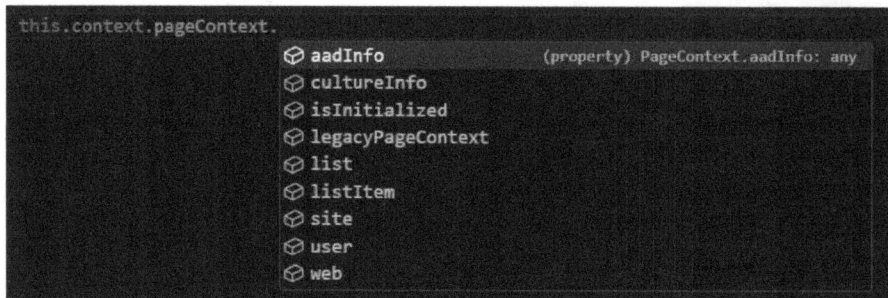

```
this.context.pageContext.
                          aadInfo              (property) PageContext.aadInfo: any
                          cultureInfo
                          isInitialized
                          legacyPageContext
                          list
                          listItem
                          site
                          user
                          web
```

Figure 5.4 – SPFx page context property

In our case, we use both strategies to demonstrate the two approaches:

- For `site-id`, we use the information from the `this.context.pageContext.site.id` property. By doing this, we assume the products list is available on the current site and the web part is meant to be used only on that site. If the web part is meant to be used on any site, storing this information as a web part property and/or making it configurable through a property pane control is a more suitable solution.

- For the list, we use the list name instead of the list ID as the Microsoft Graph endpoint also accepts this value. *The list name corresponds to the display name of the list and is more flexible than the ID, which can change depending on the site.* We store this information in the web part property bag in the `PacktProductCatalogWebPart.manifest.json` file:

```
{
    "$schema": "https://developer.microsoft.com/json-schemas/
spfx/client-side-web-part-manifest.schema.json",
    ...


    "preconfiguredEntries": [{
    ...

        "properties": {
            "productsListName": "Products"
        }
    }]
}
```

To use it in our code, we add the corresponding property in the web part properties interface:

```
export interface IPacktProductCatalogWebPartProps {
  productsListName: string;
}
```

This property can then be used using `this.properties.productsListName` from the root web part class.

Web part properties

Web part properties don't need to be necessarily configured through the property pane. They can be defined statically in the manifest file or manipulated/saved through code.

Updating the products service

The next step is to update the "products" service. We first update the `getProducts` method definition to take two additional parameters, the side ID and the list name, defined earlier:

```
export interface IProductCatalogService {
  getProducts(siteId: string, listName: string):
Promise<IProductCatalogItem[]>;
}
```

Then, we replace the static data with the actual Microsoft Graph request to the SharePoint list, selecting only the fields we need from the products list:

```
const fields = [
  "packtProductColor",
  "packtProductModelName",
  "packtProductItemPicture",
  "packtProductReference",
  "packtProductRetailPrice",
  "packtProductSize",
  "packtProductStockLastOrderDate",
  "packtProductStockLevel"
];


...


const response = await this._msGraphClient
        .api(`sites/${siteId}/lists/${listName}/items`)
        .expand(`fields($select=${fields})`)
        .get();

const items: IProductCatalogItem[] = response.value.map((item: any) =>
{
    return {
      modelName: item.fields.packtProductModelName,
      lastOrderDate: item.fields.packtProductStockLastOrderDate
        ? new Date(item.fields.packtProductStockLastOrderDate)
        : null,
      productReference: item.fields.packtProductReference,
      stockLevel: item.fields.packtProductStockLevel,
      size: item.fields.packtProductSize as ProductSizes,
      retailPrice: item.fields.packtProductRetailPrice,
      itemColour: item.fields.packtProductColor,
      itemPicture: item.fields.packtProductItemPicture
        ? JSON.parse(item.fields.packtProductItemPicture).
serverRelativeUrl
        : null,
    } as IProductCatalogItem;
});
```

To access the SharePoint list data, we use the following Microsoft Graph request using the MSGraphClientV3 client:

```
await this._msGraphClient
        .api(`sites/${siteId}/lists/${listName}/items`)
```

```
    .expand(`fields($select=${fields})`)
    .get();
```

This corresponds to the following request to be sent to the Microsoft Graph endpoint:

```
https://graph.microsoft.com/v1.0/sites/{site-id}/lists/{list_
name}/items?$expand=fields($select={fields})
```

As a best practice, when you retrieve data from an API, only the necessary information should be retrieved for performance reasons, for instance, using a $select parameter if the API implements the OData specification, as the Microsoft Graph and SharePoint REST APIs do.

In this code, you can also notice the $expand=fields parameter in the request. This means we request the special property called fields from the list item to be included in the response and its content expanded. This content corresponds to the custom SharePoint columns we defined for a product. The inner $select parameter indicates that only specific columns should be retrieved in the response.

Passing site ID and list name to sub-components

The last step is to pass the site ID and list name information retrieved from the root web part class to the PacktProductCatalog.tsx React product subcomponent. To do so, we update the component props interface, IPacktProductCatalogProps.ts, to handle these parameters:

```
export interface IPacktProductCatalogProps {
   productCatalogService: IProductCatalogService;
   siteId: string;
   listName: string;
}
```

Then, we update the getProducts method call to pass these parameters:

```
public async componentDidMount(): Promise<void> {
    const productItems: IProductCatalogItem[] = await this.props.
productCatalogService.getProducts(this.props.siteId, this.props.
listName);

    ...

}
```

Finally, we finish the flow by updating the render method in the web part root class, PacktProductCatalogWebPart.ts:

```
public render(): void {
    const element: React.ReactElement<IPacktProductCatalogProps> =
React.createElement(
```

```
  PacktProductCatalog,
  {
    productCatalogService: this._productCatalogService,
    siteId: this.context.pageContext.site.id.toString(),
    listName: this.properties.productsListName
  }
);

ReactDom.render(element, this.domElement);
}
```

Running your web part using `gulp serve`, you should now see the following:

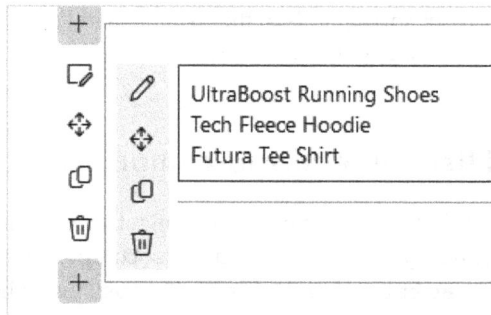

Figure 5.5 – Web part render after getting the data from the Microsoft Graph API

In this section, we saw how to get data from a SharePoint list using the Microsoft Graph API and the utility classes offered by SPFx. We also saw how to deal with dynamic parameters such as site ID and list name coming from the environment. In the next section, we'll make our product catalog prettier by updating styles and seeing how to handle different themes.

Handling styles, themes, and dark mode

> **Git branch**
>
> This section uses the `https://github.com/PacktPublishing/Mastering-SharePoint-Development-with-the-SharePoint-Framework-/tree/chapter5/handling-styles-and-theme` Git branch from the repository.

In this section, we'll see how to handle styles and make our web part a little prettier for users. As a reminder, our customer wants the products to be displayed as tiles like this:

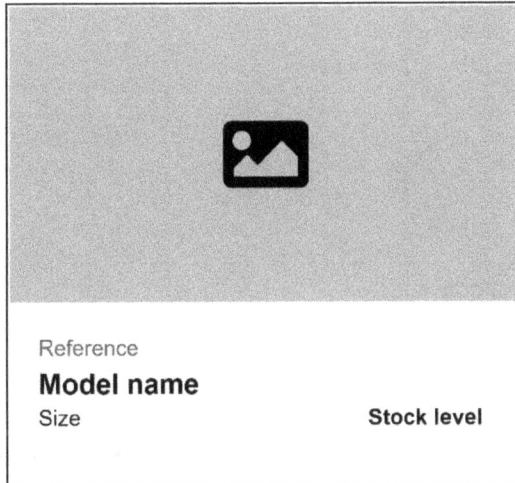

Figure 5.6 – Product tile

By default, SPFx handles CSS styles using **Syntactically Awesome Style Sheets** (**SASS**). To make it short, it makes the CSS writing process easier with a flexible syntax leveraging concepts such as variables, mixins, nested structures, and so on. It is a well-adopted framework for web development outside of SPFx.

Creating the SASS style sheet

We first start by writing our SASS code for the tile display in the `PacktProductCatalog.module.scss` file, like this:

```
.productList {
    display: grid;
    grid-auto-columns: minmax(0, 1fr);
    grid-auto-flow: column;
    gap: 20px;

    .productItem {

        box-shadow: 0 10px 10px 0 rgba(0, 0, 0, 0.2), 0 6px 10px 0
rgba(0, 0, 0, 0.19);
        background-position: 50%;
        background-size: cover;
```

```
        color: #000;
        display: flex;
        flex-direction: column;
        min-height: 210px;
        justify-content: flex-end;

        &:hover {
          box-shadow: 0 10px 25px 0 rgba(0, 0, 0, 0.2), 0 6px 25px 0
rgba(0, 0, 0, 0.19);
        }

        .productItemFooter {
          background-color: #fff;
          padding: 10px;
          display: grid;
          gap: 5px;
          grid-template-columns: repeat(auto-fit, minmax(min(250px,
100%), 1fr));

          .primaryText {
            font-size: 16px;
            font-weight: 700;
          }

          .secondaryText {
            font-size: 12px;
            display: flex;
            justify-content: space-between;
          }

          .tertiaryText {
            font-size: 12px;
          }
        }
      }
    }
}
```

> **Pro tip**
>
> In real-world projects, SPFx developers will likely have to implement styles by creating the HTML markup in React and writing the associated CSS code on their own. This task is not necessarily done by a dedicated designer. If, like me, SASS and CSS are not your thing as they require some extensive knowledge and time to do it properly, you can still use libraries such as TailwindCSS (https://tailwindcss.com), which lets you use predefined CSS classes with a ton of flexibility and without writing a single CSS line. Despite it not being detailed in this book, we strongly encourage you to look at this tool to speed up your development.

You may notice the `module.scss` in the filename instead of a regular `.scss` stylesheet. To integrate SPFx solutions seamlessly, it's crucial that your CSS styles are confined to your component and don't interfere with other page elements. Instead of manually ensuring this—which can be both cumbersome and prone to mistakes—SPFx offers an automated solution.

SPFx employs CSS modules to prevent styling conflicts. During project compilation, SPFx tools process all `.module.scss` files. It appends a unique hash to each class selector within these files, ensuring they are distinct. The tools then generate intermediate CSS files with these updated selectors, which are incorporated into the final web part bundle. This streamlines the development process and maintains style integrity across the platform.

During your development, every time you build the solution, a `module.scss.ts` (hidden by default in Visual Studio Code) is created automatically based on your stylesheet content, generating classes that you can then reference directly into your React components. Behind the scenes, SPFx also handles the vendor prefixes automatically for you, meaning it adds needed properties for certain browsers. For instance, let's look at the following:

```
.container{
  display: flex;
}
```

The preceding code becomes the following:

```
.container_7e976ae1 {
  display: -webkit-box; // older Safari on MacOS and iOS
  display: -ms-flexbox; // IE 10 - 11
  display: flex;
}
```

This way, your CSS code will look good in most browsers.

Updating the render() function

The generated classes can be consumed this way into the `render()` function of our React component, displaying products:

```
import styles from "./PacktProductCatalog.module.scss";
import { ImageHelper } from "@microsoft/sp-image-helper";
...
public render(): React.ReactElement<IPacktProductCatalogProps> {
    return (
        <div className={styles.productList}>
          {this.state.productItems.map((productItem:
IProductCatalogItem) => {
            return (
              <div
                className={styles.productItem}
                style={{
                  backgroundImage: `url(${ImageHelper.
convertToImageUrl({
                    sourceUrl: productItem.itemPicture,
                    width: 250,
                  })})`,
                }}
                key={productItem.productReference}
              >
                <div className={styles.productItem}>
                  <div className={styles.tertiaryText}>
                    <span>Reference: {productItem.productReference}</
span>
                  </div>
                  <div className={styles.primaryText}>
                    {productItem.modelName}
                  </div>
                  <div className={styles.secondaryText}>
                    <span>Size: {productItem.size}</span>
                    <span>Stock: {productItem.stockLevel}</span>
                  </div>
                </div>
              </div>
            );
          })}
        </div>
    );
}
```

We first import the TypeScript module file automatically generated and reference the classes using the `className` attribute.

We also leverage the Image Helper API via the added `@microsoft/sp-image-helper` package (under `dependencies` in `package.json`) to get an optimized version of the product images stored in the SharePoint site. Introduced with SPFx 1.14, this feature allows you to get an optimized version of an image stored in SharePoint for a requested size with the `ImageHelper.convertToImageUrl()` method. As you may know, requesting large images on the browser can drastically slow down the performance and impact user experience.

Building the solution using `gulp serve`, you should now see the new tile design for products:

Figure 5.7 – Product tile with styles

Overall, when designing styles with SPFx, here are a few general rules to comply with:

- Use one stylesheet per component, as it will be easier to read for other developers. For solutions with multiple customizations, you can share some stylesheets, but it really depends on the use case.

- Avoid using IDs in markup. Unlike CSS classes, IDs are unique to the page and won't be transformed during the build process, potentially causing conflicts on the page. Remember that your web part can be used multiple times on the same page so you can't assume the configuration or components present on the page.

- Wrap your CSS styles in a class named after the component taking benefit from the SASS nested structure (e.g., a root `productList` class).

- Use the Image Helper API to display large images not suitable for the web.

In this section, we saw how to create styles for our web part using SASS stylesheets and explained how SPFx helps with the building process. In the next section, we'll review how to make our web part work with the SharePoint theme.

Handling themes and dark mode

In our solution, we used fixed colors as an example. Ideally, you should utilize the theme colors of the host site to ensure that your solution blends seamlessly and appears as an integral part of the site.

SPFx facilitates this by allowing references to the host site's theme colors. Consequently, if your web part is on a site with a red theme, it will adopt the red color scheme, and if it's on a blue-themed site, it will automatically align with the blue palette. This adaptation occurs automatically, requiring no modifications to the web part code, ensuring consistency and visual harmony across different sites.

To handle a theme in an SPFx web part, you have multiple options, which we will see next.

Using theme tokens

The first approach is to use theme tokens in your SASS stylesheets provided by SPFx. These tokens have the format [theme: themeDark, default: #005a9e], where theme is the name of a predefined SPFx variable, and default is a fallback value if the variable is not available. Variables represent the colors used for the SharePoint site theme. During the build process, they'll be replaced automatically by the corresponding value making your web part integrated with the rest of the experience:

```
.tertiaryText {
    color: "[theme: accent, default: #0078d7]";
}
```

> **SPFx theme tokens**
>
> All the available tokens you can use are listed here: https://learn.microsoft.com/en-us/sharepoint/dev/spfx/use-theme-colors-in-your-customizations#available-theme-tokens-and-their-occurrences.

However, using this technique *will not* change the color when the theme is switched to dark. To handle dark mode, you need to use the CSS variables technique instead.

Using CSS variables

The SPFx web part root class provides a special method called onThemeChanged(currentTheme: IReadonlyTheme | undefined): void to handle the theme update, passing the new theme object as a parameter. This method is triggered every time a user changes the section background or the site theme. Using this object, we can use CSS variables to map the correct colors and use them in the SASS stylesheet. CSS variables are not specific to SPFx. Once defined in the root web part DOM element, they are propagated and accessible to child elements.

For products, we define two properties, `--productTileBackground` and `--productTileText`, mapped to the correct semantic colors from the theme object:

```
protected onThemeChanged(currentTheme: IReadonlyTheme | undefined):
void {

    if (!currentTheme) {
      return;
    }

    const { semanticColors } = currentTheme;

    if (semanticColors) {
        this.domElement.style.setProperty("--productTileBackground",
semanticColors.bodyBackground || null);
        this.domElement.style.setProperty("--productTileText",
semanticColors.bodyText || null);
    }
}
```

We can then replace fixed values with these variable references:

```
.productItemFooter {
    background-color: var(--productTileBackground);
    color: var(--productTileText);
    ...
```

This way, whenever the theme changes, the theme variables will be updated, and therefore CSS variables used for components as well. Notice the difference compared to theme tokens:

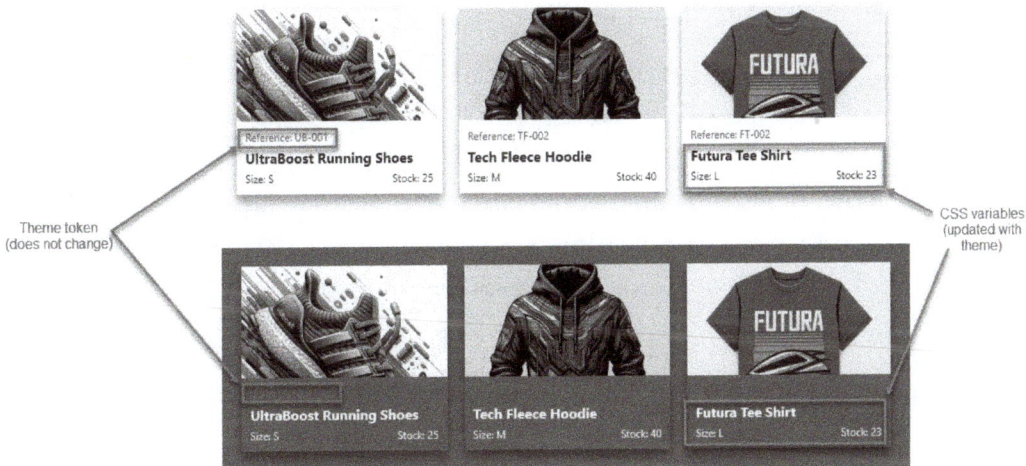

Figure 5.8 – CSS variables versus theme tokens

> **Theme object versus manual values**
>
> You have the choice to map values from the theme object to your CSS variables or use your own arbitrary values, for instance, detecting whether the current theme is in dark mode and applying fixed values depending on the mode. Here is an example:
>
> ```
> const isDarkTheme) { = !!currentTheme.isInverted;
> if (isDarkTheme) {
>   this.domElement.style.setProperty('--bodyText', "#FFF" ||
> null);
> }
> ```

In this section, we updated the web part types to match the customer requirements by updating the SASS stylesheets. We also detailed how SPFx handles styles for web parts and covered the two approaches you can use to support SharePoint themes in your components.

Localizing a web part

> **Git branch**
>
> This section uses the `https://github.com/PacktPublishing/Mastering-SharePoint-Development-with-the-SharePoint-Framework-/tree/chapter5/localize-webpart` Git branch from the repository.

A SharePoint site can support multiple languages for users. When they access the site, the UI is automatically displayed in their preferred language *if it has been enabled in the site settings*:

Site languages

The default language for this site is English. Enable translation

Enable translation into multiple languages

⬤) Off

Hide advanced settings

Available languages

Specify the languages that this site will support. Users will be

✅ Arabic	✅ French
✅ Bulgarian	✅ Hebrew
✅ Catalan	✅ Hungarian

Figure 5.9 – SharePoint site supported languages

> **User-preferred language**
>
> The user-preferred language is determined by the language set in the user profile. If not set, the current browser language is used. To force a language on a site, an admin can simply disable all available languages to keep the default one. In this case, user preferences won't be applied.

For SPFx web parts, the following elements can be localized:

- Web part content in the UI
- Web part manifest file
- Web part property pane

In the following subsections, we'll cover the first two. The web part property pane will be detailed in the next chapter.

Localizing web part content

In our "products" web part, we have some labels such as `reference`, `size`, and `stock`, which are written in plain English directly in the component UI. This means that if the user language changes, they won't be updated. To support other languages than English, we need to localize these values (i.e., add translation labels).

SPFx automatically streamlines this process by providing a localization mechanism based on resource files. When a new web part project is scaffolded, default `loc/en-us.js` and `mystrings.d.ts` files are created. The first file corresponds to the actual translation strings for a specific locale (in this case, *en-US* corresponding to English) and the latter is the TypeScript definition file, allowing you to dynamically reference these strings in your code. Behind the scenes, SPFx loads the correct resource file depending on the user language. To support multiple languages, you need to create a resource file for each one. For instance, to support the *French* locale, we need to create a `loc/fr-fr.js` file with the same properties defined in the definition file.

Even if there is only one targeted language for your web part, you should always use localized values and avoid any static text in your React components.

> **Resource file locales**
>
> You should always use the original locales instead of variants when creating resource files. If the user-preferred language is a locale variant, SharePoint will automatically fall back to the original one. For instance, if the user language is *fr-CA* (French Canada) and the *French* language is enabled on-site, the locale in the web part will be *fr-FR*. The default locale used by SPFx is *en-US*. If your web part is used on a site that uses a locale that is not supported, SPFx uses *en-US* as the default one.

Applied to our products web part, the `mystrings.d.ts` definition file looks like the following:

```
declare interface IPacktProductCatalogWebPartStrings {
  Labels: {
    Size: string;
    StockLevel: strings;
    Reference: string;
  };
}
```

The English translations are defined in the `en-us.js` file:

```
define([], function () {
  return {
    Labels: {
      Size: "Size",
      StockLevel: "Stock",
      Reference: "Reference",
    },
  };
});
```

And finally, the French translations are in the `fr-fr.js` file:

```
define([], function () {
  return {
    Labels: {
      Size: "Taille",
      StockLevel: "Quantité en stock",
      Reference: "Référence",
    },
  };
});
```

> **Important**
>
> There is no synchronization mechanism between the actual translations and the TypeScript definition defining these translations. The property names defined in the interface must exactly match the ones in the localization file, and vice versa. Also, being a JavaScript object, you can use a nested structure to better define your strings.

To use these translations in the `PacktProductCatalog.tsx` React component, we simply need to import the module file and select the corresponding property:

```
import * as PacktProductCatalogStrings from
"PacktProductCatalogWebPartStrings";
...
<div
  className={styles.productItem}
  style={{
    backgroundImage: `url(${ImageHelper.convertToImageUrl({
      sourceUrl: productItem.itemPicture,
      width: 250,
    })})`,
  }}
  key={productItem.productReference}
>
  <div className={styles.productItemFooter}>
    <div className={styles.tertiaryText}>
      <span>
        {PacktProductCatalogStrings.Labels.Reference}: {productItem.
productReference}
      </span>
    </div>
    <div className={styles.primaryText}>
      {productItem.modelName}
    </div>
    <div className={styles.secondaryText}>
      <span>
        {PacktProductCatalogStrings.Labels.Size}: {productItem.size}
      </span>
      <span>
        {PacktProductCatalogStrings.Labels.StockLevel}:{" "}
        {productItem.stockLevel}
      </span>
    </div>
  </div>
</div>
```

Localizing the web part manifest

In the *Updating the solution configuration* section of this chapter, we saw how to set a title and description of our web part to help users determine its purpose when adding new components to a page. We can also localize these values depending on the current user language. For this, you can simply add the locale name and the corresponding label to each element you want to translate in the manifest file:

```
"preconfiguredEntries": [{

    . . .

    "title": { "default": "Packt - Product Catalog", "fr-FR": "Pack -
Catalogue de produits" },

    "description": { "default": "Displays the list of products
from the Packt catalog", "fr-FR": "Affiche la liste de produits du
catalogue Packt" }

    . . .

}]
```

> **Locale names**
>
> The last part of locale names must be in uppercase (e.g., `fr-FR`).

Testing locales

We'll start with the web part content.

To verify that the resource files are correctly loaded depending on the language, SPFx provides the `--locale` parameter for the `gulp serve` command. For instance, to test labels in French for the products web part, use `gulp serve --locale=fr-fr`:

Référence: UB-001	Référence: TF-002	Référence: FT-002
UltraBoost Running Shoes	**Tech Fleece Hoodie**	**Futura Tee Shirt**
Taille: S Quantité en stock: 25	Taille: M Quantité en stock: 40	Taille: L Quantité en stock: 23

Figure 5.10 – Localized web part

Now, we'll look at the web part manifest.

Unfortunately, the SPFx Workbench doesn't currently support previewing the localized values from the web part manifest. It always uses the default translation. To test the localization in this scenario, the web part must be loaded in a live SharePoint modern page:

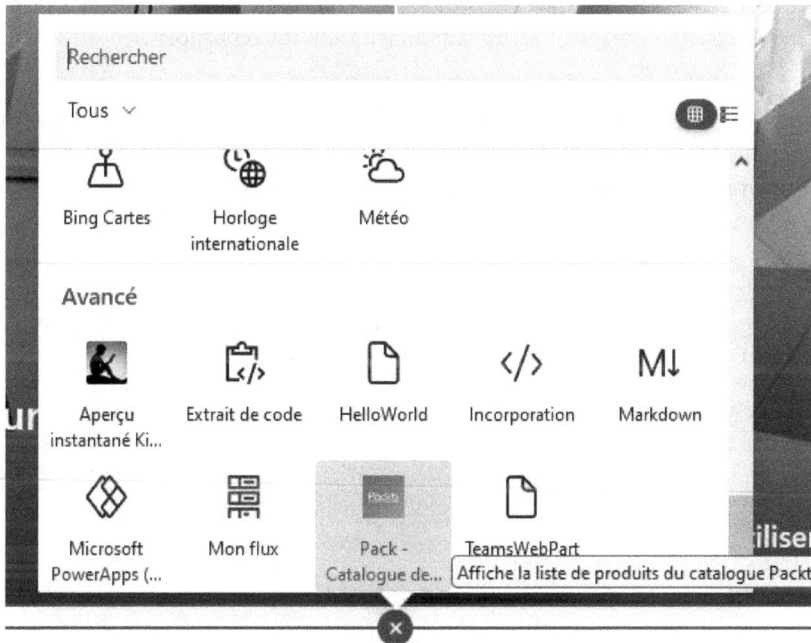

Figure 5.11 – Localized web part title and description

We will detail how to debug an SPFx solution in a SharePoint site later in this book, in *Chapter 17, Debugging Your Solution Efficiently*.

In this section, we reviewed all the localization options for an SPFx web part. We saw how to localize our web part according to the current user language by adding translations for both English and French for product labels displayed in the UI, and provided translations for the title and description updating the manifest. In the next section, we'll cover how to leverage web part top actions to let users quickly customize web part settings.

Using web part top actions

> **Git branch**
>
> This section uses the `https://github.com/PacktPublishing/Mastering-SharePoint-Development-with-the-SharePoint-Framework-/tree/chapter5/webpart-top-actions` Git branch from the repository.

Like the property pane, top actions can be used to quickly configure web part settings. However, unlike the former, they do not need to implement a specific control or open the property pane. Also, they are only displayed in edit mode in the web part command bar menu.

Defining top actions

In the solution we are creating, the customer wants to quickly change the number of products displayed in the catalog. This is a perfect use case for a web part top action.

We first define a new web part property called `itemsCount` that will be used to determine the number of products to display in the UI:

```
export interface IPacktProductCatalogWebPartProps {
  productsListName: string;
  itemsCount: number;
}
```

Top action definitions are handled by the provided `getTopActionsConfiguration()` method in the web part root class. A top action is composed of two parts:

- **The actions definition**: This defines the controls and their values to display in edit mode. Both dropdowns and button control types are supported, and you do not have control over the rendering. However, you can use the provided properties to customize the behavior of dropdowns or buttons.

- **An action handler**: This represents a function executed when actions are performed, such as a click on a button or an option selected in a dropdown, passing the new value and action name as parameters. There is only one handler for multiple actions, so it is up to you to determine what action was triggered and do the appropriate operation using the action name mapped to the `targetProperty` value.

In our example, we have three products, so the options will be one, two, or three items defined as a dropdown:

```
public getTopActionsConfiguration(): ITopActions | undefined {
    return {
      topActions: [
```

```
         {
           targetProperty: 'selectCount',
           type: TopActionsFieldType.Dropdown,
           title: 'Dropdown',
           properties: {
             options: [
               {
                 key: 1,
                 text: PacktProductCatalogStrings.TopActions.OneTile,
                 checked: this.properties.itemsCount === 1
               },
               {
                 key: 2,  text:  PacktProductCatalogStrings.TopActions.TwoTiles,
                 checked: this.properties.itemsCount === 2
               },
                           {
                 key: 3,  text:  PacktProductCatalogStrings.TopActions.ThreeTiles,
                 checked: this.properties.itemsCount === 3
               }
             ]
           }
         }
       ],
       onExecute: (actionName: string, newValue: number): void => {

         if (actionName === 'selectCount') {
           this.properties.itemsCount = newValue;
           this.render();
         }
       }
     }
   }
}
```

The action handler simply saves the new value in the itemsCount property. This value is then passed to subcomponents in the same way as we did for the "products" list name and site ID parameters:

```
public render(): void {
    const element: React.ReactElement<IPacktProductCatalogProps> =
      React.createElement(PacktProductCatalog, {
        productCatalogService: this._productCatalogService,
        siteId: this.context.pageContext.site.id.toString(),
        listName: this.properties.productsListName,
```

```
itemsCount: this.properties.itemsCount
    });

    ReactDom.render(element, this.domElement);
}
```

On the React component, we use the `componentDidUpdate` lifecycle method to determine whether products need to be fetched based on the `itemsCount` value:

```
public async componentDidMount(): Promise<void> {
    await this.getItems();
}


public async componentDidUpdate(prevProps:
Readonly<IPacktProductCatalogProps>): Promise<void> {

    if (prevProps.itemsCount !== this.props.itemsCount) {
      await this.getItems();
    }
}

private async getItems(): Promise<void> {
    const productItems: IProductCatalogItem[] = await this.props.
productCatalogService.getProducts(this.props.siteId, this.props.
listName, this.props.itemsCount);

    this.setState({
      productItems: productItems,
    });
}
```

Finally, we update the `getProducts()` method to use the count to limit the number of items to retrieve using the `$top` condition on our Microsoft Graph query:

```
public async getProducts(
    siteId: string,
    listName: string,
    itemsCount?: number
  ): Promise<IProductCatalogItem[]> {

    ...
    try {

      const response = await this._msGraphClient
```

```
            .api(`sites/${siteId}/lists/${listName}/items`)
            .expand(`fields($select=${fields})`)
            .top(itemsCount ? itemsCount : 50)
            .get();
    }
    ...
}
```

Testing top actions

Finally, the last step is to test our top actions. Unfortunately, top actions can only be tested on a live SharePoint modern page. To do it, you need to perform the following steps:

1. Run gulp clean to make sure we delete old build artifacts and start a build from scratch.

2. Run gulp bundle to bundle the application with webpack so the web part can be consumed on pages.

3. Run gulp package-solution to package the solution as a .sppkg file pointing to your localhost environment.

4. In the tenant app catalog, https://{your-tenant-domain}.sharepoint.com /sites/AppCatalog, upload the SPFx package file and check the **Make this solution available to all sites in the organization** option. You should also see the solution pointing to https://localhost:4321/dist/.

5. Run the gulp serve --nobrowser command to serve the solution locally. The --nobrowser option signifies that this shouldn't open the Workbench automatically.

6. Use or create a new modern page and add the web part. You should see the web part top actions:

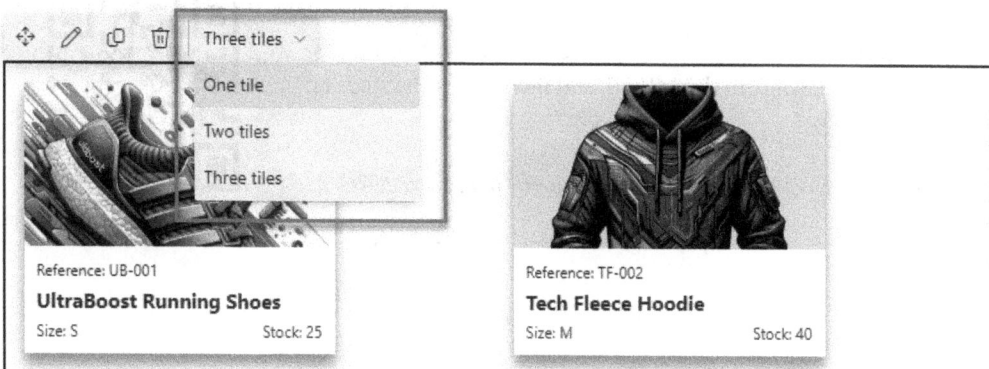

Figure 5.12 – Web part top actions

In this section, we saw how to use web part top actions to quickly configure properties without the need to implement a dedicated control in the property. We implemented an option to customize the number of tiles to show and used the value in the Microsoft Graph request to limit the number of items to retrieve from the list. Finally, we detailed how to test our top action in a live SharePoint modern page using different commands and deploying a package pointing to our localhost code.

Summary

In this (long) chapter, we built an SPFx web part to meet the customer's requirement of viewing products as a catalog. We started by creating and configuring the solution from scratch. Then, we defined our entities and services and implemented the basic render flow to handle products, using static data first.

Then, we updated the code to get the product items directly from the SharePoint list using Microsoft Graph. We continued by implementing styles to display products as tiles and added theme support according to the SharePoint site.

We also localized our web part to make sure the user-preferred language was correctly considered in the web part content as well as the title and description.

Finally, we created web part top actions to provide quick options for users to configure the number of tiles to display in the web part.

In the next chapter, we'll focus on the web part property pane and how we can build more complex configuration options.

6

Working with the Property Pane

In the previous chapter, we went through the implementation of the "viewing products as a catalog" requirement by initializing the solution and creating our first **SharePoint Framework (SPFx)** web part.

In this chapter, we will cover how to work with the web part property pane and use Microsoft-provided controls and custom controls to make our solution configurable by users. By the end of this chapter, you will be able to do the following:

- Understand the basics of the web part property pane and how to use it
- Use and configure SPFx default property controls
- Create your own custom control to integrate with the property pane
- Get advanced tips and tricks to manage the property pane for more complex solutions

Let's get started!

Technical requirements

This chapter relies on the GitHub solution accessible here: `https://github.com/PacktPublishing/Mastering-SharePoint-Development-with-the-SharePoint-Framework-`. You need to first clone the repository locally on your machine to be able to follow the steps.

The following Git branch is used for the entire chapter: `https://github.com/PacktPublishing/Mastering-SharePoint-Development-with-the-SharePoint-Framework-/tree/chapter6/working-with-the-property-pane`.

You must check out this branch before using either the Git command line or a Git client such as GitHub Desktop, SourceTree, and so on.

Code snippets

For brevity and readability considerations, only the relevant parts of the code are detailed in the provided snippets in this chapter. For these reasons, ad hoc code such as dependency imports, updates to certain files, and so on may be omitted. We recommend having the GitHub solution open alongside to get the full working version of the code and review the provided steps.

Understanding the property pane

The property pane allows users to configure web part properties by providing controls and options in a predefined experience. This is a built-in SPFx mechanism to manage settings more easily and make your web part more flexible.

The property pane only applies to the SPFx web part customization type and is only available when the page is in **Edit** mode.

In the next sections, we'll go into the property pane mechanism in depth by explaining its core concepts.

Web part property bag

Before digging into the property pane itself, it is important to understand the concept of the web part *property bag* and how web part properties are handled by SPFx.

The property bag represents the web part settings, saved directly inside the page where it belongs. Therefore, it is available and shared by all users viewing the page, meaning they all see the same configuration. The following schema explains the SPFx data stack and properties life cycle:

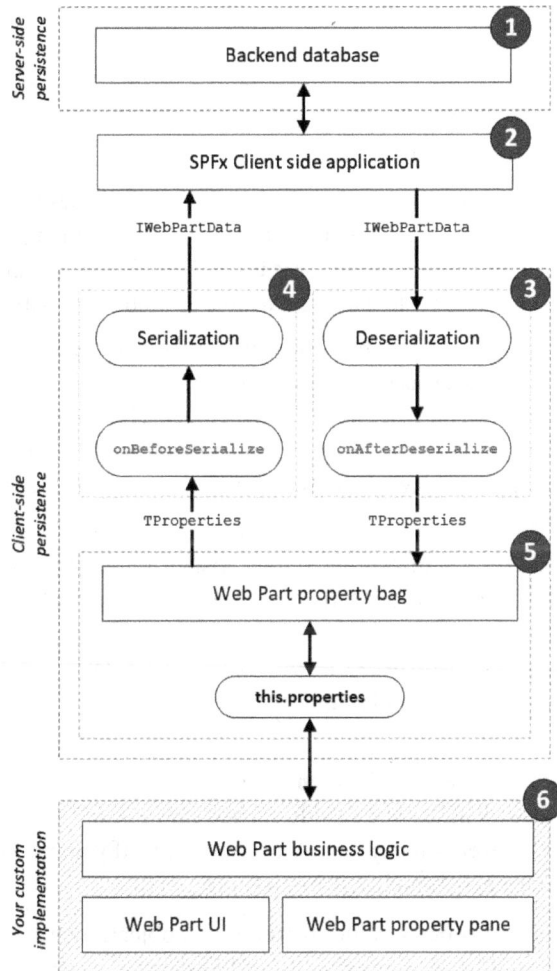

Figure 6.1 – SPFx data stack

In the case of web parts, values are saved directly into the page content where they belong (in the CanvasContent1 column) and, therefore, in the underlying database SharePoint internally uses for libraries. You don't have to worry about this as it is completely transparent to your application.

> **Warning**
>
> Never update the CanvasContent1 value manually as you risk breaking the page entirely and not being able to open it anymore.

The lifecycle steps are as follow:

1. Web parts are loaded by a client-side application on top of SPFx. It basically loads the data from the page using REST requests and passes them to web parts. Again, you don't have to worry about this part as it is transparent to you.

2. Data is deserialized and cleaned from any framework-specific values so it can be consumed in your web part. After this step, SPFx lets you handle the deserialization process final step using the `onAfterDeserialize` handler. This is particularly useful when you release a new version and need to upgrade an old data schema to a new one automatically.

3. In the same way as the deserialization process, property values set by your web part are serialized to be saved in the backend database. SPFx gives you a hook using the `onBeforeSerialize` handler to let you do modifications or verification before actually saving. Unlike the deserialization override, this method should be used only for very specific use cases and more as a last-resort safety net to avoid saving corrupted data. At this stage, data should already be validated by the web part business logic.

4. The web part property bag is materialized by a JavaScript object accessible using `this.properties` inside the web part code. This object complies with the `TProperties` interface defined in your web part code. In our business scenario, for example, this corresponds to the `IPackProductCatalogWebPartProps` interface we defined in the previous chapter specifying the product list name and number of items to retrieve.

5. Web part properties can then be manipulated according to your business requirements through the `this.properties` member. This can occur either inside the web part internal business logic (for example, in SPFx life cycle methods, such as `onInit()`), through the property pane via specific controls, or even directly from UI components. If you modify this object, it does not really matter from where this change has been triggered.

    However, when you set property values through this object, they are automatically saved whenever the page itself is saved (according to the SPFx data stack). SharePoint has a mechanism of auto-saving on modern pages so it means whenever you set a value, it will likely persist instantaneously or in a few seconds on the page. *You don't have to explicitly persist your values in the code.*

6. Web Part property pane fields values are accessed from your business logic code, for instance directly in the user interface, in custom classes or in the property pane itself.

User-specific properties

Because web part settings are available to all users having access to the page, specific user information *must not be stored* in the web part property bag. If your scenario requires you to update the behavior based on the user context, this information should be retrieved from another source (for example, the user profile) at runtime.

When consumed on a modern page, web part property bag raw values can be accessed by appending the ?maintenanceMode=true query string parameter to the URL:

PackProductCatalogWebPart

Summary   Manifest   **Data**

```
{
  "id": "ab225f70-c1a8-4d87-a527-78d74542a9d9",
  "instanceId": "838c9885-0292-444f-bad6-73a9eb8205e9",
  "title": "Packt - Product Catalog",
  "description": "Displays the list of products from the
  "audiences": [],
  "serverProcessedContent": {
    "htmlStrings": {},
    "searchablePlainTexts": {},
    "imageSources": {},
    "links": {}
  },
  "dataVersion": "1.0",
  "properties": {
    "productsListName": "Products",
    "itemsCount": 3
  },
  "containsDynamicDataSource": false
}
```

Figure 6.2 – Web part property bag viewed in maintenance mode

In the hosted workbench, this can be accessed using the **Web part data** button:

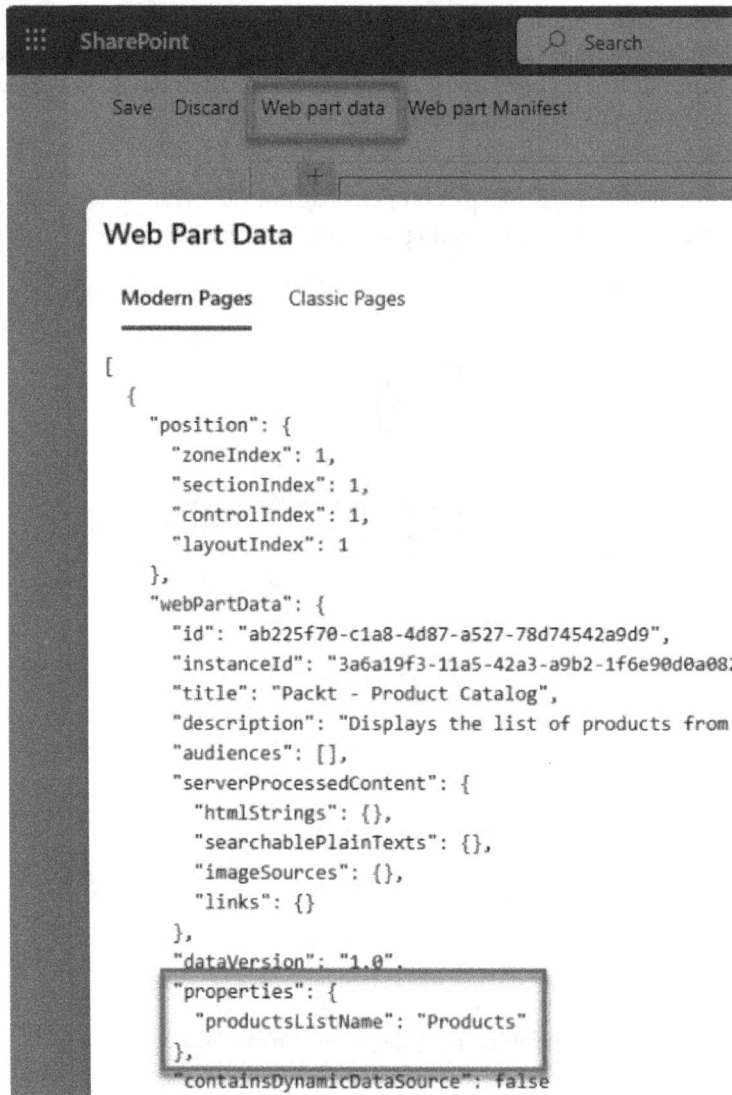

Figure 6.3 – Web part property bag in the hosted workbench

Now that we have explained what the web part property bag is, we can focus on the property pane, which is directly mapped to the this.properties JavaScript object.

Property pane structure

The property pane is used to provide a friendly experience to users to configure web part settings. Therefore, its structure is divided into pages, groups, and fields:

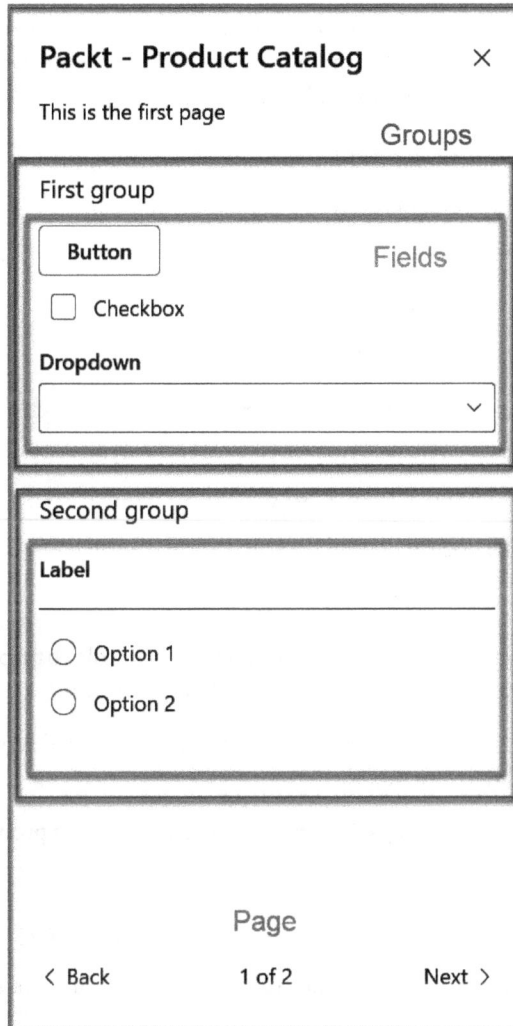

Figure 6.4 – Property pane structure

Let's go through the structuring details:

- **Pages**: These are used to regroup settings by larger categories, for instance, one page is dedicated to data/query configuration, and another is dedicated to UI parameters. Pages are composed of one or multiple groups.

- **Groups**: These contain the fields to display in the property pane. They can be regular or collapsible. When set as collapsible, you can even set their default state (expanded or collapsed). A collapsed group is usually used for settings that are less important to users (such as advanced parameters, for instance).

- **Fields**: Finally, these are used to configure web part settings. They are directly mapped to the `this.properties` object. SPFx provides a set of default controls you can use to surface your properties. Among them are the following:

  - **Slider** (`PropertyPaneSlider`)

  - **Button** (`PropertyPaneButton`)

  - **Checkbox** (`PropertyPaneCheckbox`)

  - **Dropdown** (`PropertyPaneDropdown`)

  - **Label** (`PropertyPaneLabel`)

  - **Horizontal rule** (`PropertyPaneHorizontalRule`)

  - **Choice field** (`PropertyPaneChoiceGroup`)

  - **Text field** (`PropertyPaneTextField`)

  - **Link** (`PropertyPaneLink`)

  - **Toggle** (`PropertyPaneToggle`)

Most of these controls are wrappers of Fluent UI framework controls (`https://developer.microsoft.com/en-us/fluentui#/controls/web`) and share pretty much the same properties.

Not all controls are used for settings. For instance, label or horizontal rule controls are used purely for the UI and are not mapped to any values.

For complex scenarios with many settings, it is important to leverage the property pane structure to give the best experience to users.

Reactive versus non-reactive

The property pane can work in two modes, controlling the way values are saved in the web part property bag:

- Reactive mode
- Non-reactive mode

In reactive mode, every update made on a property pane field value automatically updates the corresponding property in the property bag. This is the default mode for a web part.

In non-reactive mode, values updated in property pane fields are only saved when the user confirms the changes. When configured as non-reactive, SPFx adds an **Apply** button at the bottom of the property pane automatically:

Figure 6.5 – Non-reactive property pane

When the user applies the settings, all values are saved at once in the property bag. This process is handled automatically by SPFx.

You can control which mode to use with the `disableReactivePropertyChanges()` handler in the web part root class. For example, in the following snippet, we configure the web part property pane to be non-reactive:

```
protected get disableReactivePropertyChanges(): boolean {
  return true; // Non-reactive
}
```

In the next section, we'll detail how to use the default provided controls and create your own custom controls to integrate with the property pane.

Using property pane default controls

In the previous chapter, we defined two properties for our products web part through the `IPackProductCatalogWebPartProps` interface (`itemsCount` for the number of tiles to display and `productsListName` for the SharePoint where the data is). However, we only set the values statically in the web part manifest file and/or use web part top actions.

To provide more flexibility, we will now surface these settings in the property pane so users can set their own values for the list name and the number of tiles to display.

Defining the Slider field

We first start with the `itemsCount` property. As it is a `number` data type, we can use the default **Slider** property pane field (`PropertyPaneSlider`):

We add the following code to the main Web Part class:

```
import {
  PropertyPaneSlider,
  type IPropertyPaneConfiguration,
} from '@microsoft/sp-property-pane';

...

protected getPropertyPaneConfiguration(): IPropertyPaneConfiguration {
    return {
      pages: [
        {
          groups: [
            {
              groupName: strings.PropertyPane.SettingsGroupName,
              groupFields: [
                PropertyPaneSlider("itemsCount", {
                  min: 1,
                  max: 5,
                  label: strings.PropertyPane.ItemsCountFieldLabel,
                  showValue: true,
                  step: 1
                })
              ]
            }
          ]
        }
      ]
    };
  }
```

Adding this simple code will produce the following output in the property pane:

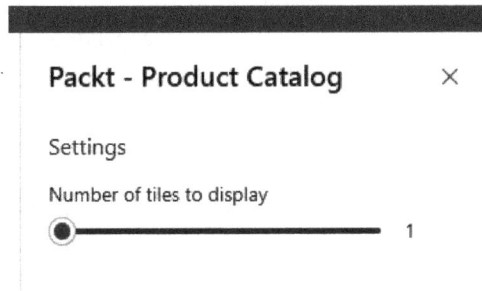

Figure 6.6 – Property pane Slider field

Web part properties' default values

At this point, when adding the web part on the page, you may have noticed that the slider default value does not reflect the number of tiles displayed in the UI. This is because we didn't set a default value for the itemsCount field. As a best practice, all web part settings should have a default value. You can set it in one of two ways. The first is setting the value directly inside the onInit() method:

```
protected async onInit(): Promise<void> {
    ...
    this.properties.myProperty = "default value"
}
```

The second way is setting it directly in the web part manifest JSON file (recommended as it can be updated externally more easily if needed, for instance, through a CI/CD pipeline):

```
properties: {
    myProperty: "default value"
}
```

A property pane field always follows the same convention when used (default or custom fields):

PropertyPane**<Field type>**("**<Property name>**", { ... **<Field properties>** })

The preceding code has the following placeholder meanings:

- Field type: The type of field (such as Slider, Toggle, etc.)

- Property name: The property name in the property bag accessible through this.properties

- Field properties: The field-specific properties (such as the label to display, description, etc.)

Behind the scenes, SPFx will update the underlying web part property using the field name specified as a string. Most of the time, you don't have to set the property pane field value manually via the field properties (sometimes you have this option, sometimes not, depending on the field type). Default-provided property pane fields will use the default value from the associated web part property.

Validating field values

For some property pane fields, it can be useful to validate the value before saving anything. For some default provided field types, the onGetErrorMessage() handler is available through field properties allowing you to validate the user input. For a control such as a slider, validation is not really needed as we set min and max boundaries, although other field types such as text fields benefit from this validation handler. For instance, if we replace our slider with a text field instead, we could use a validation like this:

```
PropertyPaneTextField("itemsCount", {
  label: strings.PropertyPane.ItemsCountFieldLabel,
  onGetErrorMessage: (value: string) => {
    if (!/^\d+$/.test(value)) {
      return "Value should be a number"
    }
    return "";
  }
})
```

This will produce the following output:

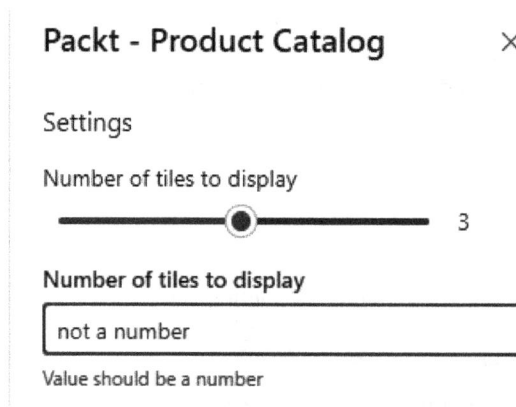

Figure 6.7 – Field validation

When default SPFx property controls are not sufficient for your requirements, you can still create your own.

Creating custom property pane controls

Previously in our solution, we hardcoded the product list name setting value in the web part manifest. Although it seems to be a convenient option, what if the list doesn't have this specific name on the site? In such a scenario, our web part will simply not work.

To give more flexibility to our solution, we created a custom property pane control to let users configure dynamically the products list to use. This control will fetch the available lists on the current site and let users choose one from a combo box.

Understanding the typical structure of a custom property pane field

Every property pane field class inherits from the `IPropertyPaneField` interface defining the common methods and properties a property pane field should implement. This interface takes as a parameter another interface representing the properties your field will expose to consumers (i.e., the web part root class through the `getPropertyPaneConfiguration()` method). These properties are also referred to as **public** properties.

To distinguish between public properties exposed to consumers and **internal** properties used for a property pane field, another interface is also declared combining both types (public properties and properties from the SPFx-provided `IPropertyPaneCustomFieldProps` interface).

For reusability purposes, the field business logic and UI are usually implemented through regular React subcomponents called directly from the property field class. As best practice, subcomponents used for a property pane field should be consumer agnostic (i.e., they could be used outside of the property pane if needed). In the end, a typical custom property pane structure looks like this:

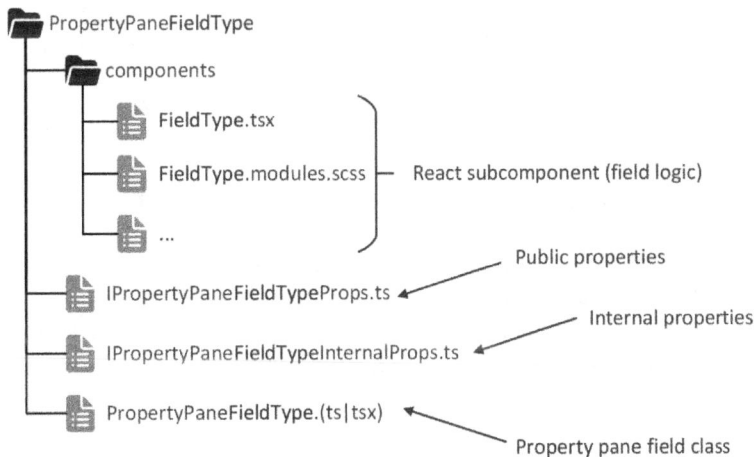

Figure 6.8 – Property pane folder structure

The first step of creating a custom property pane control is to define its input properties (aka public properties).

Creating the interface for public properties

We start by creating the `IPropertyPaneAsyncListPickerProps` interface defining the properties our field needs to receive from consumers. As our control will fetch site lists dynamically, it needs some context parameters such as the current site ID (`siteId`) and a Microsoft Graph client object (`msGraphClient`) to perform requests. Also, we specify a `defaultListName` parameter to reflect the current configuration state when users open the property pane panel for the first time:

```
export interface IPropertyPaneAsyncListPickerProps {
    msGraphClient: MSGraphClientV3;
    siteId: string;
    defaultListName: string;
}
```

Once the public properties are defined, it is time to define internal ones.

Creating the interface for internal properties

Then, we create the internal properties interface, `IPropertyPaneComboBoxInternalProps`, extending the default `IPropertyPaneCustomFieldProps` interface provided by SPFx:

```
import { IPropertyPaneCustomFieldProps } from "@microsoft/sp-property-pane";
import { IPropertyPaneAsyncListPickerProps } from "./IPropertyPaneAsyncListPickerProps";

export interface IPropertyPaneComboBoxInternalProps extends
IPropertyPaneAsyncListPickerProps, IPropertyPaneCustomFieldProps {
}
```

> **Why have two interfaces for props?**
>
> Having two interfaces is technically not mandatory, but it is considered a best practice to avoid any mistakes on the consumption side. We could have used only one interface combining both public and internal properties. However, the way Microsoft implemented the custom property pane scenario encourages the use of two distinct interfaces to avoid confusion. Properties specific to a property pane field shouldn't be used by consumers directly to avoid any mistakes.

Creating the property pane custom field class

Finally, we implement the `PropertyPaneAsyncListPicker` class using these interfaces:

```
export class PropertyPaneAsyncListPicker implements IPropertyPaneField IPropertyPaneAsyncListPickerProps {

    public type: PropertyPaneFieldType = PropertyPaneFieldType.Custom;
    public targetProperty: string;
    public shouldFocus?: boolean;
    public properties IPropertyPaneComboBoxInternalProps;
    private elem: HTMLElement;

    constructor(targetProperty: string, properties: IPropertyPaneAsyncListPickerProps {

      this.targetProperty = targetProperty;
      this.properties = {
          ...properties,                              ──► Consumer exposed properties
          key: targetProperty,
          onRender: this.onRender.bind(this),         ──► Property pane internal properties
          onDispose: this.onDispose.bind(this)
      };
    }
}
```

Figure 6.9 – Custom property pane field class declaration

As mentioned previously, the property pane field class is just a wrapper over regular React components, allowing it to be used in the property pane. In our case, we create a custom `AsyncListPicker` React control, fetching the lists from the site using a dedicated `ListService` and displaying them in a combo box. We don't detail the implementation here as it is the same concept as the `PackProductCatalog` component described in the previous chapter. You can refer to the `/controls/AsyncListPicker.ts` file to see the actual code.

React subcomponents are called in the `onRender()` method, using the properties passed by the consumer:

```
private onRender(domElement: HTMLElement, context?: unknown,
changeCallback?: (targetProperty?: string, newValue?: string) =>
void): void {

    if (!this.elem) {
        this.elem = domElement;
    }

    const element = <AsyncListPicker
                        {...this.properties}
                        onItemSelected={((item: IComboBoxOption) => {
                            if (changeCallback) {
                                changeCallback(this.targetProperty,
item.text);
```

```
                                 }
                             }).bind(this)}
                   />;

        ReactDom.render(element, domElement);
    }
```

The important part here is the `changeCallback()` method. This method allows you to save the newly configured value from the subcomponent in the web part property configured for that field. Using this technique doesn't require the consumer to save the field value on its side.

> **Notice**
>
> The `changeCallback()` method takes care of the reactive/non-reactive mode configuration.

Using the property pane custom field

In the end, the custom property pane field can be consumed like any other field in the root web part class:

```
protected getPropertyPaneConfiguration(): IPropertyPaneConfiguration {
    return {
      pages: [
        {
          groups: [
            {
              groupName: strings.PropertyPane.SettingsGroupName,
              groupFields: [
                ...
                new PropertyPaneAsyncListPicker("productsListName", {
                  msGraphClient: this._msGraphClient,
                  siteId: this.context.pageContext.site.id.toString(),
                  defaultListName: this.properties.productsListName
                })
              ]
            }
          ]
        }
      ]
    };
}
```

> **Tip – use .tsx instead of .ts**
>
> To benefit from the JSX syntax, you can use a `.tsx` extension for the property pane class instead of the regular `.ts` one.

Now, when users open the web part property pane, they'll be able to configure the list to use for the products:

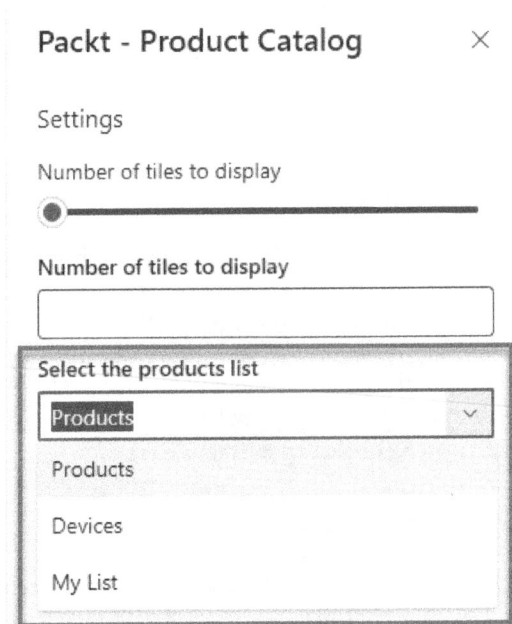

Figure 6.10 – Custom property pane list picker field for products list

We've seen in this section how to create our own property pane control to let users choose the list to use to display products. However, we only detailed the nominal scenario. In the next section, we'll review all the possibilities you can leverage working with the property pane.

Tips and tricks for working with the property pane

In the previous sections, we detailed how to use the default SPFx-provided controls or create custom ones. We will now give you some tips and tricks to go further with the property pane.

Handling property pane events

In the same way that SPFx provides handlers for the web part life cycle, it also provides multiple handler methods to manage the property pane life cycle itself. You can use them to customize its behavior according to your requirements:

- `onPropertyPaneConfigurationStart`: A handler when the property pane is opened. This can be useful to initialize shared variables used by all controls.

- `onAfterPropertyPaneChangesApplied`: When used in non-reactive mode only, this handler is triggered when values are saved. A good opportunity to review the values or set other web part properties based on property pane ones.

- `onPropertyPaneRendered`: A handler where the property pane is rendered. We don't see a real utility for this handler though.

- `onPropertyPaneFieldChanged`: When used in reactive mode only, this handler is triggered when a value is updated in the web part property bag. For instance, it is especially useful to set property values depending on other properties.

SPFx also provides direct access to the property pane object through the `this.context. propertyPane` property. This can be useful to manipulate property pane actions programmatically (such as refreshing the content, opening or closing the pane, etc.).

Handling asynchronous controls

When a field is required to load data asynchronously, it should only be when needed. For instance, considering the previously built custom control to fetch lists, data is only fetched once when the user opens the combo box for the first time. This ensures data is only retrieved when needed and does not impact performance:

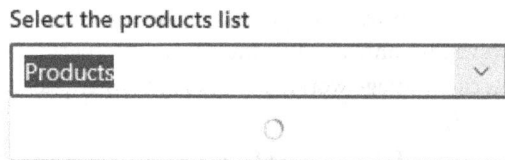

Select the products list

Products

Figure 6.11 – Asynchronously fetching property pane data

Fetching data for the property pane in `getPropertyPaneConfiguration`, `onPropertyPaneConfigurationStarts`, or, even worse, the `onInit` method is considered a bad practice as it may impact performance.

Also, once the data is fetched for the first time, it is not always worth it to fetch it for subsequent operations (for instance, lists in a SharePoint site won't likely change between two property pane panel openings).

Configuring property pane fields dynamically

Property pane field configuration shouldn't always have to be static. Depending on your requirements, you can build the property pane dynamically based on the web part context or other property values. Here is an example of how you could achieve a conditional behavior property pane field:

```
protected getPropertyPaneConfiguration(): IPropertyPaneConfiguration {

    const propertyPaneFields = [];

    if (this.properties.itemsCount >= 1) {
      propertyPaneFields.push(
        PropertyPaneSlider("itemsCount", {
          min: 1,
          max: 5,
          label: strings.PropertyPane.ItemsCountFieldLabel,
          showValue: true,
          step: 1
        })
      );
    } else {
      propertyPaneFields.push(
        PropertyPaneTextField("itemsCount", {
          label: strings.PropertyPane.ItemsCountFieldLabel,
          onGetErrorMessage: (value: string) => {
            if (!/^\d+$/.test(value)) {
              return "Value should be a number"
            }
            return "";
          }
        })
      );
    }

    return {
      pages: [
        {
          groups: [
            {
```

```
                    groupName: strings.PropertyPane.SettingsGroupName,
                    groupFields: propertyPaneFields
                }
            ]
        }
    ]
};
}
```

In this snippet, we display different property pane fields based on the value of another one, itemCount.

Setting attributes on property bag properties

For certain scenarios, some properties defined in the property bag need special treatment from SPFx when saved, such as a text property that needs to be indexed by the search engine or a property that shouldn't be persisted at all for whatever reason.

For such behaviors, SPFx lets you configure some attributes over the properties you define by overriding the propertiesMetadata property from the root WebPart class. This property instructs SPFx about a specific behavior for specific properties in the property bag. For example, here is a list of available attributes for the myPropertyName property:

```
protected get propertiesMetadata(): IWebPartPropertiesMetadata |
undefined {
    return {
        'myPropertyName': {
            dynamicPropertyType: 'string',
            isHtmlString: true,
            isImageSource: false,
            isLink: false,
            isSearchablePlainText: false,
            shouldNotPersist: false
        }
    }
}
```

The following attributes are configurable:

- dynamicPropertyType: If a web part has properties that are dynamically configurable, use this flag to declare the property as a dynamic property by specifying its type. This flag is likely used when using the SPFx dynamic data feature (detailed later in this book in *Chapter 7, Connecting to Other Web Parts*).

- `isHtmlString`: This indicates whether the property should be serialized as HTML. This flag instructs the framework to store the value as HTML so that SharePoint can perform the following services on it:

  - Normalizing HTML encodings

  - Stripping unsafe HTML tags (i.e., for usage with `Element.innerHTML`)

  - Search indexing

  - SharePoint link fix-up

- `isImageSource`: This indicates whether the property is an image so SPFx can perform some optimizing steps on it.

- `isLink`: This indicates whether the property contains a link. This allows the SharePoint server to treat the value as such and perform services such as search indexing, link fix-up, loading from CDN, and so on.

- `isSearchablePlainText`: This indicates whether the property contains plain text that should be search-indexed by SharePoint. This flag instructs the framework to store the property in a representation that supports search indexing. Unlike the `isHtmlString` flag, the content will be treated as plain text; SharePoint will not modify the string in any way, and special HTML characters may be stored, encoded, and appear in search results.

- `shouldNotPersist`: This indicates whether the framework should persist the property on the server. Use this for properties that are only important in runtime and do not need to persist on the server.

Using reusable fields from the community

Before going into the creation of a custom property pane control, we recommend you look at the *Pattern & Practices* initiative, especially the `@pnp/spfx-property-controls` npm package. This package contains a large list of ready-to-use, open source property pane controls you can use in your solution (such as a file picker, list picker, multi-select dropdown, etc.). The documentation for all controls is available at `https://pnp.github.io/sp-dev-fx-property-controls/`.

Summary

In this chapter, we covered all you need to know about the property pane for a web part. We started by explaining how web part properties were structured and handled by SPFx through the property bag and detailed the serializing/deserializing flow. Then, we focused on the default provided controls and their usage. We listed all the available controls and saw a basic usage of a slider-type field to control the number of tiles to be displayed in our product catalog web part.

Then, we went a little further by creating our own custom property pane control to dynamically fetch the available lists on the current site and let the user choose one. We detailed the typical custom field files and folder structure and provided some key code snippets to fully understand the prerequisites to build a custom field. We finished by providing tips and tricks to take full benefit of the property pane for your solution.

With this knowledge, you are now able to make your web parts more flexible by taking advantage of the default provided property pane controls or creating your own controls, depending on your business requirements.

In the next chapter, we'll focus on the dynamic data feature and how to connect multiple web parts.

Get This Book's PDF Version and Exclusive Extras

UNLOCK NOW

Scan the QR code (or go to packtpub.com/unlock). Search for this book by name, confirm the edition, and then follow the steps on the page.

Note: Keep your invoice handy. Purchases made directly from Packt don't require an invoice.

7

Connecting to Other Web Parts

In the previous chapter, we detailed how to work with the property pane to let users configure the web part settings. We will now continue the implementation of our products catalog solution by tackling the requirement exposed in the *Requirement 5 – Searching products by model, size, or color using free text keywords* section in *Chapter 4*. To meet this requirement, we leverage the SPFx dynamic data feature to connect multiple SPFx components on the same page. In this chapter, we'll cover the following concepts:

- The SPFx dynamic data feature and why you should use it

- Creating a new search box web part and exposing the data to other components on the page

- Consuming this data in an existing web part

By the end of this chapter, you'll be able to fully understand the concept and usage of dynamic data and how to leverage it to build flexible solutions.

Technical requirements

This chapter relies on the GitHub solution accessible here: `https://github.com/PacktPublishing/Mastering-SharePoint-Development-with-the-SharePoint-Framework-`. You need to first clone the repository locally on your machine to be able to follow the steps.

The following Git branch is used for the entire chapter: `https://github.com/PacktPublishing/Mastering-SharePoint-Development-with-the-SharePoint-Framework-/tree/chapter7/connecting-to-other-webparts`.

Before reading this chapter, you must check out this branch using either the Git command line or a Git client such as GitHub Desktop, Sourcetree, and so on.

> **Code snippets**
>
> For brevity and readability considerations, only the relevant parts of the code are detailed in the provided snippets in this chapter. For these reasons, ad hoc code, such as dependency imports, updates to certain files, and so on may be omitted. We recommend having the GitHub solution open alongside this chapter to get the full working version of the code and review the provided steps.

Why connect web parts?

The SPFx dynamic data feature was introduced in version 1.7. It connects multiple components on the same SharePoint page using a publish/subscribe design pattern leveraging the JavaScript events model behind the scenes.

With this model, some components are defined as *sources*, exposing information to other components defined as *consumers*.

The dynamic data feature is not limited to web parts, and any SPFx component can benefit from it, allowing multiple component combinations (e.g., an extension connected to a web part or two extensions together, etc.).

This feature gives the developer the ability to provide modular and flexible solutions to users. For instance, instead of creating one huge web part containing all the code and UI controls for every situation, solutions can be broken down into multiple independent parts that can (or not) be connected together to build a larger solution.

Dynamic data also encourages the reusability of your component. For instance, a search box web part can be used in many other situations than a products catalog solution; the data exposed is not specific to a particular use case (i.e., search keywords).

In the next sections, we'll go through a practical example to fully understand the purpose of that feature, covering the two connection scenarios:

- Exposing the data you want other components to consume
- Consuming the data exposed by other components

Exposing data from a search box web part

To meet our requirement of searching for a product, we'll create another search box web part in the same solution and connect it to the existing products catalog using the dynamic data feature. On the source side, we need to perform the following steps:

1. Create a new web part in the existing SPFx solution.

2. Implement a search box control.

3. Configure the web part to be used as a dynamic data source.

Let's do that now.

Creating and configuring the new web part

To create the new web part structure, we again use the SPFx Yeoman generator with the following command from the solution root folder:

```
yo @microsoft/sharepoint --component-type "webpart" --component-
name "PacktProductSearchBox" --framework "react" --environment "spo"
--package-manager "npm" --skip-feature-deployment
```

Unlike the first time we configured the solution, the Yeoman generator is smart enough to add only needed files for the new component and update existing ones without touching other components. In this case, a new packtProductSearchBox folder containing the web part code is to be created under the webparts one, and new entries are added to the config.json file. You don't need to install *npm* dependencies again as no new packages are used at this time.

Also, despite using an existing solution, it does not exempt us from configuring the web part-specific information. As we saw in *Chapter 5, Building a SharePoint Web Part*, we need to update the web part's PacktProductSearchBoxWebPart.manifest.json manifest file with relevant information for users, such as the title, description, and icon:

```
...
"preconfiguredEntries": [{
    "groupId": "5c03119e-3074-46fd-976b-c60198311f70",
    "group": { "default": "Advanced" },
    "title": { "default": "Packt - Product Search box", "fr-FR":
"Packt - Boîte de recherche de produits" },
    "description": { "default": "Allows searches in the products
catalog", "fr-FR": "Permet la recherche de produits dans le catalogue"
},
    "iconImageUrl": "data:image/png;base64,iVBORw0KG...
```

Running the `gulp serve --nobrowser` command will now give you two web parts in the SharePoint page callout box, as shown in *Figure 7.1*:

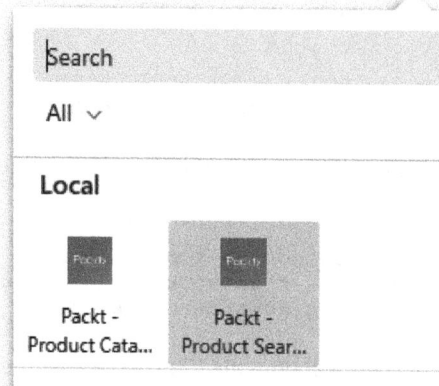

Figure 7.1 – Search box web part

For now, our web part does not display anything except the default placeholder. Let's implement the search box React control.

Creating the search box control

For the search box component, instead of creating our own control from scratch, we take advantage of the `SearchBox` control from the Fluent UI library. This way, we end up with this very simple implementation in the `PacktProductSearchBox.tsx` file:

```
...
import { SearchBox } from '@fluentui/react';

export default class PacktProductSearchBox extends React.
Component<IPacktProductSearchBoxProps, {}> {
  public render(): React.ReactElement<IPacktProductSearchBoxProps> {

    return (
      <SearchBox placeholder={strings.SearchBoxPlaceholder}
onSearch={this.props.onSearch} />
    );
  }
}
```

This produces the following output:

Figure 7.2 – Search box control UI

We define an `onSearch: (searchText: string) => void` handler to update the search query when submitted by the user.

Exposing data to other components

The dynamic data feature relies on a source/consumer model. In our case, the search box web part will act as the source for the products catalog web part by providing the search keywords submitted by the user.

The dynamic data package is not included by default, so you have to include it manually in the `package.json` file and install packages again by running the `npm i` command:

```
{
    "name": "packt-solutions-product-management",
    "version": "0.0.1",
    . . .
    "dependencies": {
      . . .
      "@microsoft/sp-dynamic-data": "1.19.0"
```

To define a component as a data source, it must implement the `IDynamicDataCallables` interface:

```
export default class PacktProductSearchBoxWebPart extends
BaseClientSideWebPart<IPacktProductSearchBoxWebPartProps> implements
IDynamicDataCallables {

    . . .
}
```

Then, the source needs to be registered on the page so other components can connect to it. This is done by using the `this.context.dynamicDataSourceManager.initializeSource(this)` method, usually called in the `onInit` web part life cycle handler :

```
protected onInit(): Promise<void> {
    this.context.dynamicDataSourceManager.initializeSource(this);
    return Promise.resolve();
}
```

A data source must implement the following methods:

- `getPropertyDefinitions`: This returns all the properties exposed by the data source. These properties will be displayed on the consumer side during configuration. The `id` value is used to uniquely reference a property and the `title` value is what is displayed to a user when connecting to the source. This means it needs to be relevant enough for the users to quickly understand what kind of data can be consumed.

  For the search box component, we define a `queryText` property representing the current search keywords:

  ```
  public getPropertyDefinitions():
  ReadonlyArray<IDynamicDataPropertyDefinition> {
      return [
          { id: 'queryText', title: strings.
  SearchQueryPropertyDefinition }
          ];
  }
  ```

> **Note**
>
> The property definitions for dynamic data sources are different from web part properties. You can use any value here; they won't be saved in the property bag.

- `getPropertyValue`: This returns a specific property's `id` value. By default, the return type of this method is set to `any`, meaning it is up to you, as a developer, to define the type of data returned by the source. It can be a primitive type (string, number, Boolean, etc.) or an object. For objects, these have to be flat, as in this example:

  ```
  {
      "searchQuery": "some keywords"
  }
  ```

  Let's say it contains nested properties, like this:

  ```
  {
      "search": {
          "query": "some keywords"
      }
  }
  ```

  SPFx will flatten it this way:

  ```
  {
      "search.query": "some keywords"
  }
  ```

To store the search query value, we use a simple `searchQuery` variable of the `string` type:

```
private _searchQuery: string = '';
...
public getPropertyValue(propertyId: string): string {
    return this._searchQuery;
}
```

In our case, we have only one property exposed so we can return the value directly. However, if you have multiple properties exposed for a source, you need to return the value corresponding to each property corresponding to the property ID, as in this example:

```
public getPropertyValue(propertyId: string): string {

    switch (propertyId) {

      case 'myProperty1':
        return "myProperty1 value"

      case 'myProperty2':
        return "myProperty2 value";

      default:
        return '';
    }
}
```

> **Good to know**
>
> The `IDynamicDataCallables` interface can be implemented by any class, not just by web parts or extension root classes. For complex sources, it means you can use dedicated TypeScript classes to handle connections. However, using it at the root web part or extension level is sufficient for most use cases.

The last implementation part for the data source consists of notifying the connected consumers that the value has been updated so they can process it. This is done in the `render` method using the handler we defined in our search control component:

```
public render(): void {
    const element: React.ReactElement<IPacktProductSearchBoxProps> =
React.createElement(
      PacktProductSearchBox,
      {
        onSearch: (searchText: string) => {
```

```
            this._searchQuery = searchText;
            this.context.dynamicDataSourceManager.
 notifyPropertyChanged('queryText');
          }
        }
      );

      ReactDom.render(element, this.domElement);
    }
```

The notification is done by calling the `this.context.dynamicDataSourceManager.notifyPropertyChanged(<property_id>)` method with the updated property ID as a parameter.

Now that you have learned how to expose data in a source component such as a web part, it is time to configure the consumer side.

Consuming data in the products catalog web part

As we mentioned earlier, the consumer component of the search box keywords will be the existing products catalog web part we developed in *Chapter 5, Building a SharePoint Web Part*.

On the consumer side, we need to do the following:

1. Define new web part properties to handle the dynamic value retrieved from the search box.
2. Create the property pane control to configure the data source connection to the search box web part.
3. Update the `ProductCatalogService` class to support the search capability.

Let's do that now.

Defining dynamic properties

We start by adding a new web part property in the `IPackProductCatalogWebPartProps` interface:

```
export interface IPackProductCatalogWebPartProps {
  ...
  searchQuery: DynamicProperty<string>;
}
```

The `searchQuery` property is set as a `DynamicProperty` of the `string` type. This special type means the property is intended to be connected to a dynamic data source on the page and can both receive a value from it (in our case, a string representing the search keywords) or use a static value. This simplifies the need to manage multiple scenarios with distinct properties (connected/not connected to a data source). Also, when defined as a web part property, SPFx automatically registers the render() method of the web part to be called whenever the value is updated by the source.

> **Managing dynamic properties manually**
>
> When used as web part properties with property pane default controls, dynamic properties are *managed automatically by SPFx*, the framework taking care of the property life cycle, such as source registration, value update, and so on. For more complex scenarios, you can also set up the dynamic properties manually using class variables instead (i.e., calling new DynamicProperty<{type}>()) and using your own property pane controls and life cycle logic (i.e., setting source reference, setting/resetting values, etc.). You can see a good example of this technique in the PnP Modern Search open source solution, which heavily relies on the dynamic data feature (https://github.com/microsoft-search/pnp-modern-search/tree/main/search-parts).

In addition to the dynamic property definition, we also need to tell SPFx what kind of data this property is. This information is used for the serialization process (i.e., saving the right value format in the property bag), and the possible values are string, number, boolean, object, or array. Of course, this type needs to correspond to the source property definition type we saw earlier.

As we already saw in *Chapter 6, Working with the Property Pane*, we use the propertiesMetadata configuration to specify the data type that needs to be saved:

```
protected get propertiesMetadata(): IWebPartPropertiesMetadata |
undefined {
  return {
    'searchQuery': {
      dynamicPropertyType: 'string'
    }
  };
}
```

Finally, to access the property value at runtime, we use either the tryGetValue() or tryGetValues() method when passing the value to subcomponents:

```
public render(): void {
    const element: React.ReactElement<IPackProductCatalogProps> =
    React.createElement(PackProductCatalog, {
        ...
searchQuery: this.properties.searchQuery.tryGetValue()
    });

    ReactDom.render(element, this.domElement);
}
```

---

tryGetValue() versus tryGetValues()

SPFx provides two methods to access a value from a dynamic property, which mainly depends on the property type.

`tryGetValue()` is used for objects or primitive types (string, number, etc.). If the value is an array, then the first element of the array is returned; otherwise, the value itself is returned.

`tryGetValues()` is used for array-type properties. However, if the value is not an array, then an array is returned with the value being the single entry; otherwise, the value itself is returned. If the property is undefined or cannot be found, an empty array will be returned. You can use this method to ensure an array will be retrieved in any case, and you can process it safely, even if empty.

At this point, we have defined the dynamic web part property to handle search keywords, but we haven't provided a way for users to connect yet. For this, we need to define a new property pane control taking care of the connection between the two web parts.

Creating property pane controls for a dynamic property

SPFx provides the default `PropertyPaneDynamicField` control to facilitate the connection to data sources present on the page from the property pane. We use it like any other property pane field:

```
protected getPropertyPaneConfiguration(): IPropertyPaneConfiguration {
    ...

    return {
      pages: [
        {
          groups: [
            {
                groupName: strings.PropertyPane.SettingsGroupName,
                groupFields: [
                    ...
PropertyPaneDynamicField('searchQuery', {
                    label: strings.PropertyPane.SearchQueryDynamicField,
                  })
                ]
            }
          ]
        }
      ]
    };
```

The control provides a default UI to select sources and their available properties:

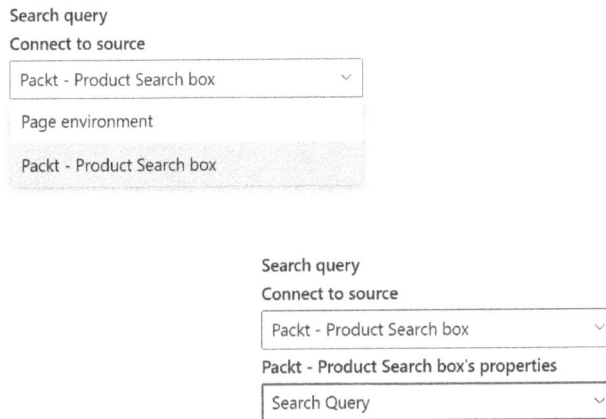

Figure 7.3 – Default dynamic field experience

By default, the `PropertyPaneDynamicField` field discovers *all* the sources and their exposed properties present on the page, even the ones that are not supposed to be connected to your web part. For example, we could connect the **Page environment** built-in source and a query string parameter instead of a search box.

If you need to show only a specific source, you can use the `filters` attribute to restrict either a component ID (i.e., web part ID or extension ID in the manifest), a property ID, or a source ID:

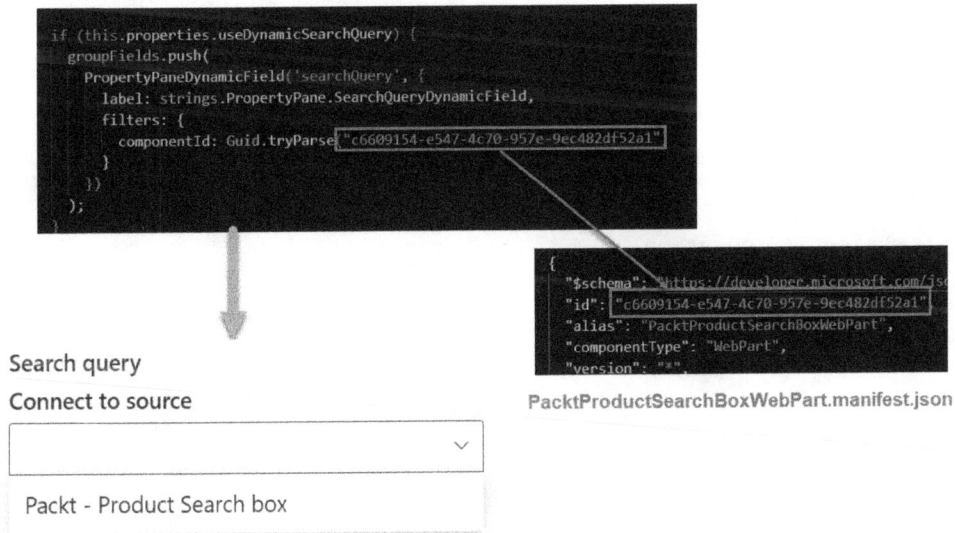

Figure 7.4 – Filtering available sources

Also, if you need to consume multiple properties for the same source, you can use the `PropertyPaneDynamicFieldSet` field type instead. For example, for a source exposing both `myProperty1` and `myProperty2` string properties, we could use the following configuration in the property pane:

```
myProperty1: DynamicProperty<string>;
myProperty2: DynamicProperty<string>;
...
protected get propertiesMetadata(): IWebPartPropertiesMetadata |
undefined {
  return {
    'myProperty1': {
      dynamicPropertyType: 'string'
    },
    'myProperty2': {
      dynamicPropertyType: 'string'
    }
  };
}
...
protected getPropertyPaneConfiguration(): IPropertyPaneConfiguration {
    ...
    PropertyPaneDynamicFieldSet({
      label: 'Select a property',
      fields: [
        PropertyPaneDynamicField('myProperty1', {
          label: "My property 1"
        }),
        PropertyPaneDynamicField('myProperty2', {
          label: "My property 2"
        }),
      ],
      sharedConfiguration: {
        depth: DynamicDataSharedDepth.Source,
        source: {
          sourcesLabel: "My source",
          filters: {
            componentId: Guid.tryParse("c6609154-e547-4c70-957e-
9ec482df52a1")
          }
        }
      }
    })
```

This will result in the following configuration experience:

My source

Packt - Product Search box	⌄

My property 1
Packt - Product Search box's properties

myProperty1	⌄

My property 2
Packt - Product Search box's properties

myProperty2	⌄

Figure 7.5 – Consuming multiple properties for a source

In general, when consuming a dynamic value, the data type for the consumer dynamic property and the property exposed by the source should match.

Handling static/dynamic value scenarios

When designing components leveraging the dynamic data feature, you also must think about the scenario where the component *is not connected to any source*. In our case, when not connected to a search box, the default behavior should be to display the list of all the products from the list. To handle this scenario, there are usually two approaches:

- Use a toggle control indicating whether the web part should be connected to a source or not and manually reset the dynamic property when switched to **Off**. This technique is useful when you don't expect users to enter a static value themselves. In our search box example, there is no sense in providing a query *hardcoded* in the web part.

- Use conditional groups in the property pane. This scenario leverages a built-in capability of SPFx and lets users enter a static value manually.

We detail these two approaches next.

Using the toggle button approach

In the first scenario, we add a new web part property, `useDynamicSearchQuery`, representing a Boolean value indicating whether the web part should use a search query from a dynamic data source. This property will serve as a toggle in the property pane to clearly identify the usage scenario:

```
export interface IPackProductCatalogWebPartProps {
  ...
  useDynamicSearchQuery: boolean;
```

```
    searchQuery: DynamicProperty<string>;
}
...
protected getPropertyPaneConfiguration(): IPropertyPaneConfiguration {
    ...

    if (this.properties.useDynamicSearchQuery) {
      groupFields.push(
        PropertyPaneDynamicField('searchQuery', {
          label: strings.PropertyPane.SearchQueryDynamicField,
          filters: {
              componentId: Guid.tryParse("c6609154-e547-4c70-957e-
9ec482df52a1")
          }
        })
      );
    }

    return {
      pages: [
        {
          groups: [
            {
              groupName: strings.PropertyPane.SettingsGroupName,
              groupFields: groupFields
            }
          ]
        }
      ]
    };
```

We then use this property to toggle the property pane dynamic field according to the desired behavior:

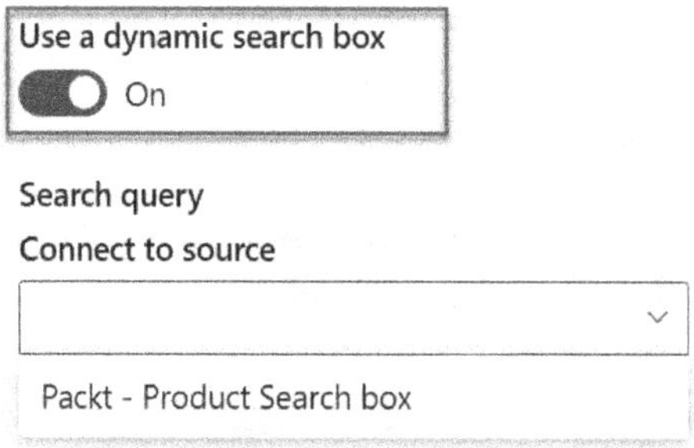

Figure 7.6 – Toggle field to control dynamic connection scenario

Using this technique will require us to manually reset the value when the control is switched to **Off**. As we manipulate dynamic property manually, we also need to take care of registering/unregistering the update event (by default, the `render()` method). We use the `onPropertyPaneFieldChanged` property pane life cycle event to reset the dynamic property value:

```
protected onPropertyPaneFieldChanged(propertyPath: string, oldValue:
any, newValue: any): void {

    if (propertyPath === 'useDynamicSearchQuery' && !newValue) {
        // Disconnect the source
        this.properties.searchQuery.setValue('');
        this.properties.searchQuery.unregister(this.render);
    }

    if (propertyPath === 'searchQuery') {
      this.properties.searchQuery.register(this.render);
    }
  }
```

This technique is recommended when you don't need to let users set a default value for the dynamic property. It also produces a clean and straightforward interface in the property pane making it clear whether the web part is connected or not.

Using the conditional groups approach

With this strategy, we leverage a built-in capability of SPFx for the property pane: the ability to conditionally display field groups based on a value. Using this technique will let users choose between a static value or connecting to a dynamic source. Notice the usage for different types of property pane fields depending on the scenario (`PropertyPaneTextField` for the static scenario and `PropertyPaneDynamicField` for the dynamic scenario):

```
protected getPropertyPaneConfiguration(): IPropertyPaneConfiguration {
    ...

    return {
      pages: [
        {
          groups: [
            {
              primaryGroup: {
                groupName: "Configure static group",
                groupFields: [
                  PropertyPaneTextField('searchQuery', {
                    label: strings.PropertyPane.
SearchQueryDynamicField,
```

```
                })
              ]
            },
          secondaryGroup: {
            groupName: "Configure dynamic value",
            groupFields: [
              PropertyPaneDynamicField('searchQuery', {
                label: strings.PropertyPane.
SearchQueryDynamicField,
                filters: {
                   componentId: Guid.tryParse("c6609154-e547-
4c70-957e-9ec482df52a1")
                 }
              })
            ]
          },
          showSecondaryGroup: !!this.properties.searchQuery.
tryGetSource()
        } as IPropertyPaneConditionalGroup
      ]
    }
  ]
};
```

This way, users will have a choice in the property pane:

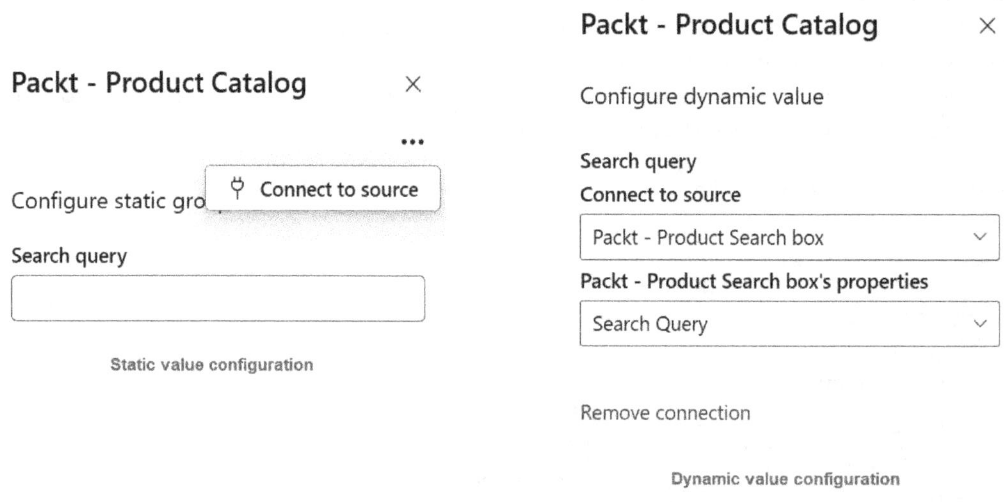

Packt - Product Catalog   ×

Configure static gro   ⚇ **Connect to source**   ...

Search query

[   ]

Static value configuration

Packt - Product Catalog   ×

Configure dynamic value

Search query
Connect to source

| Packt - Product Search box   ⌄ |

Packt - Product Search box's properties

| Search Query   ⌄ |

Remove connection

Dynamic value configuration

Figure 7.7 – Conditional groups for dynamic properties

Unlike the toggle button approach, this technique is useful if you need to let users set a default value themselves when not connected to any component. It is also easier to implement as you use the default controls provided by SPFx.

Now that we have a way to connect the two web parts, we need to update the `ProductCatalogService` class implementation to support the search capability.

Updating the products service class to support the search capability

The last step on the consumer side is to update the service class `ProductCatalogService` to support a new search feature. Instead of creating a new method, we simply add a new optional `searchQuery` parameter in the existing `getProducts()` method and build the Microsoft Graph request dynamically depending on this parameter:

```
public async getProducts(
siteId: string,
listName: string,
itemsCount?: number,
searchQuery?: string
): Promise<IProductCatalogItem[]> {
    ...
    try {

      const response = await this._msGraphClient
        .api(`sites/${siteId}/lists/${listName}/items`)
        .filter(searchQuery ? `startswith(fields/
packtProductModelName, '${searchQuery}') or startswith(fields/
packtProductColor, '${searchQuery}') or startswith(fields/
packtProductSize, '${searchQuery}')`:'')
        .expand(`fields($select=${fields})`)
        .top(itemsCount ? itemsCount : 50)
.header("Prefer", "HonorNonIndexedQueriesWarningMayFailRandomly")
        .get();
    ...
```

This way, when a query is provided, we adapt the Microsoft Graph request to add the search capability for products.

> **Notice**
>
> In this example, for convenience, we use a very basic search capability relying on the `$filter` OData parameter. However, in a real use case, you may want to use the endpoint from the Microsoft Search Graph API to allow free text searches: `https://graph.microsoft.com/v1.0/search/query`.
>
> When querying SharePoint list items and filtering on specific columns, you need to add the HTTP header, `Prefer: HonorNonIndexedQueriesWarningMayFailRandomly`, to avoid errors during the call.

Running the `gulp serve -nobrowser` command and going to the workbench page, we can now connect our two web parts and search for specific products:

Figure 7.8 – Search experience with two web parts connected with dynamic data

By adding the search capability to our products catalog web part, we've detailed the two scenarios involved in the SPFx dynamic data feature and components connection:

- Exposing data (here, search keywords) through a completely new and generic search box web part
- Consuming that data into the existing products catalog web part when users search for products, including the case where the web part is not connected

This implementation gives you a clear understanding of the SPFx dynamic data possibilities and how you can design your solutions efficiently by decoupling components.

Summary

In this chapter, we've covered all you need to know about the SPFx dynamic data feature and how to connect components. We implemented the *Searching products by model, size, or color using free text keywords* requirement for our products catalog solution by creating a new search box web part acting as a source and updating the existing products catalog web part to consume information from that source.

We've covered the necessary steps to configure both the source and consumer sides, explaining all the important implementation details.

In the next chapter, we'll detail the steps involved in a SPFx solution deployment from development to production using CI/CD tools.

Get This Book's PDF Version and Exclusive Extras

UNLOCK NOW

Scan the QR code (or go to packtpub.com/unlock). Search for this book by name, confirm the edition, and then follow the steps on the page.

Note: Keep your invoice handy. Purchases made directly from Packt don't require an invoice.

8

Deploying a SharePoint Web Part

In previous chapters, we went through all the implementation steps of the Packt product inventory management solution leveraging SPFx web part capabilities. However, the solution we developed is still only available through local development tools. In this chapter, we'll detail how to distribute the solution to end users in a Microsoft 365 environment. We'll start by breaking down the SPFx deployment pipeline and execute the required steps manually from our local machine.

Then, we will cover how to automate these into a CI/CD process through popular DevOps platforms such as GitHub Actions and Azure DevOps.

In this chapter, you will learn about the following:

- The solution lifecycle and deployment sequence

- Using SPFx built-in commands to build, bundle, and package a solution

- Customizing the build sequence by adding your own webpack rules or Gulp tasks

- Making your solution compatible with Teams, Office, and Outlook

- Automating deployment using DevOps tools such as GitHub Actions or Azure DevOps in a CI/CD process

By the end of this chapter, you'll be able to master SPFx solutions deployment, starting from your local machine to a DevOps process ready for production.

Technical requirements

This chapter relies on the GitHub solution accessible here: `https://github.com/PacktPublishing/Mastering-SharePoint-Development-with-the-SharePoint-Framework-`. You need to first clone the repository locally on your machine to be able to follow the steps.

The following Git branch is used for the entire chapter: `https://github.com/PacktPublishing/Mastering-SharePoint-Development-with-the-SharePoint-Framework-/tree/chapter8/deploying-a-webpart`.

Before reading this chapter, you must check out this branch using either the Git command line or a Git client such as GitHub Desktop, SourceTree, and so on.

> **Code snippets**
>
> For brevity and readability considerations, only the relevant parts of the code are detailed in the provided snippets in this chapter. For these reasons, ad-hoc code, such as dependencies imports, updates to certain files, and so on, may be omitted. We recommend having the GitHub solution open alongside to get the full working version of the code and review the provided steps. You also need to run the `npm i` command from the SPFx solution folder to install newly added dependencies and be able to run the sample.

Understanding the deployment cycle

The SharePoint framework provides a streamlined build and deployment pipeline relying on multiple commands to manage the lifecycle of a solution. As we explained in *Chapter 3, Your First Steps with the SharePoint Framework*, the SPFx toolchain uses Gulp and its tasks model to orchestrate build and deployment operations (i.e. `gulp <task_name>`).

These commands can be run locally for a manual deployment (for instance, in a development scenario) or automated through a **continuous integration/continuous delivery** (**CI/CD**) process. In both cases, the workflow is the same:

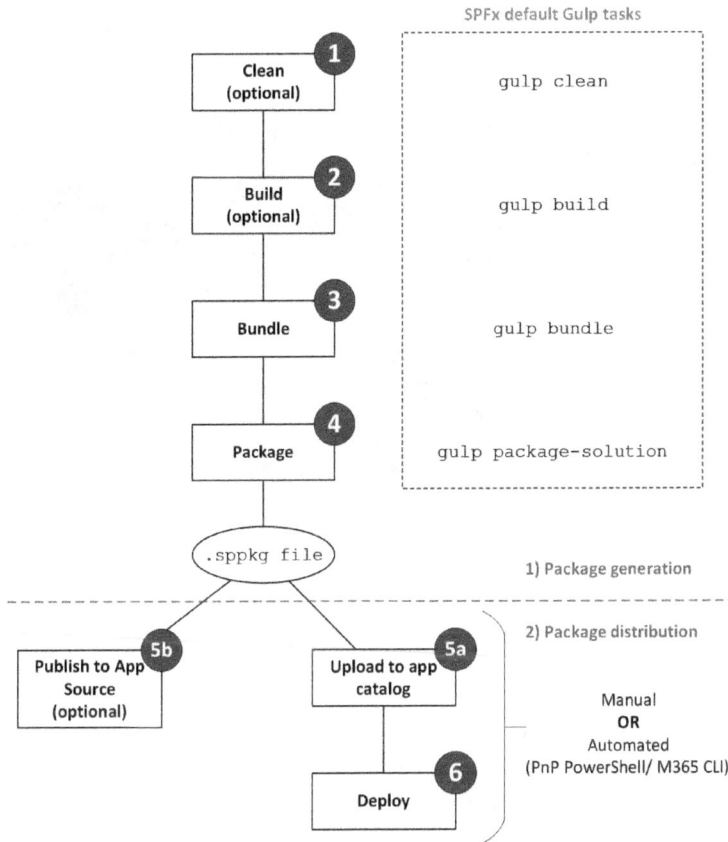

SPFx default Gulp tasks

Clean (optional) ①	gulp clean
Build (optional) ②	gulp build
Bundle ③	gulp bundle
Package ④	gulp package-solution

.sppkg file

1) Package generation

2) Package distribution

Publish to App Source (optional) 5b

Upload to app catalog 5a

Manual
OR
Automated
(PnP PowerShell/ M365 CLI)

Deploy 6

Figure 8.1 – SPFx deployment process

The SPFx solution lifecycle is divided into two distinct phases. The first one consists of *generating a package* for your solution (a .sppkg file) containing all needed resources (code, assets, etc.). This phase can be done locally or in a DevOps pipeline using SPFx-provided tasks. The second phase is to distribute that package. This can be done in any Microsoft 365 tenant by either deploying the file in an "app catalog" (manually or programmatically) or by publishing it to the Microsoft application store for Microsoft 365 applications: **AppSource**. In this case, getting the application through the store deploys it into the app catalog automatically, but in the customer's Microsoft 365 tenant.

Regarding the first phase, you can see all available tasks by running `gulp --tasks` from the solution root folder:

```
PS C:\VS\Packt\Packt.Solutions.ProductManagement> gulp --tasks
Tasks for C:\VS\Packt\Packt.Solutions.ProductManagement\gulpfile.js
├── clean
├── build
├── default
├── bundle
├── deploy-azure-storage
├── package-solution
├── test
├── serve-deprecated
├── trust-dev-cert
├── untrust-dev-cert
├── test-only
└── serve
```

Figure 8.2 – Available gulp tasks for an SPFx solution

In the next steps, we'll go through all the necessary commands to properly generate our solution package and deploy it for users.

Building the solution

The first step of the deployment process is to build the solution. This is handled by running the `gulp build` command. This command executes the **TypeScript compiler** (**tsc**) on `.ts` files, producing intermediate JavaScript files (`.js`). These files are intended to be executed directly in a browser (as they don't run TypeScript natively). The output of this transformation is done in a temporary `lib` folder.

In a production scenario, you must append the `--ship` flag to this command to perform SPFx internal additional optimization steps.

TypeScript version and compiler options

As a developer, you can access the TypeScript compiler options through the `tsconfig.json` file present at the root of the solution. However, by default, the compiler uses settings made to specifically work with SPFx through an internal tool called **Rush Stack** (`https://rushstack.io/`). This tool is a build orchestrator created by Microsoft and handles the internal project build sequence that SPFx relies on.

The Typescript version used by the SPFx solution is determined by the npm package `@microsoft/rush-stack-compiler-X.X` found in the `package.json` dependencies where `X.X` is the TypeScript version used (i.e. `@microsoft/rush-stack-compiler-4.7` for TypeScript 4.7). Theoretically, you could change the TypeScript version used by changing the package reference and updating the `tsconfig.json` file accordingly. However, in practice, it is not recommended as it is not officially documented nor supported by Microsoft.

Before running any build, the `gulp clean` command is usually used to remove the `dist`, `lib`, and `temp` folders generated by other commands from previous deployments. This step is not mandatory but recommended as it is always a good practice to clean temporary folders before deploying and to avoid including unnecessary files.

Applied to our product inventory management application, we run the following commands to build the solution:

```
gulp clean
gulp build --ship
```

Now we've built the solution, it is time to bundle it.

Bundling the solution

Unlike *building*, which strictly compiles TypeScript files into JavaScript files, *bundling* is the operation of processing all dependencies in the source code (including all kinds of file extensions) and performing multiple actions on them based on rules (for instance, transforming a SASS stylesheet into a CSS file). Then, it outputs them into larger static assets loaded by the browser and containing everything needed:

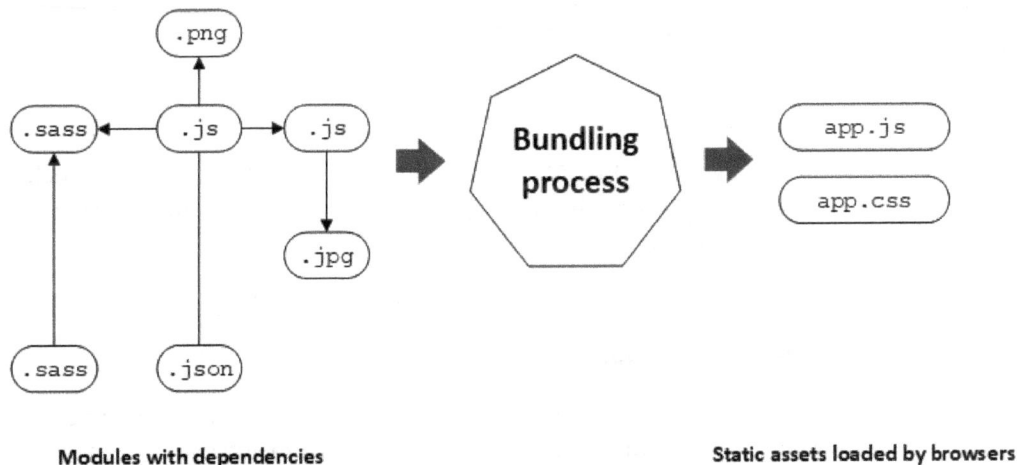

Figure 8.3 – Bundling process

The goal of bundling is to simplify the solution deployment with its dependencies (for instance, images, static files, etc.) and also optimize the performance. For instance, loading one bigger single file is more efficient than loading multiple small ones.

In SPFx, the bundling process is handled by *webpack* through the `gulp bundle` command. When this command is executed, it bundles the solution using both SPFx default webpack rules and your own custom rules, if defined. In the process, it also creates the following temporary folders:

- `dist`: This contains the static JavaScript files intended to be loaded by the browser with all necessary dependencies

- `temp`: This contains all files necessary for the deployment as manifest files describing the solution components and the SPFx packages that will be uploaded to SharePoint

> **Pro tip**
>
> In practice, you could skip running the `gulp build` command before `gulp bundle` because the bundle task will perform the build anyway. However, because the bundle operation can be quite long, depending on the size of your application (for large solutions, it can take minutes!), running `guild build` is especially useful in a CI/CD process to check for build issues and fails early to avoid wasting time running the bundle process (which would fail anyway).

Just like the `build` command, in a production scenario, you must append the `--ship` flag to include additional optimization steps (such as minification, embedding of assets, etc.).

Applied to our solution, the command to run to bundle the solution looks like this:

```
gulp bundle --ship
```

As mentioned, when running the `gulp bundle` command, SPFx uses its default set of webpack rules to bundle the solution. You can extend the bundling process by creating your own rules in the `gulpfile.js` file in the root folder of the solution.

In the next section, we detail how to create your own rules, enhancing the default webpack configuration.

Creating custom webpack configuration

SPFx exposes the entire webpack configuration through the `build.configureWebpack.mergeConfig()` method and the `additionalConfiguration` property:

```
build.configureWebpack.mergeConfig({
    additionalConfiguration: (generatedConfiguration) => {
        generatedConfiguration.module.rules.push(
                            externalsPresets?
            externalsType?
            ignoreWarnings?
            infrastructureLogging?
            loader?
            mode?
            module?          (property) Configu
    }
});
```

Figure 8.4 – Webpack configuration object

From here, you can review the current configuration and add custom settings such as loaders and plugins using the regular webpack configuration schema (`https://webpack.js.org/configuration/`).

Webpack customizations

Customizing the configuration requires a minimum of webpack knowledge. A misconfiguration can break the entire build, so only use this option if you are sure of what you are doing. The goal of this book is not to explain how webpack works.

Since SPFx v1.19.0, **Webpack 5** is now used, making it way easier to work with external JavaScript libraries. Compared to the previous **Webpack 4** version, it considerably reduces the need to customize the Webpack configuration in order to fix compatibility issues. For instance, and as a concrete example, the configuration step that was required to make the *Microsoft Graph Toolkit* library work with SPFx (`https://learn.microsoft.com/en-us/graph/toolkit/get-started/mgt-spfx#configure-webpack`) is no longer compatible with Webpack 5.

As an example, in our product inventory management solution, we add another transformation step for source files using **Babel**, an alternative JavaScript compiler used to support older browsers. We use the `babel-loader` webpack loader to process already compiled `.js` files in order to support older browsers such as Internet Explorer 11:

```
build.configureWebpack.mergeConfig({
  additionalConfiguration: (generatedConfiguration) => {
    generatedConfiguration.module.rules.push(
      {
        test: /\.js$/,
        use: {
          loader: 'babel-loader',
          options: {
            presets: [
              ["@babel/preset-env", {"targets": {"ie": "11"}}]
            ]
          }
        }
      }
    );
    return generatedConfiguration;
  }
});
```

SPFx will apply this rule at bundling time and generate files compatible with IE 11 according to our **Babel** configuration.

> **JavaScript file compilation**
>
> In this scenario, transformations made by Babel are done *after* the `.ts` files are compiled for the first time by the **tsc** TypeScript compiler according to the SPFx build sequence.

In addition to rules, custom Gulp tasks can also be created to extend the build rig.

Creating custom gulp tasks

In the same way as webpack rules, you can also create your own Gulp tasks as part of the SPFx build rig, for instance, to apply some transformations on solution files before deployment. However, unlike webpack rules, which are applied only at bundle time (when running the `gulp bundle` command), Gulp tasks can be called directly and independently from a command prompt, making them easier to integrate into the deployment sequence.

Traditionally, Gulp tasks are defined at the root of a `gulpfile.js` file using the `gulp.task()` instruction. Regarding SPFx, custom tasks must be defined in the build rig through the provided `build` object exposing the following methods:

- `build.subTask()`: This defines the task logic to be executed

- `build.task()`: This registers the task as part of the build rig so it can be called from the command line using `gulp <task_name>`, executing the sub task.

As an example, in our product inventory management solution, we define a new custom task `version`, used to update the version number in both web part manifests and the `package-solution.json` file. We rename the original files, appending the `.template.json` extension and use the `{{VERSION}}` token in them so it can be found and replaced by the custom tasks. The version number is passed in the `newversion` parameter when running the task from the command line. The Gulp task definition looks like this:

```
const replace = require("gulp-replace");
const rename = require("gulp-rename");
const semver = require('semver');


...


let versionSubTask = build.subTask('version-subtask', function(gulp,
buildOptions, done) {

  const version = buildOptions.args["newversion"];
  this.log(`Updating solution to version ${version}`);

  return gulp.src("**/*.template.json")
      .pipe(replace("{{VERSION}}", function handleReplace() {
```

```
        const semverVersion = `${semver.major(version)}.${semver.
minor(version)}.${semver.patch(version)}`;

        if (this.file.basename.indexOf("package-solution") !== -1) {
            return `${semverVersion}.0`;
        }

        return semverVersion;

    }))
    .pipe(rename((path) => {
        return {
            dirname: path.dirname,
            basename: path.basename.replace(".template",""),
            extname: ".json"
        };
    }))
    .pipe(gulp.dest("./"));
});

// Register the custom gulp task
build.task('version', versionSubTask);
```

When a task is added to the build rig, it will appear after running the `gulp  --tasks` command:

Figure 8.5 - Tasks after running the gulp --tasks command

Running the task is like any other task:

```
gulp version –newversion 1.1.0.0
```

When implementing a custom task, you can do the following:

- You can use `buildOptions.args` to get the value of passed parameters from the command line.

- You can use SPFx built-in functions to add logs to the command-line output and also determine the build outcome. The following methods are available:

  - `this.log()`: This logs a warning and adds it to the warnings list, which will cause the build to fail

  - `this.logError()`: This logs an error and adds it to the errors list, which will cause the build to fail

  - `this.fileWarning()`: This logs a warning related to a specific file and causes the build to fail

  - `this.fileError()`: This logs an error related to a specific file, causing the build to fail

- You can either return a stream (i.e. `pipe()`) or call the `done()` function passed as a parameter to mark the task as complete

Once the solution is bundled with our special rules, it is time to package it!

Packaging and deploying the solution

The packaging step takes all generated files from previous steps and packages them into a single file to be deployed in a SharePoint **app catalog**. This operation is done using the `gulp package-solution` command and creates an SPFx package (`.sppkg`) file including all the necessary files and assets from previous temporary folders.

The package is output in the `sharepoint/solution` folder and the `sharepoint/solution/debug` folder represents the content of the `.sppkg` package.

Pro tip

A `.sppkg` package is simply an archive file behind the scenes. It means you can extract and view the content by simply changing its extension to `.zip`.

Before packaging the solution, we need to understand what an app catalog is.

Understanding the app catalog

A package basically describes the solution and its contents. It also provides directions on how and where solution assets will be hosted.

All SPFx packages are deployed through an **app catalog**, a special SharePoint library that can be found at multiple levels in the Microsoft 365 tenant:

- **At the tenant level**: Accessible through this standardized URL: `https://<tenant_name>.sharepoint.com/sites/appcatalog`, the tenant app catalog is automatically available in the tenant and all solutions deployed from it can be used by all SharePoint sites within that tenant:

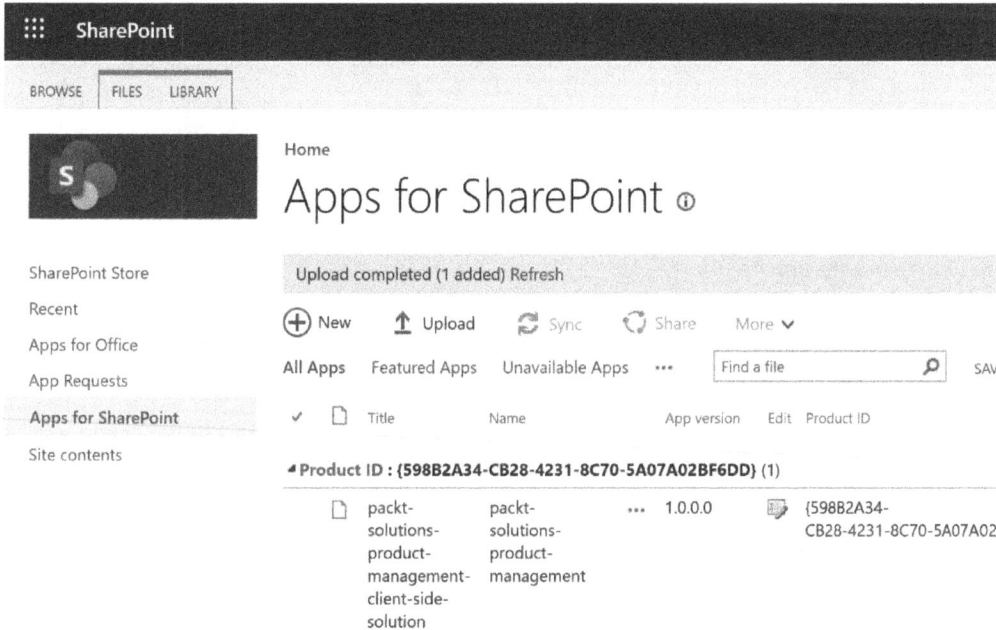

Figure 8.6 – Tenant-level app catalog

- **At the site-collections level**: Some solutions may need to be isolated in a single site collection for various reasons, for instance, because they are only relevant to a specific site and not intended to be used elsewhere. In such scenarios, an app catalog can be created only for that site collection and SPFx customizations will only be available to that site collection scope. Site administrators can enable the site collection app catalog feature by using either PnP PowerShell cmdlets or the CLI for Microsoft 365. Here is an example of how to enable the app catalog on a site collection using PnP PowerShell:

```
Connect-PnPOnline -Url https://{tenant}.sharepoint.com/sites/
{site}
Add-PnPSiteCollectionAppCatalog -Site  https://{tenant}.
sharepoint.com/sites/{site}
```

Once activated, you will have the new library in the site collection root site contents:

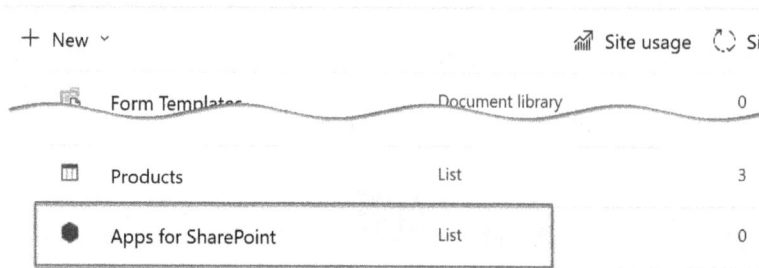

Figure 8.7 – Site collection app catalog

When deployed from the app catalog, you'll see the **Make this solution available to all sites in the organization** option. Checking this checkbox will make the solution available directly on pages without the need to install the app on the site.

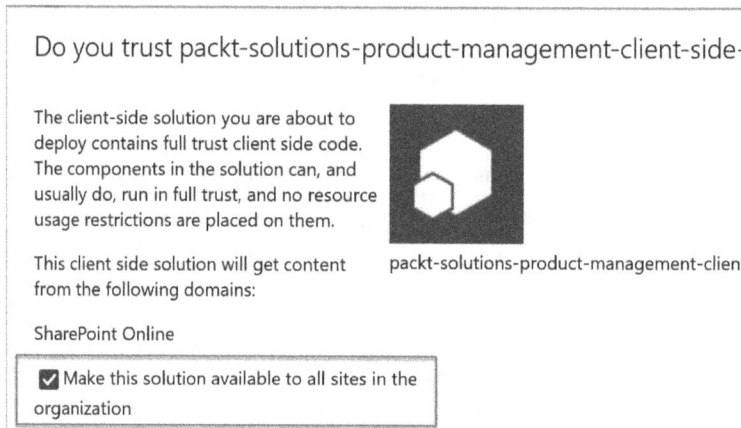

Figure 8.8 – Deploy the application

If omitted, users will have to explicitly install the application on the site from the SharePoint store to be able to use it:

My apps

Filter

All

From my organization

From SharePoint Store

Apps you can add

These are custom apps allowed by you experience.

packt-solutions-
product-managemen...

My organization

Add

Fir
Sh

→

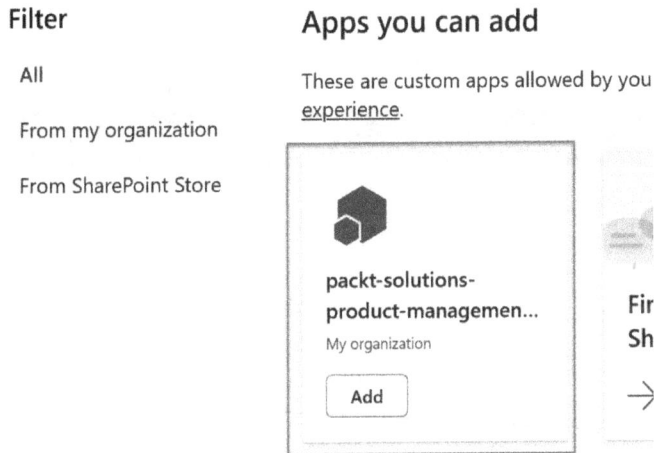

Figure 8.9 – Add application to SharePoint site

Behind the scenes, this feature is called `skipFeatureDeployment` and can be set in the `package-solution.json` file.

Choosing the hosting option for the solution assets

An important part of the packaging process is to define the location from where the solution files will be served once deployed (i.e., client-side assets such as JavaScript files, images, etc. generated from the bundling step). SPFx provides multiple options to host the solution assets. These options are controlled by the `includeClientSideAssets` property in the `package-solution.json` file. SPFx provides the following options:

- Host files in the app catalog site collection (default option)
- Host files using the Microsoft 365 **Content Delivery Network (CDN)**
- Host files using your own CDN, such as an Azure blob container or AWS S3 and CloudFront.

In our solution, we'll use the default option for convenience by simply running this command:

```
gulp package-solution --ship
```

Hosting files in the app catalog site collection

This is the default hosting option for an SPFx solution. When the `includeClientSideAssets` property is set to `true` (by default), all solution client assets are included in the `.sppkg` file. Then, when the solution is deployed from the app catalog, all these assets are copied to a hidden `ClientSideAssets` SharePoint library *in the same site collection as the app catalog* and can be then served from the following URL: `https://<tenant_name>.sharepoint.com/sites/appcatalog/ClientSideAssets`.

In there, you will find the same files as the `dist` folder generated by the `gulp bundle` command:

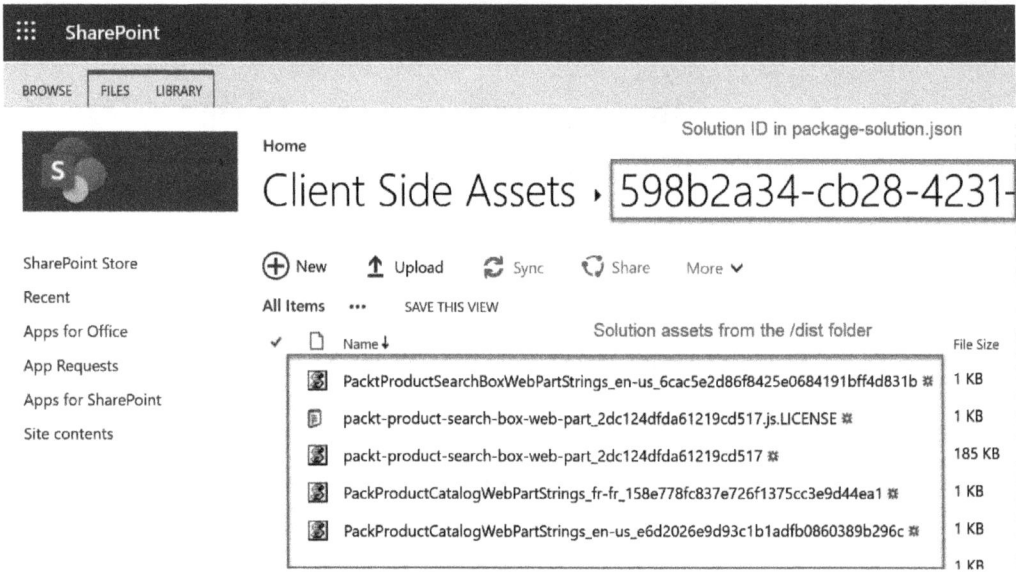

Figure 8.10 – ClientSideAssets library from App Catalog site

This behavior is the same for both global and site collection-level App Catalog. To verify assets are served from that library, simply inspect the network requests on a page where the SPFx customization is used:

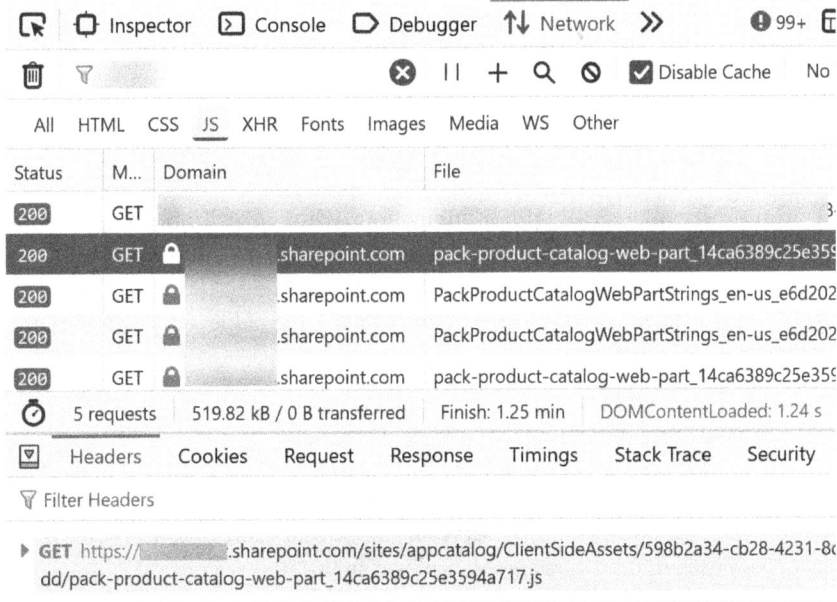

Figure 8.11 – Web parts served from the ClientSideAssets library

---

Development versus production scenarios

When `gulp package-solution` is used with the `--ship` flag, solution files will be served according to your hosting configuration (either from App Catalog, a private origin, or a custom CDN). You must also run the `gulp bundle --ship` command before to get it to work).

However, when omitted, the solution will point to the `https://localhost:4321` URL, using files from the local `dist` folder. The latter scenario is used for development purposes and should be used in conjunction with running the `gulp serve -nobrowser` command, starting a web server locally to serve the files.

Hosting files using Microsoft 365 CDN

Another convenient option to host your solution client-side assets is to use the built-in Microsoft 365 CDN feature available with every SharePoint Online subscription. This feature is not enabled by default on the tenant and needs to be enabled by an administrator using either the SharePoint Online Management Shell PowerShell cmdlets or the CLI for Microsoft 365.

Note

The Microsoft 365 CDN feature is not exclusive to SPFx and can be used by other solutions as well.

The goal of a **Content Delivery Network (CDN)** is to provide an efficient way to serve static assets to clients (for example, SharePoint pages) from a controlled location, also called the *origin*, by levering capabilities such as caching, improved compression with the HTTP/2 protocol or serving files closer to the browsers requesting them, helping to speed up downloads and reduce latency. The Microsoft 365 CDN can use either or both **public** or **private** origins:

- **Public origin**: All assets are accessible anonymously from a well-known URL. This option should be used only for non-sensitive assets, such as JavaScript files, scripts, or images. When enabled on the tenant, behind the scenes, it registers the `ClientSideAssets` library as a public CDN origin. Here is an example of how to enable the public origin on the tenant using the SPO management shell:

```
Connect-SPOService
Set-SPOTenantCdnEnabled -CdnType Public
```

- Compared to the default hosting option, the only difference is, now, when the files are requested from the library, they are served from the Microsoft CDN in the backend instead of the library itself (but the files are still deployed in that library in the first place). There is no need to change anything in your solution configuration as it will be all transparent for users.

- The public CDN URL looks like this:

```
https://publiccdn.sharepointonline.com/<TenantHostName>/sites/
site[/library][/asset.png]
```

- Again, you can check whether a solution is served from a public CDN by simply inspecting the network requests:

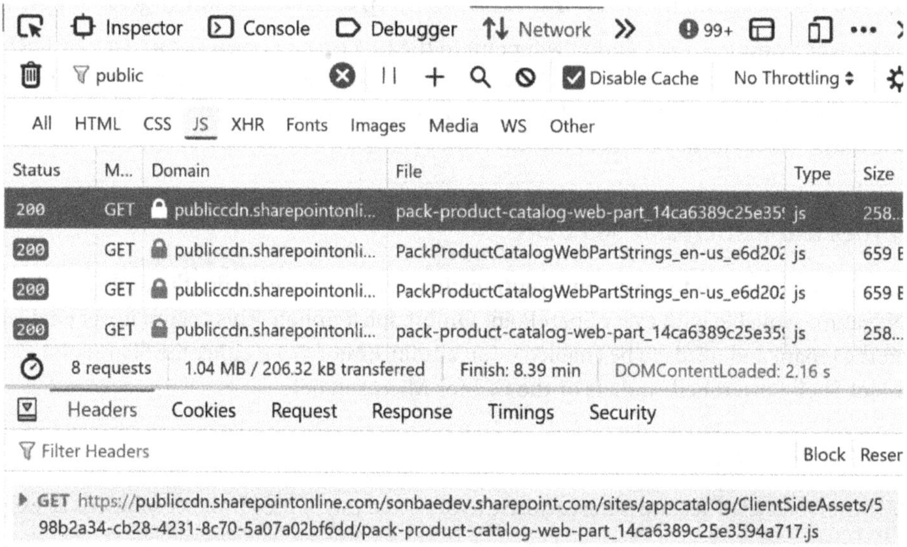

Figure 8.12 – Serving solution files from the Microsoft 365 public CDN

- **Private origin**: Assets are accessed from an arbitrary SharePoint Online site or library, or can even point to a unique file. Behind the scenes, assets are still accessed from a well-known endpoint URL, but this time, using a generated token representing the same permissions level as the current user. For example, if a user doesn't have access to a SharePoint library set as a CDN private origin, they won't be able to access assets from the corresponding private endpoint URL. It is also noteworthy that private origins don't support item-level permissions.

Unlike public origins, private ones need to be registered one by one. Here is an example of registering a SharePoint custom library as a CDN private origin:

```
Connect-SPOService
Set-SPOTenantCdnEnabled -CdnType Private
Add-SPOTenantCdnOrigin -CdnType Private -OriginUrl */sites/
packt/customcdn
```

When using a private origin URL for your SPFx solution, you must also configure the solution accordingly by performing these actions:

- Configure the `cdnBasePath` property in the `config/write-manifests.json` file, pointing to the library or folder URL. SharePoint Online automatically rewrites URLs for assets in private origins, ensuring that requests for those assets are always served from the CDN. You can't manually build URLs to CDN assets in private origins because these URLs contain tokens that must be auto-generated by SharePoint Online at the time the asset is requested.

```
{
    "$schema": "https://developer.microsoft.com/json-schemas/
spfx-build/write-manifests.schema.json",
    "cdnBasePath": "https:///{tenant_name}.sharepoint.com/sites/
packt/customcdn"
}
```

- Set `includeClientSideAssets` to `false` in the `config/package-solution.json` file.

- Upload the files from the `dist` folder in that library as they won't be included in the `.sppkg` package anymore.

A private CDN URL has the following format (where the `eat` and `oat` parameters correspond to the token generated by SharePoint Online):

```
https://privatecdn.sharepointonline.com/<TenantHostName>/sites/
site[/library1] [/folder] [/asset.png]?eat=1486154359_cc59042c5c
55c90b26a2775323c7c...&oat=1486154359_7d73c2e3ba4b7b1f9724233
2900616db0d4ff...
```

- When inspecting the network requests on a page, you won't explicitly see the private CDN URL. To ensure assets are correctly set, you can inspect the HTTP protocol version as a hint. When served from a regular library, without the CDN enabled, the version will be HTTP/1.1. However, if the library is backed by a CDN, you'll see HTTP/2:

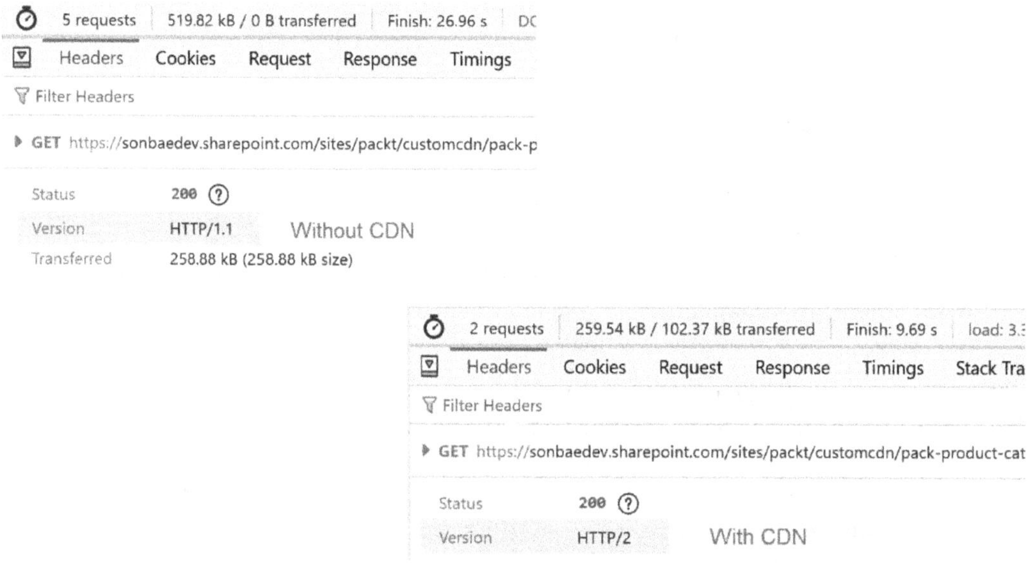

Figure 8.13 – Serving solution files from the Microsoft 365 private origin CDN

Azure CDN

Another option is to use a hosting solution completely outside of SharePoint, for instance in Azure. For that particular scenario, SPFx also provides a streamlined approach. Because configuring an Azure blob container is outside of the scope of this book, we simply provide the high-level steps to use an Azure CDN for an SPFx solution here:

1. Create an Azure storage account and a blob container.

2. Configure the container to be accessible anonymously.

3. Configure a CDN profile for that storage account. This will give you a URL from which to access containers and blobs.

4. Configure CDN cache settings.

5. Update the `config/deploy-azure-storage.json` file, filling in the `account`, `container`, and `accessKey` properties according to your Azure configuration. These parameters are used to upload the files in the container (and not to access them at runtime):

```
{
    "$schema": "https://developer.microsoft.com/json-schemas/spfx-
```

```
build/deploy-azure-storage.schema.json",
  "workingDir": "./release/assets/",
  "account": "packtstoaccount",
  "container": "packt-solutions-product-management
",
  "accessKey": "q1UsGWocj+CnlLuv9ZpriOCj46ikgBbDB...
DTVSbRGj41av1G73rynbvKizZpIKK9XpnpA=="
}
```

6. Set `includeClientSideAssets` to `false` in the `config/package-solution.json` file.

7. Update `cdnBasePath` using the CDN endpoint configured in *step 2*.

8. Run the `gulp deploy-azure-storage` command to deploy all the necessary assets to the Azure blob container.

9. Upload and deploy the `.sppkg` in the app catalog.

> **Cost consideration**
>
> When using Azure CDN, you'll have to pay the storage costs for your assets. Even though the amount won't be very significant, it is worth noticing. If you don't have a valid reason to use Azure CDN, prefer hosting your assets directly in SharePoint at no cost using built-in mechanisms.

Last but not least, SPFx also lets you use your custom existing CDN if needed.

Custom CDN

For custom CDN options, such as AWS S3 and CloudFront, all you need to do is update the `cdnBasePath` with the CDN location where the files are hosted. The rest of the procedure is the same as the private origin or Azure CDN options. This is up to you to configure the CDN properly and upload the solution files from the `dist` folder.

> **A SharePoint library is a "custom CDN"**
>
> Even if it does not make any sense, you could use a simple SharePoint library as a *custom CDN* but without any kind of CDN features, like a private origin setup.

Hosting options summary

To help you choose the right hosting configuration, here is a table summarizing all the options you can use:

Hosting scenario	includeClientSideAssets	Hosting location	cndBasePath
Default	`true`	The `ClientSideAssets` library in the App Catalog site where the solution is deployed (without being backed by a CDN)	*empty*
Microsoft 365 CDN (public origin)	`true`	Microsoft 365 CDN `public` origin through the `ClientSideAssets` library	*empty*
Microsoft 365 CDN (private origin)	`false`	SharePoint library or folder set as private origin	Absolute URL of the library or folder
Azure CDN	`false`	Azure CDN or other CDN	Absolute URL of the CDN

Table 8.1 – SPFx hosting option summary

Every time the `includeClientSideAssets` property is set to `false`, files from the `dist` folder must be uploaded manually in the CDN.

Integrating with Teams, Outlook, and Office.com

Another aspect of the packaging process is to configure the host applications where SPFx web parts will be available. We saw in the very first chapter of this book, *Introducing Microsoft 365 and SharePoint Online for Developers*, that web parts can be used in SharePoint but also in Teams, Outlook, and Office applications. This host deployment option is controlled by the `supportedHosts` property in each *web part manifest file*:

```
{
    "$schema": "https://developer.microsoft.com/json-schemas/spfx/
client-side-web-part-manifest.schema.json",
    . . .
    "supportedHosts": ["SharePointWebPart", "TeamsPersonalApp",
"TeamsTab", "SharePointFullPage"],
    . . .
```

It lets you decide where and how your web part will be consumed by users.

> **Note**
> This option is only available for the SPFx web part customization type.

When at least one of the `TeamsTab`, `TeamsPersonalApp`, or `TeamsMeetingApp` values is configured for a web part in the solution, a new **Sync to Teams** option will show up in the **tenant** app catalog (this option is not available at the site collection app catalog level), allowing you to add the application in the Teams store as well (the first time you deploy the solution or upgrade an existing one):

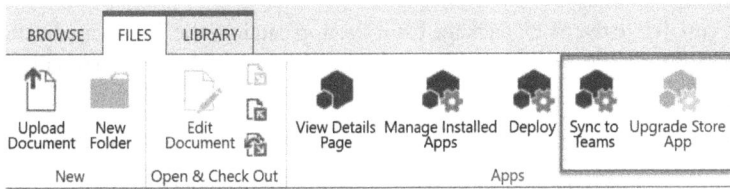

Figure 8.14 – Actions from tenant-level app catalog

When clicked, behind the scenes, SharePoint will automatically generate the Teams app package and upload it to the Teams app store using the information from web part manifests and the content of the `/teams` folder present in the `.sppkg` file (such as web part titles and descriptions and also icons for the app).

Also, if your SPFx solution contains two web parts supporting Teams capabilities, two separate Teams applications will be deployed in the Teams store:

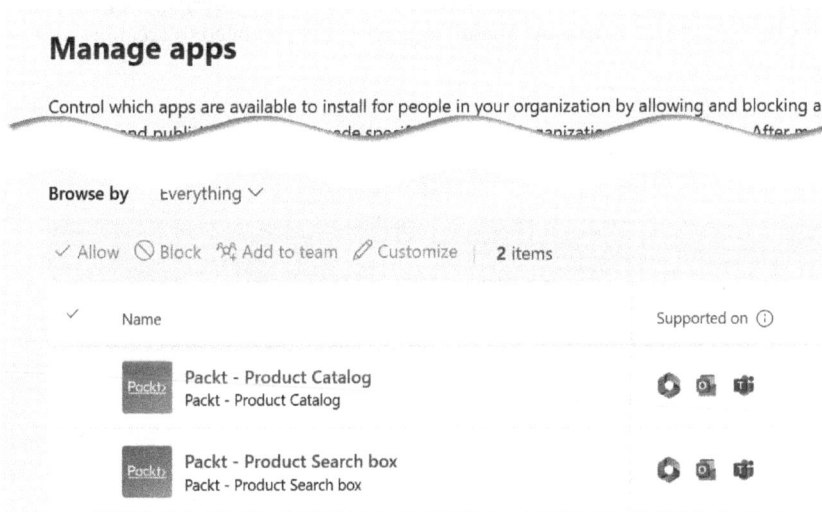

Figure 8.15 – Synced Teams applications from SPFx package

"Sync to Teams" option

Syncing an SPFx solution to Teams can sometimes be tricky. Here is some useful information to keep in mind when deploying a solution from the tenant app catalog:

- You can update an SPFx package in the app catalog using the same version number. However, whenever you want to synchronize to Teams, *the version number must be different*. Otherwise, the sync operation to the Teams app catalog will fail. This restriction is because Teams requires a different version number when updating an application in the portal. Syncing to Teams using the same solution package but an updated version number will also update the version for the associated Teams app – users won't have to install it again.

- When you delete the SPFx package from the app catalog, the Teams application is *not* deleted from the global app catalog in Teams. You must delete it manually from the Teams admin portal.

- You can only sync an SPFx package from the *tenant* app catalog, not from the site collection.

- A SPFx solution can only be synced to Teams if it has been deployed first in SharePoint.

Deploying in SharePoint

When your web part is intended to be used in SharePoint, the following values can be used in the web part manifest file:

- `SharePointWebPart`: The web part will be available as a standard web part that can be added to a modern page inside regular columns and sections

- `SharePointFullPage`: The web part will be displayed as a full-page application intended to be hosted in a special **App page** SharePoint page (that you need to create):

Page templates

From Microsoft   Saved on this site   **Apps**

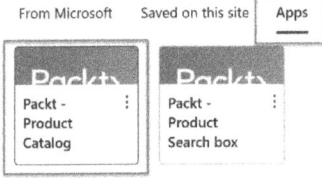

| Packt -
Product
Catalog | ⋮ | Packt -
Product
Search box | ⋮ |

Packt - Product Catalog

Displays the list of products from the Packt catalog

Learn more about app pages   ☐ Create as a private draft ⓘ   **Create page**   Cancel

Figure 8.16 – App page creation experience

- In this experience, there are no sections or columns. The web part fills the entire page canvas:

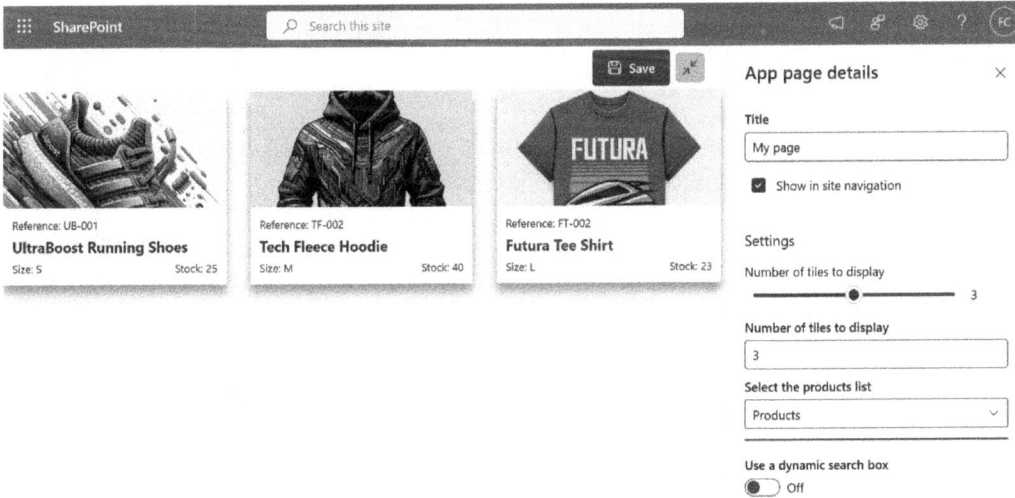

Figure 8.17 – Full-page web part

Deploying to Teams only

The following options will only make the web part available in Teams in different ways:

- `TeamsTab`: The web part will be displayed as a Teams tab in a channel. By definition, a tab is shared by multiple users and can use the underlying SharePoint site used for the team containing the tab.

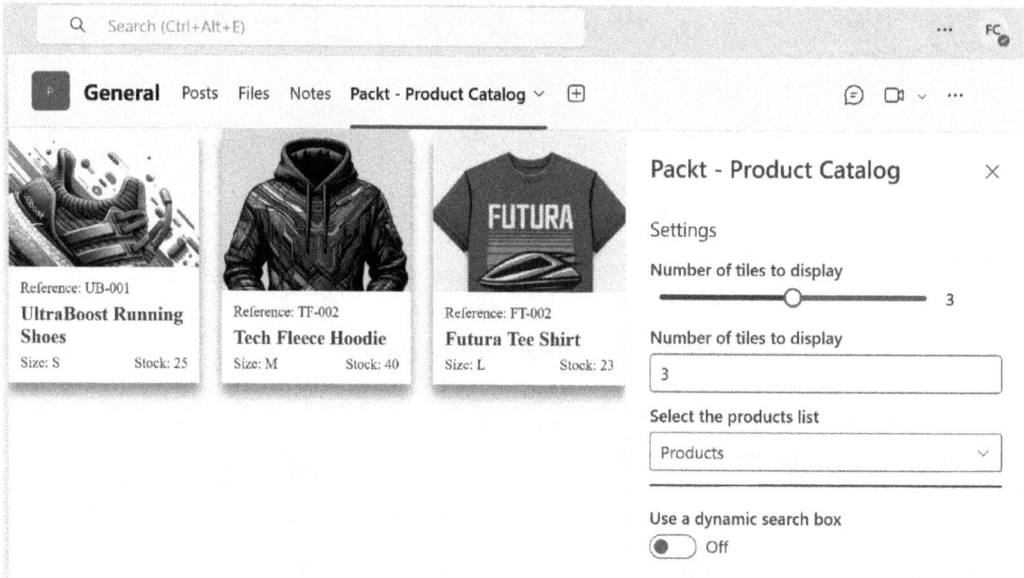

Figure 8.18 – Teams tab web part integration

- `TeamsMeetingApp`: The web part will be displayed as a meeting app:

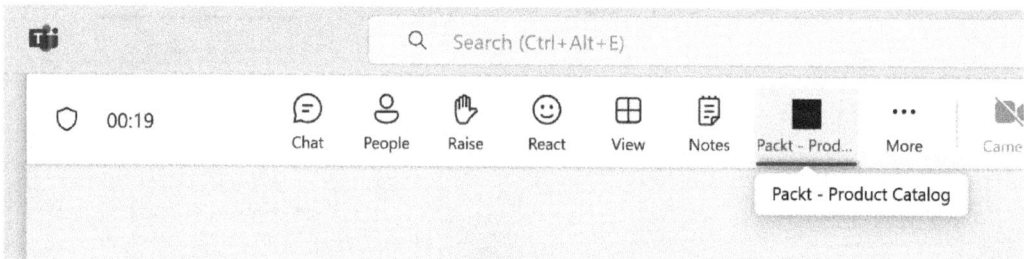

Figure 8.19 – Web part as a Teams meeting app

However, this value *can't* be used alongside `TeamsPersonalApp` and `TeamsTab` values and, unlike a Teams tab, can't rely on a SharePoint site structure.

Deploying to Teams, Outlook, and Office applications

To make your web part available in Teams, Office, and Outlook applications, it must be deployed as a personal app using the `TeamsPersonalApp` value as it is the only common customization type supported by these three tools. By default, in Microsoft 365, personal apps deployed to Teams are automatically available in Outlook and Office applications (web and desktop). You don't have to configure any other host type to get that compatibility.

> **Web parts as personal apps**
>
> Unlike a Teams tab, when deployed as a personal app, a web part can't rely on a specific SharePoint site structure behind the scenes. For instance, in the case of our product inventory management solution, the web part won't find the associated products list and, therefore, won't load anything.

Customizing the Teams app package

By default, when an SPFx package is synchronized to Teams from the app catalog, SharePoint automatically generates a Teams app package and deploys it to the Teams app store. You can inspect the content of this package by downloading it using this URL in the context of the app catalog site:

```
https://{tenant_name}.sharepoint.com/sites/appcatalog/_api/web/
tenantappcatalog/downloadteamssolution({id})/$value
```

Here, `{id}` corresponds to the ID column in the app catalog library (to see it, you need to manually add this column to the current library view).

Depending on your requirements, you can customize this package using these techniques:

- **By customizing the application icons**: For a Teams app, you have two types of icons you need to define: a color icon and an outline icon. By default, when scaffolding a new SPFx solution or adding a new web part to an existing one using the Yeoman generator, SPFx automatically generates corresponding icons for web parts (usually taking the web part ID in the filename) in the `teams` folder. If your application is intended to be used in Teams, it is recommended to update these images to better identify your solution in the Teams app store.

> **Teams icon format**
>
> Color and outline icons follow very strict rules regarding their format and sizes. Refer to the Microsoft documentation to learn more: `https://learn.microsoft.com/en-us/microsoftteams/platform/concepts/build-and-test/apps-package#app-icons`. If your images don't comply with these, the application deployment in Teams will fail.

- **By providing your own package and manifest file**: To get even more control over the Teams application, you can even provide your own package and manifest. This scenario is recommended when exposing a web part as a Teams messaging extension, an option not available in the host configuration options.

To generate a valid Teams app manifest, you can use the following techniques:

- Use the Teams Toolkit extension with Visual Studio Code (`https://learn.microsoft.com/en-us/microsoftteams/platform/toolkit/teams-toolkit-fundamentals`). This option is recommended when your web part is combined with other types of Teams-specific features, such as bots, messaging extensions, and so on.

- Use the Teams developer portal to create your manifest via a graphic interface (go to `https://dev.teams.microsoft.com/` and sign in with your Microsoft 365 account).

- Deploy your SPFx package from the app catalog using the auto-generated package and download it afterward using the `/_api/web/tenantappcatalog/downloadteamssolution({id})` API described before. Then update the part of the manifest you need in a text editor.

In the manifest, you can use the predefined dynamic tokens to reference the hosting location of SPFx client-side assets, not known at deployment time and they will be replaced automatically by Microsoft Teams:

- `{teamSiteDomain}`: The URL of the SharePoint Online tenant where the SPFx solution is deployed and installed

- `{teamSitePath}`: The path to the SharePoint site where the SPFx components are installed

- `{locale}`: The current locale of the Microsoft Teams client (web or desktop)

Here is an example of how to declare a web part as a Teams messaging extension in a custom Teams app manifest file:

```
{
  "$schema": "https://developer.microsoft.com/en-us/json-schemas/
teams/v1.16/MicrosoftTeams.schema.json",
  "manifestVersion": "1.16",
  ...
  "composeExtensions": [
      {
      "botId": "ab225f70-c1a8-4d87-a527-78d74542a9d9",
      "canUpdateConfiguration": true,
      "commands": [
          {
          "id": "packtProductCatalog",
          "type": "action",
```

```
            "title": "View product catalog",
            "description": "View current Packt product catalog",
            "initialRun": false,
            "fetchTask": false,
            "context": [
                "commandBox",
                "compose"
            ],
            "taskInfo": {
                "title": "View catalog",
                "width": "1100",
                "height": "665",
                "url": "https://{teamSiteDomain}/_layouts/15/
TeamsLogon.aspx?SPFX=true&dest=/_layouts/15/teamstaskhostedapp.
aspx%3Fteams%26personal%26componentId=ab225f70-c1a8-4d87-a527-
78d74542a9d9%26forceLocale={locale}"
            }
          }
        ]
      }
    ],
  ]
  ...
}
```

After the manifest is created, you must compress all the files from the `teams` folder color icon, outline icon, and `manifest.json` files into an archive specifically named `TeamsSPFxApp.zip` in the same folder:

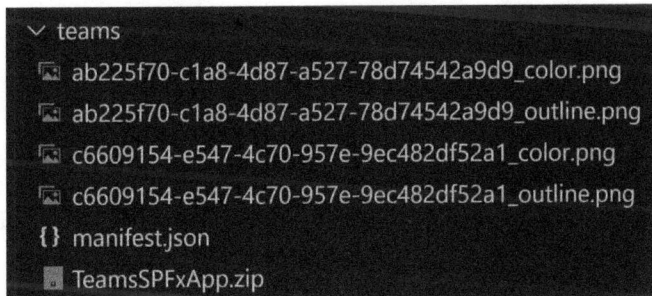

Figure 8.20 – "teams" folder structure for custom app package

When deployed from App Catalog, SharePoint will automatically look for that particular package and deploy it to the Teams app store. Again, don't forget to increase the version number between deployments to avoid sync failure.

> **Teams development versus SPFx development**
>
> Creating your own Teams app manifest requires Teams development-specific knowledge and is outside of the scope of this book.

Adapting your code according to the Teams context

Except for the `SharePointWebPart` option, all other host options can display only a single web part in the UI. This means the dynamic data feature and connections to other web parts can't be used. For our product catalog web part, we update the code to not show the connection options from the property pane when running in a Teams context. To do this, we leverage the `this.context.sdks.microsoftTeams.teamsJs` object, checking for a current Teams app context:

```
protected async onInit(): Promise<void> {
    ...
    this._runInTeams = await !!this.context.sdks.microsoftTeams?.
teamsJs.app.getContext();
}
...
protected getPropertyPaneConfiguration(): IPropertyPaneConfiguration {

    // Display only option if not in a Teams context
    if (!this._runInTeams) {
      groupFields.push(
        PropertyPaneToggle("useDynamicSearchQuery", {
          checked: this.properties.useDynamicSearchQuery,
          label: strings.PropertyPane.UseDynamicSearchQueryFieldLabel
        })
      );
      ...
```

Publish to AppSource

Most of the time, SPFx solutions are used by companies to resolve their internal business problems. However, when made by **independent software vendors (ISVs)**, they can also be monetized as commercial applications and distributed in an online store.

AppSource (`https://appsource.microsoft.com/en-us/marketplace/apps?product=office`) is the dedicated marketplace for all Microsoft-related apps, including Microsoft 365 (including SPFx), Power Platform, SaaS application, or Dynamics 365. A big advantage of SPFx solutions is that they can be published to AppSource without major modifications. This way, other organizations will be able to install your solution in their tenant as well.

> **SPFx version**
> Only solutions using **SPFx v1.11** and above can be submitted to the store.

The publishing process for applications is quite simple. We only provide the general steps here:

1. Register your company account as a Microsoft partner and get access to the partner portal: `https://partner.microsoft.com/dashboard`.

2. Ensure all steps from the submission checklist are completed for your solution (`https://learn.microsoft.com/en-us/partner-center/marketplace-offers/checklist`) – for instance, completing the `developer` information in the `package-solution.json` file.

3. Submit your solution in the partner center portal, entering the required information (platforms supported, languages, targeted markets, etc.). You will need to bundle and package your solution and then submit the `.sppkg` file. Don't forget to provide instructions on how to test your applications and all prerequisites needed (e.g., API keys or licenses, API permissions to set up in the target tenant, specific site structure, etc.).

Once submitted, most of the communications are done by email with the Microsoft support team and can take a bit of back and forth before completing. The more information you provide, the simpler the process will be.

Regardless of the target usage of your solution, you'll need to integrate its building and deployment in a DevOps process using CI/CD pipelines.

DevOps with the SharePoint Framework

In previous sections, we detailed all the steps required to build and deploy an SPFx solution. However, in a real context, these steps won't likely be executed manually from a local machine but rather integrated into a proper CI/CD process, limiting the risk of deployment errors and misconfigurations.

In the upcoming sub-sections, we'll detail how to deploy SPFx solutions using a DevOps pipeline for popular tools such as GitHub or Azure DevOps.

Understanding CI/CD

CI/CD, which stands for "Continuous Integration" and "Continuous Delivery/Deployment", is a set of practices in software development that aims to improve the speed, efficiency, and reliability of software delivery. It ensures a predictable and repeatable deployment cycle for solutions, mainly to avoid human errors due to manual operations (for instance, deploying from a developer's local machine where the technical environment can vary over time).

CI/CD practices are part of the DevOps process and can be achieved using many different tools on the market, the most popular ones being **GitHub**, **Azure DevOps**, and **GitLab**. The choice of the DevOps platform itself is up to the developer, according either to company policies or their own preferences, the deployment tasks and sequence remaining the same regardless of the tool.

Managing versions and updates

When it comes to integration into a CI/CD pipeline, version management becomes quite important as it will be tied to the solution lifecycle. Version numbers can be set at multiple places in an SPFx solution:

- In the `package.json` file at the root of the solution. This version number is only useful when building SPFx library components. Otherwise, it is not used anywhere for other types of customizations:

```
{
    "name": "packt-solutions-product-management",
    "version": "0.0.1",
    "private": true,
    ...
```

- In the `package-solution.json` file, specifying the version number for the entire solution that will be displayed in the app catalog:

```
{
    "$schema": "https://developer.microsoft.com/json-schemas/spfx-build/package-solution.schema.json",
    "solution": {
        ...
        "version": "1.3.3.0",
        ...
```

- In web parts or extensions manifest files (`*.manifest.json`):

```
{
    "$schema": "https://developer.microsoft.com/json-schemas/spfx/client-side-web-part-manifest.schema.json",
    ...
    "alias": "PackProductCatalogWebPart",
    "componentType": "WebPart",
    "version": "1.3.3",
    ...
```

- This version number is not explicitly displayed in the interface but can be useful in an upgrade scenario as it is available in the code directly using the `this.context.manifest.version` property:

```
protected get dataVersion(): Version {
    return Version.parse(this.context.manifest.version);
}
```

Web part manifest files follow a semantic versioning format (`semver`) with three digits `<major>.<minor>.<patch>`. However, the version number format of the solution itself in the `package-solution.json` file uses four digits (due to legacy reasons regarding SharePoint server .NET assemblies). In practice, always use the `semver` format and append a `0` at the end for the solution version (e.g., if the `semver` version is `1.2.0`, then the solution version will be `1.2.0.0`).

There is no specific way of managing versions in SPFx, and this topic likely falls into general software development best practices. Because it will likely depend on development policies in your organization, there are therefore multiple approaches that can be used. However, to get started, here we'll give you our proven recipe, which you can use to manage versions in your CI/CD processes for SPFx solutions (or other types of software solutions, actually). This recipe is based on the following tools and concepts and because it goes beyond the scope of this book, we unfortunately won't go into these in depth:

- **Gitflow**: A Git branching management workflow focused on project releases (`https://www.atlassian.com/git/tutorials/comparing-workflows/gitflow-workflow`). This workflow defines specific Git branches according to the state of an application.

- **GitVersion**: A utility tool to determine the version number automatically based on a Git workflow (like Gitflow, but also others, such as GitHub workflow, Mainline, etc.) and Git commit history. You can find more information here: `https://gitversion.net`.

- **SemVer**: Despite it not being a tool per se, the semantic versioning notation allows you to quickly identify the meaning of a version using the concept of `MAJOR.MINOR.PATCH` increments (`https://semver.org/`). Unlike versioning based on build numbers or identifiers (incremented each time you run a build), semantic versions won't change if the code doesn't change.

Gitflow is an interesting model to manage your versions, Git branches, and environments together, corresponding with the development state of your application. Basically, the idea behind this model is to associate well-known Git branches defined by the workflow to specific target environments, deducing the version number. The following table explains the interactions between these three concepts:

Git branch in the Gitflow workflow	Corresponding Microsoft 365 environment	Version format (semver)
`/feature/*`	**Development** (such as a developer's personal tenant).	*major.minor.patch-alpha* (ex: 1.0.0-alpha)

Git branch in the Gitflow workflow	Corresponding Microsoft 365 environment	Version format (semver)
/develop	**Staging** or **User Acceptance Test (UAT)** – typically, a shared tenant for all developers where end users can ideally test as well.	*major.minor.patch-alpha* (ex: 1.0.0-alpha)
/release/*	**Preproduction** Usually, the same as a Microsoft 365 production tenant, but deployed to a dedicated/isolated site collection. The solution is tested here with real production data, but by a subset of users. When creating a new release, **it is up to the developer to indicate the next version number based on the semantic meaning**. For example, adding a new feature without breaking changes will increment the minor number (e.g., 1.0.0 to 1.1.0). However, if a new feature introduces a breaking change, the major increment should be updated (e.g., 1.0.0 to 2.0.0).	*major.minor.patch-beta* (ex: 1.0.0-beta)
/main	**Production** tenant. The solution is used by final end users and uses production data.	*major.minor.patch* (ex: 1.1.0)
/hotfix/*	**Production** tenant. Patches and fixes on an existing production-deployed solution. Does not consider newly developed features from higher versions.	*major.minor.patch* (ex: 1.0.1)

Table 8.2 – Gitflow workflow branches and versions

Automating the deployment of your solution

We've seen in previous steps that SPFx provides built-in commands to build and package the solution. However, it does not provide a command to upload the generated .sppkg package file into the app catalog. You can use the following options to automate this step (for example, for the tenant app catalog):

- Using PnP PowerShell:

```
Connect-PnPOnline -Url https://{tenant}.sharepoint.com/sites/
appcatalog
```

```
Add-PnPApp -Path ./sharepoint/solution/myapp.sppkg -Publish
Install-PnPApp -Identity {{solution_id}}
```

- Using the CLI for Microsoft 365:

```
m365 login …
m365 spo app add --filePath ./sharepoint/solution/myapp.sppkg
m365 spo app deploy --id {{solution_id}}
```

Here, `{{solution_id}}` is the ID of the solution in the `package-solution.json` file.

> **Deployment credentials**
>
> In a CI/CD process, because deployment commands are run in the backend through the command line without any user interaction, you can't use a regular username/password combination here, as most of the time it will require multi-factor authentication. Creating an admin user account without MFA just for deployment is not an option and is considered bad practice.
>
> To handle this scenario, you must connect to the target environment using an Entra ID application and **application permissions**. As a best practice, you can leverage the *Sites.Selected* API permissions to only access the site you need to deploy (e.g., the tenant app catalog site: `https://tenant_name.sharepoint.com/sites/AppCatalog`) and use a certificate-based authentication (required by the SharePoint API). Ideally, these applications and certificate information should be stored as secrets in your CI/CD tool and accessed in the pipeline jobs at runtime. Never use hardcoded values, for security reasons.
>
> Here are some references to get you started on this configuration:
>
> `https://learn.microsoft.com/en-us/sharepoint/dev/solution-guidance/security-apponly-azuread`
>
> `https://devblogs.microsoft.com/microsoft365dev/controlling-app-access-on-specific-sharepoint-site-collections/`

Integrating with CI/CD tools

Most of the popular CI/CD tools use YAML files to define pipelines and jobs. These files are committed directly to the repository along with the source code itself and the workflow is triggered when a new commit is made (or manually, depending on the configuration you specify).

Each tool has its own syntax, but concepts are generally similar between them (jobs, steps, variables, etc.).

GitHub Actions

GitHub Actions is the name of the CI/CD feature in GitHub. Pipelines are defined under the `.github/workflows` folder at the root of your solution.

> **Pro tip**
>
> Install the Visual Studio Code `GitHub Actions` extension to benefit from syntax correction and IntelliSense features. It will drastically reduce the risk of making dummy syntax errors.

Multiple environments can be created, defining variables and secrets for each, usable directly in the pipeline:

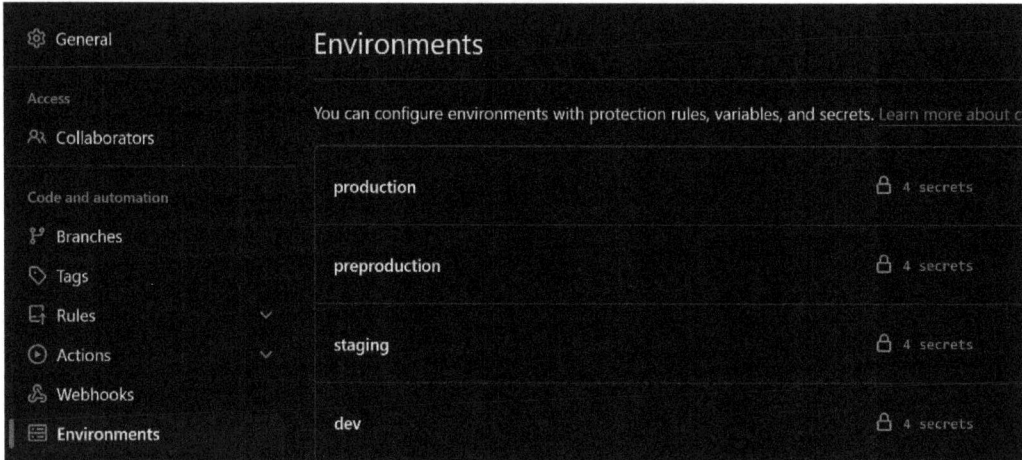

Figure 8.21 – GitHub environments

According to the GitFlow workflow, we can set the correct environment using the following expression in the pipeline definition. This will automatically use the variables declared for that environment:

```
...
on:
  push:
    branches:
      - main
      - develop
      - release/*
      - hotfix/*
jobs:
  build:
    runs-on: ubuntu-latest
    environment: "${{ (github.ref == 'refs/heads/main' ||
contains(github.ref, 'refs/heads/hotfix')) && 'production' || github.
ref == 'refs/heads/develop' && 'staging' || contains(github.ref,
'refs/heads/release') && 'preproduction' || contains(github.ref,
'refs/heads/feature' && 'dev')  }}"
    steps:
      ...
```

The rest of the pipeline follows the SPFx deployment sequence seen in previous sections with the Gulp `bundle` and `package-solution` tasks:

```
-   name: Bundle solution
    run: gulp bundle --ship

-   name: Package solution
    run: gulp package-solution --ship
```

The solution version is determined automatically by the GitVersion tool and used with our custom Gulp `gulp version` task created earlier:

```
steps:

  . . .

  - name: Determine Version
    id: gitversion
    uses: gittools/actions/gitversion/execute@v3.0.0


  . . .


  - name: Version solution
    run: gulp version --newversion ${{ steps.gitversion.outputs.
majorMinorPatch }}
```

Finally, to deploy the solution to the tenant app catalog, we use the CLI for Microsoft 365 tool with deployment credentials defined for the current environment:

```
  . . .
  - name: Deploy to tenant app catalog
    working-directory: ./sharepoint/solution
    env:
      CERTIFICATE_VALUE: ${{ secrets.ENV_spDeployAppCertificateValue
}}
      CERTIFICATE_THUMBPRINT: ${{ secrets.ENV_
spDeployAppCertificateThumbprint }}
      APP_ID: ${{ secrets.ENV_spDeployAppId }}
      TENANT_ID: ${{ secrets.ENV_spDeployTenantId }}
    run: |
      pnpm add -g @pnp/cli-microsoft365
      m365 login --authType certificate --certificateBase64Encoded
$CERTIFICATE_VALUE --thumbprint $CERTIFICATE_THUMBPRINT --appId $APP_
ID --tenant $TENANT_ID
      m365 spo app add --filePath ./packt-solutions-product-
management.sppkg -s tenant --overwrite
```

```
m365 spo app deploy --name packt-solutions-product-management.
sppkg -s tenant --skipFeatureDeployment
```

In the end, the complete deployment sequence looks like this:

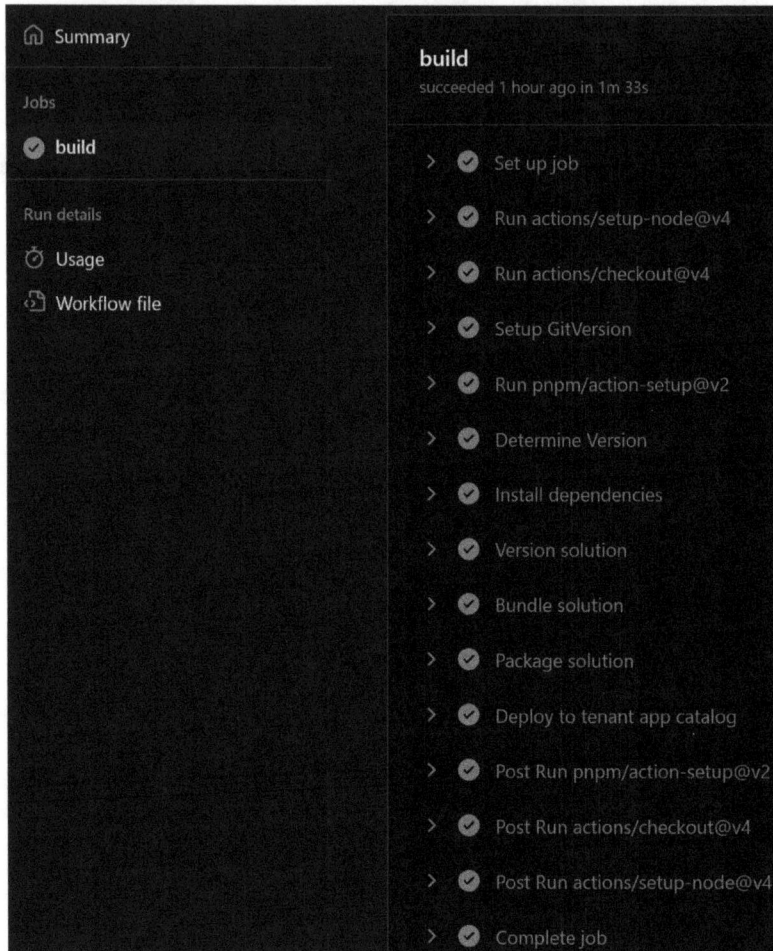

Figure 8.22 – SPFx deployment workflow with GitHub Actions

Azure DevOps

Azure DevOps (ADO) is a cloud-based DevOps platform offered by Microsoft and is probably the most used for SPFx solutions deployment as it is cheaper than GitHub.

The pipeline is defined in an `azure-pipelines.yml` file at the root of the solution repository.

> **Pro tip**
>
> Install the Visual Studio Code `Azure Pipelines` extension to benefit from syntax correction and IntelliSense features. It will drastically reduce the risk of making dummy syntax errors.

To manage environments, ADO uses the *variable groups* concept. Following the Gitflow workflow, we can define a variable group per environment we want to deploy in (dev, staging, production, etc.) according to the commit branch:

```
...
variables:
- ${{ if contains(variables['Build.SourceBranch'], 'refs/heads/
release') }}:
  - group: preproduction
- ${{ if eq(variables['Build.SourceBranch'], 'refs/heads/develop') }}:
  - group: staging
- ${{ if contains(variables['Build.SourceBranch'], 'refs/heads/
feature') }}:
  - group: dev
- ${{ if eq(variables['Build.SourceBranch'], 'refs/heads/main') }}:
  - group: production
- ${{ if contains(variables['Build.SourceBranch'], 'refs/heads/
hotfix')}}:
  - group: production
```

Variables are then loaded according to the selected variable group.

> **Store secrets in Azure Key Vault for a variable group**
>
> ADO also has a built-in capability to integrate directly with Azure Key Vault to manage secrets in a variable group. This is the recommended option to store deployment secrets instead of using plain text values.

The SPFx deployment sequence itself is the same as detailed earlier and we use the CLI for Microsoft 365 to automate the upload and deploy process into the SharePoint tenant app catalog:

```
- bash: |
    gulp bundle --ship
  displayName: Bundle solution

- bash: |
    gulp package-solution --ship
  displayName: Package solution
```

```
- bash: |
    npm i -g @pnp/cli-microsoft365

    m365 login --authType certificate --certificateBase64Encoded
$(ENV_spDeployAppCertificateValue) --thumbprint $(ENV_
spDeployAppCertificateThumbprint) --appId $(ENV_spDeployAppId)
--tenant $(ENV_spDeployTenantId)

    m365 spo app add --filePath ./packt-solutions-product-management.
sppkg -s tenant --overwrite

    m365 spo app deploy --name packt-solutions-product-management.sppkg
-s tenant --skipFeatureDeployment
  workingDirectory: ./sharepoint/solution
  displayName: Deploy to tenant app catalog
```

The GitVersion tool is also available as an extension. However, unlike GitHub Actions, it has to first be installed in the Azure DevOps organization using the marketplace (https://marketplace. visualstudio.com):

```
- task: gitversion/setup@3.0.0
  displayName: Setup GitVersion
  inputs:
    versionSpec: '6.x'

- task: gitversion/execute@3.0.0
  name: gitversion
  displayName: Determine Version

- bash: |
    gulp version --newversion  $(gitversion.majorMinorPatch)
  displayName: Version solution
```

In the end, in Azure DevOps, the deployment sequence looks like this:

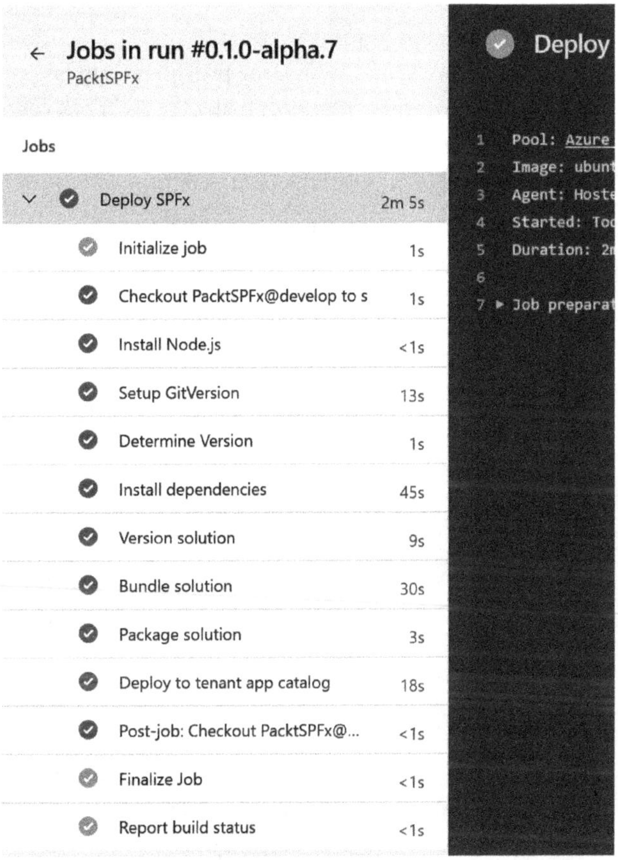

Figure 8.23 – Azure DevOps SPFx deployment sequence

We demonstrated through these two pipelines examples of how to automate the SPFx deployment process by doing the following:

- Installing deployment prerequisites such as Node.js, GitVersion, and so on

- Managing multiple environments, such as development, staging, and production, and calculating the solution version accordingly using Gitflow and GitVersion

- Building, bundling, and packaging the solution using SPFx Gulp commands

- Deploying the solution to the tenant app catalog using the CLI for Microsoft 365 tool

Summary

In this chapter, we've covered all the steps required to deploy an SPFx solution, from building to app catalog upload and deployment. We went through the provided Gulp tasks and explained how to customize the build rig by adding new tasks or customizing the webpack configuration. We also explained all the different hosting options you can use for your solution assets and how to make them available for Teams, Office, and Outlook.

We finally provided examples of deployment automation in a CI/CD process using popular tools such as GitHub Actions or Azure DevOps, managing versions using the Gitflow workflow.

That knowledge will allow you to provide robust deployments for your SPFx solution in a professional context and deliver well-managed solutions to your users.

In the next part of this book, we'll focus on SPFx extension implementation illustrated through our Packt product inventory management solution.

Part 3: Building Extensions with the SharePoint Framework

Part 3 focuses on extension development, allowing us to customize and enhance the SharePoint default user interface experience through predefined placeholders. Like the previous part, we cover each extension type through our sample business solution, from creation to deployment.

This part has the following chapters:

- *Chapter 9, Building a Form Customizer*
- *Chapter 10, Building an Application Customizer*
- *Chapter 11, Building a Field Customizer*
- *Chapter 12, Building a ListView Command Set*
- *Chapter 13, Building a Search Query Modifier*
- *Chapter 14, Building an Adaptive Card Extension*
- *Chapter 15, Deploying Extensions*

Building a Form Customizer

In the previous chapter, we saw how to deploy an SPFx web part. A web part is one of multiple elements that we can create with SPFx. In this chapter, we will look into another element of SPFx called **extensions** – in particular, the Form Customizer.

Some of the concepts in this chapter will be similar or in line with the concepts mentioned in the previous chapters on web parts. In this chapter, you will do the following:

- Learn how to create a Form Customizer from scratch using SPFx to meet the functional requirements
- Understand the Form Customizer development flow using React and SPFx-provided lifecycle methods
- Use Microsoft Graph to interact with SharePoint list items
- Learn how to custom render a form that is used to create, view, and edit SharePoint list items

Technical requirements

This chapter relies on the GitHub solution accessible here: `https://github.com/PacktPublishing/Mastering-SharePoint-Development-with-the-SharePoint-Framework-`. Similar to the earlier chapters, you need to first clone the repository locally on your machine to be able to follow the steps. As the solution is built step by step, for each section in this chapter, a dedicated Git branch has been created representing the solution at a specific state corresponding to a section. Before reading each section, you must check out the corresponding branch before using either the Git command line or a Git client such as GitHub Desktop, Sourcetree, and so on.

> **Code snippets**
>
> For brevity and readability considerations, only the relevant parts of the code are detailed in the provided snippets in this chapter. For these reasons, ad-hoc code, such as dependencies, imports, and updates to certain files, may be omitted. We recommend having the GitHub solution open to get the full working version of the code and review the steps provided.

The branch name to refer to and additional instructions are indicated at the beginning of each section. Here is a summary of Git branches to check out per section:

Section in this chapter	Git branch to check out
Building a Form Customizer	`https://github.com/PacktPublishing/ Mastering-SharePoint-Development-with- the-SharePoint-Framework-/tree/chapter9/ building-a-form-customizer`
Rendering static product data	`https://github.com/PacktPublishing/ Mastering-SharePoint-Development-with- the-SharePoint-Framework-/tree/chapter9/ adding-static-data-to-form-customizer`
Using Microsoft Graph to interact with list items	`https://github.com/PacktPublishing/ Mastering-SharePoint-Development-with- the-SharePoint-Framework-/tree/chapter9/ interact-with-list-data`

What is a Form Customizer?

An SPFx Form Customizer (a type of SPFx extension) is a component that allows developers to customize the default forms used for creating, viewing, and editing list items and documents in SharePoint. It provides the ability to create customized user experiences that align more closely with organizational needs and branding.

Why is it needed?

The necessity for an SPFx form customizer arises from the limitations of the default SharePoint forms, which may not always meet specific business requirements. The out-of-the-box forms are generic and may lack advanced functionalities or specific design elements required by an organization. By using an SPFx form customizer, developers can enhance the user interface, add validation logic, integrate with other services, and ensure a more cohesive and streamlined user experience.

Uses of an SPFx Form Customizer

An SPFx Form Customizer can be used for various purposes, including the following:

- **Adding custom fields**: It allows the inclusion of additional fields that are not available in the default forms
- **Enhancing UX**: It can be used to improve the user interface and **user experience** (**UX**) by applying custom styles and layouts

- **Implementing validation**: Custom validation logic can be added to ensure data integrity and accuracy before submission

- **Integrating with external systems**: It can facilitate the integration of form data with other systems or services, providing a seamless data flow

- **Applying business logic**: Custom business rules and workflows can be incorporated into the form submission process

Simple examples

Here are a couple of simple examples to illustrate the use of an SPFx form customizer.

Example 1 – customizing a task list form

Suppose your organization uses a task list to manage projects. You may want to add a custom field to capture the task's priority level and apply custom styling to highlight high-priority tasks. By using an SPFx Form Customizer, you can add a *priority* drop-down field and apply conditional formatting to change the background color based on the selected priority.

Example 2 – integrating with an external API

Imagine you need to capture user information in a SharePoint list and validate it against an external CRM system. With an SPFx form customizer, you can add custom validation logic that calls the CRM API to verify the user information before allowing the form submission.

By leveraging SPFx form customizers, you can tailor the SharePoint user experience to better suit your organization's unique needs and ensure more efficient and effective use of SharePoint forms.

Building a Form Customizer

> **Git branch**
>
> This section uses the `https://github.com/PacktPublishing/Mastering-SharePoint-Development-with-the-SharePoint-Framework-/tree/chapter9/building-a-form-customizer` Git branch from the repository.

Now that we have understood what a Form Customizer is and what it's used for, let's start building one.

For this chapter, we will create a Form Customizer as per the details mentioned in the *Requirement 2 – selecting color and size for a product item* section in *Chapter 4, Packt Product Management Solution: A Practical Use Case*, which will provide a custom way to display the color and size fields in the list item forms.

Adding a Form Customizer to the solution

From the existing `Packt.Solutions.ProductManagement` folder, run the following command:

```
yo @microsoft/sharepoint --component-type "extension" --extension-
type "FormCustomizer" --component-name "PacktProductFormCustomizer"
--framework "react" --environment "spo" --package-manager "npm"
--skip-feature-deployment
```

We use the following parameters (if omitted in the command, you will be prompted by the generator to provide values):

- `--component-type "extension"`: This indicates that we create an extension.

- `--extension-type "FormCustomizer"`: This indicates that we create a Form Customizer extension (there are other types of extensions, which we will see in the following chapters).

- `--component-name "PacktProductCatalogFormCustomizer"`: This is the base name of the component that will be used to create files.

- `--framework "react"`: This is the JavaScript framework we use as a starter. We use React here, as this is the framework that has the most examples and resources available related to SPFx.

- `--environment "spo"`: This indicates that we target SharePoint Online only.

- `--package-manager "npm"`: This indicates that we use npm as a package manager to install dependencies.

- `--skip-feature-deployment`: This indicates that users won't have to install the app manually on sites. As long as the solution is uploaded to the application catalog, it will be available without any other required steps.

This command will create a Form Customizer and add it to the existing solution.

> **Tip**
> If you want to add a new element (e.g., a web part or an extension) to an existing solution, simply run `yo @microsoft/sharepoint` and complete the steps accordingly.

Updating the configuration

At this point, the base Form Customizer is created, and dependencies are installed. However, we still need to configure some settings to properly set up the solution. The first setting is about the hosted workbench configuration.

This file has four configurations specified: `default`, `<your_extension_name>_NewForm`, `<your_extension_name>_EditForm`, and `<your_extension_name>_ViewForm`. As per the last part in their names, each of these configurations is related to different modes of a list item form. We will make use of these configurations in the later sections.

> **Component ID**
>
> Notice the `componentId` property present in the `config/serve.json` file and in the `<your_extension_name>.manifest.json` file. It will have the same value, which will be unique and represents the Form Customizer you created. This ID will be used in the future during deployment.

The `default` configuration needs to be updated so that it will continue pointing to the workbench page and not the form customizer. Update the `default` configuration, such that it only has the `pageUrl` property, which is set to `https://tenantDomain.sharepoint.com/_layouts/workbench.aspx`, replacing `{tenantDomain}` with the SharePoint Online site you want to use (e.g., `https://mytenant.sharepoint.com/sites/test site/_layouts/workbench.aspx`).

After that, in the `<your_extension_name>_NewForm`, `<your_extension_name>_EditForm`, and `<your_extension_name>_ViewForm` configuration, edit the `RootFolder` property to point to the `Products` list (e.g., `/sites/yoursite/lists/products`).

Now that we have set up our Form Customizer information, it is time to start the implementation.

Business requirement

As mentioned in *Chapter 4*, *Requirement 2*, the form customizer will be used to aid the users visually in selecting the color and size of a product while creating a new product or editing an existing product.

Hence, in this chapter, the New list form and the Edit list form will be customized such that the `color` field and the `size` field in these forms are rendered as per the requirement.

Initial render check

Before updating the code to meet the requirement, let's update the form customizer that was created so that it renders a simple text.

In the `src` folder, we can see that a new `extensions` folder will be added, which will have the `PacktProductFormCustomizer.tsx` file under the `components` folder. This is a React component that will have some basic code, including the `render` method. Let's update the `render` method so that it shows some simple text, as follows:

```
public render(): React.ReactElement<{}> {
    return <div className={styles.packtProductFormCustomizer}>This is
the custom form for the Packt Product list</div>;
}
```

From the command line, run `gulp serve --config=" packtProductFormCustomizer_ NewForm"`. This will open the browser and load the form customizer with the preceding text.

> **Serve configurations**
>
> The `--config` parameter of the `gulp serve` command can point to any of the four configurations specified earlier. If the `--config` parameter is not specified, then the default configuration is used.

In this section, we have seen how to create a form customizer and get it to display simple text. We added a form customizer to the project, updated the `serve` configuration, and updated the React component to render text. In the next section, we will see how to render static data for a product.

Rendering static product data

> **Git branch**
>
> This section uses the `https://github.com/PacktPublishing/Mastering-SharePoint-Development-with-the-SharePoint-Framework-/tree/chapter9/adding-static-data-to-form-customizer` Git branch from the repository.

In the previous section, we added a form customizer to the solution and got it running to display simple text. Now, let's see how we can display some static data for products.

As mentioned in the *What is a Form Customizer?* section, each item in a SharePoint list can be associated with three types of forms – New, Edit, and View. As per the names, the New form is used for creating a new item, the Edit form is used for editing an existing item, and the View form is used for viewing an existing item. In our case, the item is a product and the `ProductFormCustomizer.tsx` React component should take care of displaying the New, Edit, and View forms of a product.

The idea is such that we determine the current display mode provided to us by SharePoint (`New`, `Edit`, or `View`), and `ProductFormCustomizer.tsx` should change its rendering based on the display mode. The main element that needs to be rendered in `ProductFormCustomizer.tsx` is a product, which can be either empty (when the display mode is New) or a product with details (i.e., an existing list item) when the display mode is `Edit` or `View`. The `ProductFormCustomizer.tsx` component will need to know the details of the product, hence, its state will need to have a product of the `IProductCatalogItem` type. The value of this product will change based on the display mode and the concerned list item.

A file for the state called `IPacktProductFormCustomizerState.ts` needs to be created with the following details, and `ProductFormCustomizer.tsx` needs to be updated to reference that:

```
import { IProductCatalogItem } from "../../../models/
IProductCatalogItem";
export interface IPacktProductFormCustomizerState {
    product: IProductCatalogItem | null;
    error: string | null;
}
```

We also add a string called `error` in the state to track any errors in the later parts.

Setting static data

> **Commit reference**
>
> Please refer to the commit at `https://github.com/PacktPublishing/Mastering-SharePoint-Development-with-the-SharePoint-Framework-/commit/745c27dee27a17968f7bd492714a5f4ce3df6f25` for this section.

When `ProductFormCustomizer.tsx` mounts, we check the display mode:

- If it is New, we set the state such that it is a new product (e.g., empty model name, zero for numeric values, empty for `color` and `size`, etc.).

- If it is not New, then we set the state such that it is an existing product. For this, we will use static data.

The following code block shows how the `componentDidMount()` method will look:

```
public componentDidMount(): void {
    if (this.props.displayMode === FormDisplayMode.New) {
      this.setState({
        product: {
          modelName: '',
          retailPrice: 0,
          stockLevel: 0,
          lastOrderDate: new Date(),
          itemPicture: '',
          itemColour: '',
          size: ProductSizes.M,
          productReference: ''
        }
      });
```

```
    return;
  }

  // if we are in edit mode or display mode, we load static data
  this.setState({
    product: {
      modelName: 'Packt Product',
      retailPrice: 100,
      stockLevel: 10,
      lastOrderDate: new Date(),
      itemPicture: '',
      itemColur: 'Red',
      size: ProductSizes.M,
      productReference: 'ABC123'
    }
  });
}
```

The data that we saw in the Edit mode is only for testing. Feel free to change the values of the properties as you need them to be.

Displaying static data

> **Commit reference**
>
> Please refer to the commit at https://github.com/PacktPublishing/
> Mastering-SharePoint-Development-with-the-SharePoint-Framework-/
> commit/745c27dee27a17968f7bd492714a5f4ce3df6f25 for this section.

Now that we have static data in the state, we need to display that static data. This again depends on the display mode:

- If the display mode is Display (View), we will use Label (from Fluent UI) to display the product data.

- If the display mode is New or Edit, we will use TextField to display the product data. (Along with these, we will also display a couple of buttons for save and cancel actions.)

To display the static data, we need to update the render method, as shown here:

```
public render(): React.ReactElement<{}> {
    if (this.props.displayMode === FormDisplayMode.Display) {
      return (
```

```
            <div className={styles.packtProductFormCustomizer}>
                <Label>Model Name: {this.state.product?.modelName}</Label>
                <Label>Retail Price: {this.state.product?.retailPrice}</
Label>
                <Label>Stock Level: {this.state.product?.stockLevel}</Label>
                <Label>Last Order Date: {this.state.product?.lastOrderDate?.
toDateString()}</Label>
                <Label>Item Picture: {this.state.product?.itemPicture}</
Label>
                <Label>Item Colour: {this.state.product?.itemColour}</Label>
                <Label>Size: {this.state.product?.size}</Label>
                <Label>Product Reference: {this.state.product?.
productReference}</Label>
            </div>
        );
    }


    return (
        <div className={styles.packtProductFormCustomizer}>
            <TextField label="Model Name" value={this.state.product?.
modelName} />
            <TextField label="Retail Price" value={this.state.product?.
retailPrice.toString()} />
            <TextField label="Stock Level" value={this.state.product?.
stockLevel.toString()}  />
            <TextField label="Item Picture" value={this.state.product?.
itemPicture} />
            <TextField label="Item Colour" value={this.state.product?.
itemColour} />
            <TextField label="Item Size" value={this.state.product?.size ?
ProductSizes[this.state.product?.size] : ""} />
            <TextField label="Product Reference" value={this.state.
product?.productReference} />
            <TextField label="Last Order Date" value={this.state.product?.
lastOrderDate?.toDateString()} />
            <PrimaryButton text="Save" />
            <DefaultButton text="Cancel" />
        </div>
    );


    return <></>;
  }
```

With this code, running the `gulp serve --config=packtProductFormCustomizer_ViewForm` command will display the form as shown in the following screenshot:

Model Name: Packt Product

Retail Price: 100

Stock Level: 10

Last Order Date: Sat Jan 04 2025

Item Picture:

Item Colour: Red

Size: 2

Product Reference: ABC123

Figure 9.1 – Form in Display mode

Running the `gulp serve --config= packtProductFormCustomizer_EditForm` command will display the form as shown here:

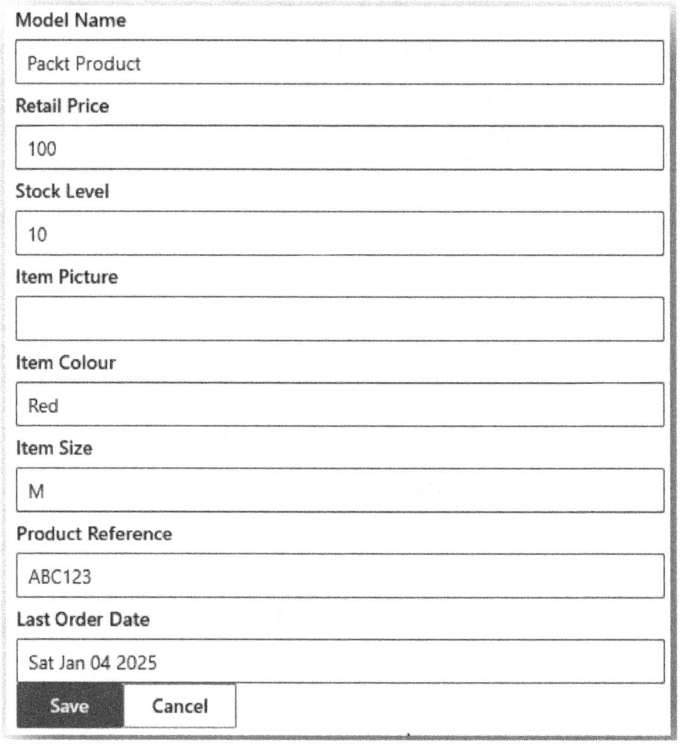

Model Name

Packt Product

Retail Price

100

Stock Level

10

Item Picture

Item Colour

Red

Item Size

M

Product Reference

ABC123

Last Order Date

Sat Jan 04 2025

Save   Cancel

Figure 9.2 – Form in Edit mode

Now that we have the static data being displayed, let's look at how we can customize the display (look and feel) of the fields in the forms.

Custom display of fields

> **Commit reference**
>
> Please refer to the commit at `https://github.com/PacktPublishing/Mastering-SharePoint-Development-with-the-SharePoint-Framework-/commit/6621e3d54f6db9b3ee5e00aa6abd9f73b140eba5` for this section.

We are now able to display textboxes in the New and Edit forms. The display of the **Color** and **Size** fields needs to be changed to match the requirement. To do that for **Color**, we will use a line of `div` HTML elements (each representing a different color), and for **Size**, we will use the `ChoiceGroup` Fluent UI component.

To store the `Size` and `Color` options, we declare two arrays, as shown here:

```
private _sizeOptions: IChoiceGroupOption[] = [
    { key: ProductSizes[ProductSizes.XS], text: 'XS', iconProps: {
iconName: 'shirt', style: { fontSize: '10px' } } },
    { key: ProductSizes[ProductSizes.S], text: 'S', iconProps: {
iconName: 'shirt', style: { fontSize: '12px' } } },
    { key: ProductSizes[ProductSizes.M], text: 'M', iconProps: {
iconName: 'shirt', style: { fontSize: '14px' } } },
    { key: ProductSizes[ProductSizes.L], text: 'L', iconProps: {
iconName: 'shirt', style: { fontSize: '16px' } } },
    { key: ProductSizes[ProductSizes.XL], text: 'XL', iconProps: {
iconName: 'shirt', style: { fontSize: '18px' } } },
    { key: ProductSizes[ProductSizes.XXL], text: 'XXL', iconProps: {
iconName: 'shirt', style: { fontSize: '20px' } } }
  ];

private _colourOptions: string[] = ['Red', 'Blue', 'Green', 'Black',
'White'];
```

We specify the font size for each icon so that it varies as per the size.

In the `render` method, we will remove the `TextField` components for `Size` and `Color` and add the following code, which renders the `Size` and `Color` fields as per the requirement:

```
<div>
        <Label>Item Colour</Label>
        <div className={styles.productColourContainer}>
          {this._colourOptions.map(colour => (
```

```
            <div
              key={colour}
              style={{
                width: '30px',
                height: '30px',
                backgroundColor: colour.toLowerCase(),
                border: this.state.product?.itemColour === colour ?
'2px solid black' : '1px solid gray',
                cursor: 'pointer'
              }}
            />
          ))}
        </div>
      </div>
      <ChoiceGroup
        label="Size"
        selectedKey={this.state.product?.size}
        options={this._sizeOptions}
      />
```

We loop through the `colorOptions` array and, for each option, we display a small `div` HTML element (30 px by 30 px) with the corresponding background color.

For `Size`, the `ChoiceGroup` Fluent UI component takes care of rendering the tiles with icons of different sizes.

With this updated code, running the `gulp serve` commands for the new form and edit form will render the updated **Size** and **Color** fields, as shown in *Figure 9.3*.

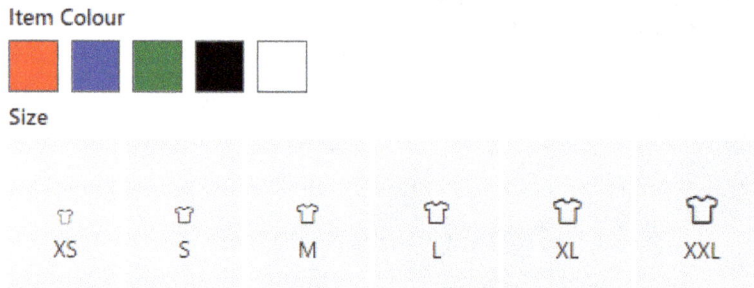

Figure 9.3 – Updated display of Color and Size fields

With the display of fields now customized, let's understand how to bind fields to events (e.g., change of text and change of selection).

Binding fields to events

Commit reference

Please refer to the commit at https://github.com/PacktPublishing/Mastering-
SharePoint-Development-with-the-SharePoint-Framework-/commit/
b7f8a863b0e27c0477cc0cc73076949c879a3b49 for this section.

We are now able to display the fields as per the requirement. Next, we have to store this data in the state so that we can use it in the next section to save the data back in the SharePoint list.

To store the data in the state, we have to bind events to the **Color** field, the **Size** field, and the other fields. We will start with other fields first.

Since all of them are textboxes, we need to add a function that gets triggered when the value changes. This function will update the respective key of the product in the state. For example, when the data in the **Model Name** text field changes, we need to call an onModelNameChanged function, which will set the modelName value of the product in state to the new value:

```
<TextField label="Model Name" value={this.state.product?.modelName}
onChange={this._onModelNameChange.bind(this)} />


private _onModelNameChange = (event: React.FormEvent<HTMLInputElement
| HTMLTextAreaElement>, newValue?: string): void => {
    const product = this.state.product;
    if (product === null) {
      return;
    }
    product.modelName = newValue || '';
    this.setState({
      product: product
    });
  }
```

The same needs to be done for the **Price**, **Stock**, **Last Order Date**, **Picture**, and **Reference** fields.

For the **Color** field, we call the function to update the color of the product in the state when a color tile is clicked. So, the code for the **Color** field will be as per the following code block:

```
<div>
    <Label>Item Colour</Label>
    <div className={styles.productColourContainer}>
    {this._colourOptions.map(colour => (
            <div
              key={colour}
```

```
                        onClick={() => this._onItemColourChange(colour)}
//Other code omitted
          </div>
</div>

// color change handler
private _onItemColourChange = (colour: string): void => {
    const product = this.state.product;
    if (product === null) {
      return;
    }
    product.itemColour = colour;
    this.setState({
      product: product
    });
  }
```

The handler for the **Size** field will be similar to the preceding code block and will handle the update to the size of the product in the state:

```
private _onSizeChange = (event: React.FormEvent<HTMLDivElement>,
option?: IChoiceGroupOption, index?: number): void => {
    const product = this.state.product;
    if (product === null) {
      return;
    }
    product.size = option ? ProductSizes[option.key as keyof typeof
ProductSizes] : ProductSizes.M;
    this.setState({
      product: product
    });
  }
```

With this, the updated values will be stored in the state. In the next section, we will look at connecting the form customizer to the `Products` list data using Microsoft Graph.

Using Microsoft Graph to interact with item

Git branch

This section uses the `https://github.com/PacktPublishing/Mastering-SharePoint-Development-with-the-SharePoint-Framework-/tree/chapter9/interact-with-list-data` Git branch from the repository.

In the previous section, we saw how to show static data in the form customizer. Now, let's see how we can interact with the data from the list (Products). We will use the Microsoft Graph API, as we did in *Chapter 5, Building a SharePoint Web Part*, for interaction with the list.

By the end of this section, we will be able to *create* an item in the Products list when the display mode is New, *edit* an existing item in the Products list when the display mode is Edit, and *view* an existing item in the Products list when the display mode is View.

The concepts are similar to those mentioned in *Chapter 5*, so please refer to the *Using the Microsoft Graph API to get items* section of that chapter for a detailed overview of the concepts.

Getting a Microsoft Graph client instance

We need to instantiate a new Microsoft Graph client object to be able to call the API and retrieve data. Service instances should be defined in the onInit () method of the Form Customizer root class and passed to services or subcomponents whenever needed:

```
public async onInit(): Promise<void> {
    this._msGraphClient = await this.context.msGraphClientFactory.
getClient(
        "3"
    );
    this._productCatalogService = new ProductCatalogService(this._
msGraphClient);

    ...
}
```

With the Microsoft Graph client instantiated, we can use the client to get items from lists.

Defining and retrieving information from the context

To get the items from the list, Microsoft Graph needs information such as the ID of the site, the name of the list, and the ID of the item. All this information will be present in the SPFx context object, which can be accessed using this.context:

- For the site ID, we use this.context.pageContext.site.id.toString()
- For the list name, we use this.context.list.title
- For the item ID, we use this.context.itemId

This information will be passed to the PacktProductFormCustomizer component. The code is similar to the code explained in the *Passing site ID and list name to subcomponents* subsection of *Chapter 5*.

Updating the products service

The next step is to update the `products service` so that we can do the following:

- Get a product by ID (this will be used when the display mode is `View`)

- Update a product by ID (this will be used when the display mode is `Edit`)

- Create a new product (this will be used when the display mode is `New`)

The methods for these will use Microsoft Graph to perform the respective operation.

We specify the definitions for these methods in the `IProductCatalogService` interface:

```
export interface IProductCatalogService {
  getProducts(siteId: string, listName: string, itemsCount?: number,
searchQuery?: string): Promise<IProductCatalogItem[]>;
  getProductById(siteId: string, listName: string, productId: string):
Promise<IProductCatalogItem | null>;
  updateProduct(siteId: string, listName: string, productId: string,
product: IProductCatalogItem): Promise<void>;
  createProduct(siteId: string, listName: string, product:
IProductCatalogItem): Promise<void>;
}
```

Then, we create these methods in the `ProductCatalogService` class.

To get a product by ID, the code uses the Microsoft Graph API, as shown here:

```
    ...
        const response = await this._msGraphClient
        .api(`sites/${siteId}/lists/${listName}/items/${productId}`)
        .get();

    return {
        modelName: response.fields.packtProductModelName,
        lastOrderDate: response.fields.packtProductStockLastOrderDate
            ? new Date(response.fields.packtProductStockLastOrderDate)
            : null,
        productReference: response.fields.packtProductReference,
        stockLevel: response.fields.packtProductStockLevel,
        size: response.fields.packtProductSize as ProductSizes,
        retailPrice: response.fields.packtProductRetailPrice,
        itemColour: response.fields.packtProductColor,
        itemPicture: response.fields.packtProductItemPicture
            ? JSON.parse(response.fields.packtProductItemPicture).
serverRelativeUrl
```

```
            : null,
        } as IProductCatalogItem;
...
```

In the first line of the code, the ID of the site, the name of the list, and the ID of the item are used by the Microsoft Graph API to get the item from the list. Following this, the details of the item (model name, last order date, product reference, stock level, size, price, color, and picture) are extracted from the response and returned.

For updating a product, the `update` function of the Microsoft Graph API is used, which will get the updated values of fields:

```
await this._msGraphClient
        .api(`sites/${siteId}/lists/${listName}/items/${productId}/
  fields
        .patch({
            packtProductModelName: product.modelName,
            packtProductStockLastOrderDate: product.lastOrderDate,
            packtProductReference: product.productReference,
            packtProductStockLevel: product.stockLevel,
            packtProductSize: ProductSizes[product.size],
            packtProductRetailPrice: product.retailPrice,
            packtProductColor: product.itemColour,
            packtProductItemPicture: product.itemPicture
              ? JSON.stringify({ serverRelativeUrl: product.itemPicture
  })
              : null,
        });
```

For creating a product, the `post` function of the Microsoft Graph API is used, which will get the values of the fields:

```
await this._msGraphClient
        .api(`sites/${siteId}/lists/${listName}/items`)
        .post({
          "fields": {
            "packtProductModelName": product.modelName,
            "packtProductStockLastOrderDate": product.lastOrderDate,
            "packtProductReference": product.productReference,
            "packtProductStockLevel": product.stockLevel,
            "packtProductSize": ProductSizes[product.size],
            "packtProductRetailPrice": product.retailPrice,
            "packtProductColor": product.itemColour,
            "packtProductItemPicture": product.itemPicture
```

```
                    ? JSON.stringify({ serverRelativeUrl: product.
itemPicture })
                    : null,
              }
          });
```

We are adding a method only for getting, updating, and creating a product. If needed, we can also add a method for deleting a product. We won't be using that method in this book; however, it can be done as a learning exercise.

Calling the service methods from the component

> **Commit reference**
>
> Please refer to the commit at https://github.com/PacktPublishing/Mastering-SharePoint-Development-with-the-SharePoint-Framework-/commit/f3f0317a9125ec48f6592ff9365a0079ab9c7da2 for this section.

Now that we have the methods defined to create, update, and get a product in the service, the next step is to use them in the PacktProductFormCustomizer component.

When the component is mounted, we set static data for the Edit or View display modes. Instead, we can now call the getProductById method and set the state with the response:

```
public componentDidMount(): void {
    …
    // load item to display on the form
    this.props.productCatalogService.getProductById(this.props.siteId,
this.props.listName, this.props.itemId)
        .then((product) => {
          this.setState({
            product: product
          });
        })
        .catch((error: string) => {
          this.setState({
            error: error
          });
        });
    }
```

With this, the corresponding product details are set in the state and can be seen when we run `gulp serve --config= packtProductFormCustomizer_EditForm`. In the `serve.json` file, this configuration has an ID set to `1`. Hence, it will load the product item with the ID of `1` (which, in this case, is **UltraBoost Running Shoes**).

Model Name

UltraBoost Running Shoes

Retail Price

180

Stock Level

25

Item Picture

/sites/Packt/SiteAssets/Lists/40734a45-c048-4232-8eb3-d2c1cf2f9e1b/ultraboost.jpg

Item Colour

Size

XS   S   M   L   XL   XXL

Product Reference

UB-001

Last Order Date

Save   Cancel

Figure 9.4 – Product item with ID 1 in Edit mode

Saving the data in the list

> **Commit reference**
>
> Please refer to the commit at https://github.com/PacktPublishing/
> Mastering-SharePoint-Development-with-the-SharePoint-Framework-/
> commit/924e9a11588ce57a2f49e481e3d31b13b3b2d01d for this section.

The final step is to save the data (either new or changed) back to the SharePoint list.

We introduce two new functions in the component for creating and updating products, which, in turn, call the respective `service` methods:

```
private _createProduct = (product: IProductCatalogItem): Promise<void>
=> {
    return this.props.productCatalogService.createProduct(this.props.
siteId, this.props.listName, product)
  }
private _updateProduct = (product: IProductCatalogItem): Promise<void>
=> {
    return this.props.productCatalogService.updateProduct(this.props.
siteId, this.props.listName, this.props.itemId, product)
  }
```

These functions need to be called when the **Save** button is clicked, based on the display mode. If the display mode is New we call the `_createProduct` function; if we know that we are in `Edit` mode, we call the `_updateProduct` function.

The logic here is like any standard React code. When the form is filled or updated, the changes are saved in the state (product). This is detailed in the earlier subsection, *Binding fields to events*. On clicking **Save**, the details in the state are used to either create or update the product.

To call these, we create a function called `onSave`, as follows:

```
private _onSave = (): void => {
    ...
    if (this.props.displayMode === FormDisplayMode.New) {
      this._createProduct(this.state.product)
        .then(() => {
            this.props.onSave();
        })
    } else {
      this._updateProduct(this.state.product)
        .then(() => {
            this.props.onSave();
        })
```

```
        }
    }
```

SharePoint provides a `formSaved()` function, which must be called after saving. Hence, after saving, we call `this.props.onSave()`, which, in turn, calls the `formSaved()` function in the root component:

```
private _onSave = (): void => {
    // You MUST call this.formSaved() after you save the form.
    this.formSaved();
}
```

With this, when we run `gulp serve --config= packtProductFormCustomizer_ EditForm`, the product item with an ID of 1 is loaded (which, in this case, is **UltraBoost Running Shoes**). Making changes to the fields and clicking **Save** will update the item.

Error handling

The code in the `service` needs to be updated to handle errors gracefully. This can be done separately based on the requirements.

In this section, we have seen how to use the Microsoft Graph API to get a product and update a product.

Note

The code in the repository has a condition to check whether we are running in debug mode, and if we are, then an alert is displayed on update and the product item is not updated. This is done so that, while debugging, the control does not redirect to the list page every time we click **Save**.

With the help of functions provided by Microsoft Graph for SharePoint items, our task is made easier.

Summary

Form Customizers are one of the ways to customize the list forms in which we have full control over the rendering of the fields of the item and `save` and `cancel` events.

In this chapter, we have seen how to create a Form Customizer to meet the requirements. We started by understanding what a Form Customizer is and how it can be used to update the view, edit, and display forms of list items.

We added a form customizer to the existing solution and added static data to display a product. After that, we used Microsoft Graph to get and edit a product from the `Products` list.

In the next chapter, we will see how to visually notify users when the stock is low using an Application Customizer.

Get This Book's PDF Version and Exclusive Extras

UNLOCK NOW

Scan the QR code (or go to packtpub.com/unlock). Search for this book by name, confirm the edition, and then follow the steps on the page.

Note: Keep your invoice handy. Purchases made directly from Packt don't require an invoice.

10

Building an Application Customizer

In the previous chapter, we saw how to create a form customizer (one of the multiple elements that we can create using SPFx), which was used to control the new, edit, and display forms of a list item in the Products list. In particular, we learned how to change the display of the fields rendered in the forms and have complete control of their actions and the forms' actions. In this chapter, we will look at another element of SPFx – an extension called **Application Customizer**.

Some of the concepts in this chapter will be similar or in line with the concepts mentioned in the previous chapters on web parts and form customizers. This chapter contains the following topics:

- Learn how to create an Application Customizer from scratch using SPFx to meet the functional requirements.

- Understand the Application Customizer development flow using React and SPFx provided lifecycle methods.

- Use Microsoft Graph to get data from a SharePoint list.

Technical requirements

This chapter relies on the GitHub solution accessible here: `https://github.com/ PacktPublishing/Mastering-SharePoint-Development-with-the-SharePoint- Framework-`. Similar to the earlier chapters, you need to first clone the repository locally on your machine to be able to follow the steps. As the solution is built step-by-step, for each section in this chapter, a dedicated Git branch has been created representing the solution at a specific state corresponding to a section. Before reading the section, you must check out the corresponding branch before using either the Git command line or a Git client such as GitHub Desktop or SourceTree.

> **Code snippets**
>
> For brevity and readability considerations, only the relevant parts of the code are detailed in the provided snippets in this chapter. For these reasons, ad hoc code, such as importing dependencies and updates to certain files may be omitted. We recommend having the GitHub solution open to get the full working version of the code and review the steps.

The branch name to refer to and additional instructions are indicated at the beginning of each section. Here is a summary of Git branches to check per section:

Section in this chapter	Git branch to check out
Building an application customizer	`https://github.com/PacktPublishing/Mastering-SharePoint-Development-with-the-SharePoint-Framework-/tree/chapter10/build-an-application-customizer`
Adding a React component to the application customizer	`https://github.com/PacktPublishing/Mastering-SharePoint-Development-with-the-SharePoint-Framework-/tree/chapter10/adding-react-component-to-application-customizer`
Using Microsoft Graph to get data from a list	`https://github.com/PacktPublishing/Mastering-SharePoint-Development-with-the-SharePoint-Framework-/tree/chapter10/using-microsoft-graph-to-get-products`

What is an application customizer?

An SPFx application customizer (a type of SPFx extension) is a component that enables developers to extend and customize the user interface of SharePoint sites by injecting custom scripts or HTML elements. It provides a way to add persistent UI elements, such as headers, footers, or custom notifications, across pages within a site or site collection.

Why is it needed?

The need for an SPFx application customizer arises from the limitations of the standard SharePoint interface, which may not always align with an organization's branding or functional requirements. By using an application customizer, developers can introduce consistent UI elements, implement custom behaviors, or integrate additional functionality into SharePoint without altering the core platform. This enhances user engagement, branding consistency, and the overall user experience.

Uses of an SPFx application customizer

An SPFx application customizer can serve various purposes, including the following:

- **Adding global UI elements**: It enables developers to create persistent UI components such as site-wide headers, footers, and navigation bars.

- **Displaying notifications or alerts**: Application customizers can be used to show important announcements, alerts, or system messages across the site.

- **Injecting scripts**: They can insert custom scripts (e.g., analytics or tracking scripts) to enhance functionality or gather insights.

- **Integrating external services**: Application customizers can connect SharePoint with third-party systems or APIs, displaying external data or functionality within the SharePoint interface.

- **Customizing branding**: They allow the application of consistent branding elements, such as logos, color schemes, or typography, across a SharePoint site.

- **Implementing custom user experiences**: Developers can create tailored experiences by adding dynamic components or interactive elements that meet business-specific needs.

When to use an SPFx application customizer

An SPFx application customizer should be used when an organization requires consistent, site-wide customizations that the default SharePoint interface does not provide. This could include branding updates, global notifications, or integration with external systems that need to be accessible across multiple pages.

Simple examples

Here are a couple of examples to illustrate the use of an SPFx application customizer:

Example 1 – adding a custom footer

Suppose your organization wants to display a custom footer on every page that includes copyright information, quick links, and a company logo. Using an SPFx application customizer, you can inject a fully styled footer element that remains consistent across all pages within the SharePoint site.

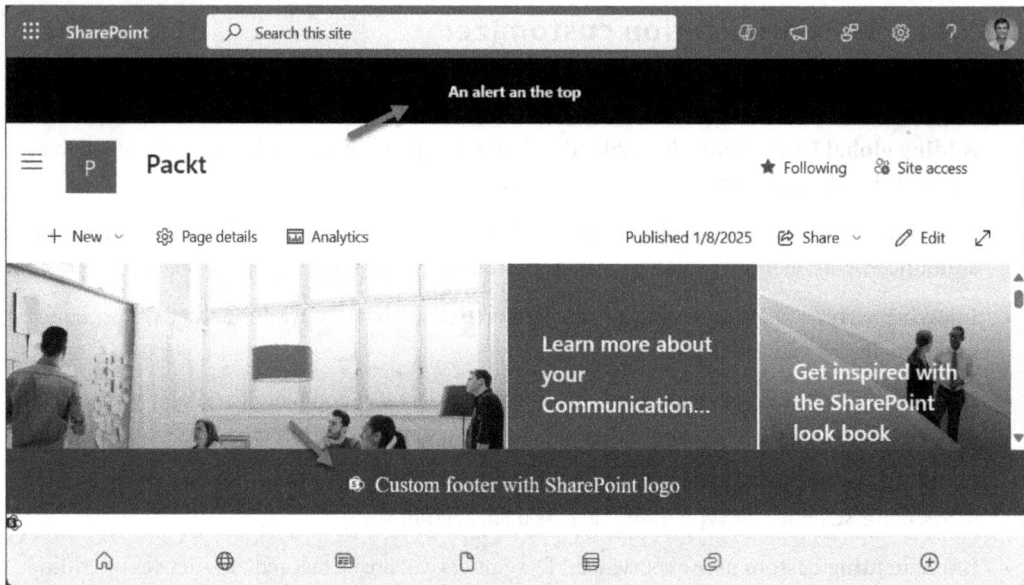

Figure 10.1 – Example application customizer in header and footer

Example 2 – displaying site-wide alerts

Imagine you need to inform all users about scheduled maintenance or policy updates. With an SPFx application customizer, you can create a notification bar that appears at the top of every page. This bar can be styled to match your site's branding and include dismiss functionality for better user experience.

By leveraging SPFx application customizers, organizations can ensure a cohesive, branded, and functional SharePoint environment that enhances productivity and aligns with business goals.

By now, you have learned what an application customizer is, why is it needed, what to use it for, and a couple of simple examples. Next, we will focus on how to create an application customizer.

Building an application customizer

> **Git branch**
>
> This section uses the `https://github.com/PacktPublishing/Mastering-SharePoint-Development-with-the-SharePoint-Framework-/tree/chapter10/build-an-application-customizer` Git branch from the repository.

Now that we know what an application customizer is and what it's used for, let's start building one.

For this chapter, we will create an application customizer as per the details mentioned in the *Requirement 3 – getting a visual notification when a product is low in stock* section of *Chapter 4*, which will provide a warning message at the top of all the pages of a site when one or more products are low in stock.

Adding an application customizer to the solution

From the existing Packt.Solutions.ProductManagement folder, run the following command:

```
yo @microsoft/sharepoint --component-type "extension"
--extension-type "ApplicationCustomizer" --component-name
"PacktProductApplicationCustomizer" --framework "none" --environment
"spo" --package-manager "npm" --skip-feature-deployment
```

The parameters are similar to the command that we have seen in previous chapters for web part and form customizer.

Note that for --framework, the parameter is set to none as the SPFx generator doesn't provide React scaffolding for application customizers out of the box. We will create a react component separately in the section, *Adding a React component to an Application Customizer*.

Updating the configuration

At this point, the base application customizer is created, and the dependencies have been installed. We will need to update the solution configuration so that we can test the application customizer.

Open the config/serve.json file and notice a new configuration called packtProductApplicationCustomizer. Update the pageUrl property in this configuration, replacing the {tenantDomain} placeholder with the SharePoint Online site you want to use (such as https://mytenant.sharepoint.com/sites/testsite/_layouts/workbench.aspx).

This URL will be used to test the application customizer and will be launched with some query parameters when using the gulp serve --config=packtProductApplicationCustomizer command.

> **Custom action ID**
>
> Notice the ID under customActions present in the config/serve.json file and in the PacktProductApplicationCustomizerApplicationCustomizer.manifest.json file. It will have the same value, which represents the application customizer created. This ID will be used in the future during deployment.

With this, the application customizer has been set up for testing, and it is time to start the implementation.

Initial render check

Commit reference

Please refer to the https://github.com/PacktPublishing/Mastering-SharePoint-Development-with-the-SharePoint-Framework-/commit/3965eead11ad2b0240d7260ae6811040286dd6fb commit for this section.

Before updating the code to meet the requirements, let's run the application customizer to see its default behavior.

From the command line, run the following:

```
gulp serve --config=packtProductApplicationCustomizer
```

This will open the browser and load the application customizer.

It may take a few minutes for the code to build. Once you see that the reload subtask has finished in the command line, the code will be ready to be tested in the browser.

```
Finished subtask 'webpack' after 14 s
Starting subtask 'reload'...
Finished subtask 'reload' after 1.76 ms
```

Figure 10.2 – Verification of the reload subtask completing in the command line

Once the subtask reload has finished, reload the page, and a dialog will be displayed with the text **Hello from PacktProductApplicationCustomizerApplicationCustomizer: Test message**.

The code in the PacktProductApplicationCustomizerApplicationCustomizer.ts file is responsible for the dialog to be displayed. In that file, the onInit method simply says that when the application customizer loads, show a dialog with a message:

```
public onInit(): Promise<void> {
  let message: string = this.properties.testMessage;
  Dialog.alert(`Hello from ${strings.Title}:\n\n${message}`)
  return Promise.resolve();
}
```

With the application customizer now initialized, let's look at one of the important elements of application customizers called **placeholders**.

Placeholders

Commit reference

Please refer to the `https://github.com/PacktPublishing/Mastering-SharePoint-Development-with-the-SharePoint-Framework-/commit/a915be5f6571439124dd77ee38d1080ad886cd88` commit for this section.

Placeholders are predefined regions in the SharePoint page layout where we can inject custom content or functionality. These placeholders are used to extend the **user interface** (**UI**) of SharePoint pages without modifying the core structure of the page itself.

Placeholders in SPFx are dynamically located regions within the page where customizations can be added. These regions are defined by SharePoint and are part of its modern page model. The two most used placeholders in SPFx application customizers are as follows:

- **Top placeholder**: This placeholder is typically located at the top of the page, above the main content area

- **Bottom placeholder**: This placeholder is typically located at the bottom of the page, below the main content area

Placeholders are accessed in SPFx using the `this.context.placeholderProvider` API.

Placeholders help us dynamically add content such as headers, footers, banners, or notifications without disrupting the rest of the page.

We will be using the top placeholder to meet the requirement. In this subsection, we will see how to access the top placeholder and add text to it with some CSS.

In the `PacktProductApplicationCustomizerApplicationCustomizer.ts` file, we create a function to render the placeholders (`_renderPlaceHolders`), which will check whether the top placeholder is present, and if it is, then set it to a private member of the class (`_topPlaceholder`).

Once this has been set, we can access the `innerHTML` of the top placeholder and set it to the HTML content that we desire. In this case, that is some text:

```
private _renderPlaceHolders(): void {
    // Handling the top placeholder
    if (!this._topPlaceholder) {
       this._topPlaceholder = this.context.placeholderProvider.
tryCreateContent(
          PlaceholderName.Top,
          { onDispose: this._onDispose }
       );
    }
```

```
    if (!this._topPlaceholder) {
      console.error("The expected placeholder (Top) was not found.");
      return;
    }
    if (this._topPlaceholder.domElement) {
      this._topPlaceholder.domElement.innerHTML = `
      <div class="${styles.applicationCustomizer}">
        <p class="${styles.topPlaceHolder}">This is the Packt Product
Management Application Customizer</p>
      </div>`;
    }
  }
```

This `_renderPlaceHolders` function will be called in the `onInit` method of the application customizer only after the placeholders are created by SharePoint.

The way to determine whether placeholders have been created or not is by using the `this.context.placeholderProvider.changedEvent` property:

```
  public onInit(): Promise<void> {
    // Wait for the placeholders to be created (or handle them being
changed) and then render
    this.context.placeholderProvider.changedEvent.add(this, this._
renderPlaceHolders);
    return Promise.resolve();
  }
```

Along with this, an `scss` file can be added optionally to control the look and feel of the `innerHTML` of the top placeholder:

```
.applicationCustomizer {
  .topPlaceHolder {
    height: 60px;
    text-align: center;
    display: flex;
    align-items: center;
    justify-content: center;
    background-color: black;
    color: white;
    margin: 0px;
  }
}
```

Running `gulp serve --config=packtProductApplicationCustomizer` from the command line will open the browser and load the application customizer.

Once the `reload` subtask has finished, reload the page and the text will be displayed at the top of the page in the top placeholder:

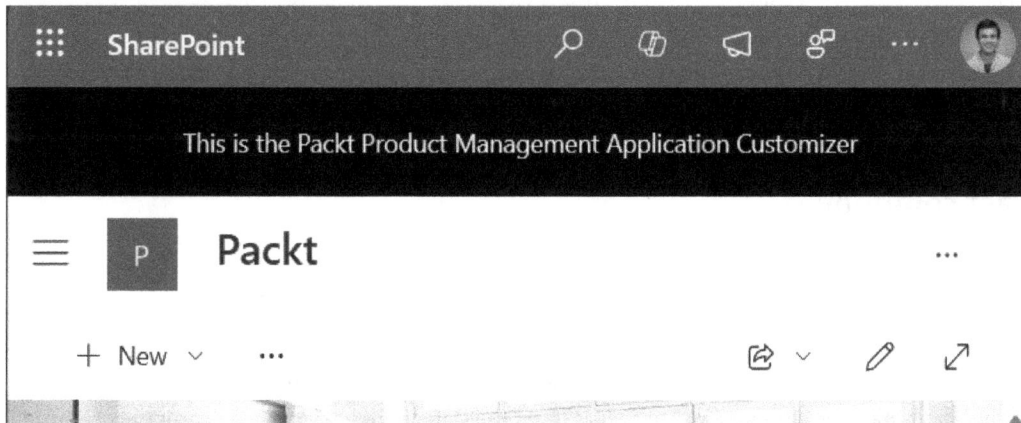

Figure 10.3 – Application customizer with text in the top placeholder

We have seen how to create an application customizer using SPFx, learned what placeholders are, and are able to render text in the top placeholder. The content in the top placeholder was directly rendered HTML. Instead of rendering HTML directly, in the next section, we will see how to use a React component to render the content in the top placeholder.

Adding a React component to an application customizer

> **Git branch**
>
> This section uses the `https://github.com/PacktPublishing/Mastering-SharePoint-Development-with-the-SharePoint-Framework-/tree/chapter10/adding-react-component-to-application-customizer` Git branch from the repository.

In this section, we will see how to add a React component in an application customizer to render the content in the top placeholder. By the end of this section, we will be able to see text in the top placeholder, rendered using React instead of simple HTML.

As stated in *Chapter 4, Requirement 3*, the requirement is related to showing the application customizer at the top of the page when products are low in stock (i.e., below 10). To do this, we will create a React component called `LowStockInformer` and show some text to say that products A, B, and C are low in stock.

> **React installation**
>
> Since React has already been installed in the solution, we can start using it straight away. However, if you are building an application customizer separately, then React needs to be installed to the solution using npm. Please refer to the information mentioned at `https://learn.microsoft.com/en-us/sharepoint/dev/spfx/compatibility` for the correct React version.

React component

Like with any React project, we create a new folder called `components` in the `packtProductApplicationCustomizer` folder and create a new file called `LowStockInformer.tsx`.

This component will have a state with only one property to begin with, called `show`, which controls showing and hiding the component. The idea is to set the state to `false` when the component loads. Once the component is mounted, it will check whether there are any products with low stock; if there are products with low stock, then it will set `show` to `true`.

In this section, we purposely set `show` to `true` as we are only displaying the text:

```
export default class LowStockInfomer extends React.
Component<ILowStockInformerProps, ILowStockInformerState> {
    constructor(props: ILowStockInformerProps) {
        super(props);
        this.state = {
            show: false
        };
    }
    public componentDidMount(): void {
        this.setState({
            show: true
        });
    }
}
```

The `render` method will check the value of show in the state and render HTML that shows the text:

```
public render(): React.ReactElement<ILowStockInformerProps> {
    if(!this.state.show) {
        return <></>;
    }
    return (
        <div className={styles.main}>
```

```
          <div className={styles.content}>
              <span>Products A, B, C are low in stock.</span>
          </div>
        </div>
     );
   }
```

Root class update

Now that the component is ready, we need the root (application customizer) to call it. The code will be similar to that of the web part and form customizer, which we saw in the previous chapters:

```
if (this._topPlaceholder.domElement) {
     const lowStockInformer: React.
ReactElement<ILowStockInformerProps> = React.createElement(
       LowStockInformer,
       {}
     );
     ReactDOM.render(lowStockInformer, this._topPlaceholder.
domElement);
   }
 }
```

Commit reference

Please refer to the `https://github.com/PacktPublishing/Mastering-SharePoint-Development-with-the-SharePoint-Framework-/commit/66aa56c3e910ffa1c276788c7e1c5860e5ed9e51` commit for more details on the exact changes.

Running `gulp serve --config=packtProductApplicationCustomizer` from the command line will open the browser and load the application customizer.

Once the reload subtask has finished, reload the page, and the text will be seen at the top of the page in the top placeholder.

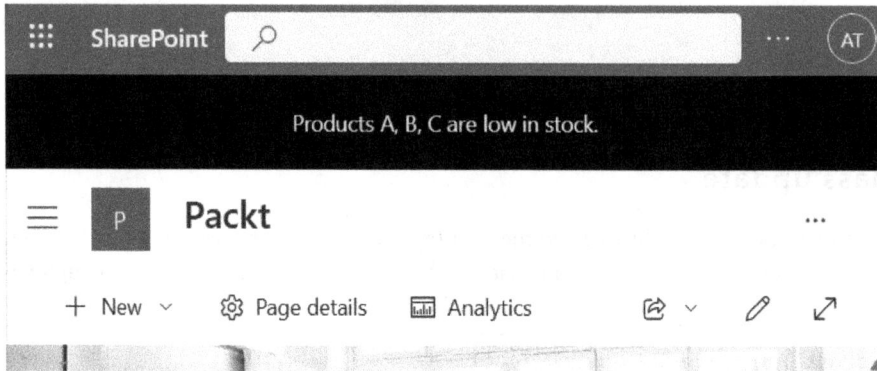

Figure 10.4 – Top placeholder with a React component

Tip

Try setting the value of `show` to `false` in the `componentDidMount` function of the `LowStockInformer` component. Saving the code and reloading the page after subtask reload is finished will not render the `LowStockInformer` component.

In this section, we saw how to add a React component to the application customizer and make that component render sample text by setting its state. In the next section, we get the products that are low in stock from the `Products` list and control the state of the component based on the response.

Using the Microsoft Graph API to get items

Commit reference

Please refer to the https://github.com/PacktPublishing/Mastering-SharePoint-Development-with-the-SharePoint-Framework-/commit/9287d2f1e7978393ab41903669828f677d0c07fb commit for more details on the exact changes.

Now that we can display text in a React component of the application customizer, the next step needed to meet the requirements is to query the `Products` list to check whether there are any products that are low in stock (i.e., below 10). If that is the case, then we will show the React component with the names of the products that are low in stock.

Filtering items

We can use the Microsoft Graph API to filter the items from a SharePoint list. This can be done by passing a filter clause to the /items endpoint (which gets the items list).

In our case, we need to filter those products from the Products list whose Stock Level is less than 10. So, the filter clause will be fields/packtProductStockLevel lt 10.

Since the ProdictCatalogService.ts file already has a method to get products, we need to update it to introduce a filter clause. We do that by passing filter as one of the parameters:

```
public async getProducts(
  siteId: string,
  listName: string,
  itemsCount?: number,
  searchQuery?: string,
  filterClause?: string
): Promise<IProductCatalogItem[]> {

  // SharePoint columns for a product
  const fields = [

    ...
  ];

  try {
    const response = await this._msGraphClient
      .api(`sites/${siteId}/lists/${listName}/items`)
      .filter(filterClause)
      .expand(`fields($select=${fields})`)
      .top(itemsCount ? itemsCount : 50)
      .header("Prefer",
"HonorNonIndexedQueriesWarningMayFailRandomly")
      .get();

    const items: IProductCatalogItem[] = response.value.map((item:
any) => {
      return {
        modelName: item.fields.packtProductModelName,
        productReference: item.fields.packtProductReference,
        stockLevel: item.fields.packtProductStockLevel,

        ...
      } as IProductCatalogItem;
    });
```

```
      return items;
    }
  }
```

We also introduce another method called `getLowStockProducts`, which will call `getProducts` with a filter clause:

```
public async getLowStockProducts(
  siteId: string,
  listName: string,
  itemsCount?: number
): Promise<IProductCatalogItem[]> {
  try {
    return this.getProducts(
      siteId,
      listName,
      itemsCount,
      undefined,
      `fields/packtProductStockLevel lt 10`
    );
  }
}
```

Calling the API from the component

> **Commit reference**
>
> Please refer to the https://github.com/PacktPublishing/Mastering-SharePoint-Development-with-the-SharePoint-Framework-/commit/2d98cc2afbce672e02e81e5d191d67bbc9fdd085 commit for more details on the exact changes.

Now that the service has been updated, all that is left to do is to call the method in the service from the component.

The initial setup (i.e., getting the Microsoft Graph client, initializing the service, and passing it as props to the component) remains similar to how it is done in the web part in *Chapter 5, Building a SharePoint Web Part*.

Since we need to know the name of the `products` list, we will introduce a new property for the application customizer called `productsListName` and set its value to `Products` (in the `packtProductApplicationCustomizer` configuration of `config/serve.json`). In *Chapter 15, Deploying Extensions*, we will see how this property can be changed dynamically if needed.

The service, site ID, list name, and URL of the list are passed as props to the component. Their purpose is as follows:

- The service needs the site ID and list name to get the items

- URL of the list is needed so that we can show it in the top placeholder as a link to easily navigate to the list

The following code block shows passing the service, site ID, list name, and URL of the list:

```
React.ReactElement<ILowStockInformerProps> = React.createElement(
      LowStockInformer,
      {
          productCatalogService: this._productCatalogService,
          siteId: this.context.pageContext.site.id.toString(),
          listName: listName,
          listUrl: `${this.context.pageContext.site.
serverRelativeUrl}/Lists/${listName}`
      }
    );
```

In the `LowStockInformer` React component, a new state called `lowStockProductNames` is added to store names of the products that are low in stock.

When the component mounts, the `getLowStockProducts` method of the service is called. If the method returns any products, then `show` in the state is set to `true` and `lowStockProductNames` in `state` is set to the comma-separated names of the products:

```
public componentDidMount(): void {
      this.props.productCatalogService.getLowStockProducts(this.
props.siteId, this.props.listName)
          .then((products) => {
              if (products.length > 0) {
                  // Get the names of the low stock products
                  let lowStockProductNames = products.map(product =>
product.modelName).join(", ");
                  this.setState({
                      show: true,
                      lowStockProductNames: lowStockProductNames
                  });
              }
```

```
        })
        .catch((error) => {
            console.error(error);
        });
    }
```

The `render` method checks the value of `show` in the state and renders HTML based on that. This HTML includes a message with the name of the products that are low in stock and an *anchor tag* to point to the `Products` list:

```
public render(): React.ReactElement<ILowStockInformerProps> {
        if (!this.state.show) {
            return <></>;
        }
        return (
            <div className={styles.main}>
                <div className={styles.content}>
                    <span>{this.state.lowStockProductNames} low in
stock. <a href={this.props.listUrl} data-interception="off">Click
here</a> to view the list.</span>
                </div>
            </div>
        );
    }
```

Navigate to the `Products` list in the browser and change the `Stock Level` column of a product to a number below 10.

After that, running `gulp serve --config=packtProductApplicationCustomizer` from the command line will open the browser and load the application customizer.

Once the `reload` subtask has finished, reload the page and the text will be seen at the top of the page in the top placeholder.

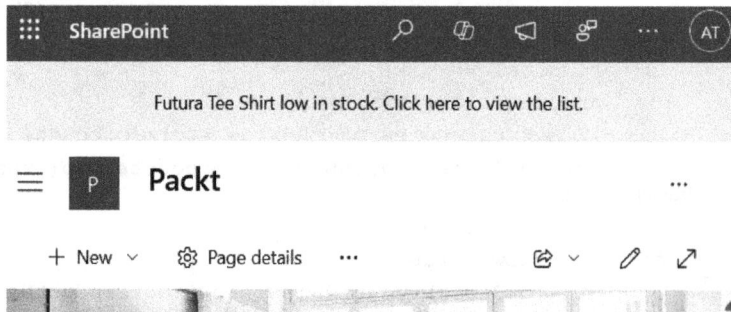

Figure 10.5 – Application customizer showing products that are low in stock

In this section, we have seen how to get the products that are low in stock from the `Products` list using the Microsoft Graph API by supplying a filter clause to it. After retrieving the products that are low in stock, we saw how to use the state of the React component to display those products in the top placeholder.

Summary

In this chapter, we learned about an SPFx extension called application customizer. We started by understanding what an application customizer is, when it is needed, and what it is used for. Then, we moved on to creating an application customizer using SPFx; we learned how it is rendered and what placeholders are.

After that, we looked at adding a React component to the application customizer by going into the details of what the component does and how it can render simple text.

Once the React component was ready, we updated the service to get filtered items using Microsoft Graph and used it in the component to render products that are low in stock.

In the next chapter, we will look at a field customizer that will give control over rendering a field as per our requirements.

11

Building a Field Customizer

In the previous chapter, we understood what an Application Customizer is (one of the multiple elements that we can create with SPFx) and how to create one. We looked into the different placeholders in a SharePoint page where the Application Customizer can be rendered. With that information, we created an Application Customizer that was used to show a banner at the top of the pages on a site with information on products that were low. The Application Customizer also displayed a link to the **Products** list.

In this chapter, we will continue with the theme of low-stock products and look into another element of SPFx called the **Field Customizer**, which will provide visual information on the products that are low in stock. We will do this by customizing the display of the **Stock level** field in the **Products** list.

Some of the concepts in this chapter will be similar or in line with the concepts mentioned in the previous chapters on web parts, form customizers, and Application Customizers. In this chapter, you will do the following:

- Learn how to create a Field Customizer from scratch using SPFx to meet the functional requirements
- Understand the Field Customizer development flow and SPFx-provided lifecycle methods
- Use custom **Sassy CSS (SCSS)** to control the display of a field

Technical requirements

This chapter relies on the GitHub solution accessible here: `https://github.com/ PacktPublishing/Mastering-SharePoint-Development-with-the-SharePoint- Framework-/tree/chapter11/building-a-field-customizer`. Similar to the earlier chapters, you need to first clone the repository locally on your machine to be able to follow the steps. As the solution is built step by step, for each section in this chapter, a dedicated Git branch has been created representing the solution at a specific state corresponding to a section. Before reading the section, you must check out the corresponding branch before using either the Git command line or a Git client such as GitHub Desktop, Sourcetree, and so on.

> **Code snippets**
>
> For brevity and readability considerations, only the relevant parts of the code are detailed in the provided snippets in this chapter. For these reasons, ad hoc code, such as dependencies, imports, and updates to certain files, may be omitted. We recommend having the GitHub solution open alongside to get the full working version of the code and review the provided steps.

The branch name to refer to and additional instructions are indicated at the beginning of each section. Here is a summary of Git branches to check out per section:

Section in this chapter	Git branch to check out
Building a Field Customizer	`https://github.com/PacktPublishing/Mastering-SharePoint-Development-with-the-SharePoint-Framework-/tree/chapter11/building-a-field-customizer`
Updating the Field Customizer	`https://github.com/PacktPublishing/Mastering-SharePoint-Development-with-the-SharePoint-Framework-/tree/chapter11/updating-field-customizer`

What is a Field Customizer?

An SPFx Field Customizer (a type of SPFx extension) is a component that allows developers to modify how fields in SharePoint lists and libraries are displayed. It provides the ability to customize the rendering of specific field values, enabling a more tailored and visually appealing user experience.

Why is it needed?

The default rendering of fields in SharePoint lists and libraries may not always meet specific business or design requirements. Field Customizers address this limitation by enabling us to display field values in a way that enhances usability, visual appeal, or functionality. They allow for dynamic, context-aware displays that align with organizational needs and improve the overall user experience.

Uses of an SPFx Field Customizer

An SPFx Field Customizer can be used for various purposes, including the following:

- **Conditional formatting**: Highlighting field values based on specific conditions, such as color-coding task statuses or emphasizing overdue items
- **Enhanced visuals**: Displaying field data using custom icons, charts, or other graphical representations

- **Interactive elements**: Adding interactive components such as buttons, dropdowns, or progress bars directly within list views

- **Data transformation**: Transforming raw field data into a more user-friendly format, such as converting a date to a relative time (e.g., "3 days ago") or formatting a monetary value

- **Integration with external data**: Displaying external data or functionality, such as pulling data from an API and rendering it within a list field

- **Custom actions**: Embedding action buttons or links within a field to trigger workflows, navigate to related content, or interact with external systems

Simple examples

Here are a couple of examples to illustrate the use of an SPFx Field Customizer.

Example 1: Status field with conditional formatting

Say we have a list for the management of tasks that has a **Status** field with values such as **Not Started**, **In Progress**, and **Completed**. With the help of an SPFx Field Customizer, we can apply conditional formatting to display these statuses with different background colors or icons. This will make it easy for end users to identify task progress.

Example 2: Displaying progress bars

Say we have a list that is used for project tracking that has a field called **Completion Percentage**. With the help of an SPFx Field Customizer, we can render the value of this field as a progress bar. This is easily identifiable for end users and they can understand the progress of the project.

By leveraging SPFx Field Customizers, organizations can create visually appealing, interactive, and functional list views that better suit their unique business needs, enhancing the overall usability and efficiency of SharePoint.

Now that we have understood what a Field Customizer is and what it's used for, let's start building one.

Building a Field Customizer

> **Git branch**
>
> This section uses the `https://github.com/PacktPublishing/Mastering-SharePoint-Development-with-the-SharePoint-Framework-/tree/chapter11/building-a-field-customizer` Git branch from the repository.

For this chapter, we will create a Field Customizer as per the details mentioned in the *Requirement 3: Getting a visual notification when a product is low stock* section in *Chapter 4, Packt Product Management Solution: A Practical Use Case*. As per the requirement, in the *Products* list, the display of the **Stock level** column of an item should change based on its value. If, for a product, the value is lower than 10, then the **Stock level** display for that product will change to a different background color with a warning icon.

Figure 11.1 – Field Customizer requirement

Next, let's see how to add a Field Customizer to the SPFx solution.

Adding a Field Customizer to the solution

From the existing `Packt.Solutions.ProductManagement` folder, run the following command:

```
yo @microsoft/sharepoint --component-type "extension" --extension-
type "FieldCustomizer" --component-name "PacktProductFieldCustomizer"
--framework "none" --environment "spo" --package-manager "npm" --skip-
feature-deployment
```

> **Note on similarity**
>
> The parameters are similar to the commands that we have seen in previous chapters for web parts, form customizers, and Application Customizers, and will be seen in further chapters. There are only a couple of minor tweaks.

Note that the `--framework` parameter is set to `none`; this is because we will not be using any framework (React or Angular) here for the requirement. If the requirement is complex, then a decision can be made to use the framework of choice.

Updating the configuration

At this point, the base Field Customizer is created, and dependencies are installed. We will need to update the `serve` configuration so that we can test the Field Customizer.

Open the `config/serve.json` file and notice that a new configuration called `packtProductFieldCustomizer` has been added. We need to update that section as per the following points:

- Update the `pageUrl` property in this configuration to point to the **Products** list of your site (e.g., `https://mytenant.sharepoint.com/sites/testsite/Lists/Products/AllItems.aspx`). This is because we cannot use the workbench page to debug SPFx extensions.

- Update `InternalFieldName` to `packtProductStockLevel`, as that will be the field we will be customizing.

The *Products* list URL will be used to test the Field Customizer and will be launched with some query parameters when using the `gulp serve --config=packtProductFieldCustomizer` command.

> **Field Customizer ID**
>
> Notice the ID under `packtProductStockLevel` present in the `config/serve.json` file and in the `PacktProductFieldCustomizerFieldCustomizer.manifest.json` file. It will have the same value, which will be a unique ID that represents the Field Customizer created. This ID will be used in the future during deployment.

With this, the Field Customizer is set up for testing, and it is time to start the implementation.

Initial render check

> **Commit reference**
>
> Please refer to the `https://github.com/PacktPublishing/Mastering-SharePoint-Development-with-the-SharePoint-Framework-/commit/2bf0a7d8c947d624914f37b04385d680d632b3ce` commit for this section.

Before updating the code to meet the requirement, let's run the Field Customizer to see its default behavior.

From the command line, run the following:

```
gulp serve --config=packtProductFieldCustomizer
```

This will open the browser and load the Field Customizer (in the **Products** list page with debug query parameters).

It may take a few minutes for the code to build. Once you see that the subtask reload is finished in the command line, the code will be ready to be tested in the browser.

```
Finished subtask 'webpack' after 14 s
Starting subtask 'reload'...
Finished subtask 'reload' after 1.76 ms
```

Figure 11.2 – Verification of subtask reload complete in the command line

An existing issue in SPFx 1.19.0

> **Note**
>
> This will not be an issue for SPFx 1.20.0 and above.

Once the subtask reload is finished, reload the page. If there are no changes in the display of the **Stock level** field, then it is because of an existing issue related to SPFx 1.19.0.

To fix the issue, in the URL, change `packtProductStockLevel` to `Stock level` (i.e., change the **internal name** of the field to the **display name**) and reload the page.

If that doesn't load the Field Customizer (i.e., it doesn't change the display of the **Stock level** field), then it might be because of the case sensitivity of a query string in the URL called `loadSPFX`. Make sure that it is set to `loadSPFX` (not `loadSPFx` or `loadspfx`).

This will load the Field Customizer by changing the display of the **Stock level** field, as shown here:

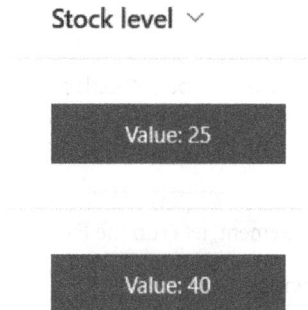

Stock level ∨

Value: 25

Value: 40

Figure 11.3 – Default customized display of the Stock level field

> **Note**
>
> The values may be different from what you see in *Figure 11.3*.

Lifecycle methods

There are three important methods related to the lifecycle of a Field Customizer. They are `onInit()`, `onRenderCell()`, and `onDisposeCell()`. These can be seen in the `PacktProductFieldCustomizerFieldCustomizer.ts` file. Let's see what each one does:

- The `onInit()` method is called when the Field Customizer is initialized. It sets up any necessary resources or configurations required for the Field Customizer to function.

- The `onRenderCell()` method is called for each cell in the list or library where the Field Customizer is applied. This method allows us to customize the rendering of the field value.

  Do look at the code in this method, which is responsible for the display of the **Stock level** field, as per *Figure 11.3*:

  ```
  public onRenderCell(event: IFieldCustomizerCellEventParameters):
  void {
      const text: string = `${this.properties.sampleText}:
  ${event.fieldValue}`;
      event.domElement.innerText = text;
  event.domElement.classList.add(styles.
  packtProductFieldCustomizer);
      }
  ```

- The `onDisposeCell()` method is called when a cell is no longer needed, such as when the list view is updated or the user navigates away from the list. It ensures the proper cleanup of resources or event handlers associated with the cell.

This concludes our understanding of building a Field Customizer. In the next section, we will take a look at changing the display of the Field Customizer (i.e., updating the code in the `onRenderCell` method) to meet the requirement.

Updating the Field Customizer

> **Git branch and commit reference**
>
> This section uses the `https://github.com/PacktPublishing/Mastering-SharePoint-Development-with-the-SharePoint-Framework-/tree/chapter11/updating-field-customizer` Git branch from the repository.
>
> Please refer to the `https://github.com/PacktPublishing/Mastering-SharePoint-Development-with-the-SharePoint-Framework-/commit/9fb8dacdc71b8b2db213d254c1fd3d193accadd5` commit for this section.

In this section, we will see how to update the Field Customizer (which we created in the previous section) to meet the requirement, which is showing a different background color for the **Stock level** field when its value is less than 10. With this, we will be easily able to see which products are low in stock.

As mentioned in the earlier section, the `onRenderCell()` method is the one that allows us to customize the rendering of a field. Hence, we will be updating that with the following steps:

1. Get the value of the field

2. Parse it to an integer and check whether the integer value is less than 10

3. If it is less than 10, then render a <div> element with custom CSS applied

4. This element will show the value and a warning icon

5. If not, render the value as is

The custom CSS will have code for the required background color of the cell.

As per the preceding points, the onRenderCell() method will have the following code:

```
public onRenderCell(event: IFieldCustomizerCellEventParameters):
void {
    event.domElement.classList.add(styles.
packtProductFieldCustomizer);
    const text: string = `${event.fieldValue}`;
    let value: number = parseInt(event.fieldValue);
    if (value < 10) {
      event.domElement.innerHTML = `
        <div class='${styles.lowStockContentContainer}'>
          <div class='${styles.lowStockValue}'>${text}</div>
          <div class='${styles.lowStockWarningIcon}'>&#9888;</div>
        </div>`;
      return;
    }
    event.domElement.innerText = text;
}
```

The scss file will have the following code, which sets the background color to the intended value:

```
.packtProductFieldCustomizer {
  .lowStockContentContainer {
    background-color: #f8a392;
    color: #000;
    height: 20px;
    display: flex;
    align-items: center;
    justify-content: center;
    border-radius: 5px;
  }
  .lowStockValue {
    margin: 0 auto; /* Push this item to the center */
  }
  .lowStockWarningIcon {
    margin-right: 5px; /* Push this item to the right end */
  }
}
```

In the **Products** list, update one or two products by changing their **Stock level** value to a value less than 10.

Running `gulp serve --config=packtProductFieldCustomizer` from the command line will open the browser and load the Field Customizer.

Once the subtask reload is finished, reload the page (refer to the *An existing issue in SPFx 1.19.0* subsection earlier in this chapter), and the updated display of the **Stock Level** field can be seen for those items that have a **Stock level** value less than 10.

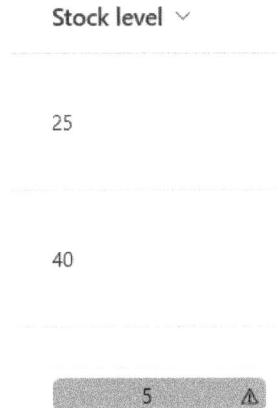

Figure 11.4 – Updated display of the Stock level field

In this section, we saw how to update a Field Customizer (i.e., updating the code in the `onRenderCell()` method to change the display of a field). We changed the code such that the display of a field (in this case, **Stock level**, as set in `config/serve.json`) renders differently when its value is less than 10.

Summary

In this chapter, we were able to understand the details of an SPFx extension called the Field Customizer. We started by understanding what a Field Customizer is, its requirements, and its use cases. Then, we moved on to creating a Field Customizer using SPFx, in which we understood its different lifecycle methods and how the Field Customizer is rendered.

After that, we looked into updating the display of a Field Customizer by updating the code in the `onRenderCell()` method to render HTML based on a condition (a value less than 10).

In the next chapter, we will look at another extension, called **ListView Command Set**, which will help us in taking actions on list items.

Get This Book's PDF Version and Exclusive Extras

UNLOCK NOW

Scan the QR code (or go to packtpub.com/unlock). Search for this book by name, confirm the edition, and then follow the steps on the page.

Note: Keep your invoice handy. Purchases made directly from Packt don't require an invoice.

12

Building a ListView Command Set

In the previous chapter, we learned what a field customizer is (one of the multiple elements we can create with SPFx). We looked into how to create a basic one and the different life cycle methods of a field customizer in detail and then modified the code of the field customizer such that its display changes based on its value. This was in line with our requirement, which was to allow users to easily see the products low in stock.

In this chapter, we will continue to the next stage of the low stock theme, in which we will understand how we can take action for products that are low in stock. Taking action means executing a command, hence, we will be looking at an element of SPFx called the **ListView Command Set**. This Command Set will be available when browsing a list page, and we will make the command(s) available only for certain list items, in our case, for products that are low in stock.

Some of the concepts in this chapter will be similar or in line with the concepts mentioned in the previous chapters on web parts and extensions. In this chapter, you will do the following:

- Learn how to create a ListView Command Set from scratch using SPFx to meet the functional requirements

- Understand the ListView Command Set development flow and SPFx-provided life cycle methods

- Understand how to call an external system (Power Automate flow or a third-party HTTP service) from a ListView Command Set

Technical requirements

This chapter relies on the GitHub solution accessible here: `https://github.com/PacktPublishing/Mastering-SharePoint-Development-with-the-SharePoint-Framework-`.

Similar to the earlier chapters, you need to first clone the repository locally on your machine to be able to follow the steps. As the solution is built step by step, for each section in this chapter, a dedicated Git branch has been created representing the solution at a specific state corresponding to a section. Before reading the section, you must check out the corresponding branch before using either the Git command line or a Git client such as GitHub Desktop, SourceTree, and so on.

Code snippets

For brevity and readability considerations, only the relevant parts of the code are detailed in the provided snippets in this chapter. For these reasons, ad hoc code, such as dependencies imports and updates to certain files may be omitted. We recommend having the GitHub solution open to get the full working version of the code and review the provided steps.

The branch name to refer to and additional instructions are indicated at the beginning of each section. Here is a summary of Git branches to check out per section:

Section in this chapter	Git branch to check out
Building a ListView Command Set	`https://github.com/PacktPublishing/Mastering-SharePoint-Development-with-the-SharePoint-Framework-/tree/chapter12/building-a-listview-command-set`
Updating the ListView Command Set to meet the requirement	`https://github.com/PacktPublishing/Mastering-SharePoint-Development-with-the-SharePoint-Framework-/tree/chapter12/updating-a-listview-command-set`

What is a ListView Command Set?

An SPFx ListView Command Set (a type of SPFx extension) is a component that allows us to add custom options to the command bar or context menu of SharePoint lists and libraries. These custom commands provide additional functionality that we can perform on selected items or lists.

Why is it needed?

The default command bar and context menu in SharePoint may not always meet all the requirements for an organization. SPFx ListView Command Sets enable us to extend these menus with custom actions that meet the requirements of specific business processes that might be around integrating with external systems or enhancing user productivity.

Uses of a ListView Command Set

A ListView Command Set can be used for various purposes, including the following:

- **Custom actions**: Adding new actions such as "Export to PDF" or "Convert to X format"
- **Integration with external systems**: Triggering workflows or calling APIs to send data to external platforms
- **Batch operations**: Enabling actions on multiple selected items, such as bulk updates to list items or documents
- **Conditional commands**: Displaying specific commands based on the user roles
- **Custom workflows**: Integrating with SharePoint workflows or Power Automate to run custom business processes

Simple examples

Here are a couple of examples to illustrate the use of a ListView Command Set:

Example 1: Export to CSV

We can add an **Export to CSV** command in the command bar, which can allow users to download a CSV file of the selected items in the list. The command would work in a way such that it collects the selected items, formats the data, and then generates a downloadable file.

Example 2: approve items

Say we have an approval workflow. We could think of adding a **Mark as Approved** context menu command, which will update the status of selected items to **Approved** and then trigger a notification to relevant approvers.

Now that we have understood what a ListView Command Set is and what it's used for, let's start building one.

Building a ListView Command Set

> **Git branch**
>
> This section uses the `https://github.com/PacktPublishing/Mastering-SharePoint-Development-with-the-SharePoint-Framework-/tree/chapter12/building-a-listview-command-set` Git branch from the repository.

For this chapter, we will create a ListView Command Set as per the details mentioned in the *Requirement 4: Placing a new order when a product is low in stock* section of *Chapter 4, Packt Product Management Solution: A Practical Use Case*, which, in the **Products** list, will display a command called **Update Stock**. Clicking on this command will run a Power Automate flow, which then performs the action of updating the stock.

> **A Power Automate flow will not be built**
>
> Note that we will not be creating a Power Automate flow here as it is out of scope for the topic of this book. However, we will assume that there will be a Power Automate flow that gets triggered when a URL is called, and that flow will update the stock of the selected product successfully.

Adding a ListView Command Set to the solution

From the existing `Packt.Solutions.ProductManagement` folder, run the following command:

```
yo @microsoft/sharepoint --component-type "extension" --extension-type
"ListViewCommandSet" --component-name "PacktProductListViewCommandSet"
--framework "none" --environment "spo" --package-manager "npm" --skip-
feature-deployment
```

The parameters are similar to the commands that we have seen in previous chapters for web parts and extensions.

Note that the `--framework` parameter is set to `none`. This is because we will not be using any framework (React or Angular) here for the requirement. If the requirement is complex, then a decision can be made to use the framework of choice.

Updating the configuration

With this, the base ListView Command Set is created, and all the dependencies are installed. The next step is to update the *serve configuration*, so that we can start testing the field customizer.

To do that, open the `config/serve.json` file, and you will see that a new configuration called `packtProductListViewCommandSet` is created.

In that section, update the `pageUrl` property in this configuration to point to the *Products* list of your site (for example, `https://mytenant.sharepoint.com/sites/testsite/Lists/Products/AllItems.aspx`). This is because we cannot use the workbench page to debug SPFx extensions.

The *Products* list URL will be used to test the ListView Command Set and will be launched with some query parameters when using the `gulp serve --config=packtProductListViewCommandSet` command.

> **ListView Command Set ID**
>
> Notice the ID under `customAction` in `packtProductListViewCommandSet`
> present in the `config/serve.json` file and in the `PacktProductListView`
> `CommandSetCommandSet.manifest.json` file. It will have the same value, which
> will be a unique ID that represents the ListView Command Set created. This ID will be used
> in the future, during deployment.

With this, the ListView Command Set is set up for testing and it is time to start the implementation.

Initial render check

> **Commit reference**
>
> Please refer to the `https://github.com/PacktPublishing/Mastering-`
> `SharePoint-Development-with-the-SharePoint-Framework-/commit/`
> `e7d531bd0f090435838041ef20b118e8ac4e789b` commit for this section.

Before updating the code to meet the requirement, let's run the ListView Command Set to see its
default behavior.

From the command line, run the following:

```
gulp serve --config=packtProductListViewCommandSet.
```

This will open the browser and load the ListView Command Set (on the *Products* list page with debug
query parameters).

It may take a few minutes for the code build. Once you see that the subtask reload is finished in the
command line, the code will be ready to be tested in the browser.

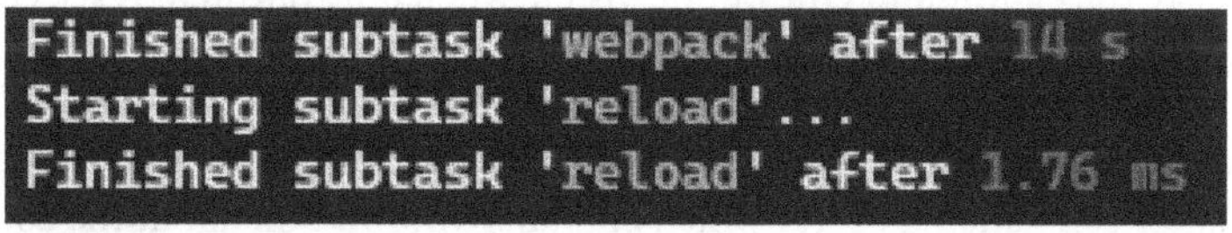

Figure 12.1 – Verification of reload subtask complete in the command line

Upon selecting an item in the *Products* list, you should see two new commands in the command bar
(creatively) named **Command One** and **Command Two**.

Figure 12.2 – Initial rendering of the ListView Command Set

These names get displayed because they are specified in the manifest file of the ListView Command Set (`PacktProductListViewCommandSetCommandSet.manifest.json`). The reason why we see the commands in the command bar is that, in `config/serve.json` under the `packtProductListViewCommandSet` config, the location is set to `ClientSideExtension.ListViewCommandSet.CommandBar`. The other option here is `ClientSideExtension.ListViewCommandSet.ContextMenu`, which will make the commands show in the context menu of the items, and another option is `ClientSideExtension.ListViewCommandSet`, which shows the commands both in the context menu and in the command bar.

Life cycle methods

There are two important methods related to the life cycle of a field customizer. They are `onInit()` and `onExecute()`. These can be seen in the `PacktProductListViewCommandSetCommandSet.ts` file.

- The `onInit()` method initializes the ListView Command Set, setting up any dependencies or configurations. The following points explain more details of this method, in this particular implementation:

  - It attaches a listener (a function) to `listViewStateChangedEvent`. This event is triggered whenever the state of the list view changes, such as when the following happens:

    - A user selects or deselects rows in the list

    - The list view is refreshed or updated

  - By attaching this listener, the extension can react to changes in the list view's state, such as the number of selected rows, and update the visibility of commands accordingly.

  - The listener in the code is the `_onListViewStateChanged` function, which has the logic to make the **Command One** button visible when only one item is selected. We will be updating the code in this function in a later section.

- The `onExecute()` method executes the logic for a specific command when it is clicked. This has a parameter called `event`, which contains information about the command being executed and the context of the action. The default code simply displays a dialog with some messages (set as properties of the ListView Command Set). We will update this code in the next section to meet the functional requirements.

Like other extensions, the ListView Command Set can also optionally have its own **properties**, which can be set at the time of deployment or in the `config/serve.json` file at the time of development. These properties can be used in the logic as per the requirement.

With this, we now know how to build a ListView Command Set. In the next section, we will take a look at changing the code of the ListView Command Set to meet the requirement, which is, for products low in stock, call an external system (in this case, an HTTP-triggered Power Automate flow) that updates the stock.

Updating the ListView Command Set

Git branch and commit reference

This section uses the `https://github.com/PacktPublishing/Mastering-SharePoint-Development-with-the-SharePoint-Framework-/tree/chapter12/updating-a-listview-command-set` Git branch from the repository.

Please refer to the `https://github.com/PacktPublishing/Mastering-SharePoint-Development-with-the-SharePoint-Framework-/commit/8965e1ac9fb0f0abfde62928d351f083c893809a` commit for this section.

In this section, we will see how to change the code of the ListView Command Set. The following points provide an outline of this section:

- The HTTP-triggered Power Automate flow can be called using `Get` or `Post` methods of an HTTP request, hence, we will be adding a simple HTTP service to the code.

- We have only one command as part of this ListView Command Set, called **Update Stock**, so related updates will be made in the manifest file of the ListView Command Set and in `config/serve.json`, which will be used during development.

- The `_onListViewStateChanged` will be updated such that it will show the **Update Stock** command only when a product with low stock is selected. This will be done by checking whether **Stock Level** is lower than **10**.

- The `onExecute` method will be updated to call the post method of the HTTP service with the endpoint as that of the Power Automate flow.

Note

As mentioned earlier, we will assume that an HTTP Power Automate flow exists that updates the product. We will also assume that this flow accepts **Id** and **Stock Level** of a product as inputs to perform its operations.

HTTP service

A new service for HTTP methods needs to be added to handle HTTP requests. The following code block shows only the post method as that's the one being used:

```
export default class HttpService implements IHttpService {
  private httpClient: HttpClient;

  constructor(httpClient: HttpClient) {
    this.httpClient = httpClient;
  }

  // Generic method for making a GET request
  ...

  // Generic method for making a POST request
  public async post(
    url: string,
    body: any,
    headers: Record<string, string> = { "Content-Type": "application/
json" }
  ): Promise<any> {
    const response: HttpClientResponse = await this.httpClient.
post(url, HttpClient.configurations.v1, {
      headers,
      body: JSON.stringify(body),
    });

    return this.handleResponse(response);
  }

  // Generic method for making a PUT request
  ...

  // Generic method for making a DELETE request
  ...

  // Handle response and parse JSON
  private async handleResponse(response: HttpClientResponse):
Promise<any> {

    if (!response.ok) {
      const errorDetails = await response.text();
      throw new Error(`HTTP error ${response.status}: ${response.
statusText}\nDetails: ${errorDetails}`);
```

```
    }

    try {
      return await response.json();
    } catch (error) {
      return null; // Return null if response is not JSON
    }
  }
}
```

This is a generic HTTP service class that can be used in any project. As you might have seen in other projects, we use this service to make the main HTTP calls – `Get`, `Post`, `Patch`, and `Delete`. The `httpClient` variable has all the methods, which will be called by the methods in the HTTP service class.

Command and properties

Since we need only one command, **Update Stock**, `manifest.json` can be updated accordingly.

The following code block shows this update in the `manifest.json` file:

```
"items": {
    "UPDATE_STOCK_COMMAND": {
        "title": { "default": "Update stock" },
        "iconImageUrl": "icons/request.png",
        "type": "command"
    }
}
```

This shows the name of the command, `UPDATE_STOCK_COMMAND`, its title, and icon (as shown in *Figure 12.3*).

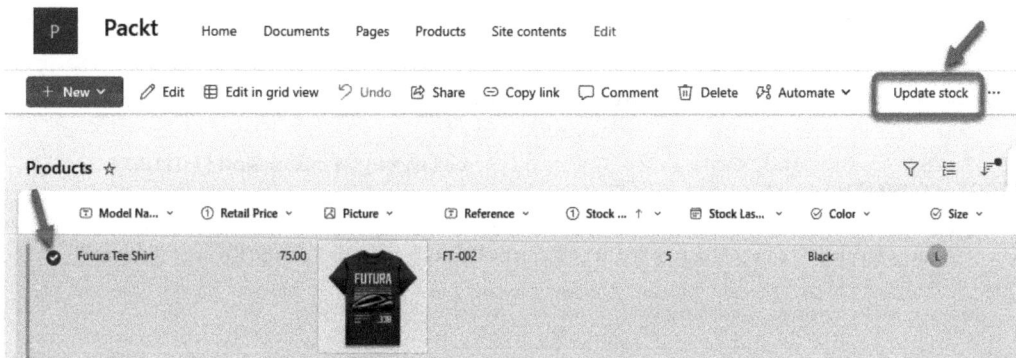

Figure 12.3 – The Update stock ListView Command Set

Understanding the role of properties in a ListView Command Set

A ListView Command Set in SPFx can have properties defined in its manifest file (or in the `config/serve.json` file while developing). These properties act like configurable variables that can be used within the logic of the Command Set. They allow us to set values externally without modifying the code itself.

Why use properties?

If we do not use properties, any time we want to test or work with new values, we would need to change the code and redeploy the solution. By using properties, we can configure these values directly in the manifest file or through tenant-wide deployment settings. This will make the solution more flexible and easier to maintain.

Listing down the properties we need

In this case, to meet the requirement, we make use of three properties:

1. `lowStockThreshold`: This determines the threshold for low stock. A product with `Stock Level` of less than `lowStockThreshold` is considered as low in stock.

2. `powerAutomateUrl`: The URL of the HTTP-triggered Power Automate flow that needs to be called when the **Update Stock** command is clicked.

3. `stockUpdatedMessage`: A message to display after a successful response is returned by the flow.

Instead of changing the code every time, we can simply update the property values, and the Command Set will use the new value dynamically.

Updating the code

We update the `onInit` method to initialize the HTTP service and get the **Update Stock** command:

```
public onInit(): Promise<void> {
    // Initialize the HttpService
    this._httpService = new HttpService(this.context.httpClient);
    // initial state of the command's visibility
    const updateStockCommand: Command = this.tryGetCommand('UPDATE_
STOCK_COMMAND');
    updateStockCommand.visible = false;
    this.context.listView.listViewStateChangedEvent.add(this, this._
onListViewStateChanged);
    return Promise.resolve();
}
```

The `_onListViewStateChanged` method can be updated such that the **Update Stock** command should be shown only when the selected product is low in stock:

```
const selectedRows = this.context.listView.selectedRows;
      // Ensure exactly one item is selected
      if (selectedRows?.length === 1) {
        const stockLevel = selectedRows[0].
getValueByName('packtProductStockLevel');
        const lowStockThreshold = this.properties.lowStockThreshold ||
10;
        // Show the command only if stockLevel is less than
lowStockThreshold
        if (stockLevel !== undefined && stockLevel <
lowStockThreshold) {
          updateStockCommand.visible = true;
        } else {
          updateStockCommand.visible = false;
        }
      } else {
        updateStockCommand.visible = false;
      }
```

Finally, the `onExecute` method, which handles the click of commands, can be updated such that the HTTP-triggered Power Automate flow is called when the **Update Stock** command is clicked:

```
switch (event.itemId) {
      case 'UPDATE_STOCK_COMMAND':
        const selectedRows = this.context.listView.selectedRows;
        const selectedRow = selectedRows[0];
        const productId = selectedRow.getValueByName('ID');
        const productStockLevel = selectedRow.
getValueByName('packtProductStockLevel');

        // Update the stock level of the selected product
        const powerAutomateUrl = this.properties.powerAutomateUrl;
        const powerAutomatePayload = {
          id: productId,
          stockLevel: productStockLevel
        };

        this._httpService.post(powerAutomateUrl, powerAutomatePayload)
          .then(() => {
            Dialog.alert(`${this.properties.stockUpdatedMessage}`);
          })
          .catch((error) => {
            Dialog.alert(`Error updating stock level: ${error}`);
```

```
        });
    }
```

Update `packtProductListViewCommandSet` in `cofig/serve.json` with example properties as shown in the following code block:

```
"packtProductListViewCommandSet": {
    "pageUrl": "https://yourtenantname.sharepoint.com/sites/Packt/
Lists/Products/AllItems.aspx",
    "customActions": {
      "2ba4a965-53bb-43d2-8dbc-55f7ae344a95": {
        "location": "ClientSideExtension.ListViewCommandSet.
CommandBar",
        "properties": {
          "lowStockThreshold": 10,
          "stockUpdatedMessage": "Stock updated successfully",
          "powerAutomateUrl": "https://prod-00.westus.logic.azure.
com/workflows/your-flow-id/triggers/manual/paths/invoke"
        }
      }
    }
  }
```

Run the following command from the command line to open the browser and load the ListView Command Set:

```
gulp serve --config=packtProductListViewCommandSet
```

Once the subtask reload is finished, reload the page, and select an item with a **Stock Level** value of less than **10**.

The **Update Stock** command shows up, and clicking on that should call the Power Automate flow.

Figure 12.4 – Update stock ListView Command Set

In this section, we saw how to update the ListView Command Set's `onInit` and `onExecute` methods to call an HTTP endpoint based on a condition – which, in this case, was when **Stock Level** is less than **10**.

Summary

In this chapter, we were able to understand the details of an SPFx extension called a ListView Command Set. We started by understanding what a ListView Command Set is, its needs, and its uses. Then, we moved on to creating a ListView Command Set using SPFx, understanding its different life cycle methods and how the ListView Command Set is rendered.

After that, we looked into updating the behavior of a ListView Command Set by updating the code in the `onInit()` and `onExecute()` methods to render the command based on a condition and to call an HTTP endpoint.

In the next chapter, we will look at another extension, called "Search Query Modifier."

13

Building a Search Query Modifier

In the previous chapter, we saw how to create a ListView Command Set (one of the multiple elements that we can create with SPFx) – a component that allows us to add custom menu options to the command bar or context menu of SharePoint items. We made that component visible only for those products that were low in stock and provided a command that would help the user place a new order. In this chapter, we will move away from the theme of low stock and switch the context to searching for products. For that, we will look into a search-related element of SPFx called **Search Query Modifier**.

Some of the concepts in this chapter will be similar to, or in line with, the concepts mentioned in the previous chapters on Web Parts. In this chapter, you will do the following:

- Learn how to create a Search Query Modifier from scratch using SPFx to meet functional requirements
- Understand the Search Query Modifier development flow using SPFx-provided lifecycle methods
- Use Microsoft Graph to filter SharePoint list items using a modified search query

Technical requirements

This chapter relies on the GitHub solution accessible here: `https://github.com/PacktPublishing/Mastering-SharePoint-Development-with-the-SharePoint-Framework-/tree/chapter13/build-a-seach-query-modifier`. Similar to the earlier chapters, you need to first clone the repository locally on your machine to be able to follow the steps. As the solution is built step by step, for each section in this chapter, a dedicated Git branch has been created, representing the solution at a specific state corresponding to a section. Before reading each section, you must check out the corresponding branch before using either the Git command line or a Git client such as GitHub Desktop, SourceTree, and so on.

> **Code snippets**
>
> For brevity and readability considerations, only the relevant parts of the code are detailed in the provided snippets in this chapter. For this reason, ad hoc code, such as importing dependencies, and updates to certain files may be omitted. We recommend having the GitHub solution open to get the full working version of the code and review the steps provided.

The branch name to refer to and additional instructions are indicated at the beginning of each section. Here is a summary of Git branches to check out per section:

Section in this chapter	Git branch to check out
Building a Search Query Modifier	`https://github.com/PacktPublishing/Mastering-SharePoint-Development-with-the-SharePoint-Framework-/tree/chapter13/build-a-seach-query-modifier`
Updating the Search Query Modifier to use the filtered search query	`https://github.com/PacktPublishing/Mastering-SharePoint-Development-with-the-SharePoint-Framework-/tree/chapter13/update-search-query-modifier`

What is a Search Query Modifier?

An SPFx Search Query Modifier is a type of SPFx extension that allows developers to modify the search queries executed in SharePoint before they are processed by the search engine (or custom search functions). It enables the customization of search behavior by refining/altering queries dynamically based on business requirements.

Why is it needed?

Out-of-the-box SharePoint search functionality is powerful but may not always meet specific organizational requirements. The default search queries might return too many or too few results. They *might* lack filtering or may not boost relevant content effectively, based on the requirement. (Note that there is no criticism of SharePoint search here – it is only to emphasize the custom requirement.)

Using an SPFx Search Query Modifier, organizations can do the following:

- **Improve search relevance**: Modify queries to prioritize certain content, such as recently modified documents or high-priority items
- **Apply business rules**: Dynamically filter or boost results based on metadata of the items, or roles of users

- **Enhance user experience**: Adjust queries to ensure users find the most useful results quickly without modifying search settings manually

- **Integrate with external systems**: Modify queries to include results from organization-integrated data sources or APIs.

Simple examples

Let's look at a couple of examples to illustrate the use of a Search Query Modifier:

Example 1: Filtering search results by department

Scenario: An organization wants to ensure employees see search results relevant to their department.

Solution: The Search Query Modifier automatically appends a filter such as `Department:HR` when an HR employee performs a search, ensuring results are specific to the HR department.

Example 2: Prioritizing recently modified documents

Scenario: Let's presume that users often need the most up-to-date documents first.

Solution: The Search Query Modifier boosts results with a higher ranking for documents modified within the last 30 days.

Now that we have understood what a Search Query Modifier is and what it's used for, let's start building one.

Building a Search Query Modifier

> **Git branch**
>
> This section uses the `https://github.com/PacktPublishing/Mastering-SharePoint-Development-with-the-SharePoint-Framework-/tree/chapter13/build-a-seach-query-modifier` Git branch from the repository.

For this chapter, we will create a Search Query Modifier as per the details mentioned in the *Requirement 6: Searching for a product from a site* section in *Chapter 4, Packt Product Management Solution: A Practical Use Case*, which will allow users to search a product(s) by the product reference value using the site search box at the top of the page.

Prerequisites

Before creating a Search Query Modifier, we need to make a few updates to the SharePoint site.

Page for search results

We need to create a page that will be used to show the search results. By default, when a user enters a query in the top search box of a SharePoint site, the user is redirected to the out-of-the-box search results page, which is the same for all the sites in a tenant. For the search query modifier, we cannot use that page. Instead, we need to create a custom page at the site level and use that page to show the search results:

1. First, create an empty page on the site.

2. Once that is done, we need to change its layout to **HeaderlessSearchResults** (this is for reduced header content in the page) because that is the only layout supported for pages associated as custom search result pages.

3. We use PnP PowerShell (which we used in *Chapter 8, Deploying a SharePoint Web Part*) to set the page layout:

```
Set-PnPPage -Identity "<Page Name>" -LayoutType
HeaderlessSearchResults
```

> **Note**
>
> After running the preceding command, the page will not load correctly. This is because we need to set the page as a search results page, which we will be doing in the following section.

4. Replace < Page Name > with the name of the custom page created earlier.

Update the search results page of the site

After creating the custom page, the next step is to update the settings of the site such that search results are sent to that page:

1. Navigate to the Packt site's **Site Settings** option and select **Search Settings** under **Site Collection Administration**.

Site Collection Administration
Recycle bin
Search Result Sources
Search Result Types
Search Query Rules
Search Schema
Search Settings
Search Configuration Import
Search Configuration Export

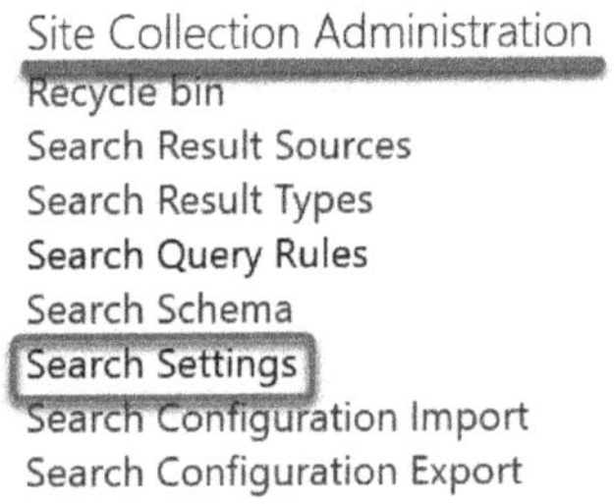

Figure 13.1 – Navigating to Search Settings

2. On the **Search Settings** page, update **Results page URL** to point to the custom page that we created earlier.

Which search results page should queries be sent to?

Custom results page URLs can be relative or absolute.

URLs can also include special tokens, such as {SearchCenterURL}. This token will be replaced by the value in the "Search Center URL" property. If the value in this property ever changes, any URL using the token will update automatically.

Example:
{SearchCenterURL}/results.aspx

☐ Use the same results page settings as my parent.
◉ Send queries to a custom results page URL.
Results page URL:

/sites/Packt/SitePages/SQM.aspx

Example: /SearchCenter/Pages/results.aspx or
http://server/sites/SearchCenter/Pages/results.aspx

◯ Turn on the drop-down menu inside the search box, and use the first Search Navigation node as the destination results page.

OK   Cancel

Figure 13.2 – Setting the custom results page URL

> **Note**
>
> This can also be done using PnP PowerShell with the `Set-PnPSearchSettings` command.

That concludes the prerequisites, and now we can start building a Search Query Modifier.

Adding a Search Query Modifier to the solution

From the existing `Packt.Solutions.ProductManagement` folder, run the following command:

```
yo @microsoft/sharepoint --component-type "extension"
--extension-type " SearchQueryModifier" --component-name "
PacktProductSearchQueryModifier" --framework "none" --environment
"spo" --package-manager "npm" --skip-feature-deployment
```

> **Note on similarity and Component ID**
>
> The parameters are similar to a command that we have seen in previous chapters on extensions, with some minor tweaks.
>
> Notice the value of `Id` key present in the `config/serve.json` file and in the `PacktProductSearchQueryModifierSearchQueryModifier.manifest.json` file. It will have the same value, which will be unique and represents the Search Query Modifier you created. This ID will be used in the future, during deployment.

It has been observed that using the debug URL to test the Search Query Modifier doesn't load the code in the page. Hence, we need to add the Search Query Modifier to the site and then use the debug URL. To do that, run the following command:

```
Add-PnPCustomAction -Title "PacktProductSearchQueryModifier" -Name
"PacktProductSearchQueryModifier" -Location "ClientSideExtension.
SearchQueryModifier" -ClientSideComponentId "<Component Id>"
```

Replace `<Component Id>` with the value of Id from `PacktProductSearchQuery ModifierSearchQueryModifier.manifest.json`.

This command will add a custom action to the site and get rendered. The custom action in this case is the Search Query Modifier.

> **Note**
>
> To learn more about custom actions, see `https://learn.microsoft.com/en-us/sharepoint/dev/spfx/extensions/guidance/migrate-from-usercustomactions-to-spfx-extensions`.

Initial render check

> **Commit reference**
>
> Please refer to the commit at `https://github.com/PacktPublishing/Mastering-SharePoint-Development-with-the-SharePoint-Framework-/commit/025f6cff8629fb9cb019dc91191f645d043ad728` for this section.

Let's now look at how the Search Query Modifier is rendered as is with some minor logging:

1. Add a logging statement in the `PacktProductSearchQueryModifierSearch QueryModifier.ts` file's `onInit` method as follows:

```
public onInit(): Promise<void> {
    console.log(`Initialized
PacktProductSearchQueryModifierSearchQueryModifier`);
    return Promise.resolve();
}
```

2. From the command line, run the following command:

```
gulp serve
```

This will open the browser and load the Search Query Modifier.

It may take a few minutes for the code build. Once you see that the subtask reload is finished in the command line, the code will be ready to be tested in the browser.

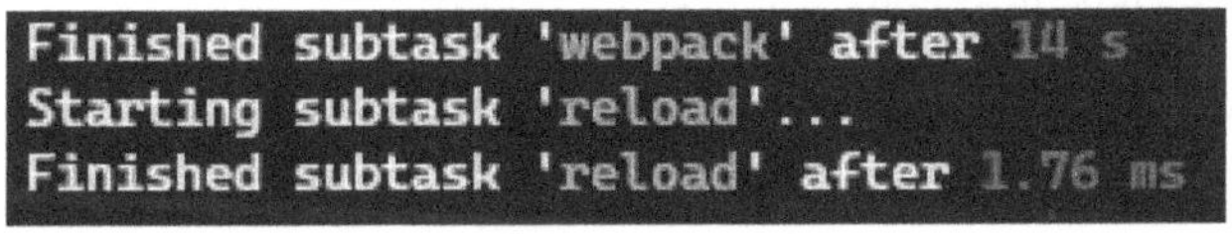

Figure 13.3 – Verification of reload subtask complete in the command line

3.   In the same tab, navigate to the custom page for search results created earlier. Open the browser developer tools, type a query in the search box at the top, and hit *Enter*. This will log a message in the browser console.

Figure 13.4 – Message logged in the browser console

If you want to test this in a different tab, then do the following:

1.   Navigate to the custom page for search results created earlier.

2.   Append the following to the URL: `?loadSPFX=true&debugManifestsFile=https://localhost:4321/temp/manifests.js`

3.   Reload the page.

4.   Open the browser developer tools.

5.   Type a query in the search box at the top and hit *Enter*. This will log a message in the browser console.

With this, we can confirm that the Search Query Modifier is loading on the site.

Lifecycle methods

There are two methods associated with a Search Query Modifier, which can be seen in the `PacktProductSearchQueryModifierSearchQueryModifier.ts` file:

- `onInit`: This method initializes the Search Query Modifier by setting up dependencies or configurations.

- `modifySearchQuery`: This method modifies the user's search query before it is executed by SharePoint. It has a parameter called `query` of the type `IQuery` that has a property called `queryText`, which is the one we will need to modify.

Next, we will take a look at how to modify the code to update the search query to meet the requirement.

Updating the Search Query Modifier

> **Git branch**
>
> This section uses the `https://github.com/PacktPublishing/Mastering-SharePoint-Development-with-the-SharePoint-Framework-/tree/chapter13/update-search-query-modifier` Git branch from the repository.

In this section, we will see how to update the search query with the Search Query Modifier so that we can achieve the business requirement mentioned in *Requirement 6: searching for a product from site* of *Chapter 4*. The search query needs to be updated in such a way that the search term entered by the user points to the product reference.

In an ideal scenario, we would want to use the modified query in a Web Part that uses the SharePoint Search API to return results. Since we are not using the SharePoint search API in this book, we will use the Products Catalog Web Part as the search results Web Part, such that it filters the results (products) based on the modified query.

In this case, the Web Part should show products whose product reference matches or begins with the term that the user has entered in the search box. For example, if the user types UB-001 in the search box, then the Products Catalog Web Part should show the products with a reference number of UB-001.

From the code in *Chapter 5*, *Building a SharePoint Web Part*, and *Chapter 7*, *Connecting to Other Web Parts*, we know that the Web Part will not know that the term entered in the search box is a product reference; all it can do is filter products based on the search term. If the search term explicitly specifies the reference (e.g., `startswith(fields/packtProductReference, 'UB-001')`), then the Web Part filters products based on the reference. However, an end user will not know the syntax to filter. All end users will know is a product reference. Hence, we need to modify an end user's query such that it becomes the product reference filter query. This is where the Search Query Modifier comes into action and modifies the user's search term (for example, UB-001) to a product reference filter query (e.g., `startswith(fields/packtProductReference, 'UB-001')`).

Updating the code of the Search Query Modifier is very simple in this case. The `modifySearchQuery` property needs to be updated as follows:

```
public modifySearchQuery(query: IQuery, scenario:
SearchQueryScenario): Promise<IQuery> {
    query.queryText = `startswith(fields/packtProductReference,
'${query.queryText}')`;
```

```
        console.log(`Modified query: ${query.queryText}`);
        return Promise.resolve(query);
}
```

In the preceding code, `query.queryText` is being updated to `startswith(fields/packtProductReference, '${query.queryText}')`. So, when the user enters `UB-001`, the updated `queryText` will be `startswith(fields/packtProductReference, 'UB-001')`.

Custom search results page updates

To test the updated code, navigate to the page created for search results in the earlier *Prerequisites* sub-section, edit the page, and add the `Packt - Product Catalog` Web Part.

Update the settings of the Web Part as per *Figure 13.5*, to the following:

- Toggle on the **Use a dynamic search box** option
- Select **Page environment** as the search query source
- Select **Search** for **Page environment's properties**
- Select **Search query** for **Search's properties**

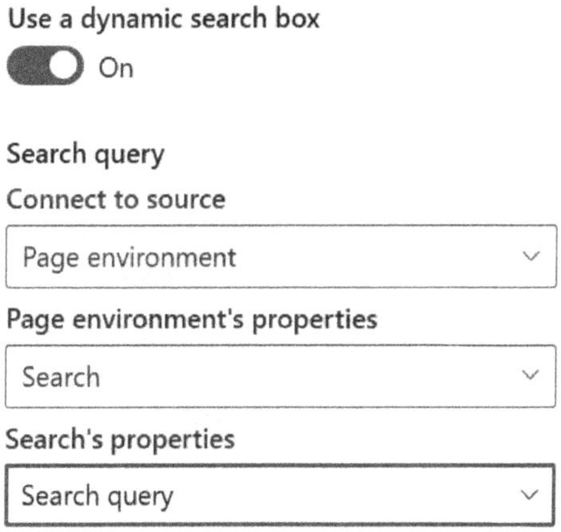

Use a dynamic search box

⬤ On

Search query
Connect to source

Page environment ⌄

Page environment's properties

Search ⌄

Search's properties

Search query ⌄

Figure 13.5 – Search properties of the Product Catalog Web Part

These settings will ensure that the Web Part behaves as per the search associated with the search box in the top bar.

If you do not see **Page environment** under **Connect to source**, it will be because of the filters of the `PropertyPaneDynamicField` property of the Web Part. So, comment out the filters part so that the search query source will not be filtered:

```
PropertyPaneDynamicField('searchQuery', {
label: strings.PropertyPane.SearchQueryDynamicField/* ,
filters: {
            componentId: Guid.tryParse("c6609154-e547-4c70-957e-
9ec482df52a1")
} */
}),
```

With the preceding code update, **Page environment** can be seen under **Connect to source**.

Using the modified query

> **Commit reference**
>
> Please refer to the commit at `https://github.com/PacktPublishing/ Mastering-SharePoint-Development-with-the-SharePoint-Framework-/ commit/7fa64525bef04bc0877f5d29347e27e3450e177c` for this section.

We need to make some updates to the Web Part code to use the modified search query. Firstly, we need to know if we need to use the query from the page environment's search or not. To do that, we check the "reference" property of the `searchQuery` property and see if it has a certain value:

```
// if useDynamicSearchQuery is true, the searchQuery property will be
a dynamic property
    // and if this.properties.searchQuery.reference is
"PageContext:SearchData:searchQuery" then useSearchQueryModifier will
be true
const useSearchQueryModifier = this.properties.
useDynamicSearchQuery && this.properties.searchQuery.reference ===
"PageContext:SearchData:searchQuery";
```

> **Tip**
>
> In the code, either debug or log the `this.properties.searchQuery` line to see the various values of reference, based on different settings of the Web Part.

Based on the value of useSearchQueryModifier, we update the getItems function in the Web Part so that we pass the modified query:

```
const productItems: IProductCatalogItem[] =
        this.props.useSearchQueryModifier ?
        await this.props.productCatalogService.getProducts(this.props.
siteId, this.props.listName, this.props.itemsCount, undefined, this.
props.searchQuery)
        : await this.props.productCatalogService.getProducts(this.
props.siteId, this.props.listName, this.props.itemsCount, this.props.
searchQuery);
```

With the preceding code, the getProducts function will not use the default filter query that was used in *Chapter 5* and *Chapter 7*. Instead, it will simply use the modified search query that we pass. The following code is the filter snippet in the getProducts function:

```
.filter(searchQuery ? `startswith(fields/packtProductModelName,
'${searchQuery}') or startswith(fields/packtProductColor,
'${searchQuery}') or startswith(fields/packtProductSize,
'${searchQuery}')` : filter ? filter : '')
```

In this case, we are passing undefined as the value of searchQuery and passing the modified search query as the value of filter.

Example flow

Let's clarify the preceding code (i.e., how the Microsoft Graph API is called) with an example:

1. The user types UB-001 in the search box.
2. The Search Query Modifier changes that to startswith(fields/packtProduct Reference, 'UB-001').
3. The Product Catalog Web Part checks if it has been asked to use the Page Environment's search (by checking its properties).
4. Since that is the case, the Web Part calls the getProducts function with the filter as startswith(fields/packtProductReference, 'UB-001').

5. The `getProducts` function then uses the Microsoft Graph API to get all the products based on that filter.

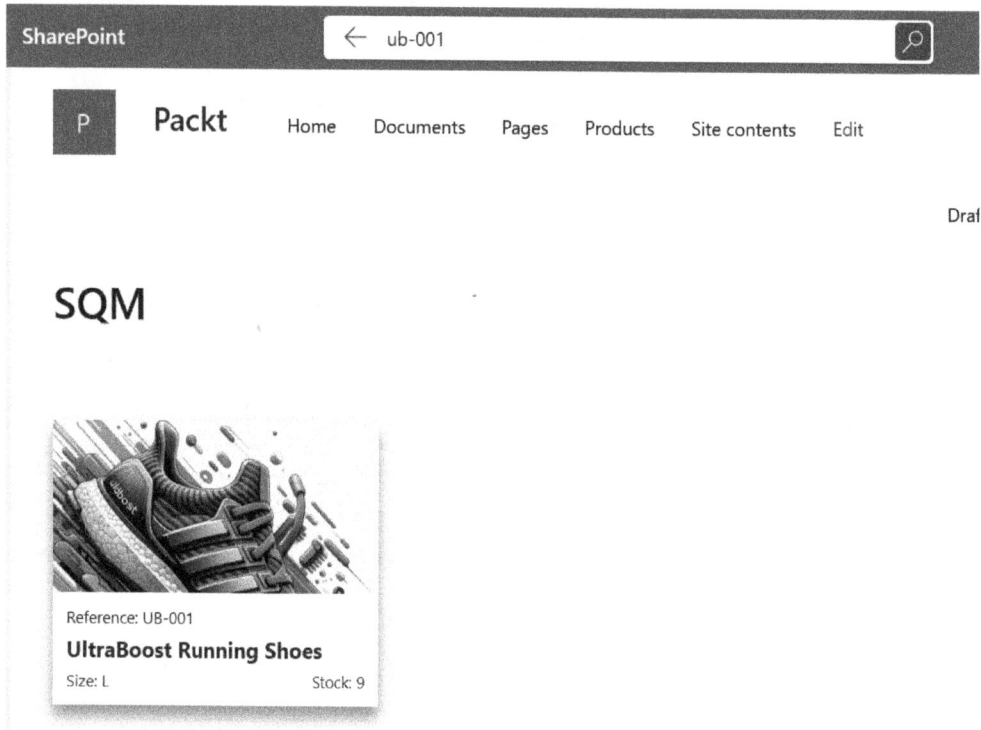

Figure 13.6 – Search Query Modifier in action

From the command line, run the following command:

```
gulp serve
```

This will open the browser and load the Search Query Modifier.

It may take a few minutes for the code to build. Once you see that the subtask reload is finished in the command line, the code will be ready to be tested in the browser.

Figure 13.7 – Verification of reload subtask complete in the command line

In the same tab, or in a new tab, do the following:

1. Navigate to the custom page for search results created earlier.

2. Append the following to the URL: `?loadSPFX=true&debugManifestsFile=https://localhost:4321/temp/manifests.js`.

3. Reload the page.

4. Open the browser developer tools.

5. Type a query in the search box (e.g., `UB-001`) at the top and hit *Enter*.

6. This will load the product with a reference number of *UB-001*.

In this section, we have seen how the user's search query is modified and is used to filter results. The modified query is passed to Microsoft Graph, which ultimately filters the results.

Summary

The Search Query Modifier, as per the name, modifies the user-entered search query, which can then be used to refine the results as per the requirement. It takes away the burden from the end user of modifying the query.

In this chapter, we saw how to create a Search Query Modifier to meet the requirements. We started by understanding what a Search Query Modifier is and what its uses are.

We then created a Search Query Modifier and added it to a site by creating a custom search results page. After understanding the lifecycle methods, we updated our understanding of how to modify the user-entered query and use that modified query in a Web Part, which changed its behavior based on the modified query.

In the next chapter, we will look at the final SPFx extension, which is called an Adaptive Card Extension.

14

Building an Adaptive Card Extension

In the previous chapter, we understood what a search query modifier is (one of the multiple elements we can create with SPFx). We looked into creating a basic one, understood the different lifecycle methods of a search query modifier, and then modified the code such that the query is updated to use product reference as the query text and get the products based on that.

In this chapter, we will shift our attention from SPFx extensions to **Adaptive Card Extensions** (**ACEs**). Before understanding what ACEs are, please familiarize yourself with Viva Connections (https://learn.microsoft.com/en-us/viva/connections/viva-connections-overview). Viva Connections in an organization can be personalized and extended. One way of personalizing or extending Viva Connections is through ACEs, which enable users to view information at a glance or interact with cards. Information surfaced can be from different systems within an organization (e.g., annual leave system, expenses system, and so on) or from external sources. Microsoft provides some ACEs out of the box. We can create our own custom ACEs using SPFx. This chapter focuses on custom ACEs.

Some of the concepts in this chapter will be similar or in line with the concepts mentioned in the previous chapters on web parts and extensions. In this chapter, you will understand the following:

- What ACEs are and how to create an ACE from scratch using SPFx to meet the functional requirement
- The ACE development flow and SPFx-provided lifecycle methods
- How to integrate data in ACE using Microsoft Graph

Technical requirements

This chapter relies on the GitHub solution accessible here: `https://github.com/PacktPublishing/Mastering-SharePoint-Development-with-the-SharePoint-Framework-/tree/chapter14/building-an-ace`. Similar to the earlier chapters, you need to first clone the repository locally on your machine to be able to follow the steps. As the solution is built step by step, for each section in this chapter, a dedicated Git branch has been created representing the solution at a specific state corresponding to a section. Before reading the section, you must check out the corresponding branch before using either the Git command line or a Git client such as GitHub Desktop or Sourcetree.

> **Code snippets**
>
> For brevity and readability considerations, only the relevant parts of the code are detailed in the provided snippets in this chapter. For these reasons, ad-hoc code, such as dependencies, imports, and updates to certain files, may be omitted. We recommend having the GitHub solution open alongside to get the full working version of the code and review the provided steps.

The branch name to refer to and additional instructions are indicated at the beginning of each section. Here is a summary of Git branches to check per section:

Section in this chapter	Git branch to checkout
Building an ACE	`https://github.com/PacktPublishing/Mastering-SharePoint-Development-with-the-SharePoint-Framework-/tree/chapter14/building-an-ace`
Updating the ACE	`https://github.com/PacktPublishing/Mastering-SharePoint-Development-with-the-SharePoint-Framework-/tree/chapter14/updating-an-ace`

What is an SPFx ACE?

An SPFx ACE is a component in the SPFx that allows us developers to create custom cards for Microsoft Viva Connections dashboards. These cards use the Adaptive Cards framework to provide interactive and visually appealing user experiences, delivering key information and actions directly to users.

> **Note**
>
> In the later versions of SPFx (beyond 1.19.0), these cards use custom HTML as well. Hence, custom HTML will be a second option along with the Adaptive Card framework to render the ACEs.

Why is it needed?

SPFx ACEs are essential for enhancing the functionality and user experience of Microsoft Viva Connections. Out-of-the-box cards are limited in functionality and customization and sometimes may not meet the organizational requirements. That is where ACEs come into the picture and enable us to customize the content, layout, and actions of cards to meet specific organizational needs.

By using ACEs, organizations can do the following:

- Deliver actionable insights and quick links to users in a personalized way

- Integrate with internal or external systems to display real-time data

- Streamline workflows by embedding key actions directly in the dashboard

Uses of an SPFx ACE

An SPFx ACE can be used for various purposes, including the following:

- **Displaying key metrics**: Show real-time metrics such as sales numbers, project statuses, or key performance indicators

- **Quick actions**: Provide buttons for users to perform actions, such as submitting reports or approving requests

- **Personalized content**: Display user-specific content such as personalized tasks, notifications, or recommendations

- **Integration with other systems**: Pull data from external APIs or internal systems and display it in a visually pleasing way

Key features of SPFx ACEs

ACEs have two card views (we will cover these in detail later in this chapter):

- **Card View**: A smaller, summarized view displayed on the dashboard. This is the view that the end users first see when they visit the dashboard.

- **Quick View**: A detailed view that allows for richer content and user interactions. The Quick View will show up by clicking on the Card View or by clicking on a button in the Card View. This is the customizable element of an ACE.

Simple examples

Let's look at a couple of examples to illustrate the use of an SPFx ACE:

- **Example 1 – Sales Dashboard card**:
- **Scenario**: Let's say the requirement is to display a sales summary for the current month, including total revenue and top-performing regions

  - **Solution**: Using ACEs, the Card View can be set up to show a summary (e.g., **Revenue: $1.2M**) and the Quick View can be customized to provide detailed statistics and charts for the user

- **Example 2 – Task Management card**:
- **Scenario**: Let's say we need to provide a personalized card showing the number of pending tasks for the user

  - **Solution**: Using ACEs, the Card View can show the number of tasks (e.g., **You have 5 tasks**) and the Quick View can display a list of tasks with links to take an action for each task

As you can see, using SPFx ACEs, organizations can deliver personalized, actionable, and visually appealing experiences to their users within Microsoft Viva Connections dashboards. With this in mind, let's start building one.

Building an ACE

> **Git branch**
>
> This section uses the `https://github.com/PacktPublishing/Mastering-SharePoint-Development-with-the-SharePoint-Framework-/tree/chapter14/building-an-ace` Git branch from the repository.

For this chapter, we will create an ACE as per the details mentioned in the *Requirement 7: Visualizing products dashboard in Viva Connections* section in *Chapter 4, Packt Product Management Solution: A Practical Use Case*, which will display a simple insight into products by color. The Card View (i.e., the view of the card on the dashboard) will show the number of colors, and the Quick View (i.e., the view that gets displayed on clicking the Card View) will show the stock levels per color.

Adding an ACE to the solution

From the existing `Packt.Solutions.ProductManagement` folder, run the following command:

```
yo @microsoft/sharepoint --component-type "adaptiveCardExtension"
--ace-template-type "Generic"  --component-name
"PacktProductAdaptiveCardExtension" --framework "none" --environment
"spo" --package-manager "npm" --skip-feature-deployment
```

The parameters are similar to the commands that we have seen in previous chapters for web parts and extensions. The parameter that is specific to ACEs is "ace-template-type", which can have the values as "Generic" or "DataVisualization" or "Search". These correspond to different look and feel of the ACE. In this chapter we will cover only the "Generic" card type.

This doesn't create any configurations specific to an ACE in the `config/serve.json` file. So, to debug the ACE, we can use the `gulp serve` command and open the workbench page (as we did for debugging web parts).

Initial render check

> **Commit reference**
>
> Please refer to the `https://github.com/PacktPublishing/Mastering-SharePoint-Development-with-the-SharePoint-Framework-/commit/2b34442c40f2bf4d87bb2880e7e877dd8acb03d3` commit for this section.

Before updating the code to meet the requirement, let's run the ACE to see its default behavior:

1. From the command line, run `gulp serve`. This will open the browser and load the workbench page.

    It may take a few minutes for the code to build. Once you see that the subtask reload is finished in the command line, the code will be ready to be tested in the browser.

Figure 14.1 – Verification of reload subtask complete in the command line

2. On the workbench page, click on the **Add** button to see the ACE appearing under the **Local** section.

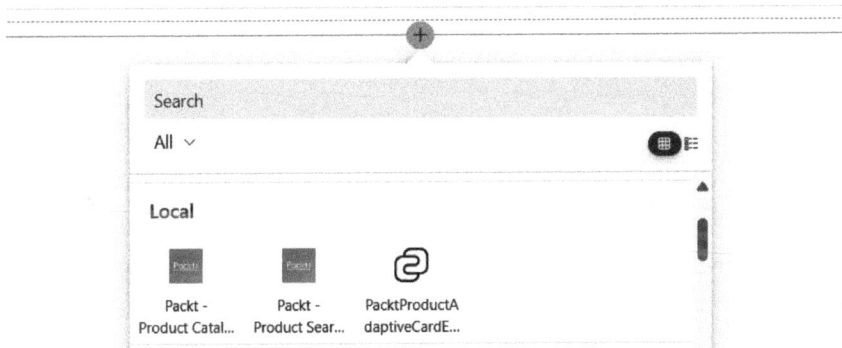

Figure 14.2 – Adding the ACE

3. Select the ACE to add it to the workbench page. Once done, click on **Preview** in the top-left corner to make the workbench page go into preview mode.

The view of the ACE that we see is called the **Card View**, which has the title of the ACE, a primary text, and the **Quick view** button. Clicking on the **Quick view** button opens the **Quick view** window, which shows some basic text.

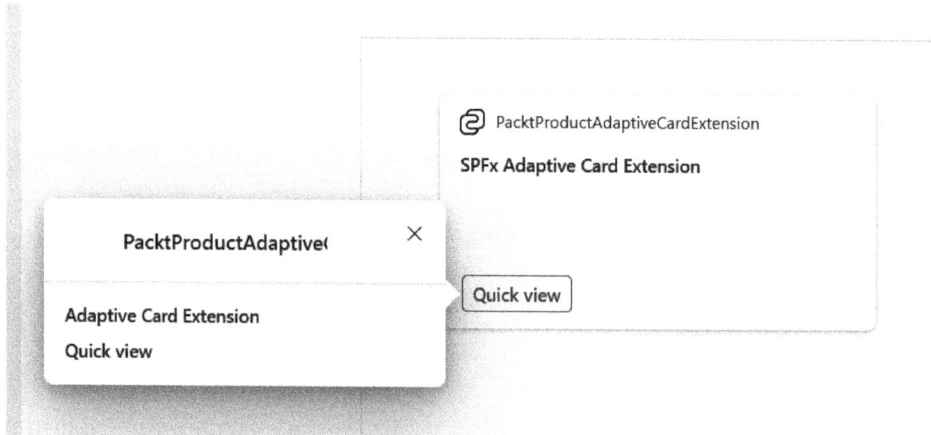

Figure 14.3 – Card view and Quick view of the default ACE

Let's take a look at the Card View and Quick View in detail.

Card View

The Card View that gets rendered in this case is called the basic Card View, which is made up of the following elements:

- Title
- Header (which contains text)
- Footer (which can have one or more buttons)

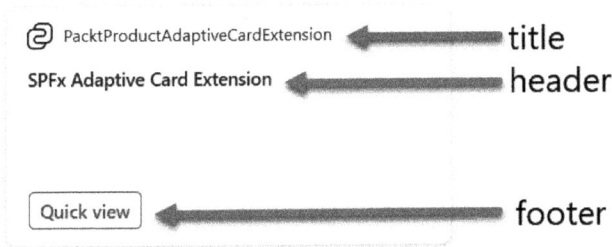

Figure 14.4 – Parts of the basic Card View

This can be seen in the `CardView.ts` file in which the `CardView` class returns an object of the `BasicCardView` type:

```
export class CardView extends BaseComponentsCardView<
  IPacktProductAdaptiveCardExtensionAdaptiveCardExtensionProps,
  IPacktProductAdaptiveCardExtensionAdaptiveCardExtensionState,
  ComponentsCardViewParameters
> {
  public get cardViewParameters(): ComponentsCardViewParameters {
    return BasicCardView({
      cardBar: {
        componentName: 'cardBar',
        title: this.properties.title
      },
      header: {
        componentName: 'text',
        text: strings.PrimaryText
      },
      footer: {
        componentName: 'cardButton',
        title: strings.QuickViewButton,
        action: {
          type: 'QuickView',
          parameters: {
            view: QUICK_VIEW_REGISTRY_ID
          }
        }
      }
    });
  }
}
```

Microsoft offers other types of card views that can be used based on the following requirements:

- Image card view

- Primary text card view

- Text input card view

The level of customization (of UI elements) is restricted in the Card View. Hence, it is up to us which Card View to choose based on the information we want to display.

Quick View

The Quick View is the part of an ACE in which we have full control of the customization. Quick View uses adaptive cards to render.

> **Note**
>
> From SPFx 1.20 onward, HTML or any framework such as React can be used to render the quick view as another option.

The code for the Quick View will be present in the `QuickView.ts` file and the UI aspect of the Quick View will be in the `template/QuickViewTemplate.json` file.

The data for the Quick View will be set in the `.ts` file and the `.json` file will have the Adaptive Card JSON, which has special slots to display the data.

In the following example, the `title` and `subTitle` properties are being set in the `QuickView. ts` file and the `template()` method specifies which JSON file to use to render the data:

```
public get data(): IQuickViewData {
    return {
      subTitle: strings.SubTitle,
      title: strings.Title
    };
  }


public get template(): ISPFxAdaptiveCard {
    return require('./template/QuickViewTemplate.json');
  }
```

That data (`title` and `subTitle`) will be rendered using special slots in the `template/QuickViewTemplate.json` file:

```
{
     "type": "TextBlock",
```

```
        "weight": "Bolder",
        "text": "${title}"
    },
    {

        "type": "TextBlock",
        "weight": "Bolder",
        "text": "${subTitle}"

    }
```

SharePoint combines these files to render the view when we see the ACE on a page.

These views need to be registered for them to be displayed in the ACE. That registration process happens in the main file of the ACE, which, in this case, is PacktProductAdaptiveCardExtensionAdaptiveCardExtension.ts.

Here, the main class extends from BaseAdaptiveCardExtension (provided by SPFx) in which the onInit method has the code to run when the ACE initializes and the code for registering the views:

```
this.cardNavigator.register(CARD_VIEW_REGISTRY_ID, () => new
CardView());
this.quickViewNavigator.register(QUICK_VIEW_REGISTRY_ID, () => new
QuickView());
```

With the basic knowledge of Card View and Quick View, let's move on to understanding how the data flows in an ACE.

Data flow

ACEs are made up of properties and states, which are responsible for holding the data needed to be displayed.

Properties are used to define static configuration settings that are managed at design time (e.g., in the **Property** pane). They are typically set once and do not change during the lifetime of the ACE. They are used for *static values* such as labels, titles, and so on.

State in an ACE is used to define *dynamic data* that changes during the lifetime of the ACE. It allows the ACE to update dynamically based on user actions, data fetching, or other events. The state is used to get runtime data such as API responses.

Properties and states are shared across the entire ACE (i.e., Card View and Quick View).

An example data flow might be the following:

1. API endpoints that need to be called are obtained from properties.

2. Data is obtained from APIs after the ACE is initialized.

3. After that, the state is updated with the data.

4. Card View and Quick View make use of the data in the state and/or properties to display the relevant information.

With this, we've seen how to build an ACE. In the next section, we will see how to get the product data using Microsoft Graph and set that in the state, so that this data can be displayed in the Card View and Quick View.

Updating the ACE

> **Git Branch and commit reference**
>
> This section uses the `https://github.com/PacktPublishing/Mastering-SharePoint-Development-with-the-SharePoint-Framework-/tree/chapter14/updating-an-ace` Git branch from the repository.
>
> Please refer to the `https://github.com/PacktPublishing/Mastering-SharePoint-Development-with-the-SharePoint-Framework-/commit/e4796eaef4d126cbd46c7c463823b85581ee62a4` commit for this section.

In this section, we will see how to update the ACE to meet the requirements (showing the product stock by color). This is done as per the following steps:

1. After the ACE initializes, we will use the `Products` service to get all the products from the product list (by getting the name of the list from the properties).

2. Format the data such that they are grouped by color and have stock against each color.

3. Store this data in the state.

4. Utilize the data in the state to show the Quick View.

Let's start by looking into the state of the ACE.

State

We create a state for the ACE to store the products by color and their stock:

```
export interface IProductStock {
  color: string;
  stock: number;
}
export interface
IPacktProductAdaptiveCardExtensionAdaptiveCardExtensionState {
  productStocks: IProductStock[];
}
```

The `state` object will be populated later. Let's now look into the ACE properties.

Properties

We add a new property to get the name of the products list (the same as getting data from the **Property** pane, which we saw in *Chapter 5, Building a SharePoint Web Part*):

```
export interface
IPacktProductAdaptiveCardExtensionAdaptiveCardExtensionProps {
  title: string;
  productsListName: string;
}
```

Getting data

As part of the `onInit` function, the `ProductCatalogService` class is initialized. After this, we need to call methods which call APIs to get the needed data:

```
public async onInit(): Promise<void> {
    this.state = {
      productStocks: []
    };
    this._msGraphClient = await this.context.msGraphClientFactory.
getClient(
      "3"
    );
    this._productCatalogService = new ProductCatalogService(this._
msGraphClient);
    await this.loadProductStocks();
    return Promise.resolve();
  }
```

In the case of an ACE, the calling of the service methods needs to happen as part of `onInit`. Hence, we call the `loadProductStocks` function, which will use the `ProductCatalogService` class to get the products. All this is done asynchronously.

Once the products are obtained, they are grouped by color, and the state is set accordingly:

```
private async loadProductStocks(): Promise<void> {
    const products = await this._productCatalogService.getProducts(
      this.context.pageContext.site.id.toString(),
      this.properties.productsListName
    )
```

```
const allProductStocks = products.map(product => {
  return {
    color: product.itemColour,
    stock: product.stockLevel
  };
});

// if the productStocks array has colors with the same name,
then sum the stock levels use groupBy
const groupedProductStocks = groupBy(allProductStocks, 'color');
const productStocksResult: IProductStock[] = [];

for (const color in groupedProductStocks) {
  const stock = groupedProductStocks[color].reduce((acc,
productStock) => acc + productStock.stock, 0);
  productStocksResult.push({
    color: color,
    stock: stock
  });
}

this.setState({
  productStocks: productStocksResult
});
}
```

Now that we have retrieved the data, let's bind it where needed.

Binding data in the quick view

> **Commit reference**
>
> Please refer to the https://github.com/PacktPublishing/Mastering-SharePoint-Development-with-the-SharePoint-Framework-/commit/f761b747114e9e8c2f4b1c0c06fb1295b09a97e1 commit for this subsection.

Once the data is present in the state, it needs to be utilized in the Quick View. The Quick View's data can be set to that as in the state (in this case, it is an array of products by color and their stock). In complex scenarios, only the relevant data from the state can be extracted and set as the data for Quick View:

```
public get data(): IQuickViewData {
    const { productStocks } = this.state;
    return {
```

```
        productStocks
    };
}
```

In the corresponding JSON file of the Quick View that renders the Adaptive Card, we update it such that it displays the color and stock information in columns.

Since the data of Quick View is set as the productsStocks type, we make use of that in the JSON file and set $data to that. With that, the Adaptive Card knows that it needs to loop through the productStocks type.

For each item in the state, we use an **Scalable Vector Graphics (SVG)** square to represent its color, setting the square's fill value to match the color value stored in the state. Next to the square, we display the corresponding stock value from the state:

```
{
...
    "body": [
        {
            "type": "ColumnSet",
            "columns": [
                {
                    "$data": "${productStocks}",
                    "type": "Column",
                    "width": "auto",
                    "verticalContentAlignment": "bottom",
                    "items": [
                        {
                            "type": "Image",
                            "url": "data:image/svg+xml,...
fill=${color}...",
                            "size": "small"
                        },
                        {
                            "type": "TextBlock",
                            "text": "${formatNumber(stock, 0)}",
                            "horizontalAlignment": "left"
                        }
                    ]
                }
            ]
        }
    ]
}
```

Running the `gulp serve` command from the command line will open the browser with the workbench page. Once the subtask reload is finished, reload the page and add the ACE.

Put the workbench in preview mode. Opening **Quick View** will display the products by color with stock.

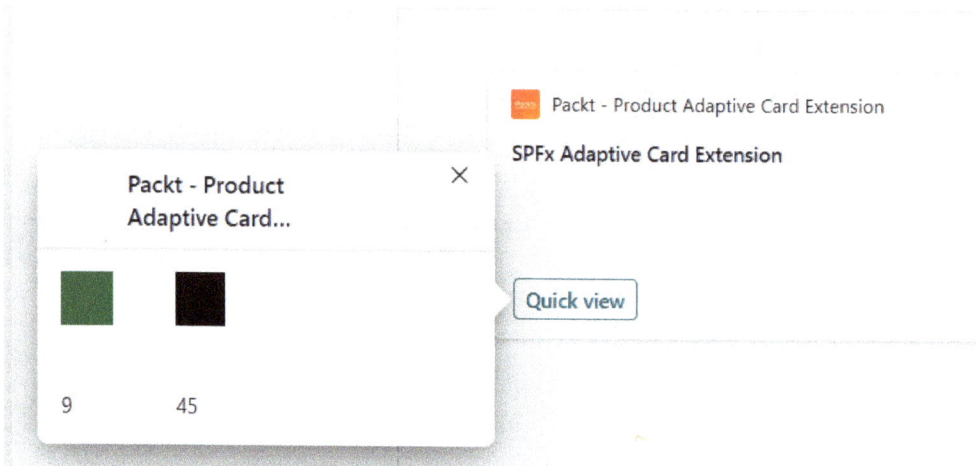

Figure 14.5 – The ACE showing products by color with stock

Please note that the information displayed in the preceding figure might be different from what you see.

> **Tip**
>
> Try updating the data in the products list to make the colors of a couple of products the same.
>
> Try updating the code in the Card View to make use of information in the state to display the number of colors.

Summary

In this chapter, we were able to understand the details of an SPFx ACE. We started by understanding what an ACE is – a component of SPFx that allows us to create custom cards for Microsoft Viva Connections dashboards. We then looked into how to create an ACE using SPFx and understood the different views of an ACE (Card View and Quick View). After this, we understood the properties and state of an ACE, which are used to handle the data flow in an ACE. We then updated the ACE to get the data using the Microsoft Graph API, set that in the state, and changed the Quick View to display the information in the state.

In the next chapter, we will look at information on deploying the extensions, which is on similar lines to deploying web parts.

Get This Book's PDF Version and Exclusive Extras

UNLOCK NOW

Scan the QR code (or go to packtpub.com/unlock). Search for this book by name, confirm the edition, and then follow the steps on the page.

Note: Keep your invoice handy. Purchases made directly from Packt don't require an invoice.

15

Deploying Extensions

In the previous chapter, we learned about **Adaptive Card Extensions** (**ACEs**) – one of the multiple elements we can create using SPFx. We understood what they are (custom cards for the Microsoft **Viva Connections** dashboard) and then saw how to create one from scratch. We looked into the different views of an ACE (card view and quick view) and then looked into the properties and state of an ACE and what role they play in rendering the data of an ACE. We then concluded the chapter by creating an ACE that showed the products grouped by color, along with the number in stock for those.

That was the last chapter showing the various elements of SPFx. Until now, as part of SPFx extensions, we have seen the following:

- Form customizer (*Chapter 9*)

- Application Customizer (*Chapter 10*)

- Field Customizer (*Chapter 11*)

- ListView Command Set (*Chapter 12*)

- Search Query modifier (*Chapter 13*)

- ACEs (*Chapter 14*)

In this chapter, we will understand how we package these elements and deploy them. Before proceeding, please make sure to quickly re-read *Chapter 8, Deploying a SharePoint Web Part*. The knowledge of the concepts covered in that chapter is essential to get the most out of this chapter. In this chapter, you will learn about the following:

- How to package the extensions

- The scopes of deployments for SPFx extensions – tenant scope and site collection scope

- How we can use PnP PowerShell and CLI for Microsoft 365 to deploy extensions

Technical requirements

This chapter relies on the GitHub solution accessible here: `https://github.com/PacktPublishing/Mastering-SharePoint-Development-with-the-SharePoint-Framework-/tree/chapter15/deploying-extensions`. Similar to the earlier chapters, you need to first clone the repository locally on your machine to be able to follow the steps.

Packaging solution with extensions

In *Chapter 8*, we saw how to package a solution. At that point, the solution only contained web parts within it. From *Chapter 9*, *Building a Form customizer*, to *Chapter 14*, *Building a SharePoint Adaptive Card Extension*, we have added more elements to the solution, which are mainly extensions. So now, the next step is to package these elements into the solution as well so that we can deploy them and use them in the site(s). The commands to build and package the solution remain the same as in *Chapter 8*. Those commands are as follows:

- `gulp bundle --ship`
- `gulp package-solution --ship`

Running these commands will create the solution package (the `.sppkg` file) that will be used for deployment.

Scope of deployment for extensions

As explained in *Chapter 8*, SPFx packages can be deployed at two levels – tenant level and site collection level.

Tenant-level scope

The meaning of the tenant-level scope is that when a package is deployed at the tenant level and is enabled to be available across all the sites within a tenant immediately, all the elements in that package can be accessed immediately across all the sites.

Now, in our package, all the elements in the solution, which now includes all the SPFx extensions we have created, also get packaged. When we deploy this package at the tenant level and enable it, the expectation is that all the SPFx extensions will be available immediately. However, that is not the case for extensions. Only the Application Customizer and ListView Command Set are available immediately for use. The rest of the extensions need to be added via scripts to the site(s) where we need them.

With respect to ACEs, in the SPFx world, they are not considered as SPFx extensions. The availability of ACEs on the dashboard is similar to that of the web part. We will look into the deployment of ACEs in a separate section later.

Site collection-level scope

When the package is deployed to the site collection app catalog and is enabled to be available immediately, the pattern of availability of extensions for use is similar to the tenant-level scope (i.e., the Application Customizer and ListView Command Set are available immediately for use in that particular site where the package is added). The rest of the extensions need to be added via scripts to the site. More information related to this can be found at `https://learn.microsoft.com/en-us/sharepoint/dev/general-development/site-collection-app-catalog`.

The skipFeatureDeployment property

In the `package-solution.json` file, we can see a property called `skipFeatureDeployment`. This property gives the option to the admin to decide whether the elements within a solution must be available for use immediately or not.

If this property is set to `true`, then when the solution is deployed, the admin gets an option to enable the solution (app) and add it to all sites. If the admin selects that, then the elements within the solution are available immediately for use.

App availability

This app contains an organization-wide extension. To make sure all features in the app work as designed, add the app to all sites.

◯ Only enable this app
    Selecting this option makes the app available for site owners to add from the My apps page. Learn how to add an app to a site

◉ Enable this app and add it to all sites
    Selecting this option adds the app automatically so site owners don't need to.

    ☑ Add to Teams
        This app can be added to Teams. You can add it now as you enable the app or anytime later.

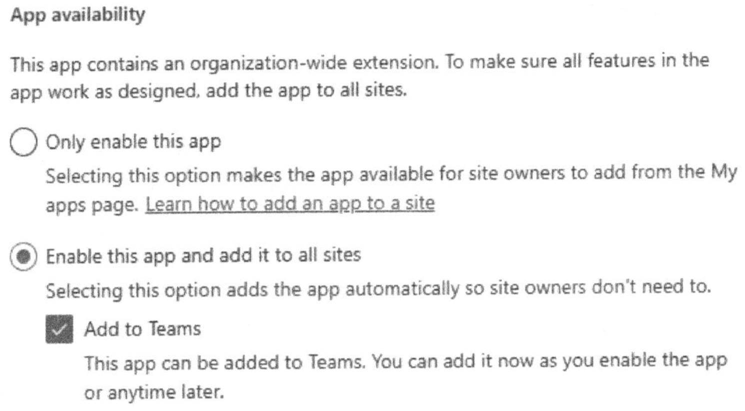

Figure 15.1 – Solution availability

In the case of extensions, as explained in the subsection before, it will be only Application Customizers and ListView Command Set to which this property is applicable.

> **Note**
>
> For more details on this property and its naming origin, please refer to this article: `https://pnp.github.io/blog/post/spfx-05-tenant-or-site-scoped-spfx-solutions/`.

Deploying extensions

When a solution is deployed, be it at the tenant level or at the site collection level, the extensions within that solution are ready to be used. The way they are enabled and their availability for use vary based on the decision made by the admin.

If the admin has decided the extensions should be available immediately, then the Application Customizer and ListView Command Set are available immediately across all the sites in the tenant. This is because of the entries present in the `ClientSideInstance.xml` file.

> **Note**
>
> More details on this file can be found here: `https://learn.microsoft.com/en-us/sharepoint/dev/spfx/extensions/basics/tenant-wide-deployment-extensions#automating-tenant-wide-deployment-from-solution-package`.

If the admin has decided the extensions should not be available immediately, then all the extensions need to be enabled via a script by the admin (or site owner) for the extensions to be used.

If the entries are not present in the `ClientSideInstance.xml` file, then the Application Customizer and ListView Command Set *can* be added to the sites via a script.

Form customizers, Field Customizers, and Search Query modifiers always need to be enabled via scripts by the admin (or site owner).

Usage of scripts during deployment

Throughout this chapter, we will be using scripts for deployment. We have a couple of command-line tool options to run the scripts – **PnP PowerShell** and **CLI for Microsoft 365**.

Both the command-line tools come with a rich set of *cmdlets* related to SPFx extension deployment that simplify the deployment process. Using the scripts with these cmdlets ensures consistency across different environments (e.g., development, UAT, and production), and we can reuse the scripts for uniform deployment. These command-line tools are cross-platform compatible (i.e., they can run on Windows, macOS, and Linux).

With that overview on deployment, let's now look into deploying each of the extensions in the solution one by one, starting with the Application Customizer.

Deploying the Application Customizer

The Application Customizer is one of those SPFx extensions that can be deployed either at the tenant level or at the site collection level. In the SPFx solution that we have, it is configured to be deployed at the tenant level.

When the `.sppkg` file (`packt-solutions-product-management.sppkg`) is added to the app catalog site of the tenant and is enabled at the time of deployment, the Application Customizer (in this case, `PacktProductApplicationCustomizer`) gets enabled across all the sites in the tenant. This can be seen by navigating to the Packt site or any other site in the tenant.

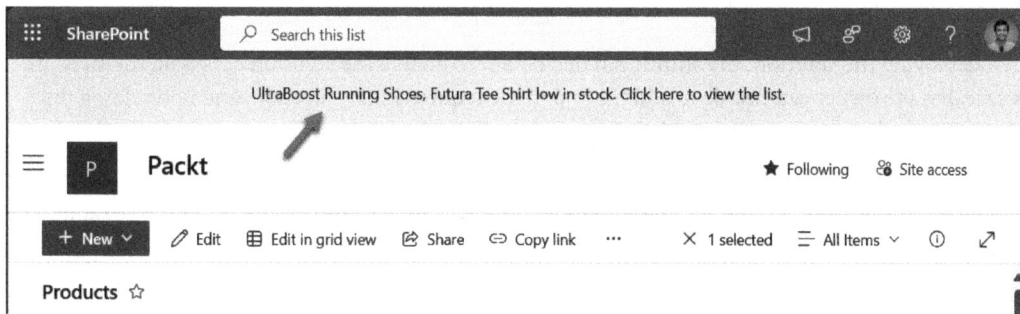

Figure 15.2 – Packt Application Customizer

As part of the deployment, an entry for the Application Customizer is created in a list called **Tenant Wide Extensions** in the app catalog site. This list contains the entries for the tenant-wide deployed extensions, and the properties of the extensions can be controlled from this list.

> **Note**
>
> More details on this list and its behavior can be found at this link: `https://learn.microsoft.com/en-us/sharepoint/dev/spfx/extensions/basics/tenant-wide-deployment-extensions#controlling-tenant-wide-deployment-from-app-catalog-site-collection`.

In our case, there will be an entry for the Application Customizer as shown in the following figure:

PacktProductApplicationCustomizer	dec4a2b3-564c-430e-b968-70096ca19d6a	{"lowStockThreshold":"10"}	0	ClientSideExtension.ApplicationCustomizer

Figure 15.3 – Application Customizer in the tenant-wide extensions list

We can change the `productsListName` property's value to a different value other than `Products` and see the Application Customizer not loading, as it will not be able to find the list with that name.

If the entry from the list is removed, then after a few minutes, the Application Customizer will not load on the sites.

Decision on scope

Until now, in this section, we have seen that the Application Customizer can be deployed to a tenant and is available across all sites. However, we may not need that. We might need it to be present on only some sites. To do that, we have a couple of options.

When deploying the solution, the admin can decide not to enable the solution across all the sites. In this case, the site owner can decide to add the app to the required site collection, and upon doing that, the Application Customizer gets enabled only on that site collection.

The second option is a separate solution. In our case, we have an Application Customizer as part of the same solution in which web parts and other extensions are present. If needed, a separate SPFx solution can be created containing only the Application Customizer. This solution can then be deployed to the site collection app catalog where the Application Customizer is needed and enabled.

Controlling the behavior using a script

To add the Application Customizer back to the site, we can either add the entry in the **Tenant Wide Extensions** list or we can use a script.

> **CustomActions**
>
> You will see references to `CustomAction` in the following scripts. To understand more about `CustomAction`, make sure to read this article by Microsoft: `https://learn.microsoft.com/en-us/sharepoint/dev/spfx/extensions/guidance/migrate-from-usercustomactions-to-spfx-extensions`.

PnP PowerShell

With the help of PnP PowerShell, we can connect to the site and run the `Add-PnPCustomAction` cmdlet to see the Application Customizer. More details on that cmdlet can be found here: `https://pnp.github.io/powershell/cmdlets/Add-PnPCustomAction.html`. The command in our case will be as follows:

```
Add-PnPCustomAction -Title "PacktProductListApplicationCustomizer"
-Name "PacktProductApplicationCustomizer" -Location
"ClientSideExtension.ApplicationCustomizer" -ClientSideComponentId
dec4a2b3-564c-430e-b968-70096ca19d6a  -ClientSideComponentProperties
"{`"productsListName`":`"Products`"}"
```

Do take a look at the parameters passed to the command, which, as per the name, signify their purpose. `ClientSideComponentId` can be found in the `manifest.json` file of the Application Customizer.

To remove the Application Customizer, the command is `Remove-PnPCustomAction`. More details can be found here: `https://pnp.github.io/powershell/cmdlets/Remove-PnPCustomAction.html`.

CLI for Microsoft 365

Another way to add an Application Customizer is by using the CLI for Microsoft 365: `https://pnp.github.io/cli-microsoft365`. Once set up, the command to run would be as follows:

```
spo customaction add - https://pnp.github.io/cli-microsoft365/cmd/spo/
customaction/customaction-add
```

In our case, the command would be similar to the following:

```
m365 spo customaction add --webUrl https://yourtenant.sharepoint.
com/sites/Packt --title "PacktProductApplicationCustomizer" --name
"PacktProductApplicationCustomizer" --location "ClientSideExtension.
ApplicationCustomizer" --clientSideComponentId dec4a2b3-
564c-430e-b968-70096ca19d6a --clientSideComponentProperties
'{"productsListName":"Products"}'
```

Running this command with the correct web URL will add the Application Customizer to the respective site.

The scripts mentioned here state "custom action." Custom actions in SPFx refer to extensions. So, the scripts used are applicable for all extensions. Based on the value of the parameters, we target the extension that is needed.

Let's look into deploying the ListView Command Set in the next section.

Deploying the ListView Command Set

The procedure to deploy the ListView Command Set is similar to that of an Application Customizer, with respect to the scope of deployment. The behavior can be controlled from the **Tenant Wide Extensions** list.

PnP PowerShell

The PnP PowerShell cmdlet needed for adding a ListView Command Set to a site is `Add-PnPCustomAction`. In our case, the command would be as follows:

```
Add-PnPCustomAction -Title "PacktProductListViewCommandSetCommandSet"
-Name "PacktProductListViewCommandSetCommandSet"
-Location "ClientSideExtension.ListViewCommandSet.
CommandBar" -ClientSideComponentId 2ba4a965-53bb-
```

```
43d2-8dbc-55f7ae344a95  -ClientSideComponentProperties
"{`"lowStockThreshold`":`"5`", `"stockUpdatedMessage`":`"Stock
updated`"}" -RegistrationType List
```

Note that we are setting `lowStockThreshold` to 5 here. So, after running this command, the ListView Command Set will be visible only on selecting those products whose stock value is less than 5.

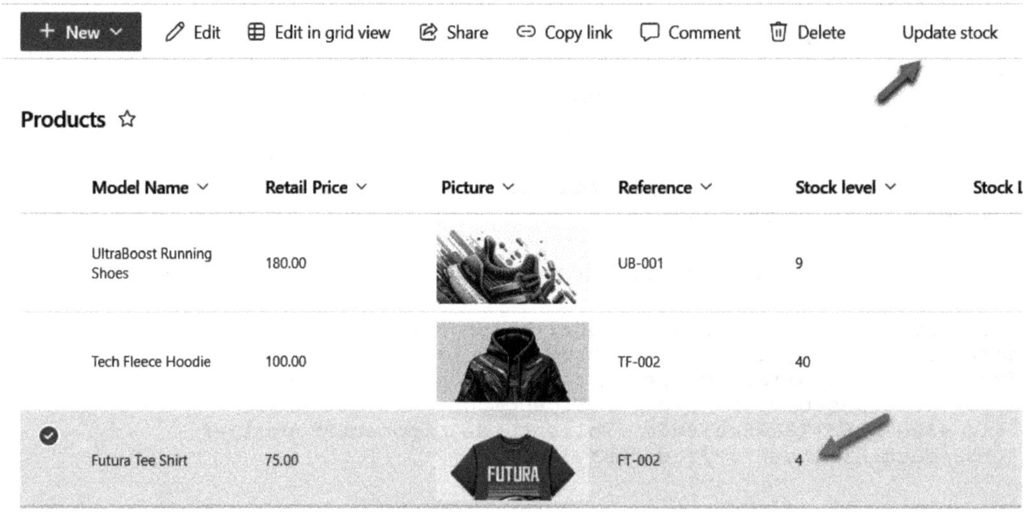

Figure 15.4 – ListView Command Set for products with a stock level less than 5

We can change the script as per the requirement to have a different threshold value.

CLI for Microsoft 365

The command to run would be `spo customaction add`: `https://pnp.github.io/cli-microsoft365/cmd/spo/customaction/customaction-add`. In our case, the command would be similar to the following:

```
m365 spo customaction add --webUrl https://yourtenant.sharepoint.
com/sites/Packt --title "PacktProductListViewCommandSet" --name "
PacktProductListViewCommandSet " --location " ClientSideExtension.
ListViewCommandSet.CommandBar" --clientSideComponentId 2ba4a965-
53bb-43d2-8dbc-55f7ae344a95 --clientSideComponentProperties '{"
lowStockThreshold ":"5", "stockUpdatedMessage":"Stock updated"}'
--registrationId 100 --registrationType List
```

Running this command with the correct web URL will add the ListView Command Set to the respective site.

We will take a look at deploying the Search Query modifier in the next section.

Deploying the Search Query modifier

Unlike the previous two extensions, the Search Query modifier can be added only at the site collection level. This makes sense because we do not want to affect the Search Query modification at the tenant level and override the search behavior of the tenant.

Just like earlier, we can use scripts to add this extension to a site collection.

PnP PowerShell

The PnP PowerShell cmdlet needed for adding a Search Query modifier to a site is `Add-PnPCustomAction`. In our case, the command would be as follows:

```
Add-PnPCustomAction -Title "PacktProductSearchQueryModifier" -Name
"PacktProductSearchQueryModifier" -Location "ClientSideExtension.
SearchQueryModifier" -ClientSideComponentId 37f614c8-2e8a-43f9-abb1-
d924ea9fab26
```

Running this command will add the Search Query modifier to the site.

CLI for Microsoft 365

The command to run would be `spo customaction add`. In our case, the command would be similar to the following:

```
m365 spo customaction add --webUrl https://yourtenant.sharepoint.
com/sites/Packt --title "PacktProductSearchQueryModifier" --name
"PacktProductSearchQueryModifier" --location " ClientSideExtension.
SearchQueryModifier " --clientSideComponentId 2ba4a965-53bb-43d2-8dbc-
55f7ae344a95
```

Running this command with the correct web URL will add the Search Query modifier to the respective site.

Let's switch to deploying a Field Customizer in the next section.

Deploying a Field Customizer

A Field Customizer is scoped at the field in a site. Similar to the previous sections, we will use scripts to add a Field Customizer to a field.

PnP PowerShell

The command needed for adding a Field Customizer to a field is as follows:

```
Set-PnPField - https://pnp.github.io/powershell/cmdlets/Set-PnPField.
html
```

We need to specify the internal name of the field and the list where we want the customization. The following command will do this:

```
Set-PnPField -Identity packtProductStockLevel -List Products -Values @
{ClientSideComponentId=[GUID]"2824bbec-56b9-4d95-acd3-3ac0e961e5cb"}
```

With that, the Field Customizer gets associated with the **Stock Level** field.

CLI for Microsoft 365

The command to run would be as follows:

```
spo field set - https://pnp.github.io/cli-microsoft365/cmd/spo/field/
field-set
```

In our case, the command would be similar to the following:

```
m365 spo field set --webUrl https://yourtenant.sharepoint.com/sites/
Packt --internalName "packtProductStockLevel" --listTitle "Products"
--ClientSideComponentId '2824bbec-56b9-4d95-acd3-3ac0e961e5cb'
```

Running this command with the correct web URL will add the Field Customizer to the **Stock Level** field.

We are now familiar with the pattern for the deployment of extensions – which is mainly running related commands. Next, let's understand the details related to deploying form customizers. The commands for this are slightly different from the previous commands we have seen.

Deploying Form customizers

To deploy form customizers, they need to be associated with a content type. Hence, the scripts we need to run will include updating the content type.

PnP PowerShell

In the case of PnP PowerShell, the cmdlet to update a content type is as follows:

```
Set-PnPContentType(https://pnp.github.io/powershell/cmdlets/
Set-PnPContentType.html)
```

The command we need is the following:

```
Set-PnPContentType -Identity "Packt Product" -List "Products"
-NewFormClientSideComponentId "f6ec214d-9520-48a8-86c6-806c6898e10f"
-EditFormClientSideComponentId "f6ec214d-9520-48a8-86c6-806c6898e10f"
-DisplayFormClientSideComponentId "f6ec214d-9520-48a8-86c6-
806c6898e10f"
```

The IDs can be found in the manifest of the form customizer in the solution. Running the preceding command associates the New, Edit, and Display custom forms to the **Packt Product** content type.

CLI for Microsoft 365

The command required here is as follows:

spo contenttype set (More details on that cmdlet can be found here - `https://pnp.github.io/cli-microsoft365/cmd/spo/contenttype/contenttype-set`)

The following command is the one we require:

```
m365 spo contenttype set --name "Packt Product"
--webUrl https://yourtenant.sharepoint.com/sites/Packt
--DisplayFormClientSideComponentId " f6ec214d-9520-48a8-86c6-
806c6898e10f " --EditFormClientSideComponentId " f6ec214d-9520-48a8-
86c6-806c6898e10f " --NewFormClientSideComponentId " f6ec214d-9520-
48a8-86c6-806c6898e10f " --updateChildren
```

The preceding command will associate the form customizer with all the forms of the **Packt Product** content type.

Finally, we will look at deploying ACEs.

Deploying ACEs

ACEs can only be added to a site that is designated as the home site of the tenant. Information on how to do that is provided here: `https://learn.microsoft.com/en-us/viva/connections/create-sharepoint-home-site-for-viva-connections`. For our scenario, we can set the Packt site as the home site, and we will have the **Dashboard** panel available, on which we can add the ACE.

Irrespective of the solution being deployed at the tenant level or at the site collection level, the ACE becomes available to be added to the dashboard.

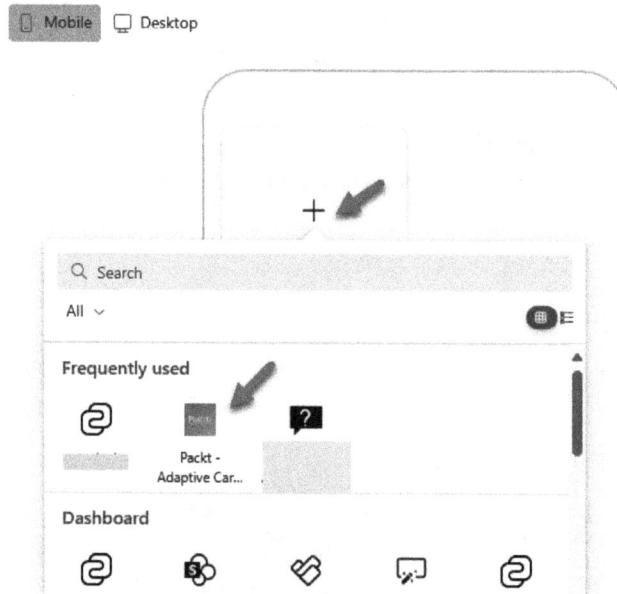

Figure 15.5 – Adding an ACE to the dashboard

As shown in *Figure 15.5*, the ACE can be added manually to the dashboard of the site.

The other option is using PnP PowerShell with the following cmdlet:

```
Add-PnPVivaConnectionsDashboardACE
```

More details on this cmdlet can be found here: https://pnp.github.io/powershell/ cmdlets/Add-PnPVivaConnectionsDashboardACE.html. The script option can be used in automation scenarios. However, in most cases, it will be the owner of the dashboard who will control the display of ACEs.

Summary

In this chapter, we looked at deploying extensions. We understood the scope of deployment and covered the general idea around deploying extensions. After that, we looked at the details of the deployment of each extension one by one with the help of cmdlets in PnP PowerShell and the CLI for Microsoft 365.

The main decision would be deciding the scope, and based on that, running the scripts as and how needed.

In the next chapter, we will look at library components that will help in reusing the code.

Get This Book's PDF Version and Exclusive Extras

Scan the QR code (or go to `packtpub.com/unlock`). Search for this book by name, confirm the edition, and then follow the steps on the page.

Note: Keep your invoice handy. Purchases made directly from Packt don't require an invoice.

Part 4:
Going Further with the
SharePoint Framework

Part 4 is about advanced concepts around SPFx to improve your overall development experience and improve the quality of your solutions. We cover topics such as API consumption, debugging practices, unit testing, and code reusability using SPFx library components. We also review the tools and other libraries offered by the open source community around SPFx that you can take advantage of.

This part has the following chapters:

- *Chapter 16, Sharing Your Code Using Library Components*
- *Chapter 17, Debugging Your Solution Efficiently*
- *Chapter 18, Consuming APIs*
- *Chapter 19, Writing Tests with SPFx*
- *Chapter 20, Upgrading Your Solutions*
- *Chapter 21, Leveraging Community Tools and Libraries*
- *Chapter 22, Development Platforms*

16

Sharing Your Code Using Library Components

In the three previous parts of this book, we saw how to work with both web parts and extensions, the two main types of customizations SPFx offers. In this part, we'll focus now on advanced SPFx techniques that you can use to push your solutions to the next level.

In the very first chapter of this part, we'll start by detailing another type of customization you can use: a **library component**. To fully detail this capability, we'll cover the following main topics:

- Understanding what a library component is and what it is used for
- Building a library component by adapting the existing code base of our product catalog solution to share some code parts
- Deploying a library component
- Providing some guidance about usage and scenarios for library components compared to npm packages

Technical requirements

This chapter relies on the GitHub solution accessible here: `https://github.com/PacktPublishing/Mastering-SharePoint-Development-with-the-SharePoint-Framework-`. You need to first clone the repository locally on your machine to be able to follow the steps. As the solution is built step by step, for the sections in this chapter, a dedicated Git branch has been created representing the solution at a specific state. Before reading the sections, you must check out the corresponding branch before using either the Git command line or a Git client such as GitHub Desktop or Sourcetree.

> **Code snippets**
>
> For brevity and readability considerations, only the relevant parts of the code are detailed in the provided snippets in this chapter. For these reasons, ad hoc code, such as dependency imports and updates to certain files, may be omitted. We recommend having the GitHub solution open while going through the chapter to get the full working version of the code and review the provided steps.

The branch name to refer to and additional instructions are indicated at the beginning of each section. Here is a summary of Git branches to check out per section:

Section in this chapter	Git branch to check out
Building a library component	`https://github.com/PacktPublishing/Mastering-SharePoint-Development-with-the-SharePoint-Framework-/tree/chapter16/sharing-code-with-library-component`

Understanding what a library component is

The library component, introduced in SPFx v1.9.1, is an additional component type available when creating a new SPFx solution using the **Yeoman** generator. The main goal of this customization is to share and reuse JavaScript code across multiple SPFx customizations deployed on the tenant (web part, extensions, and so on). It answers a common need in software development in general: *avoiding code duplication*.

To give you a clear example, let's take the following use case.

A company creates and deploys a web part, Web Part A, to display information contained in a SharePoint list as a dashboard. For that purpose, they implement a dedicated TypeScript class called ListService.ts to fetch data from a SharePoint list called List A.

A few months later, they decide to create another web part, Web Part B, but this time displaying information for another list, List B, with another view. Again, they implement another ListService.ts class to fetch data for the SharePoint list, resulting in code duplication of the data-fetching logic:

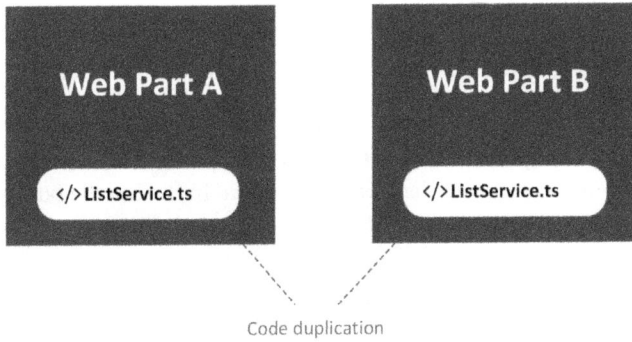

Figure 16.1 – Code duplication across web parts

In that case, by using a library component, they could have shared the common piece of code responsible for fetching data to a list so it could be consumed by other solutions:

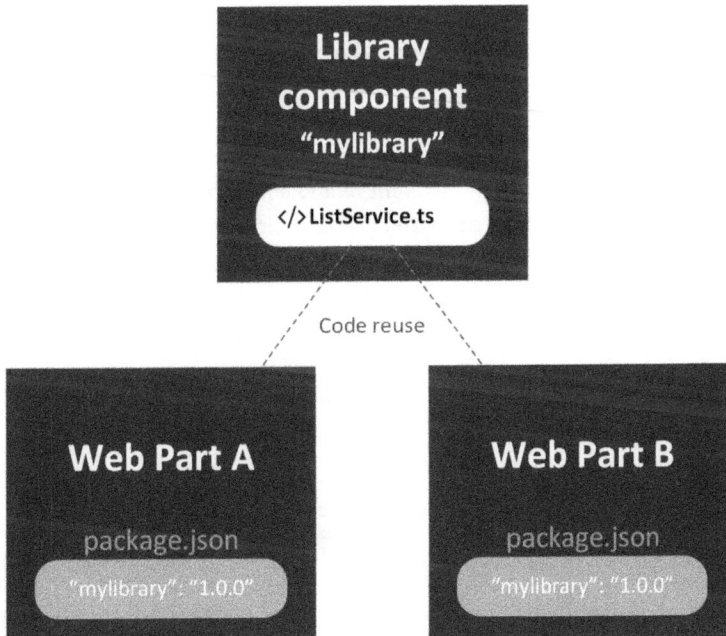

Figure 16.2 – Sharing code with a library component

You reference a library component in an SPFx solution by defining the dependency in the `package.json` file. Then, the bundling process detects this dependency and adds it to the consuming component's manifest.

Unlike a traditional npm package where a dependency is resolved at build time and included in the final bundle, a library component dependency *is not included* in the bundle but rather detected by SPFx *at runtime*, loading the library before loading the consuming component's bundle.

Library components can be deployed in the app catalog at the *tenant* or *site collection* level just like web parts and extensions. In that regard, they follow the same deployment process, so it is easier to manage.

The typical usage for library components is to share common interfaces, services, or even React components, to centralize pieces of code that are *generic* and *reusable*.

In the next chapter, we'll update the code we already implemented for our product's inventory catalog solution by creating a new library component and decoupling some reusable JavaScript classes that will be consumed by web parts.

Building a library component

As it is intended to be shared with other solutions, a library component should always have its own solution folder. We start by reorganizing our solution folders a little bit by moving the web parts already developed in *Part 2, Build Web Parts with the SharePoint Framework*, in a dedicated `Packt.Solutions.ProductManagement.Parts` folder. The desired folder structure now looks like this.

```
/<root>
  └ Packt.Solutions.ProductManagement
      ├  Packt.Solutions.ProductManagement.Library
      └  Packt.Solutions.ProductManagement.Parts
```

Figure 16.3 – SPFx library component project structure

Library components and consuming projects must use the *same SPFx version* to get it to work (otherwise, you could face compilation/bundling issues due to a type mismatch between two different versions). Prior to creating the library project, you must ensure you use the correct version of the SPFx Yeoman generator. In this example, web parts are using SPFx 1.19.0, so the version of the generator must be the same. You can install it using this command:

```
npm i -g @microsoft/generator-sharepoint@1.19.0
```

To create the library solution, from the `Packt.Solutions.ProductManagement` folder, we now initialize a new SPFx solution by using the Yeoman generator and running the following command:

```
yo @microsoft/sharepoint --component-type "library" --component-
name "PackSharedServices" --solution-name "Packt.Solutions.
ProductManagement.Library" --environment "spo" --package-manager "npm"
--skip-feature-deployment
```

We use the following parameters:

- `--component-type "library"`: Indicates we now create a library.

- `--component-name "PackSharedServices"`: Base name of the library that will be used to create files. SPFx will automatically append `Library` to the end of the file, so you don't need to add that suffix.

- `--solution-name "Packt.Solutions.ProductManagement.Library"`: The name of the folder that will be created.

- `--environment "spo"`: Indicates that we target SharePoint Online only.

- `--package-manager "npm"`: Indicates that we use npm as the package manager to install dependencies.

- `--skip-feature-deployment`: Indicates users won't have to install the app manually on sites. In the case of a library, this should always be enabled as there is no integration in the UI whatsoever. You just want to make the library available to other solutions directly.

Now that we've created the library project, let's take a look at its file structure.

Configuring the library

The Yeoman generator will scaffold a new solution containing our library. The file and folder structure for an SPFx library is quite simple. In the case of a library, the following files are particularly important:

- `index.ts`: Defines what the library exports to consumers. All elements you want to expose (TypeScript classes, interfaces, types, etc.) need to be prefixed by the `export` directive. Otherwise, they won't be visible to consumers. By default, it points to the automatically generated library class, but can be literally anything under the `src` folder.

- `package.json`: Unlike other SPFx customization types, such as web parts or extensions, this file is quite important in the case of a library as it defines how your library can be used. The two main values to set are as follows:

  - name: The name of your library when consumers use an import expression, `import * as myLib from 'my-library'`. In our case, we define the name `@packt/spfx-shared-services` for our library.

- version: The current version of the library. This value is not the same as the version set in package-solution.json!

```
"name": "@packt/spfx-shared-services",
"version": "0.0.1",
...
```

> **Naming your library**
>
> Even if your library is not shared publicly, it is a good practice to use an organization scope (the @ prefix) in your npm package name, such as @company/library-name. It helps to quickly identify organization-shared packages and their purpose.

The next step is to implement the library content.

Sharing utility classes and interfaces

In our product catalog scenario, what we want to share is the ListService.ts utility class we created earlier, as it is a generic service that can be used by other solutions. Under the src folder, we create new services and models folders and move all necessary JavaScript classes and interfaces we created earlier for web parts. We also add necessary dependencies to the package.json file, such as @microsoft/sp-http.

Because library components are specific to SPFx, it means you can use the same dependencies as consumers (such as sharing a web part or extension context object).

Finally, we expose these classes through the index.ts file:

```
export { IListService } from './services/IListService';
export { ListService } from './services/ListService';
export { IList } from './models/IList';
```

In the first section, *Understanding what a library component is*, we mentioned the linking process was done automatically by SPFx at runtime when solutions were deployed. However, during the development phase, the solutions need to be linked together on the local machine to resolve dependencies correctly. The next step is now to link the library and web parts solutions together.

Linking solutions locally

An SPFx library component is no more than a regular npm library and follows the same rules regarding the linking process using the npm link command. This command, working in two steps, allows referencing from a solution a library dependency from a local folder instead of a remote packages repository (such as npmjs) using **symbolic links**.

Step 1 – configuring the library

First, in the library solution root folder, `Packt.Solutions.ProductManagement.Library`, we run the following command:

```
> npm link
```

Without any parameter, it creates a symbolic link (aka *symlink*) for the library name, `@packt/spfx-shared-services`, pointing to this specific folder.

Then, from the same folder, we build the solution:

```
> gulp bundle --ship
```

This step is mandatory because of the `main": "lib/index.js"` value present in `package.json`, indicating the entry point of the library. We must build, at least once, the library to generate the `lib` folder and associated files. Otherwise, the linking process won't work.

> **Listing all created links**
>
> You can see the packages you already linked by using the `npm ls -g --depth=0 --link=true` command.

Step 2 – consuming the library

Second, in the `Packt.Solutions.ProductManagement.Parts` folder, we run the following command:

```
> npm link @packt/spfx-shared-services
```

This will add the `@packt/spfx-shared-services` library, available from the `node_modules` folder, using a symbolic link.

We can now update our previous imports in the web parts solutions, and the classes and interfaces will be resolved correctly:

```
import { IListService } from "@packt/spfx-shared-services";
import { ListService } from "@packt/spfx-shared-services";
import { IList } from "@packt/spfx-shared-services";
...
```

At this point, the two solutions are linked together locally on our machine and we could continue the development of both solutions in parallel. However, whenever we need to update the library implementation, we need to run the `gulp bundle --ship` command to reflect changes on the consumer side. To make the development process easier, you can use the `gulp serve` command from the library solution. Even if there is nothing to "serve," per se, as there is no UI component involved, it will start the build in watch mode, reflecting the changes automatically for consumers.

Once the development is complete and the library is ready to be used, it is time to deploy it.

Deploying a library component

Deployment of a library component can be done in the tenant app catalog or in a site collection app catalog using the same process as any SPFx solution. From the `Packt.Solutions.ProductManagement.Library` folder, containing our library, we run the following commands:

```
> gulp bundle --ship
> gulp package-solution --ship
```

This will bundle and create the `*.sppkg` file.

The next step is to upload that package into the tenant app catalog or site collection app catalog. An important remark here: when deploying a library component, always check **Make this solution available to all sites in the organization**. This is because libraries are meant to be global and not deployed manually per site.

> **Note**
> You can only host one library component version at a time in a tenant.

The next step is to deploy our web parts solution with a dependency to the library.

From the `Packt.Solutions.ProductManagement.Parts` folder, we update the `package.json` file to add the `"@packt/spfx-shared-services": "0.0.1"` reference explicitly:

```
"dependencies": {
    ...
    "@microsoft/sp-core-library": "1.19.0",
    ...
    "@packt/spfx-shared-services": "0.0.1"
},
```

This reference will be used by SPFx *at runtime* to correctly link the library. You must set the *exact* version number of the *expected* deployed library, or it won't work.

There is no need to run the `npm i` command as we only want to package the solution.

This version number is different from the `.sppkg` version number; it is up to you to know which version number is the current one as it appears nowhere in the UI within SharePoint.

You can run the following commands to bundle and package the application:

```
> gulp bundle --ship
> gulp package-solution --ship
```

Then, upload the package to the app catalog the same way as the library component.

> **Mixed deployment locations**
>
> Packages don't have to be deployed in the same app catalog. For instance, a consuming SPFx solution deployed in a site collection app catalog can use a library deployed at the tenant level. However, the opposite can't be done.

When browsing a SharePoint page and adding the product catalog web part, the library component should now be resolved correctly. To ensure this is the case, you can inspect the loaded JavaScript files in the browser's **Network** tab:

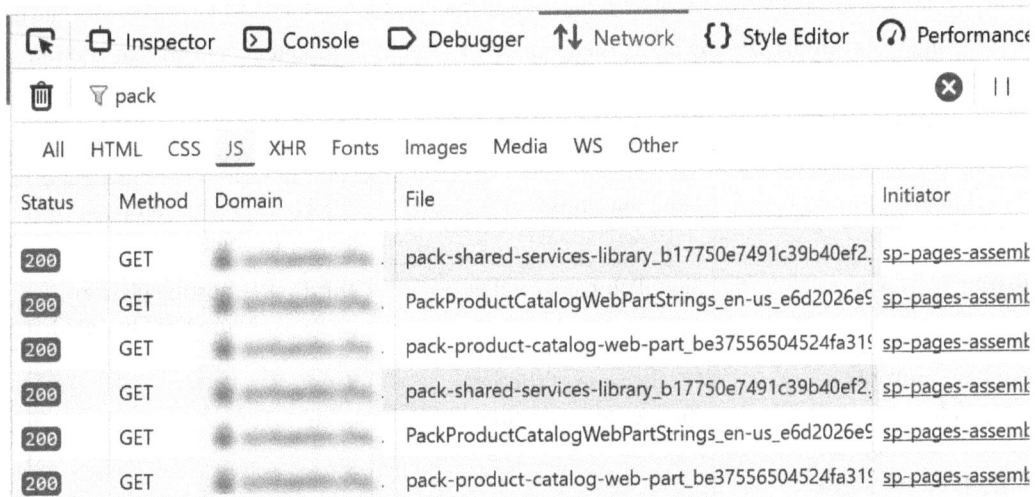

Figure 16.4 – Inspecting a network JavaScript file to ensure the library is loaded

You should see the library component loaded correctly, meaning the dependency has been resolved by SPFx.

At this point, we have described what a library component is and how to use it practically through a real example. However, as a developer, you might still wonder about the difference between a library component and a traditional npm package and, more importantly, when to use what. We'll dig into this topic in the next section.

Comparing npm packages with SPFx library components

Library components are not the only way to mutualize software code for SPFx solutions. You can also use traditional npm packages and consume them as dependencies in your code through the package.json file, using the same linking mechanism (using npm link). However, in such cases, you will be responsible for the package publishing process (for instance, as part of your DevOps process) and need to use a dedicated platform to host and distribute these packages to your consuming solution. Also – and because in an enterprise scenario, you likely won't publish your packages publicly – the chosen hosting platform needs to support *private* packages. Among them, we can mention the most popular ones:

- npmjs.com through private packages
- Azure Artifacts on Azure DevOps
- GitHub Packages on GitHub Enterprise
- JFrog Artifactory

The following table summarizes the npm package and SPFx library component options that you can use to share common code between solutions:

	SPFx library component	**npm package**
Compatible consuming solution types	SPFx solutions > v1.9.1 only.	SPFx (all versions) and non-SPFx solutions.
Hosting platform	SharePoint app catalog.	Third-party hosting platform (npmjs, Azure DevOps, etc.).
Can have multiple independent versions available for consuming solutions	No (because of the app catalog infrastructure).	Yes.
Private consumption	Yes, by default. The library is only available from the scope you deploy it (tenant or site collection app catalog).	Yes, but requires private package support in the hosting platform and additional configurations at build time (such as credentials configuration to access the packages repository).

	SPFx library component	npm package
Dependencies resolution type	At runtime. The library dependency is resolved when consuming components are executed in the browser. It is not included in the bundle.	At build time. The dependency is included in the component bundle before deployment.
Deployment type	Using SPFx commands (`gulp bundle`, `gulp package-solution`, etc.).	Custom publishing process to a package repository.

Table 16.1 – npm package and SPFx library component options

Additionally, SPFx library components have the following limitations:

- **SPFx version compatibility**: If an SPFx library component and a consuming solution rely on SPFx common dependencies (for instance, `@microsoft/sp-http`), you can't mix SPFx versions (e.g., a `1.19.0` version consuming a `1.20.0` version and vice versa) as the types won't match and you'll get an error at compilation time.

  It means whenever you want to reuse the existing library for a *new solution* (e.g., a new web part), you need to either downgrade it to the current library version or upgrade the SPFx library component itself to the newest SPFx version. In the latter, it means you must update all solutions relying on that library as well or they will break when the new version of the library is deployed.

- **No easy way to know the currently deployed version**: As an SPFx library component relies on the app catalog, only the version number present in the `package-solution.json` file will be displayed. The currently deployed version number set in the `package.json` file (which can be different) is not explicitly displayed. An (ugly) way to view the currently deployed version of a library is to inspect the deployed files directly, for instance, browsing the `https://<tenant_name>.sharepoint.com/sites/appcatalog/ClientSideAssets` URL, opening the JavaScript file, and inspecting the version number:

```
define("58c95cf0-7bab-4e78-9cbd-117f25b83dfa_0.0.1",["@
library"],e=>(()=>{"use strict";var t={878:t=>{t.export
a(e){var i=n[e];if(void 0!==i)return i.exports;var r=n[
t[e](r,r.exports,a),r.exports}a.d=(e,t)=>{for(var n in
a.o(e,n)&&Object.defineProperty(e,n,{enumerable:!
0,get:t[n]})},a.o=(e,t)=>Object.prototype.hasOwnPropert
defined"!=typeof
Symbol&&Symbol.toStringTag&&Object.defineProperty(e,Sym
```

Figure 16.5 – Inspecting the version number for a deployed library

- **Can't have multiple deployed versions**: Because library components are deployed through a regular `.sppkg` package file with only one deployed version at a time in an app catalog, you can have only *one* version of the library available, limiting the flexibility.

After seeing these limitations, you might wonder in what type of scenario the library component would be good. In our opinion, SPFx library components can be a good choice for the following use cases:

- To share pure SPFx utility code relying on SPFx-specific dependencies (such as `@microsoft/sp-http`) or context (e.g., the `WebPartContext` class).

  Using a npm package here could be more complex as SPFx packages can be complicated to use outside of an SPFx solution.

- To be used as a *plugin system* for other solutions. This is, for instance, the approach taken by the open-source *PnP Modern Search solution*, using library components as a plugin to add specific elements and enhance the base solution if present. You can see an example of this approach here: `https://github.com/microsoft-search/pnp-modern-search-extensibility-samples/`.

Other than these scenarios, we recommend using regular npm packages instead for all the reasons mentioned in the preceding comparison table.

Summary

In this chapter, we've described what an SPFx library component is and how to use it to mutualize common code and avoid duplication. We've detailed the library creation and linking process with other solutions through a practical example. Finally, we've compared library components to npm packages, seen another way to reuse code across solutions, and provided guidance on when to choose what, depending on your scenario.

In the next chapter, we'll detail how to debug your SPFx solutions efficiently for all types of components.

17

Debugging Your Solution Efficiently

Debugging is an inherent part of software development, and SPFx is no exception. It is rare that a complete solution works on the first try without any errors, and when these errors or odd behaviors occur, each developer has their own approach to troubleshooting. Without appropriate tools and techniques, a basic error can turn into hours of troubleshooting.

This chapter aims to guide you in the SPFx debugging process and give you the best practices to become efficient in your troubleshooting sessions. By the end of this chapter, you'll be able to do the following:

- Debug an SPFx Web Part using multiple techniques
- Debug an SPFx extension
- Use the SPFx developer dashboard and maintenance mode
- Benefit from other software tools to help you debug your solutions

Technical requirements

This chapter has no specific technical requirements as it details general debugging techniques for SPFx solutions. These can be used in any SPFx solution depending on the component type you implement (Web Parts or extensions).

Understanding how debugging works

Before knowing how to debug, it is important to know how debugging works for JavaScript applications and what the core concepts behind this process are.

As mentioned at the very beginning of this book in *Chapter 1*, *Introducing Microsoft 365 and SharePoint Online for Developers*, SPFx solutions are client-side solutions, meaning they use JavaScript code executed directly in a web browser (among various other assets, such as CSS and images). To be able to debug them efficiently, JavaScript solutions rely on **source map** files.

Source maps are an essential feature in modern web development that greatly simplify the debugging process. Because the SPFx build toolchain uses many intermediate steps before producing the final JavaScript bundle, making several transformations on it (transpiling, minifying, etc.), the code structure you wrote in your editor won't be the code executed in the browser. This makes it difficult to follow and understand for a human being when executed by the browser.

Source maps solve this problem by mapping the transformed code back to the original code. A source map is essentially a file (with a `.map` extension) that contains information about how the minified or transpiled code corresponds to the original source code. This allows developers to see the original code while debugging in a browser, making it easier to identify and fix issues. Source maps are generated by most build tools, such as **webpack**, **Babel**, and **TypeScript**, and can be consumed by modern browsers' developer tools, such as those in Chrome, Edge, and Firefox, that understand this format.

> **Note**
>
> Source maps are not only for JavaScript files. You can also have source maps for CSS files.

In the case of SPFx, source map generation follows this process:

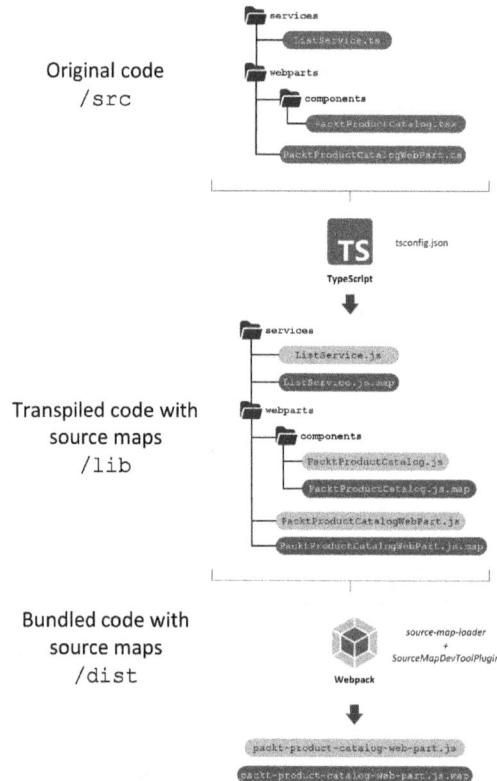

Figure 17.1 – Source map generation process with SPFx

Source maps are generated first by the TypeScript compiler. This is controlled via the `sourceMap` setting in the `tsconfig.json` file, explicitly telling the compiler to produce a source map file for each transpiled JavaScript file:

```
{
    . . .
    "compilerOptions": {
        . . .
        "sourceMap": true,
        . . .
    }
}
```

By executing the `gulp build` command from the root solution folder and inspecting the generated `lib` folder, you will find the JavaScript-compiled version of the `.ts` file and its corresponding source file.

Here is an example of the `ListService.ts` file we created earlier in this book. After running the command, a file named `ListService.js` is created referencing the corresponding `ListService.js.map` source map file:

```
    . . .
    return ListService;
}());
export { ListService };
//# sourceMappingURL=ListService.js.map
```

Here's the `ListService.js.map` file's content:

```
{
    "version": 3,
    "file": "ListService.js",
    "sourceRoot": "",
    "sources": [
        "../../src/services/ListService.ts"
    ],
    "names": [],
    "mappings": ";;;;;;;;;;;;;;;;;;;;;;;;;;;;;;;;;;;;;;;;;;;AAGA,OAAO,EAAE,
GAAG,EAAE,MAAM,4BAA4B,CAAC..."
}
```

The key component of a source map is the `mappings` field. This field employs a VLQ base 64 encoded string to link lines and positions in the compiled file to their counterparts in the original file. As a developer, *it is not mandatory to know how to read a source map*. However, you can examine these mappings using tools such as source-map-visualization (`https://sokra.github.io/source-map-visualization`).

Because SPFx uses webpack to bundle the solution, source maps are not used as is. They are processed by the internal SPFx webpack routine using the **source-map-loader** loader and the **SourceMapDevToolPlugin** plugin, which resolves all existing `.map` files to be correctly interpreted by the browser. When the bundle is generated, a single source map is emitted, resolving source maps produced earlier for each individual file.

By running the `gulp bundle` command, you can inspect the `dist` folder, and at the very end of the bundle file, you'll find the reference to the source maps:

```
/* harmony default export */ const __WEBPACK_DEFAULT_EXPORT__ = (PackProductCatalogWebPart);
})();

/******/    return __webpack_exports__;
/******/ })()
;
});;
//# sourceMappingURL=pack-product-catalog-web-part.js.map
```

Figure 17.2 – Source map file generated for a Web Part JavaScript bundle

By default, with SPFx, *source maps are only generated for development scenarios* when running `gulp serve` or `gulp bundle` commands.

There are no source maps generated for production scenarios (`gulp bundle --ship`). The reason is mainly about performance. Because source maps considerably increase the size of the bundle, it makes it slower to load for end users (who don't need/care about source maps in the end as they are a developer tool).

For instance, you can see source maps in action by running the `gulp serve` command from an SPFx Web Part project. It will open the **hosted workbench** page (`https://{tenantdomain}/sites/yoursite/_layouts/workbench.aspx`). If you open the browser developer tools (*F12*) and select **Debugger** (Edge) or **Sources** (Chrome) tab, you'll see a `webpack` folder displaying the original source code. Here is an example with Edge:

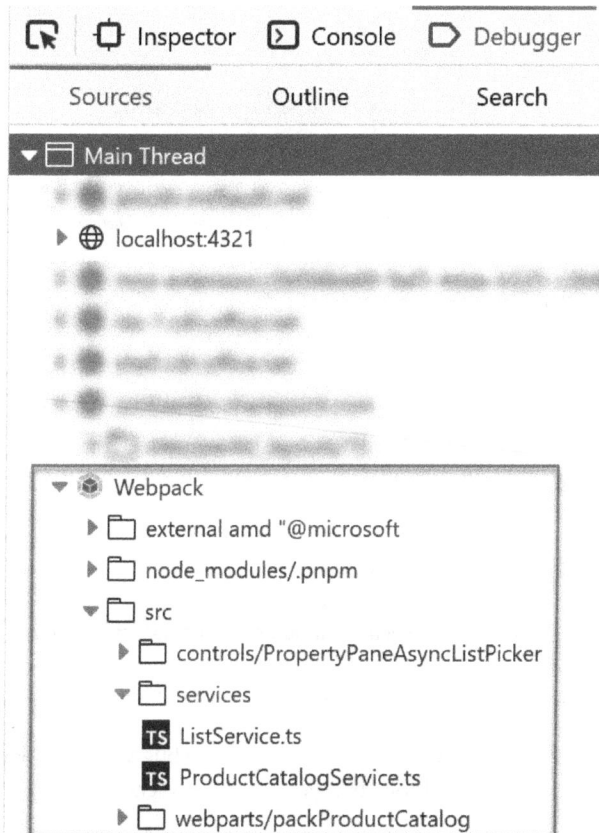

Figure 17.3 – Source maps with Edge

Opening one of these source files and putting a breakpoint in it will automatically trigger the debugger when you reload the page:

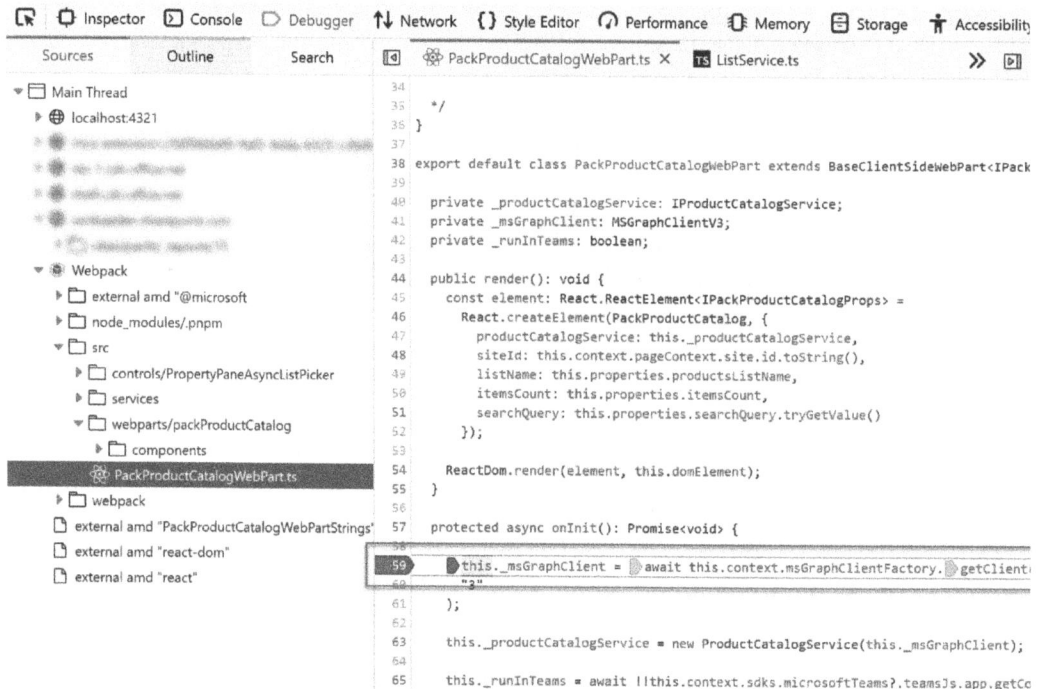

Figure 17.4 – Example of a breakpoint in a browser debugger

As you may understand, the web browser is your primary debug tool as an SPFx developer.

In the next section, we'll see how to use these source maps to debug your Web Parts an extension in a SPFx solution using more convenient tools than your web browser.

Debugging Web Parts

When you create an SPFx solution, the scaffolded project comes with a default Visual Studio Code debug configuration. This configuration is located in the `launch.json` file in the `.vscode` folder. This file contains debug configuration for your current project only, for instance, for browsers such as Edge or Chrome (by default, SPFx provides a configuration for Edge only). All the configurations defined in that file are available on the Visual Studio code interface, so you can start them.

A debug configuration in Visual Studio Code has the following fields:

- `name`: The name of your debug configuration that will appear on the Visual Studio Code dropdown.

- `type`: Web browser to use (Edge or Chrome). For Firefox, you'll need a specific Visual Studio code extension. For Edge and Chrome, the rest of the configuration is exactly the same.

- `request`: The type of debug behavior. Here, `launch` will open the browser and attach the Visual Studio code debugger automatically.

- `url`: The web page URL to launch. For a SPFx Web Part, it corresponds to the hosted workbench page, but it can be any URL.

- `webRoot`: The root folder from where to map the original source code

- `sourceMaps`: Indicates that the debugger should use source maps

- `souresourceMapPathOverrides`: Path overrides for source maps. By default, webpack creates its own structure for source maps with a `webpack` folder. We tell how to map the `webpack` folder structure to the original code structure, taking into account folder depths.

- `runtimeArgs`: The argument to pass to the web browser when opening, for instance, incognito mode.

Debugging Web Parts in Visual Studio Code is a straightforward process. It is likely the same as debugging directly in the web browser as the tool just performs a remote debugging session from the web browser. The only difference is that the breakpoints can be set directly into your code without leaving the editor.

In the next sections, we'll review all the options you have for debugging your Web Part code using Visual Studio and SPFx features.

Debugging using the hosted workbench

The most common scenario when debugging a Web Part is to use the **hosted workbench** page provided by SPFx. This special page allows you to test your Web Part in isolation from the rest of the site without having to deploy it before, with the page automatically looking for code served locally. This page includes basic capabilities such as sections, Web Part addition, and edit/display mode, but is different from a traditional modern page (no navigation, no theming).

To debug a Web Part in development mode using the hosted workbench page, use the following steps:

1. Put a breakpoint in the code where you want the debugger to stop.

2. Run the `gulp serve --nobrowser` command. The `--nobrowser` option indicates SPFx to not open any page by default and just serve the application in the background.

3. Run the hosted workbench configuration from Visual Studio. It will open the page you specified in `launch.json`. You have two ways of starting the debugging process: either by clicking on the green play button near the dropdown or by pressing *F5*.

4. Sign into your SharePoint site and add the Web Part to the canvas. If your code is supposed to be executed at load, the breakpoint will trigger in Visual Studio Code.

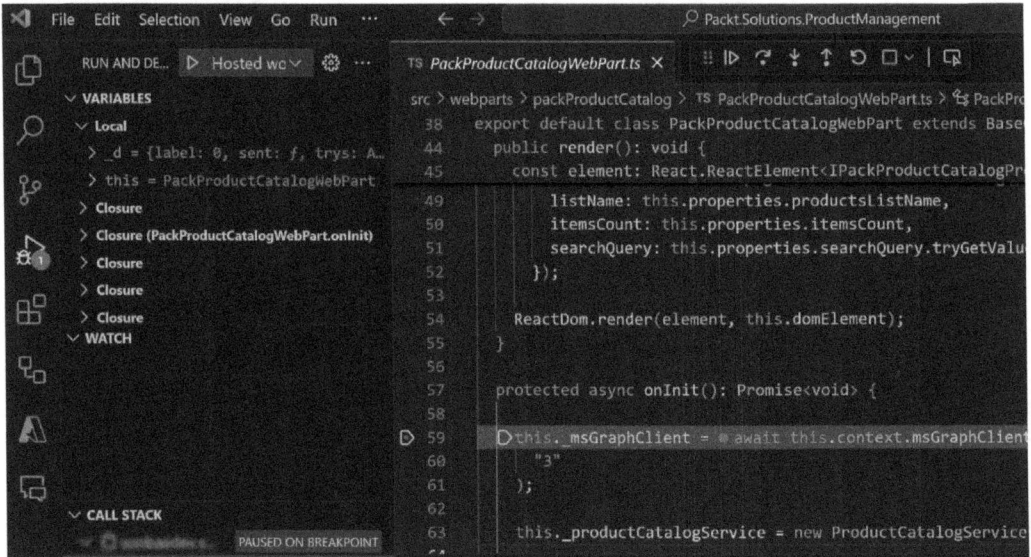

Figure 17.5 – Debugging from Visual Studio Code

5. From there, you can use traditional debug commands with *F10* to step over (i.e., do not enter a method's logic but just wait for its execution) and *F11* to step into the code (such as monitoring the code execution in a method).

The debugging scenario with the default hosted workbench page mainly aims to test a Web Part behavior alone, without any context or other Web Parts alongside. But what if your Web Part relies on a specific context value, for instance, the current page list item? In this case, you'll need to use a real modern SharePoint page to achieve this.

Debugging Web Parts from a real modern page

When implementing a Web Part, it can be quite common to rely on specific values from the current context given by the provided `this.context` object. As an example, we can use the current SharePoint list item associated with the current page where the Web Part is added through `this.context.pageContext.listItem`.

Debugging your Web Part using the hosted workbench page will result in an *undefined* value, as this page is not associated with a SharePoint list item.

In this scenario, we can use another debugging technique to get real context values. It consists of deploying the solution in the app catalog but still referencing the local code. To achieve this, you need to use the following commands without the `--ship` parameter:

```
gulp bundle
gulp package-solution
```

This will bundle and package the solution, but will still reference the code from a localhost machine. Adding this package to the app catalog will allow you to add the Web Part to any page with any specific setup you want to test, for instance, coupling it to other Web Parts on the page or relying on values that are only available from an existing modern page.

Then, to debug the solution, replace the `url` field in the debug configuration in the `launch.json` file with the URL of the actual SharePoint page:

```
{
    "name": "Hosted workbench",
    "type": "msedge",
    "request": "launch",
    "url": "https://{tenantDomain}.sharepoint.com/sites/{yourSite}/
SitePages/{yourPage}.aspx",
    ...
```

Then run the following command:

```
gulp serve --nobrowser
```

This will serve your code locally so it can be accessed by Web Parts from the page, allowing you to debug it the same way as the hosted workbench scenario.

Another interesting debugging scenario for Web Parts is when your solution is already deployed in production mode (using the `--ship` flag) and you need to debug an issue occurring in the real production context. In this case, the techniques mentioned above won't work.

Debugging Web Parts in production

Issues in production happen. When they occur, it can be difficult for developers to find the root cause as they generally can't rely on source maps. Luckily, SPFx provides a clever way to help you debug these issues without deploying anything or having to reproduce the context in a separate environment.

What about source maps in production?

Despite the fact that it is technically feasible and may sound like a good idea at first glance, it is not. Source maps significantly increase the size of the bundle and are only relevant for developers. They will slow performance for users for no reason and will be useless most of the time (unless your code is really buggy but, in this case, you have other problems). SPFx already provides a way to debug code in production so you don't have to include them in your final bundle.

To debug a Web Part in production context, you can use this procedure:

1. Run the following command first to serve the solution locally from your machine:

```
gulp serve --nobrowser
```

2. Then, append the following query string to the page URL you want to debug:

```
?loadSPFX=true&debugManifestsFile=https://localhost:4321/temp/
manifests.js
```

   This tells SPFx to reference the code from the local machine instead of the regular hosted bundle file.

3. Use that URL in the debug configuration in the launch.json file and launch the debug process like any other scenario:

```
{
    "version": "0.2.0",
    "configurations": [
        {
            "name": "Hosted workbench",
            "type": "chrome",
            "request": "launch",
            "url": "https://{yourTenantDomain}.sharepoint.
com/sites/{yourSite}/SitePages/{yourPage}.
aspx?loadSPFX=true&debugManifestsFile=https://localhost:4321/
temp/manifests.js",
            ...
```

As a safety measure, you'll be prompted to allow debug scripts to be loaded on the browser:

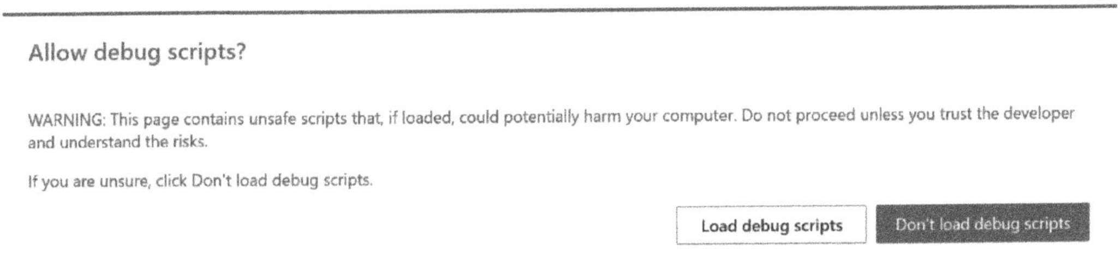

Allow debug scripts?

WARNING: This page contains unsafe scripts that, if loaded, could potentially harm your computer. Do not proceed unless you trust the developer and understand the risks.

If you are unsure, click Don't load debug scripts.

Load debug scripts   Don't load debug scripts

Figure 17.6 – Allow debug scripts

Once debug scripts have been allowed, the extension is loaded on the page and executed. Any breakpoints set in your code will be triggered.

> **Notice**
> It may be obvious, but this technique implies you have a well-managed application life cycle with correctly versioned solutions. To get it to work, you must use the same Web Part code version as the one currently deployed on the site you wish to debug!

We've seen in this section how to debug SPFx Web Parts, which are the easiest customization type to debug. In the next section, we'll do the same but this time, with extensions.

Debugging extensions

Debugging SPFx extensions is slightly different from Web Parts, as they can't be tested on the hosted workbench page. They must be tested on a real modern page context on a SharePoint site using a *specific URL format* dictated by SPFx.

Because extensions don't have a property bag like Web Part, any configuration they rely on must be passed through that URL via a query string parameter (such as a specific property's value you would normally use when registering the extension in the site).

When you create or add an extension to an SPFx project, a `config/serve.json` file is created like this:

```
{
  "$schema": "https://developer.microsoft.com/json-schemas/spfx-build/
spfx-serve.schema.json",
  "port": 4321,
  "https": true,
  "serveConfigurations": {
    "default": {
```

```
        "pageUrl": "https://{tenantDomain}/SitePages/myPage.aspx",
        "customActions": {
          "0c768ce1-f1ae-4a6a-93e5-6446c4ccd164": {
            "location": "ClientSideExtension.ApplicationCustomizer",
            "properties": {
              "testMessage": "Test message"
            }
          }
        }
      },
      "packtLowStockBanner": {
        "pageUrl": "https://{tenantDomain}/SitePages/myPage.aspx",
        "customActions": {
          "0c768ce1-f1ae-4a6a-93e5-6446c4ccd164": {
            "location": "ClientSideExtension.ApplicationCustomizer",
            "properties": {
              "testMessage": "Test message"
            }
          }
        }
      }
    }
  }
}
```

This file will be used by SPFx to build this test URL for you so you can open it on a modern SharePoint page with all the required parameters and execute the extension in the context of the hosting site. You must replace the `pageUrl` field with an existing modern page.

Depending on the type of extension you create (application customizer, field customizer, list view command set, or form customizer), the options for the JSON entry will differ.

The first `default` entry corresponds to the first extension you created in the project. The other ones represent all extensions in your project. You don't usually need it as it is better to debug a specific configuration using its name.

To debug a specific extension, run the `gulp serve` command with `--config={serve_configuration}` where the `{serve_configuration}` parameter corresponds to the desired entry in the `config/serve.json` file. For instance, to test the application customizer banner extension in the above example, we run the following command:

```
gulp serve –config=packtLowStockBanner
```

This will generate the URL that will appear in the terminal and will launch the modern page you specified for that configuration:

Figure 17.7 – Debug URL for extension

The first time you open the page, you'll be prompted to allow debug scripts, loaded from your local machine. *You need to allow them to debug.*

> **Resetting debug script permission**
>
> By default, if debug scripts are enabled and permitted once on a page, they will remain enabled for the entire browser session. To prevent the debug scripts from loading without ending your browser session or manually clearing the session data, add the URL parameter `reset=true` to your request.

At this point, you are only able to test the extension, not debug it (i.e., breakpoints put in your code in Visual Studio won't be triggered).

To debug it and see the code execution step-by-step, you need to use the same technique as with the Web Parts with the Visual Studio Code `launch.json` file. In the `url` field in the default debug configuration, just put the URL generated by the `gulp serve --config=<name>` command (you can literally copy/paste the encoded URL from the terminal):

```
{
    "version": "0.2.0",
    "configurations": [
    {
        "name": "SPFx extension debug",
        "type": "msedge",
```

```
    "request": "launch",
    "url": "https://sonbaedev.sharepoint.
com/sites/Packt/SitePages/debugExtension.
aspx?debugManifestsFile=https%3A%2F%2Flocalhost%3A4321%2Ftemp%2Fmani
fests.js&loadSPFX=true&customActions=%7B%220c768ce1-f1ae-4a6a-
93e5-6446c4ccd164%22%3A%7B%22location%22%3A%22ClientSideExtension.
ApplicationCustomizer%22%2C%22properties%22%3A%7B%22testMessage%22%3
A%22Test+message%22%7D%7D%7D",

    ...
```

Launching the debug process from Visual Studio code (from the interface dropdown or by pressing *F5*) will open the page and attach the debugger, this time, triggering breakpoints, if any.

Don't forget you must run the `gulp serve` command alongside the debugger to make it work. Otherwise, your code won't be accessible locally. Also, when opening the page through the Visual Studio Code debugger, it doesn't really matter which configuration you loaded with the `gulp serve` command, as long as the code is served locally. You won't use the default open page launched by the command anyway.

Your code is not the only thing you can debug. Sometimes, the issue can come from the execution environment. In that case, you need to rely on other tools than classic source maps.

Using the SPFx developer dashboard and maintenance mode

When it comes to inspecting the context where the solutions are executed, SPFx provides handy tools you can use as a developer to help you in your debug session: the SPFx developer dashboard and maintenance mode.

Using the SPFx developer dashboard

The SPFx developer dashboard can be opened by pressing *Ctrl + F12* on a page displaying console at the bottom of the page:

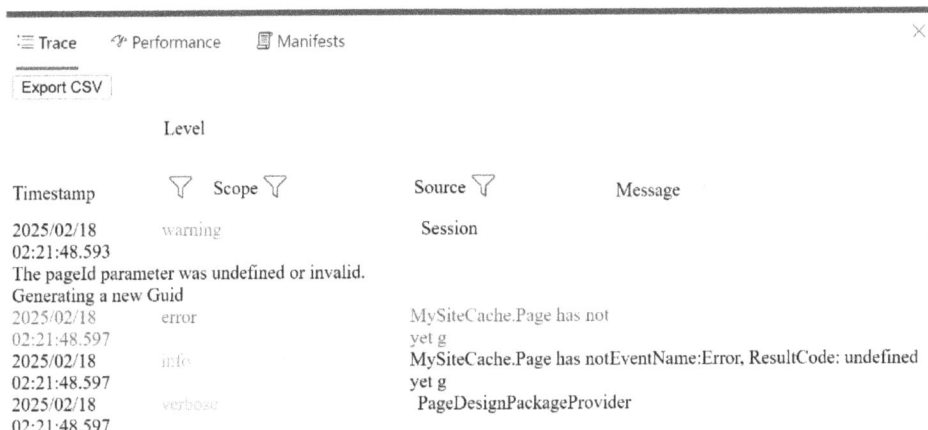

Figure 17.8 – SPFx developer dashboard

The dashboard provides a lot of information about the current execution context. It is composed of three tabs:

- **Trace**: Captures the logs emitted by all the components loaded on the page and categorized by severity (verbose, info, warning, error).

- **Performance**: Provides insights about page performance, such as load duration per component and per sequence (render, initialization, etc.).

- **Manifests**: Displays the list of components manifests currently loaded on the page. It mainly helps you to see whether components have been loaded correctly (i.e., the JavaScript bundles), from which location (CDN, library, etc.), and which dependencies have also been loaded (external libraries, etc.).

In the upcoming sections, we'll review these three tabs in more depth.

Navigating the Trace tab

By default, this tab displays logs from native SharePoint components, but *it can also display logs from your own SPFx custom solutions*. It helps you to quickly narrow down an issue if logs are well placed in your code.

Note

Although it may happen, flagged issues are rarely because of default SPFx components loaded on the page. This dashboard is primarily designed for debugging custom components.

In order to integrate with the developer console dashboard, you need to use the special `Log` utility class from `@microsoft/sp-core-library`. Logs can have multiple severity levels: `error`, `warning`, `info`, and `verbose`. For instance, let's look at the following code in a Web Part:

```
import { Log } from '@microsoft/sp-core-library';

...

protected async onInit(): Promise<void> {

    Log.info("PackProductCatalogWebPart", "Info log", this.context.
serviceScope);
    Log.verbose("PackProductCatalogWebPart", "Verbose log", this.
context.serviceScope);
    Log.warn("PackProductCatalogWebPart", "Warning log", this.context.
serviceScope);
    Log.error("PackProductCatalogWebPart", new Error("Error log"),
this.context.serviceScope);

    ...
```

This will produce the following output in the SPFx developer dashboard:

Timestamp	Level	Scope	Source	Message
2024/11/21 02:26:57.762	info	WebPart.PackProductCatalogWebPart.external.9c7bfcc7-PackProductCatalogWebPart 9c75-48db-b2d3-9650d6b2a873		
Info log				
2024/11/21 02:26:57.762	verbose	WebPart.PackProductCatalogWebPart.external.9c7bfcc7-PackProductCatalogWebPart 9c75-48db-b2d3-9650d6b2a873		
Verbose log				
2024/11/21 02:26:57.762	warning	WebPart.PackProductCatalogWebPart.external.9c7bfcc7-PackProductCatalogWebPart 9c75-48db-b2d3-9650d6b2a873		
Warning log				
2024/11/21 02:26:57.762	error	WebPart.PackProductCatalogWebPart.external.9c7bfcc7-PackProductCatalogWebPart 9c75-48db-b2d3-9650d6b2a873		
Error log				

Figure 17.9 – Example of custom logs

The method from the `Log` object corresponds to the severity (`Log.error()`, `Log.warn()`, `Log.info()`, `Log.verbose()`). Then, the parameters are as follows:

- The first parameter is the source name and will be displayed in the **Source** column, for instance, the name of your Web Part or extension.

- The second parameter is the message to display. In the case of an error, you can pass an `Error` object to get even more information about the inner exception. This will be displayed in the **Message** column.

- The last parameter is the service scope, meaning the execution context from where the message is logged. You should always set this parameter (by default, using the `this.context.serviceScope` property or use a sub scope if desired) as it allows you to isolate messages from a specific component by displaying its instance ID on the page, facilitating the debug process. For instance, if a component is present multiple times on the page (such as a Web Part), you'll be able to identify logs for them individually:

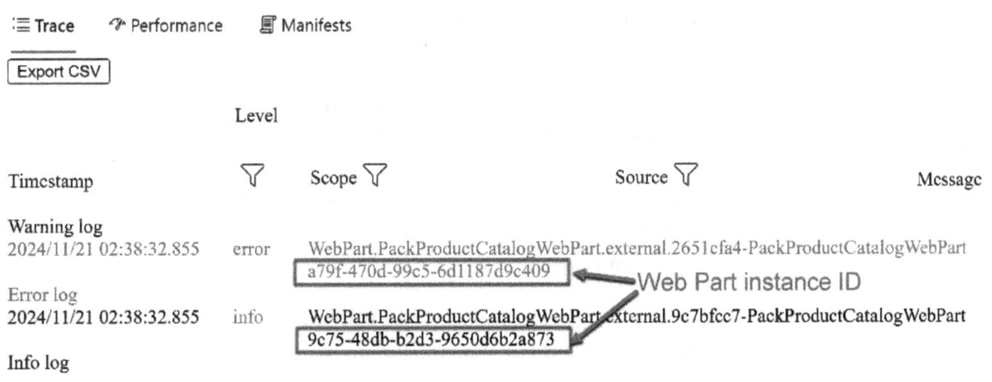

Figure 17.10 – Identifying Web Part instances in logs

> **Tips for logging**
>
> Logs are not only for errors. You can also use *info* and/or *verbose* logs to follow the execution sequence more easily in the dashboard, for instance, by identifying key execution steps (such as when a component is initialized, or when data is fetched). Unlike source maps, logs don't cost on performances, so feel free to abuse them!
>
> To quickly identify your components, use column filters. If too much data is logged, use the CSV export function.
>
> The Web Part instance ID can be retrieved using maintenance mode (as we will see later).

Now that we've seen the **Trace** tab, let's focus on the **Performance** tab.

Understanding the Performance tab

This tab will mainly tell you about the loading duration of components on the page:

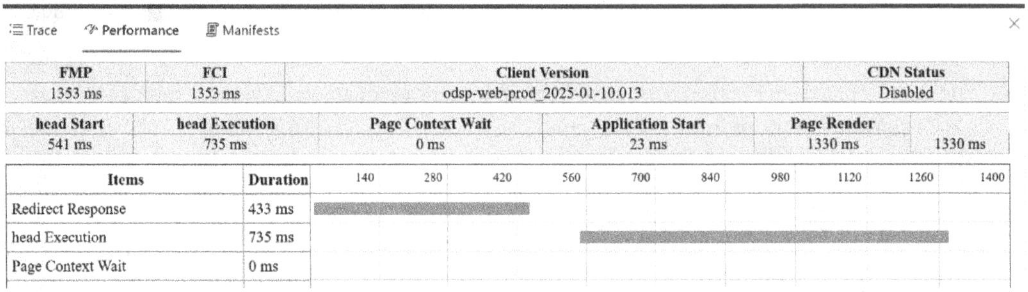

Figure 17.11 – SPFx developer dashboard Performance tab

To be honest, most of the information displayed here won't be very useful. The main interest here is to quickly identify what takes a long time to load on the page if you are experiencing latency issues on page loads.

Once narrowed down to specific components, the other information you may want to look at is the loading sequence duration for it. The dashboard provides information about the following loading phases:

- **Modules loaded**: How long it took to load all necessary modules. If this value is abnormally high, it may indicate that your solution has too many dependencies or Web Part **Tree Shaking** (i.e. dead code eliminations) is not optimal.

- **Initialization**: How long it took for your component to initialize. In the case of a Web Part, this corresponds to the `onInit()` method.

- **Render time**: How long it took for your component to render for the first time. An abnormally high value here may indicate an issue with React state management causing multiple unnecessary renders to occur.

- **Data fetch**: last but least, how long did it take for your component to load data. A high value here can indicate your component try to fetch too much data at once. If this is the case, you should consider batched or paged operations instead.

After the **Performance** tab, let's look at the last tab.

Exploring the Manifests tab

The **Manifests** tab provides information about the component's manifests loaded on the page. The manifest will display information about the load configuration for a component, for instance, where it is served from and what dependencies are loaded (i.e., JavaScript bundles):

Figure 17.12 – SPFx developer dashboard Manifests tab

Be careful here; a loaded component isn't necessarily used on the page. It just lists all components that are available on the page, for instance, a Web Part deployed in the app catalog that you could add to the page.

In our opinion, this is the least useful of the SPFx developer dashboard tabs. Only look at it to ensure your components are correctly deployed and available on the page.

Now that we've covered the SPFx developer dashboard feature, let's review another handy tool that SharePoint provides: maintenance mode.

Using maintenance mode

Maintenance mode is a special feature of SharePoint allowing developers to inspect raw data for SPFx components present on a specific page. To enable it, simply append the query string parameter `?maintenancemode=true` to the page's URL.

Once maintenance mode has been enabled, all the Web Parts present on the page will display raw configuration data. Among this data, we find three distinct tabs:

- **Summary**: Displays basic information about the Web Part, such as the alias, the version, and the unique instance ID on the page:

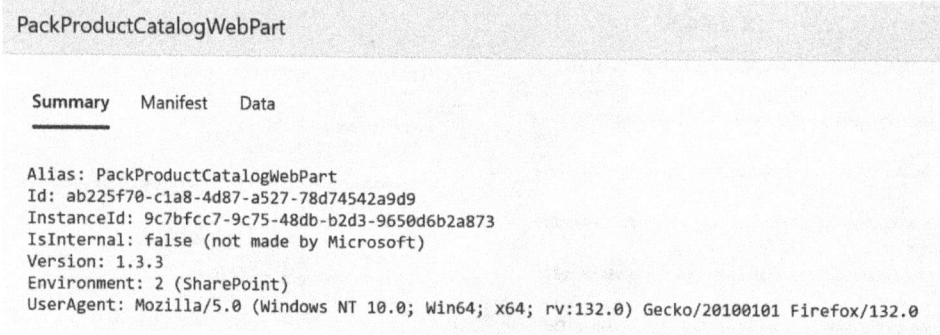

PackProductCatalogWebPart

Summary   Manifest   Data

```
Alias: PackProductCatalogWebPart
Id: ab225f70-c1a8-4d87-a527-78d74542a9d9
InstanceId: 9c7bfcc7-9c75-48db-b2d3-9650d6b2a873
IsInternal: false (not made by Microsoft)
Version: 1.3.3
Environment: 2 (SharePoint)
UserAgent: Mozilla/5.0 (Windows NT 10.0; Win64; x64; rv:132.0) Gecko/20100101 Firefox/132.0
```

Figure 17.13 – Maintenance mode – Summary

- **Manifest**: The Web Part manifest file loaded by the page. This tab is useful for inspecting what JavaScript bundles have been currently loaded and from which locations. This is the same information as provided by the SPFx dashboard.

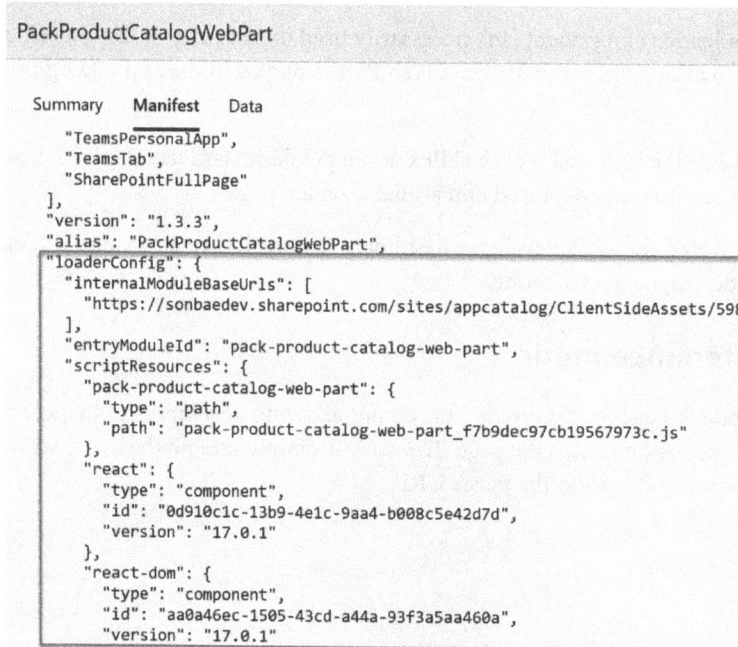

PackProductCatalogWebPart

Summary   **Manifest**   Data

```
    "TeamsPersonalApp",
    "TeamsTab",
    "SharePointFullPage"
],
"version": "1.3.3",
"alias": "PackProductCatalogWebPart",
"loaderConfig": {
  "internalModuleBaseUrls": [
    "https://sonbaedev.sharepoint.com/sites/appcatalog/ClientSideAssets/598
  ],
  "entryModuleId": "pack-product-catalog-web-part",
  "scriptResources": {
    "pack-product-catalog-web-part": {
      "type": "path",
      "path": "pack-product-catalog-web-part_f7b9dec97cb19567973c.js"
    },
    "react": {
      "type": "component",
      "id": "0d910c1c-13b9-4e1c-9aa4-b008c5e42d7d",
      "version": "17.0.1"
    },
    "react-dom": {
      "type": "component",
      "id": "aa0a46ec-1505-43cd-a44a-93f3a5aa460a",
      "version": "17.0.1"
```

Figure 17.14 – Maintenance mode – Manifest tab

- **Data**: Probably the most useful tab, this allows you to inspect the content of the Web Part property bag and the configuration values saved on the page:

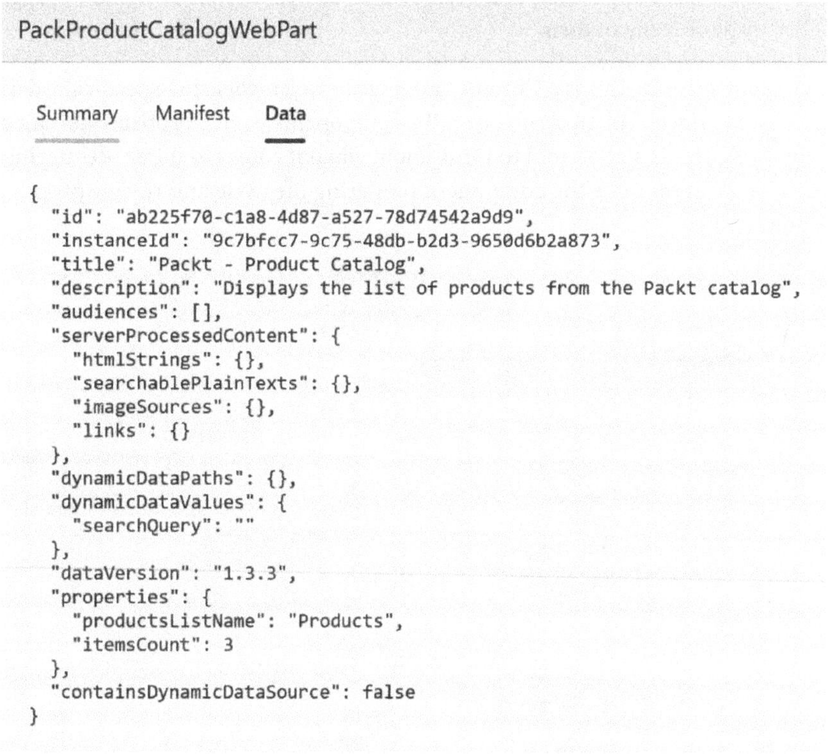

PackProductCatalogWebPart

Summary   Manifest   **Data**

```
{
    "id": "ab225f70-c1a8-4d87-a527-78d74542a9d9",
    "instanceId": "9c7bfcc7-9c75-48db-b2d3-9650d6b2a873",
    "title": "Packt - Product Catalog",
    "description": "Displays the list of products from the Packt catalog",
    "audiences": [],
    "serverProcessedContent": {
        "htmlStrings": {},
        "searchablePlainTexts": {},
        "imageSources": {},
        "links": {}
    },
    "dynamicDataPaths": {},
    "dynamicDataValues": {
        "searchQuery": ""
    },
    "dataVersion": "1.3.3",
    "properties": {
        "productsListName": "Products",
        "itemsCount": 3
    },
    "containsDynamicDataSource": false
}
```

Figure 17.15 – Maintenance mode – Data tab

> **Notice**
>
> Maintenance mode works for both native and custom SPFx Web Parts. It is not available for extensions.

In addition to built-in SharePoint and SPFx utility tools, you can also use third-party tools to help you in your debugging process. We won't go deep into them as this is not the purpose of this book, but they are worth mentioning to complete your knowledge.

Leveraging other tools to debug

Dedicated tools other than SPFx or SharePoint can be used as well when it comes to debugging your components. Let's explore some of them:

- **React Developer Tools**: This is a Chrome and Edge browser extension specifically designed to debug React interfaces. As most of your SPFx components will be probably developed using this framework, this is a good tool to think about when it comes to purely debugging the UI. With this, you can monitor the component rendering life cycle and review props and state values quite easily:

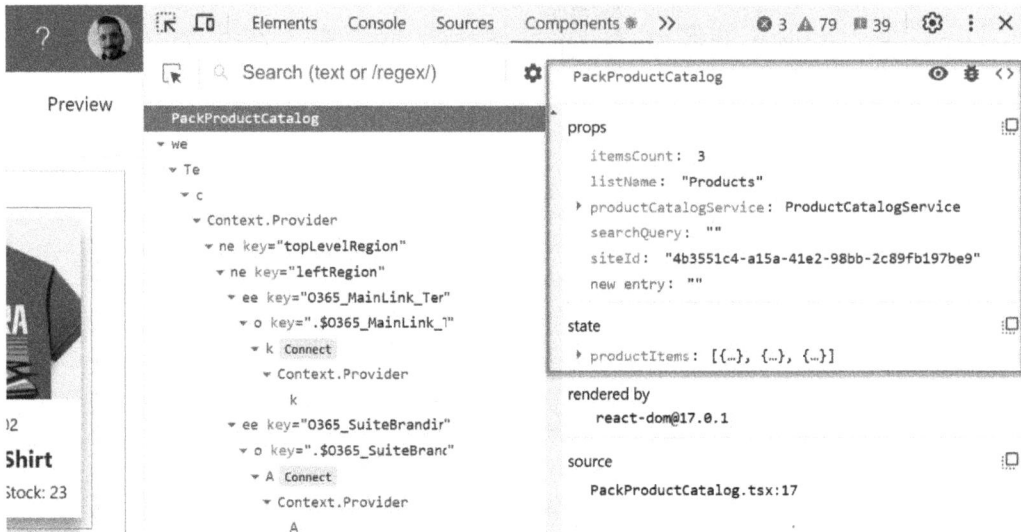

Figure 17.16 – React Developer Tools

- **SP Editor**: Another Google Chrome extension, but this time from a community open source initiative. Even though it can't be categorized as a debug tool directly, this extension can be very handy to speed up your debug process, for instance, by providing predefined actions related to debugging operations (such as loading a debug SPFx manifest to debug in production):

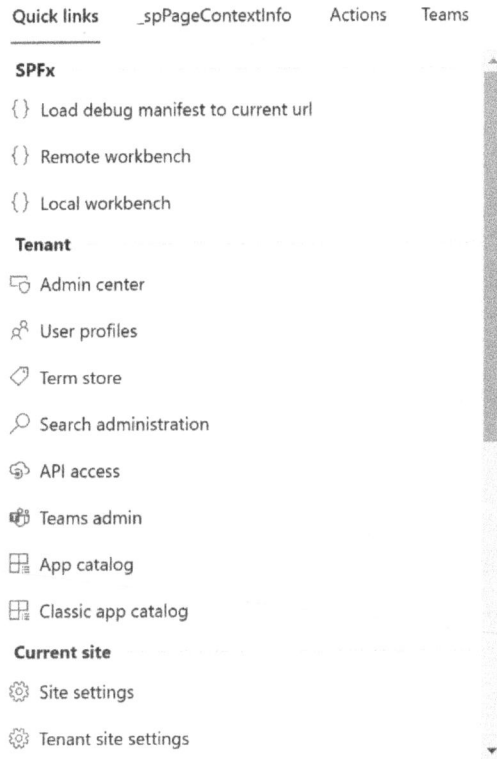

Figure 17.17 – SP Editor interface

In the end, using built-in SPFx debugging tools and community-made tools gives you a powerful combination to debug and troubleshoot your solutions.

Summary

In this chapter, we covered everything you need to know to efficiently debug your SPFx solutions. We started by explaining the underlying concepts behind the debugging process using source maps. Then, we detailed how to debug both SPFx Web Parts and extensions using Visual Studio Code and provided some tips and tricks for each.

We continued by explaining how to debug the execution environment by leveraging built-in SPFx and SharePoint tools such as the SPFx developer dashboard and maintenance mode.

Finally, we covered other third-party tools that you can use as well to help you in your debug sessions.

In the next chapter, we'll cover another important topic regarding SPFx solutions: consuming APIs to interact with data.

Get This Book's PDF Version and Exclusive Extras

UNLOCK NOW

Scan the QR code (or go to packtpub.com/unlock). Search for this book by name, confirm the edition, and then follow the steps on the page.

Note: Keep your invoice handy. Purchases made directly from Packt don't require an invoice.

18
Consuming APIs

Retrieving data or communicating with other systems via APIs is a common requirement in web development and, therefore SPFx solutions. In JavaScript in general, any API can be called using the tool-agnostic `fetch()` API (`https://developer.mozilla.org/en-US/docs/Web/API/Fetch_API/Using_Fetch`) implemented by all modern browsers.

However, most of the time, SPFx components will get data directly from SharePoint (for example, a list or a site using the SharePoint REST API) or the Microsoft 365 ecosystem (for example, Teams, Outlook, and so on using the Microsoft Graph API). Because this data is protected and always retrieved on behalf of the currently logged-in user, these API calls require an additional authentication layer to work.

Although the standard `fetch()` API could be used in SPFx solutions, dealing with this authentication process manually, or specificities of each API in the context of SPFx, can be quite cumbersome. That is why SPFx provides a set of utility classes to get data easily from authenticated contexts such as SharePoint and Microsoft 365, making these prerequisite tasks transparent to you, as a developer. Beyond these scenarios, it also provides utilities to consume external APIs (such as public or custom internal APIs) or APIs secured with Microsoft Entra ID (for example, an Azure function), covering all your needs regarding data retrieval scenarios.

In this chapter, we will detail all the different ways of using various API types using SPFx's built-in capabilities, such as the following:

- The Microsoft Graph API
- SharePoint APIs
- Entra ID-secured APIs
- Anonymous APIs

Technical requirements

This chapter relies on the GitHub solution accessible here: `https://github.com/PacktPublishing/Mastering-SharePoint-Development-with-the-SharePoint-Framework-`. You need to first clone the repository locally on your machine to be able to follow the steps.

The following Git branch is used for the entire chapter: `https://github.com/PacktPublishing/Mastering-SharePoint-Development-with-the-SharePoint-Framework-/tree/chapter18/consuming-apis`.

You must check out this branch before using either the Git command line or a Git client such as GitHub Desktop or Sourcetree.

> **Code snippets**
>
> For brevity and readability, only the relevant parts of the code are detailed in the provided snippets in this chapter. For these reasons, ad hoc code, such as dependency imports and updates to certain files, may be omitted. We recommend having the GitHub solution open as you're going along to get the full working version of the code and review the provided steps.

Getting started with SPFx clients

In SPFx components, all utility class instances to consume APIs are exposed through the root `this.context` property regardless of the type of SPFx solution (web part or extension). These JavaScript object instances are called **clients** and can be used to make HTTP requests (GET, POST, etc.) to the associated API.

Depending on their use case, developers can use the following SPFx-provided properties and their associated clients:

Property	Client type(s)	Used to...
`this.context.spHttpClient`	`SPHttpClient`	Consume the SharePoint REST API.
`this.context.httpClient`	`HttpClient`	Consume regular HTTP APIs, for instance, internal custom APIs or third-party APIs.

Property	Client type(s)	Used to...

`this.context.`
`aadHttpClientFactory.`
`getClient()`
	`AadHttpClient`	Consume Entra ID (formerly Azure Active Directory) protected APIs, such as Azure functions or Azure Web API. Can also be used to consume the Microsoft Graph API.

`this.context.`
`msGraphClientFactory.`
`getClient()`
	`MSGraphClientV3`	Consume the Microsoft Graph API.

Table 18.1 – SPFx's available HTTP base client properties

> **Use SPFx-provided properties**
>
> These clients are initialized and provided to you automatically by SPFx. This is not recommended for creating your own instances (for example, `new AddHttpClient()`).

In the next sections, we'll detail how to use each type of client depending on the scenario.

Connecting to secured APIs

Consuming APIs secured with Entra ID within an SPFx web part or extension is a fairly common business scenario. This is, for example, the case whenever your solution needs to access data using the Microsoft Graph API, or any API secured with an Entra ID application, such as a custom enterprise application or web service.

Because this type of application relies on the **Open Authorization (OAuth 2.0)** standard to authenticate the client and access underlying resources (i.e., APIs such as `https://graph.microsoft.com/` or `https://your_api/`), the client needs to first obtain a valid **access token** to access them (also referred as a **bearer token**).

This token is obtained as part of the OAuth 2.0 authorization flow that the client solution needs to implement, in this case, your SPFx component. This token must also provide the correct API permission scopes according to the requested operation (for instance, the `Files.Read.All` scope to be able to read files from a SharePoint library using the Microsoft Graph API). To be used, those scopes must be *declared and approved* directly in the Entra ID application, securing the target resources. In the case of SPFx, only *delegated permissions* are used.

> **Delegated API permissions ≠ application API permissions ≠ user permissions**
>
> Be careful here; a *delegated API permission* on a resource is different from the connected user effective permission on the resource itself. For instance, giving the `Sites.Read.All` delegated API permission to an Entra ID application won't give users access to all the sites in the tenant. It simply means we "allow" reading all the sites and resources on behalf of the logged-in user through the API. If a user doesn't have any permission on a library or an item itself, the result of the request will be an HTTP `401` code (unauthorized) regardless of the API permission given.
>
> However, using the *application API permissions* type *will actually give access* to the Entra ID application regardless of the effective permissions on the resource. For instance, giving the `Sites.Read.All` permission to an Entra ID application will allow it to read all the sites in the tenant.
>
> In SPFx, you must always use *delegated permissions* and never, ever use *application permissions* as it represents a major security risk. Such permissions imply secrets that can't be securely stored in a JavaScript application executed in a browser. For example, if an application secret is compromised and you give `Sites.FullControl.All` application permissions, someone could take over your entire SharePoint content.

In the *Authentication and permissions* section of *Chapter 2, Ecosystem and Building Blocks around the SharePoint Framework*, we already provided a high-level overview of the OAuth 2.0 specifications, so we won't repeat ourselves here. Just keep in mind that this protocol provides several flows for many different scenarios depending on the application type (web applications backed by a web server, daemon services, or simply pure JavaScript applications), and it is up to the client application requesting the resource to implement the corresponding flow and obtain a valid access token passed along the request in the *Authorization* HTTP header to access the resource. To implement such flows, Microsoft provides the **Microsoft Authentication Library** (**MSAL**) covering all possible OAuth 2.0 scenarios for all major languages (JavaScript, Node.js, C#, Python, etc.).

SPFx, being a framework for client-side applications only, uses the **OAuth 2.0 implicit flow** to get tokens and handles the authentication process behind the scenes via the `MSGraphClientV3` and `AadHttpClient` clients. However, you still need, as a developer, to declare the required API permission scopes depending on the resource and operation you want to perform as it is specific to your application.

The needed permission scopes can be declared in the `package-solution.json` file in the `webApiPermissionRequests` property. For instance, to read items from a SharePoint list using the `https://graph.microsoft.com/v1.0/sites/{site_id}/lists/{list_name}/items` endpoint, we declare the following scopes:

```
{
  "$schema": "https://developer.microsoft.com/json-schemas/spfx-build/
package-solution.schema.json",
  "solution": {
    ...
```

```
    "webApiPermissionRequests": [
      {
        "resource": "Microsoft Graph",
        "scope": "Sites.Read.All"
      }
    ],
    ...
```

For a scope, you need to define at least the following two properties:

- resource: The Entra ID application name or object ID (different in every tenant) securing the resource you want to access. For Microsoft Graph, the name is **Microsoft Graph**, and for a custom Entra ID application, it is the name of the application itself.

- scope: The name of the permission scope (or the unique ID). This value comes directly from the API documentation. For the Microsoft Graph API, every endpoint defines its own scopes, so you need to check the API reference at https://learn.microsoft.com/en-us/graph/api/overview?view=graph-rest-1.0.

Then, when the solution is packaged and deployed to the app catalog (tenant or site collection level), SharePoint administrators will get prompted to approve or reject the scopes your solution is requesting. This is done from the SharePoint administration center:

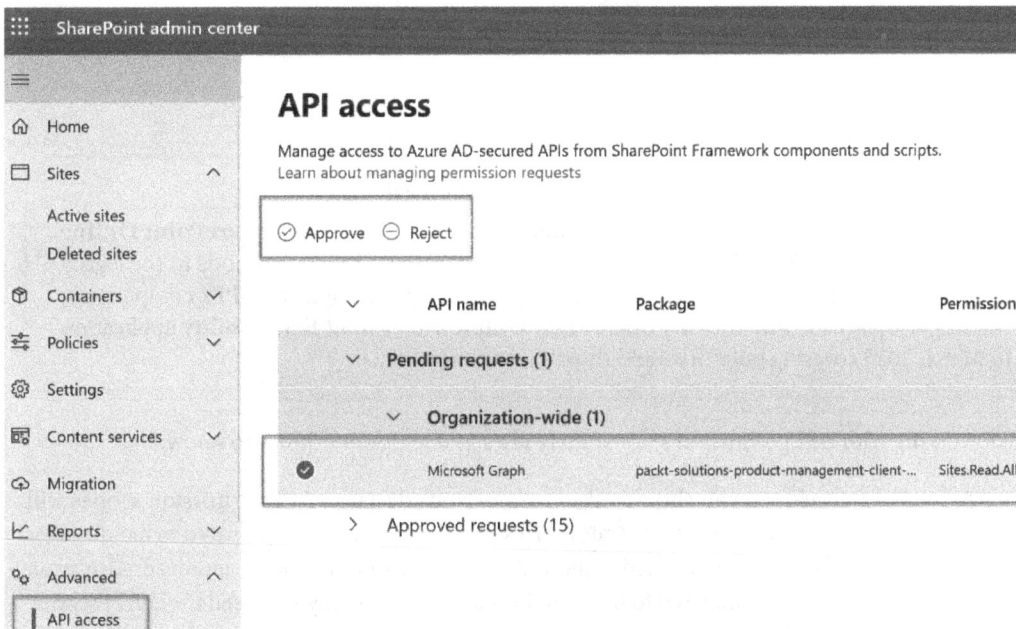

Figure 18.1 – Approve or reject API permission scopes from the SharePoint admin center

Behind the scenes, SPFx uses an Entra ID application named **SharePoint Online Web Client Extensibility**. This application, provided by Microsoft, is automatically registered as a service principal in your Azure tenant and used by the `MSGraphClientV3` and `AadHttpClient` clients. This service principal is shared for both third-party components (i.e., custom SPFx components) and first-party components (Microsoft-native ones). You can't grant API permissions directly through this service principal using the Entra ID interface; you must use the API access administration page.

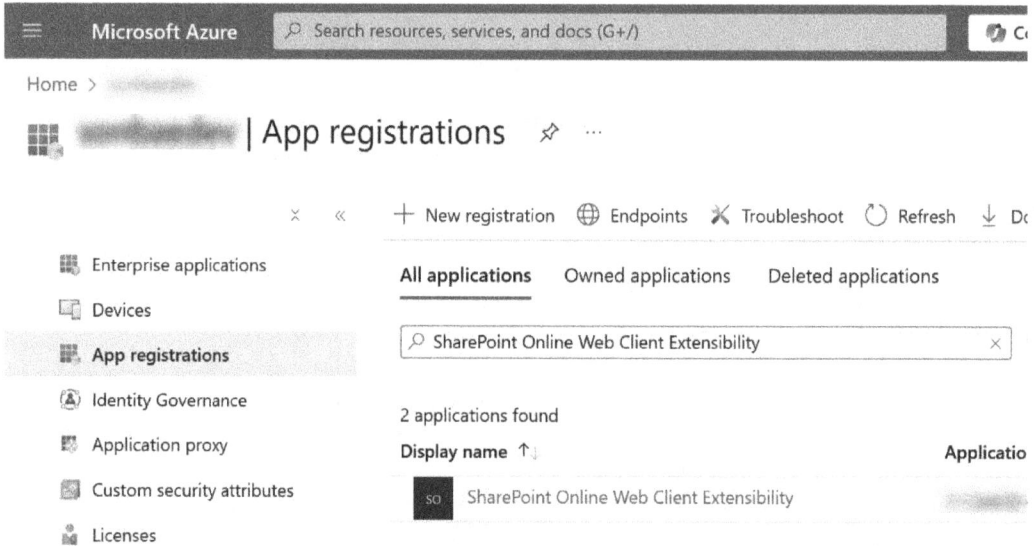

Figure 18.2 – Entra ID application used by SPFx for authentication

> **SharePoint Online Client Extensibility Web Application Principal**
>
> When browsing Azure application registrations, you may also see the **SharePoint Online Client Extensibility Web Application Principal** application. This corresponds to the legacy service principal previously used to exclusively grant API permissions for SPFx components. Microsoft replaced it with the new **SharePoint Online Web Client Extensibility** application in March 2025 covering both first- and third-party components.

When working with API permission scopes, there are some important things to know:

- As an SPFx developer, you should *never assume* your declared API permission scopes will necessarily be approved by administrators. This means you need to be prepared to handle error scenarios in code as a result of failed requests due to permissions not being approved. Also, in an enterprise scenario, be prepared to be asked by administrators why you need these API scopes. Using the **least-privilege principle** will increase the chance of your scope getting approved!

- Once an API permission is approved, *it is valid for the entire tenant*, meaning other SPFx solutions can use it as well without declaring them explicitly in the `package-solution.json` file. If not managed correctly, this could lead to a major security risk as other solutions could access resources they are not supposed to access. This is why it is again recommended to use the least-privilege principle to limit that risk.

- You should never manipulate the **SharePoint Online Web Client Extensibility** service principal manually in the Azure portal as it is completely managed by SharePoint and synchronized with the administration center. Doing this could lead to unexpected behaviors not supported by Microsoft.

- Declaring scopes in the `package-solution.json` file and using the admin portal is not the only way to get API permission scopes approved for SPFx solutions. You can also use the **CLI for Microsoft 365** to directly approve permission, for instance, through an automated CI/CD pipeline:

```
> m365 login
> m365 spo serviceprincipal grant add --resource 'Microsoft
Graph' --scope 'Sites.Read.All'
```

Or use **PnP PowerShell** to do so:

```
> Connect-PnPOnline -Url https://{your_site}-admin.sharepoint.
com/ -Interactive
> Grant-PnPTenantServicePrincipalPermission -Scope "Sites.Read.
All" -Resource "Microsoft Graph"
```

However, even if approved programmatically, it is still recommended to always declare the needed permissions in the `package-solution.json` file, to clearly identify what permissions the solution is using.

> **What about the SharePoint REST API?**
>
> The traditional SharePoint REST API is also secured by Entra ID. However, this API is not affected by this setup as it uses cookie-based authentication using `SPHttpClient` due to SharePoint on-premises legacy reasons. This means you don't need to declare API permission scopes in your solution for this API.

In the next sections, we will detail all possible clients and their usage for consuming the corresponding APIs.

Using the Microsoft Graph API

In *Chapter 5*, we demonstrated how to use the Microsoft Graph API to fetch a list of products coming from a SharePoint list in the `ProductCatalogService` class. In this section, we will simply summarize all the important steps.

As explained in the previous section, the very first step before calling the Microsoft Graph API is to approve the API permission scopes needed for the requested operation. In our case, we declare and approve the `Sites.Read.All` API permission.

Then, to perform requests against the Microsoft Graph API from an SPFx component, we need to get a client for the Microsoft Graph API to be able to make calls. We use the `msGraphClientFactory.getClient("3")` method from the `this.context` SPFx property to get one:

```
..
const msGraphClient = await this.context.msGraphClientFactory.
getClient("3");
..
```

Finally, using that client instance, we use the appropriate `/sites/{site-id}/lists/{list-id}/items` endpoint URL and the `GET HTTP` method to get the data we need from the SharePoint products list:

```
..
const response = await msGraphClient
            .api(`sites/${siteId}/lists/${listName}/items`)
            .expand(`fields($select=${fields})`)
            .get();
```

When using the `MSGraphClientV3` class, you have the choice to specify the request and OData parameters directly in the URL, or to use modifiers to do the same. For instance, take the following request:

```
await this._msGraphClient.api(`sites/${siteId}/lists/${listName}/
items?$expand=fields($select=${fields})&$filter=fields/
packtProductStockLevel gt 0`).headers({'Prefer':
'HonorNonIndexedQueriesWarningMayFailRandomly'}).get();
```

This is equivalent to the following with modifiers:

```
await this._msGraphClient.api(`sites/${siteId}/lists/${listName}/
items`).expand(`fields($select=${fields})`).filter("fields/
packtProductStockLevel gt 0").headers({'Prefer':
'HonorNonIndexedQueriesWarningMayFailRandomly'}).get();
```

For readability, we recommend using the second option.

Now that we've seen how to consume the Microsoft Graph API and how easy it is, let's update our example, this time using the SharePoint REST API.

Using the SharePoint REST API

To demonstrate how to use the SharePoint REST API, we will now update the `getProducts()` method of the `ProductCatalogService` class to use the `SPHttpClient` client to fetch the list of products from a SharePoint list instead of the Microsoft Graph API.

First, we update the constructor of the class to take an `SPHttpClient` parameter and the absolute web URL from where the products list is located:

```
export class ProductCatalogService implements IProductCatalogService {

  private _spHttpClient: SPHttpClient;
  private _webUrl: string;

  constructor(spHttpClient: SPHttpClient, webUrl: string) {
    this._spHttpClient = spHttpClient;
    this._webUrl = webUrl;
  }
  ...
```

Unlike the Microsoft Graph API, all HTTP requests with the SharePoint REST API are made relative to the site where the data is located. We use the `/_api/web/lists/GetByTitle('Products')/items` endpoint from the API to retrieve the list of products from SharePoint:

```
public async getProducts(
    siteId: string,
    listName: string
  ): Promise<IProductCatalogItem[]> {
    const fields = ...
    const response = await this._spHttpClient.get(
      `${this._webUrl}/_api/web/lists/GetByTitle('${listName}')/
items?$select=${fields}`,
      SPHttpClient.configurations.v1);

    if (response.ok) {
      const responseJson = await response.json();

      const items: IProductCatalogItem[] = responseJson.value.
map((item: any) => {
        return {
            modelName: item.packtProductModelName,
            lastOrderDate: item.packtProductStockLastOrderDate
              ? new Date(item.packtProductStockLastOrderDate)
              : null,
            productReference: item.packtProductReference,
```

```
                stockLevel: item.packtProductStockLevel,
                size: item.packtProductSize as ProductSizes,
                ...
            } as IProductCatalogItem;
        });

        return items;
    } else {
        Log.error("ProductCatalogService", new Error(response.
statusText));
        return [];
    }
}
```

Finally, we tie this all up by passing the `SPHttpClient` client instance and web URL from the root web part context in the `PackProductCatalogWebPart.ts` file in the `onInit()` method:

```
protected async onInit(): Promise<void> {
    ...
    this._productCatalogService = new ProductCatalogService(
            this.context.spHttpClient,
            this.context.pageContext.web.absoluteUrl
        );
```

Behind the scenes, `SPHttpClient` will take care of the authentication by leveraging existing session cookies. This operation is completely transparent to you, and unlike Entra ID-secured APIs such as Microsoft Graph, you don't need to specify any API permission scopes in the `package-solution.json` file.

By default, `SPHttpClient` uses **OData** version 4 for all requests. However, some endpoints in the SharePoint REST API (such as the `/_api/search/postquery` SharePoint search endpoint) only support version 3 to work properly. In this case, to configure the client correctly, you can leverage the third parameter of either the `get()`, `post()`, or `fetch()` method to customize the request options. For example, you can configure the request HTTP headers via the `headers` property to set the OData version to use:

```
const response = await this.spHttpClient.post(`${this.pageContext.web.
absoluteUrl}/_api/search/postquery`, SPHttpClient.configurations.v1, {
                    body: ...,
                    headers: {
                        'odata-version': '3.0',
                        'accept': 'application/json;odata=nometadata'
                    }
                });
```

For HTTP POST requests, you can also specify the payload as a stringified JavaScript object via the body property.

In the next section, we'll see how to call an API protected by Entra ID outside of Microsoft 365 or SharePoint.

Using Entra ID-protected APIs

In an enterprise scenario, it is quite common to consume custom APIs protected by Entra ID, for instance, to call an Azure function triggering an external business process. Like the Microsoft Graph API, SPFx provides a way to easily consume such APIs to avoid having to carry out the authentication process manually.

To demonstrate this use case, we will now assume the product information from our products inventory is now retrieved from an Azure function app called `demospfxfunction` instead of a SharePoint list.

> **Note**
>
> The goal of this book is not to explain how to create an Azure function or configure an app service. The following sections only explain the major configuration steps required to integrate your application with SPFx.

In the next section, we detail its configuration and usage with SPFx.

Configuring an Azure function with EasyAuth

From the Azure portal, we first create a function called `GetProducts` of the **HTTP** trigger type, which will return all the products:

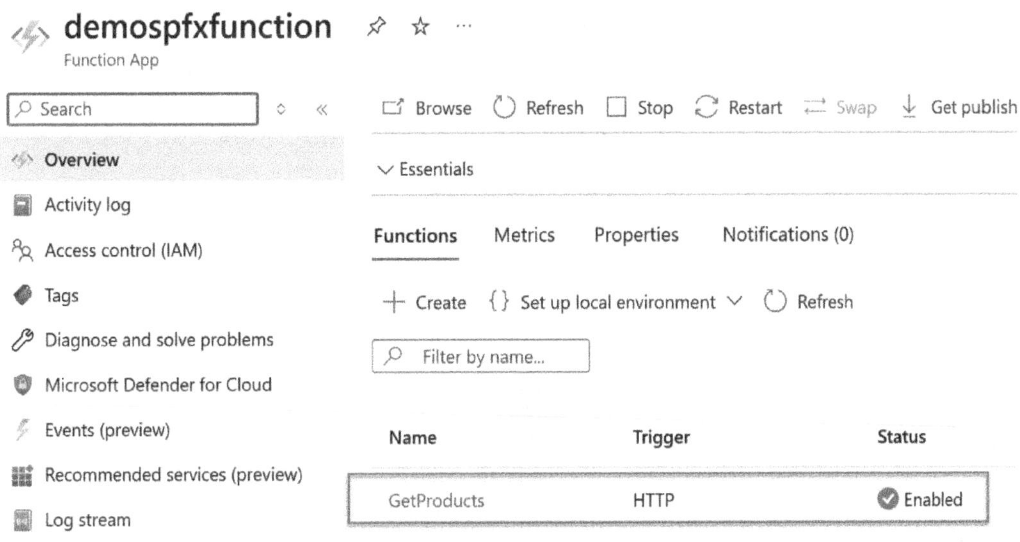

Figure 18.3 – Azure function to retrieve the list of products

In our case, we use a Node.js function in a Linux host environment (the host environment doesn't really matter here). For example purposes, we will simply return a static array of fake products. The function code looks like the following (an `index.js` file):

```js
module.exports = async function (context, req) {
    context.res = {
        body: [
            {
                packtProductModelName: "UltraBoost Running Shoes",
                packtProductRetailPrice: 180,
                packtProductStockLevel: 25,
                packtProductStockLastOrderDate: "2023-04-01",
                packtProductItemPicture: "ultraboost.jpg",
                packtProductColor: "Black",
                packtProductSize: "M",
                packtProductReference: "UB-001",
            },
            {
                packtProductModelName: "Tech Fleece Hoodie",
                packtProductRetailPrice: 100,
                packtProductStockLevel: 40,
                packtProductStockLastOrderDate: "2023-03-28",
                packtProductItemPicture: "techfleece.jpg",
                packtProductColor: "Grey",
                packtProductSize: "L",
                packtProductReference: "TF-002",
            },
            {
                packtProductModelName: "Water Bottle",
                packtProductRetailPrice: 25,
                packtProductStockLevel: 100,
                packtProductStockLastOrderDate: "2023-03-15",
                packtProductItemPicture: "waterbottle.jpg",
                packtProductColor: "Blue",
                packtProductSize: "S",
                packtProductReference: "WB-003",
            }
        ]
    };
}
```

Then, we configure the built-in Azure App Service authentication feature called **EasyAuth**, providing a predefined set of identity providers allowing us to secure a *web application* or a *function* without needing to implement any specific code:

Add an identity provider   ···

Basics   Permissions

Choose an identity provider from the dropdown below to start.

Identity provider *

Select identity provider	∨

■■ Microsoft

Sign in Microsoft and Microsoft Entra identities and call Microsoft APIs

Figure 18.4 – Adding Entra ID authentication for an Azure function via EasyAuth

When configured in **express mode**, an Entra ID application is automatically registered in the Azure tenant and the `user_impersonation` API scope is automatically exposed as well. This is the scope we're going to use in our SPFx solution to consume the function API:

Home > demospfxfunction

demospfxfunction | Expose an API   🖈   ···

- ⌕ Search   ↻   «
- ▦ Overview
- 🏁 Quickstart
- 🎯 Integration assistant
- ✖ Diagnose and solve problems
- ∨ Manage
  - 🖼 Branding & properties
  - 🔁 Authentication
  - 🔑 Certificates & secrets
  - ┃┃┃ Token configuration
  - ⊸ API permissions
  - 🗂 **Expose an API**

🗨 Got feedback?

Application ID URI :   api://4df79ed7-c568-499a-b1c2-6abdcab5d4bf   📋   Edit

Scopes defined by this API

Define custom scopes to restrict access to data and functionality protected by the API. An applica: API can request that a user or admin consent to one or more of these.

Adding a scope here creates only delegated permissions. If you are looking to create application-: application type. Go to App roles.

+ Add a scope

Scopes	Who can consent
api://4df79ed7-c568-499a-b1c2-6abdcab5d4bf/user_impersonation 📋	Admins and users

Figure 18.5 – Default user_impersonation scope for an Entra ID app

Azure function quick tips

When **EasyAuth** is enabled for a function, make sure to set its authorization level to **Anonymous** in the function settings. Otherwise, you'll get an HTTP 401 code when making the request. This is because by default, functions use the **Function** authorization level, requiring a secret code as a query parameter when invoked.

Also, in the configuration of this Entra ID application, make sure you allow all client applications or specific applications to perform a request with the **Client application requirement** setting. If configured to a specific application, add the **SharePoint Online Web Client Extensibility** application ID. By default, the registered app for the function will deny requests other than the application itself and you'll get an HTTP 403 code when making the request.

To be able to call the function URL from the SPFx web part hosted on SharePoint, we need to configure the **Cross-Origin Request Sharing (CORS)** settings on the function itself. It allows requests coming from a different origin, such as `https://{your-tenant}.sharepoint.com`. If not configured, the app service will simply reject the request:

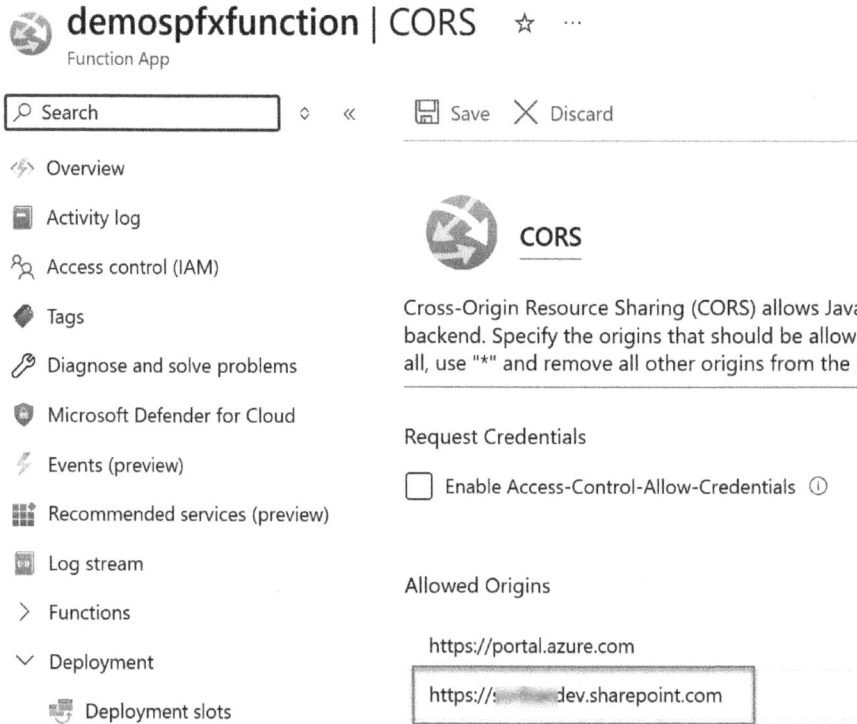

Figure 18.6 – CORS settings on the Azure function

Now that the API is ready to be consumed, in the SPFx solution, we declare the API permission scope in `package-solution.json` using the Entra ID application name and the exposed scope:

```
{
  "$schema": "https://developer.microsoft.com/json-schemas/spfx-build/
package-solution.schema.json",
  "solution": {
    . . .
    "webApiPermissionRequests": [
      {
        "resource": "demospfxfunction",
        "scope": "user_impersonation"
      }
    ],
    . . .
```

After bundling the solution (`gulp bundle --ship`), packaging it (`gulp package-solution --ship`), and finally, uploading the package to the tenant app catalog, we approve the API permission from the SharePoint admin center:

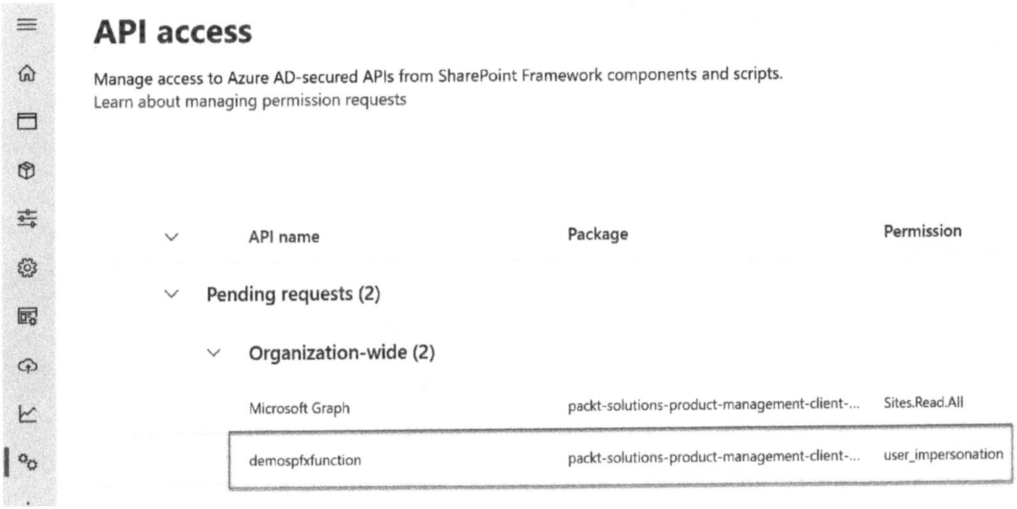

Figure 18.7 – Approve custom scope

Now that our Azure function is ready, it is time to call our API.

Using AadHttpClient

To call an Entra ID-protected API, SPFx provides the `AadHttpClient` client. Like the `MSGraphClient` seen earlier, it handles all authentication for you behind the scenes.

In the `PackProductCatalogWebPart.ts` web part entry file, we start by getting the reference of `aadHttpClientFactory` from the SPFx context object to get the client. We use as a parameter the Entra ID application ID configured as part of the **EasyAuth** feature:

```
protected async onInit(): Promise<void> {

    const aadHttpClient = await this.context.aadHttpClientFactory.
getClient("4df79ed7-c568-499a-b1c2-6abdcab5d4bf");
    this._productCatalogService = new
ProductCatalogService(aadHttpClient);

    return super.onInit();
}
```

We then update the `ProductCatalogService` class constructor to take an instance of the `AadHttpClient` that will be used to call the API:

```
export class ProductCatalogService implements IProductCatalogService {

  private _aadHttpClient: AadHttpClient;

  constructor(aadHttpClient: AadHttpClient) {
    this._aadHttpClient = aadHttpClient;
  }

  ...
```

Finally, we update the `getProducts()` method to call the function URL using the client (notice that we don't use a query string parameter in the URL):

```
public async getProducts(
    siteId: string,
    listName: string
  ): Promise<IProductCatalogItem[]> {

    const response = await this._aadHttpClient.get("https://
demospfxfunction.azurewebsites.net/api/GetProducts", AadHttpClient.
configurations.v1);

        if (response.ok) {
```

```
            const responseJson = await response.json();

            const items: IProductCatalogItem[] = responseJson.map((item:
    any) => {
                return {
                    modelName: item.packtProductModelName,
                    lastOrderDate: item.packtProductStockLastOrderDate

                    ...
                } as IProductCatalogItem;
            });

            return items;
        } else {
            Log.error("ProductCatalogService", new Error(response.
    statusText));
            return [];
        }
    }
```

This code will call the Azure function with the correct OAuth access token retrieved from Entra ID.

Using the `AadHttpClient` client is not the only way to interact with Entra ID-secured APIs. In the next section, we detail how to get access token values directly for specific resources.

Using AadTokenProvider

For some use cases, you just need to retrieve the OAuth access token value directly to access a specific resource (i.e., the API).

As an example, that would be the case when you need to communicate with a chatbot using the **Microsoft Bot Framework** and perform a server request on behalf of the currently logged-in user. Instead of implementing **Single Sign-On (SSO)** in your bot, you could simply pass the required access token retrieved from SPFx to the bot using the direct line channel.

For this type of use case, SPFx provides a utility called `AadTokenProvider`, which allows you to retrieve OAuth access tokens for particular resources where API permission scopes are already approved in **SharePoint Online Web Client Extensibility**service principal.

For instance, to retrieve a token for the Microsoft Graph API, you can use the following code to get the access token and use it in the **Authorization HTTP** header without using `MSGraphClientV3`:

```
const aadTokenProvider = await this.context.aadTokenProviderFactory.
getTokenProvider();

aadTokenProvider.getToken("https://graph.microsoft.com").then((token)
=> {
```

```
    console.log(token);
 });
```

Considering our previous example with Microsoft Graph, the token would contain the approved scopes in the service principal for that resource, in that case, Sites.Read.All:

```
    "app_displayname": "SharePoint Online Client
Extensibility Web Application Principal",
    "appid": "5112eb50-6ced-4888-92b7-1122cf570c17",
    "appidacr": "1",
    "family_name": "Cornu",
    "given_name": "Franck",
    "idtyp": "user",
    "ipaddr": "66.131.218.112",
    "name": "Franck Cornu",
    "oid": "78e08807-509f-40c9-951e-848427e09a0c",
    "platf": "3",
    "puid": "10032001BFAB3697",
    "rh":
"1.AUYAxlfp19LA406I1b9cClYmiwMAAAAAAAAwAAAAAAAACAAIxGA
A.",
    "scp": "Sites.Read.All profile openid email",
    "sub": "zKp7Almc3-fkD_u5BZS1NyoLs0RIqkdcnrHqHHH6_QQ",
```

Figure 18.8 – Access token breakdown using the jwt.io tool

This works for a custom API protected by Entra ID as well (using the application ID as the resource name). The following code retrieves the access token containing the user_impersonation scope from our custom API resource defined previously:

```
aadTokenProvider.getToken("4df79ed7-c568-499a-b1c2-6abdcab5d4bf").
then((token) => {
    console.log(token);
});
```

In the last section of this chapter, we detail how to use anonymous APIs or APIs not protected by Entra ID.

Using anonymous APIs

To consume any other type of API, such as public ones or ones that don't use Entra ID for authentication, SPFx provides the `HttpClient` client. The implementation is very close to the native `fetch()` API provided by the browser, allowing you to completely customize the request, such as headers, body, and query parameters. There are no SPFx specificities here. Like the SharePoint-dedicated `SPHttpClient` client, the usage is straightforward:

1. You first get a reference to `httpClient` for the `this.context` property:

    ```
    this._productCatalogService = new ProductCatalogService(this.
    context.httpClient);
    ```

2. Then, you can make any call to your API. The following example demonstrates the usage of `HttpClient` using the Azure function we defined in the previous section, but without the authentication part:

    ```
    const response = await this._httpClient.get("https://
    demospfxfunction.azurewebsites.net/api/GetProducts ",
    HttpClient.configurations.v1);
            if (response.ok) {

        const responseJson = await response.json();
            const items: IProductCatalogItem[] =
    responseJson.map((item: any) => {
            return {
              ...
            } as IProductCatalogItem;
          });
          return items;
      } else {
          Log.error("ProductCatalogService", new Error(response.
    statusText));
          return [];
      }
    ```

When using `HttpClient`, there is no authentication mechanism handled by SPFx. For instance, authentication cookies are not included in the requests, so it is up to you to implement any required authentication for your API.

> **What about third-party libraries?**
>
> In some SPFx samples or solutions, you'll often see the popular **Axios** library (`https://axios-http.com`), an open source HTTP client. Even though it can be quite useful for some use cases, we don't necessarily recommend using such libraries systematically for simple requests as SPFx already provides all you need with the `HttpClient` client. Using a third-party library will just increase the size of the webpack bundle for no real gain (but feel free to use it if really needed).

Summary

In this chapter, we've detailed how to use various types of APIs in an SPFx solution. We started by listing possible HTTP clients provided by the framework and where to access them. For Entra ID-secured APIs, such as the Microsoft Graph API, we explained the underlying mechanisms and prerequisites, discussing how SPFx is capable of doing the heavy lifting for you and getting access tokens on behalf of the current user to call protected APIs. For each type, we provided a clear usage example and highlighted important points to remember as a developer.

In the next chapter, we'll see how to write tests to improve the development quality.

Get This Book's PDF Version and Exclusive Extras

UNLOCK NOW

Scan the QR code (or go to `packtpub.com/unlock`). Search for this book by name, confirm the edition, and then follow the steps on the page.

Note: Keep your invoice handy. Purchases made directly from Packt don't require an invoice.

Writing Tests with SPFx

In the previous chapter, we learned how to debug our solutions if something goes wrong. What if we could avoid the issue in the first place? That is where tests come into play! Testing is always a taboo subject among developers: everybody agrees on the importance of testing but almost nobody does it. Most of the time, in real-life projects, testing is seen as something costly, hard to integrate, and hard to implement, especially with SPFx. Let's be clear: *that is partially true.*

The more critical your application is, the more important testing is. If your application is supporting thousands of users daily for a critical line-of-business process, maybe having tests is a good idea. However, as a developer, you shouldn't be ashamed of not having tests in your solution. *They are not always required.* For instance, simple use cases such as getting and displaying data on a dummy web part for two or three users and without any kind of business logic do not necessarily require automated tests. To give you an idea, the vast majority of the open source samples provided by the community (`https://pnp.github.io/sp-dev-fx-webparts/`) don't provide any tests. That does not mean the code is bad.

In this chapter, we'll learn how to write tests for our SPFx solutions. We'll focus on web parts as they are the most commonly used components in the framework. In the next few sections, you'll learn how to do the following:

- Understand what type of tests you can do with SPFx
- Write tests with the Jest framework for your components

Technical requirements

This chapter relies on the GitHub solution available at `https://github.com/PacktPublishing/Mastering-SharePoint-Development-with-the-SharePoint-Framework-`. You need to clone the repository locally on your machine to be able to follow the steps provided.

The following Git branch will be used throughout this chapter: `https://github.com/PacktPublishing/Mastering-SharePoint-Development-with-the-SharePoint-Framework-/tree/chapter19/testing-with-spfx`.

Before reading this chapter, you *must* check out this branch remove using either the Git command line or a Git client such as GitHub Desktop, SourceTree, or similar.

> **Code snippets**
>
> For brevity and readability considerations, only the relevant parts of the code are detailed in the snippets provided in this chapter. For these reasons, ad hoc code, such as dependencies and imports, as well as updates to certain files, may be omitted. We recommend that you keep the GitHub solution open while completing this chapter so that you can achieve the full working version of the code and review the steps provided.

Understanding the importance of testing

In software development, testing can take many forms. The two main ones regarding SPFx are as follows:

- **Unit tests**: These tests aim to verify that individual units of our code perform as expected when isolated from other components. For example, if we have an argument, A, our function should return true, while another argument, B, should result in false. Similarly, a single button click might trigger sequence A, whereas another button click should trigger sequence B. This is the same reasoning for UI components. Regarding SPFx, unit tests shouldn't have to rely on any SPFx context (i.e., testable outside of a SharePoint page). For this type of test, we usually use the **Jest** testing framework as it integrates well with SPFx. We won't deep dive into the framework itself here as that is outside the scope of this book, but we will cover its usage in SPFx in more detail later.

- **Integration tests**: Integration tests focus on a higher application level than unit tests in that they assess how different units collaborate and interact with each other. For instance, in the context of SPFx, integration tests allow you to run a real SharePoint page, with a logged-in user, and test end-to-end interactions with the component without having to dive into the details of the implementation. These types of tests usually require tools such as **Cypress** or **Playwright** to automate actions in the UI. However, they also require much more work as they involve many moving parts and setup (authentication, latency, and so on).

We'll only focus on unit tests in this chapter.

Regardless of their type, tests are mainly designed to help us avoid *regressions*. When a solution is updated, it's common for new issues to emerge. Without reliable ways to validate the features that were there before continue to work properly after an update, we can inadvertently deploy faulty code to production that could break the entire solution. As a developer, this is not necessarily something we want. When this happens, end users become angry, developers become angry, and it leads to frustration and technical debt (due to the need to fix those issues instead of working on new features). Nobody wants this.

That is exactly the purpose of testing: to anticipate issues before deploying anything to production.

In the next section, we'll learn how to implement unit tests for React components with SPFx.

Implementing tests with Jest

Jest is a popular testing framework for TypeScript and React projects. It provides everything you need (functions, assertions, and so on) to test your code, including regular TypeScript classes and React components for UI tests. This is typically the preferred test framework for SPFx.

Preparing the test environment

The first step is to add the necessary dependencies so that we can test our code. In the `package.json` file, add the following packages:

```
"devDependencies": {
    ...
    "jest": "^29.5.0",
    "ts-jest": "^29.1.0",
    "@types/jest": "~29.5.3"
    "jest-environment-jsdom": "^29.5.0",
    "identity-obj-proxy": "^3.0.0",
    "@testing-library/jest-dom": "~5.16.5",
    "@testing-library/react": "12.1.5"
}
```

Let's take a closer look at these packages:

- `jest`: The Jest testing library
- `ts-jest`: The Jest compiler for TypeScript projects
- `@types/jest`: TypeScript types relevant to Jest so that Visual Studio Code won't complain about the syntax that's used
- `jest-environment-jsdom`: This allows us to test the DOM for React components – for instance, ensuring a specific element is present on the page
- `identity-obj-proxy`: This is a utility library that can mock problematic imports in code, especially dependencies coming from SPFx (e.g., `@microsoft/sp-core-library`)
- `@testing-library/jest-dom`: This library extends Jest assertions so that they're closer to what real users would see or expect on a page, instead of testing specific parts of DOM elements that are tied to implementation details (e.g., to ensure an element is present in the current page with the `toBeInDocument()` assertion)

- @testing-library/react: This package provides utility functions to test React components (e.g., to get an element by its text value – that is, getByText)

> **Package versions**
>
> Be careful here – package versions are important as they need to be compatible with the versions of TypeScript and React that SPFx uses. Don't necessarily use the latest version!

After adding these dependencies, install them by running the following command:

```
> npm i
```

The next step is to update the tsconfig.json file to ensure our tests can be executed correctly:

```
"compilerOptions": {
    ..
    "esModuleInterop": true,
    ...
    "types": [
        ...
        "jest"
    ]
}
```

Then, we must create a Jest configuration file by running the following command in the root folder of our SPFx solution:

```
> npx ts-jest config:init
```

This creates a new jest.config.js file. For now, we can replace the generated content with the following:

```
/** @type {import('ts-jest').JestConfigWithTsJest} **/
module.exports = {
  roots: ['<rootDir>/src'],
  transform: {
    '^.+\\.tsx?$': 'ts-jest',
  },
  testRegex: '(/__tests__/.*|(\\.|/)(test|spec))\\.tsx?$',
  moduleFileExtensions: ['ts', 'tsx', 'js', 'jsx'],
  verbose: true,
  testEnvironment: "jsdom"
};
```

> **Jest configuration file**
>
> Please refer to the official Jest documentation to see all available options: `https://jestjs.io/docs/configuration`.

In our case, we'll focus on a simple test use case. Only the following fields are required:

- `roots`: Defines the root folder from where test files should be searched

- `transform`: Indicates that the Jest TypeScript compiler should be used for files with the `.tsx` extension that correspond to React components.

- `testRegex`: A regular expression that's used to look for test files that must be executed from the root folder. By default, our test files will have the `<filename>.test.ts` extension.

- `moduleFileExtensions`: Defines all types of imports our modules use (such as other TypeScript classes, plain JavaScript files, and so on).

- `verbose`: Used to provide test execution details. It's recommended to leave it set to `true` if you wish to see all outputs (this is useful for debugging purposes).

- `testEnvironment`: The test environment that's used for tests. By default, Jest assumes we're running tests for a regular Node.js environment (with no UI). However, in our case, we want to test React components that can be tested against DOM elements. That is why we have set it to `jsdom`.

The final step is to update the `package.json` file so that it can call Jest and run our tests once we run the `npm run test` command:

```
"scripts": {
    ...
    "test": "jest"
}
```

Now that our environment is ready, we can implement our first test.

Writing your first test

Under the `/src/webparts/packProductCatalog/components` folder, create a new file called `PackProductCatalog.test.tsx` for testing the `PackProductCatalog.tsx` component. It is responsible for displaying products in the web part. In the following section, we'll cover the implementation details and highlight the important elements you need to understand as an SPFx developer.

Organizing your tests

In our case, we want to test the product catalog component (the React component, not the web part), ensuring it displays the products in the UI correctly. We'll start our test file by ensuring it has the following structure:

```
describe("Product catalog tests suite", () => {
    it('Display the list of products retrieved from the list', async
() => {
        // Test implementation
    });
});
```

The Jest framework provides multiple directives to help you organize your tests inside a file. For example, the `describe` directive is used to group multiple tests under the same category, and test implementations are performed with the `it` or `test` directive (here, `it` is an alias of the `test` directive).

These directives are not only useful when used in code – they also produce a structured output when the test file is executed. You can refer to the official Jest documentation to see all possible directives: `https://jestjs.io/docs/api`.

Follow these guidelines to ensure you have a clean test structure in your solution:

- Ensure there's only one component/class per file.

- Filenames should follow the original name of the component/class filename but with the `.test.ts` extension – for example, `MyComponent.tsx`/`MyComponent.test.ts`.

- Use Jest API directives such as `describe` and `it`/`test` to structure your tests logically.

- Use the same pattern for your test files as per your preferences (technically, it doesn't matter). Either create `.test.ts` files alongside the original files or create a dedicated tests folder that contains all the test files, but don't do both.

Now that we have defined our test structure, it is time to implement it.

Rendering the component and mocking the products data

The next step is to configure and render the React component in the test, like so:

```
describe("Product catalog tests suite", () => {
   it('Display the list of products retrieved from the list', async ()
=> {

     const productCatalogService = new ProductCatalogService({} as
MSGraphClientV3);
```

```
    jest.spyOn(productCatalogService, 'getProducts').
mockResolvedValue([
        {
          modelName: "Product 1",
          itemColour: "Red",
          itemPicture: "https://via.placeholder.com/150",
          lastOrderDate: new Date("2021-01-01"),
          productReference: "REF-001",
          retailPrice: 100,
          size: ProductSizes.L,
          stockLevel: 10
        },
        {
          modelName: "Product 2",
          itemColour: "Blue",
          itemPicture: "https://via.placeholder.com/150",
          lastOrderDate: new Date("2021-01-01"),
          productReference: "REF-002",
          retailPrice: 50,
          size: ProductSizes.L,
          stockLevel: 10
        },
        {
          modelName: "Product 3",
          itemColour: "Yellow",
          itemPicture: "https://via.placeholder.com/150",
          lastOrderDate: new Date("2021-01-01"),
          productReference: "REF-003",
          retailPrice: 78,
          size: ProductSizes.L,
          stockLevel: 10
        }
    ]);

    render(
        <PackProductCatalog
          itemsCount={10}
          listName='ProductCatalog'
          productCatalogService={productCatalogService}
          siteId='00000000-0000-0000-0000-000000000000'
        />
    );
  });
})
```

In the preceding code, the `PackProductCatalog` component uses a `productCatalogService` instance to fetch the necessary data from a SharePoint list. The `ProductCatalogService` class itself takes a dependency on `MSGraphClientV3` that comes from the SPFx context.

In the context of a test, neither the Microsoft Graph API nor the Graph client is available. To make our test work, *we need to mock the data that's returned by the service instance* (i.e., use the `getProducts()` method). First, we created a `ProductCatalogService` instance, passing an empty object as a parameter so that we don't have to create an instance of `MSGraphClientV3` ourselves. Passing an empty object here means that we don't have to use this object in the code. To ensure this, we used the `jest.spyOn()` method to mock the `getProducts()` method so that it returns fake product data instead of calling the Graph API.

With our mocks completed, we can now use our React component as a standalone component without relying on the SPFx context. Now, it is time to define some assertions on behaviors we want to test.

Defining test assertions

Test assertions will determine whether your test is passing or failing. Defining the right assertions is crucial as this will ensure your code is doing what it is supposed to do, avoiding regression across updates.

Defining incorrect assertions, such as just testing whether a component is simply rendering or not or checking whether a method has been called, won't make your tests very valuable. In general, you should focus your tests on user outcomes – for instance, UI elements/values directly impacted by input parameters or specific actions (e.g., someone clicking on something).

For our product catalog component, we want to test the following assertions:

- All three products that have been defined as input are rendered in the component (by checking explicitly for their name (e.g., `Product 1` should appear)):

```
expect(screen.getByText("Product 1")).toBeInTheDocument();
    expect(screen.getByText("Product 2")).toBeInTheDocument();
    expect(screen.getByText("Product 3")).toBeInTheDocument();
```

- The number of elements in the list corresponds to the number of products that have been set as input (e.g., having three products defined means there will be three elements in the list):

```
expect(screen.getAllByRole("listitem")).toHaveLength(3);
```

For these assertions to work, we also need to consider the asynchronous behavior of our component. In real-world scenarios, data is fetched from a SharePoint list using the Graph API, meaning the data is not available in the component immediately. So, calling assertions too early would result in failure as the data wouldn't be rendered yet.

To take this delay into account, we must explicitly wait for the `getProducts()` method to be called at least once and for the results to be returned, thereby simulating the real life cycle of the component:

```
await waitFor(() => {
expect(productCatalogService.getProducts).toHaveBeenCalledTimes(1);
});
```

> **Testing library**
>
> To define assertions, we can use the **Testing Library** (`https://testing-library.com/`). The big advantage of this library is that it focuses on outcomes from the user's perspective instead of pre-defined structures, which means we don't have to rely on actual implementation details – for instance, relying on a specific DOM structure and querying elements based on that structure (e.g., `document.querySelector(".myClass")`). This way, your code changes, but your tests remain the same. Handy.

Now that we have defined our test, we are ready to execute it (and fix potential issues that may occur regarding SPFx).

Fixing SPFx-related issues with Jest

Now that we've created a basic test structure, we can execute the test for the first time by running the following command, which we defined earlier:

```
> npm run test
```

At this point, you should see a bunch of errors in the terminal (Windows). Here's the first one:

```
SyntaxError: Unexpected token '.'

    5 | } from "../../../models/IProductCatalogItem";
    6 | import { IPacktProductCatalogState } from "./IPacktProductCatalogState";
>   7 | import styles from "./PackProductCatalog.module.scss";
        ^
    8 | import { ImageHelper } from "@microsoft/sp-image-helper";
    9 | import * as PackProductCatalogStrings from "PackProductCatalogWebPartStrings";
   10 |
```

Figure 19.1 – Jest error regarding importing styles

This error has occurred because Jest is trying to load the `.scss` stylesheet file directly as a dependency. As mentioned in *Chapter 8*, *Deploying a SharePoint Web Part*, SCSS stylesheets are processed by webpack and transformed into TypeScript modules (`.scss.ts`) to be used in components. Because Jest does not rely on webpack, it tries to import the raw SASS file, causing this error (this file can't be imported *as-is* into TypeScript files).

To bypass this issue, we need to add some configurations to the Jest config file – that is, `jest.config.js`:

```
module.exports = {
    ...
    moduleNameMapper: {
        '\\.(scss)$': 'identity-obj-proxy'
    }
}
```

The `moduleNameMapper` property allows us to *stub* specific module names. **Stubbing** is the process of replacing the original content of the module with something else so that the test can resolve the dependency correctly. In this case, we're using the `identity-obj-proxy` utility package to correctly resolve the CSS classes in the React component.

Now, upon running the `npm run test` command again, we get another error:

```
Cannot find module '@ms/odsp-utilities/lib/alternativeUrls/
SPAlternativeUrls' from 'node_modules/@microsoft/sp-image-helper/
lib-commonjs/index.js'
```

This is where we hit our first pain point of testing with SPFx: **dependencies.**

This error has been raised because we have the following import in the `PackProductCatalog.tsx` component:

```
import { ImageHelper } from "@microsoft/sp-image-helper";
```

Behind the scenes, SPFx uses some internal modules that are not accessible via npm nor exposed directly to your code (for instance, `@ms/odsp-utilities` is an internal Microsoft package). When it comes to testing, this can cause a lot of issues if your components use SPFx packages, such as utility classes, as the dependencies chain cannot be resolved by the compiler, making the packages inaccessible.

To bypass this issue, we can use the `moduleNameMapper` property once more in the Jest config file to ignore this dependency in the test compilation (we'll also add other problematic SPFx dependencies):

```
module.exports = {
    ...
    moduleNameMapper: {
        '\\.(css|less|scss|sass)$': 'identity-obj-proxy',
        '@microsoft/sp-core-library|
': 'identity-obj-proxy'
    }
}
```

However, this step is not sufficient. Doing this only resolves `ImageHelper` and makes it *undefined* in the component code. Because we're using a specific method from that class – that is, `ImageHelper.convertToImageUrl()` – the test will fail:

```
. . .
style={{
    backgroundImage: `url(${ImageHelper.convertToImageUrl({
      sourceUrl: productItem.itemPicture,
      width: 250,
    })})`,
}}
. . .
```

To avoid this, we need to mock the result of this method as well. We can do this by using the `jest.mock()` function. Let's add it to the test file:

```
. . .
jest.mock('@microsoft/sp-image-helper', () => ({
  ImageHelper: {
    convertToImageUrl: jest.fn().mockResolvedValue('https://via.
placeholder.com/150')
  }
}));

describe("Product catalog tests suite", () => {
. . .
```

This way, when the method is called from the component, a mocked value will be returned.

> **Mocking SPFx dependencies**
>
> Because SPFx provides a lot of utility classes and functions, this technique can't always be applied to your tests. Depending on the methods and classes you are using, issues can vary. Keep in mind that the more you rely on SPFx classes and methods, the more difficult the tests will be. Unfortunately, we can't provide a one-size-fits-all resolution as it will be very case-specific.

Running the `npm run test` command again, we get one final error:

```
Cannot find module 'PackProductCatalogWebPartStrings' from 'src/
webparts/packProductCatalog/components/PackProductCatalog.tsx'
```

This error has occurred because the localization modules can't be resolved as they are declared as global modules. Again, to bypass this issue, we must add the physical path of the module to the Jest config file in the `moduleNameMapper` property:

```
moduleNameMapper: {
    '\\.(scss)$': 'identity-obj-proxy',
    '@microsoft/sp-core-library|@microsoft/sp-image-helper$':
'identity-obj-proxy',
    'PackProductCatalogWebPartStrings': '<rootDir>/src/webparts/
packProductCatalog/loc/mystrings.d.ts',
}
```

Like the SPFx utility classes, we also need to mock this data so that the necessary values can be resolved correctly:

```
...
jest.mock('PackProductCatalogWebPartStrings', () => {
  return {
    Labels: {
      Size: "Size",
      StockLevel: "Stock",
      Reference: "Reference",
    },
  }
});
...
```

At this point, if we execute the test with the `npm run test` command, it will be successful!

```
PS                                          > npm run test

> packt-solutions-product-management@0.0.1 test
> jest

 PASS  src/webparts/packProductCatalog/components/PackProductCatalog.test.tsx
  Product catalog tests suite
    √ Display the list of products retrieved from the list (68 ms)

Test Suites: 1 passed, 1 total
Tests:       1 passed, 1 total
Snapshots:   0 total
Time:        4.105 s
Ran all test suites.
```

Figure 19.2 – Successful SPFx test with Jest

As you've seen in this section, testing with SPFx is not as straightforward as it should be. Sometimes, several workarounds are required to make them work properly. Unfortunately, these workarounds will greatly depend on your code structure.

Summary

In this chapter, we covered the importance of testing in SPFx and detailed the prerequisites for test integration within your SPFx solution. We focused on web part testing using Jest and the Testing Library and provided examples of how to test React components and mock data to create standalone tests.

We also provided some guidelines and resolutions for common issues you may encounter with SPFx specificities. In the next chapter, we'll cover how to upgrade your solutions to a newer version of SPFx.

20

Upgrading Your Solutions

In *Chapter 1, Introducing Microsoft 365 and SharePoint Online for Developers*, we explained that Microsoft had to make sure all versions of SPFx were compatible with SharePoint Online, from the very first to the latest.

However, staying on the same version of SPFx indefinitely, even if technically possible, isn't a good idea. Upgrading is an essential part of any software maintenance, and SPFx is no exception. As a developer, it's important to make a habit of regularly checking for new updates as part of your application maintenance process so that you can address any security or performance issues or simply benefit from the latest features.

In this chapter, we'll discuss how to upgrade your SPFx solution and cover the following topics:

- Staying up to date with new SPFx releases and updates
- Upgrading your solution manually or using the CLI for Microsoft 365

Staying up to date with SPFx releases and updates

Being aware of new features and releases of SPFx is not that easy. As we mentioned earlier, you can stay on a specific version for a very long time without the need to upgrade. If you don't perform manual checks, the tool itself won't notify you that a new version is available. To find out whether you can upgrade, you must find information about new versions by yourself. Here are the different ways you can stay up to date regarding SPFx releases and updates:

- **Look for outdated packages using npm:** This is the most straightforward approach. In your SPFx root solution folder, run the following command:

```
> npm outdated
```

This will list all outdated packages (including SPFx ones) looking at the `package.json` file:

```
® PS C:\VS\Packt\Packt.Solutions.ProductManagement> npm outdated
Package                              Current  Wanted  Latest  Location
          Depended by
@babel/preset-env                    7.25.4   7.25.4  7.26.7  node_modules/@babel/preset-env
@fluentui/react                      8.122.1  8.122.8 8.122.8 node_modules/@fluentui/react
@microsoft/eslint-config-spfx        1.20.1   1.20.1  1.20.2  node_modules/@microsoft/eslint-config-spfx
@microsoft/eslint-plugin-spfx        1.20.1   1.20.1  1.20.2  node_modules/@microsoft/eslint-plugin-spfx
@microsoft/rush-stack-compiler-4.7   0.1.0    0.1.0   0.1.1   node_modules/@microsoft/rush-stack-compiler-4.7
@microsoft/sp-build-web              1.20.1   1.20.1  1.20.2  node_modules/@microsoft/sp-build-web
@microsoft/sp-component-base         1.19.0   1.19.0  1.20.0  node_modules/@microsoft/sp-component-base
@microsoft/sp-core-library           1.19.0   1.19.0  1.20.0  node_modules/@microsoft/sp-core-library
@microsoft/sp-dynamic-data           1.19.0   1.19.0  1.20.0  node_modules/@microsoft/sp-dynamic-data
@microsoft/sp-http                   1.19.0   1.19.0  1.20.0  node_modules/@microsoft/sp-http
@microsoft/sp-image-helper           1.19.0   1.19.0  1.20.0  node_modules/@microsoft/sp-image-helper
@microsoft/sp-lodash-subset          1.19.0   1.19.0  1.20.0  node_modules/@microsoft/sp-lodash-subset
```

Figure 20.1 – Example of outdated npm packages

Regarding `@microsoft/sp-*` packages, if the version number in the **Latest** column is different from the **Current** one, then a new update of SPFx is available. We'll learn how to do this upgrade in the next section.

> **What about updating the SPFx Yeoman generator (@microsoft/generator-sharepoint)?**
>
> Updating the generator is different than updating SPFx npm dependencies in the `package.json` file of a project. The generator is used to scaffold a *new project* or *add components* to an existing project using the latest available version of SPFx. Upgrading it won't change anything regarding your existing project. Therefore, you are not required to update the generator when you are upgrading to a newer SPFx version. However, we recommend updating it alongside other SPFx npm packages to avoid any errors (for instance, if you want to add a new component to your newly updated solution afterward) and/or to compare the new SPFx project structure with your existing one to counter-verify upgrade modifications.

- **Regularly review the SPFx release notes on the documentation website** (`https://learn.microsoft.com/en-us/sharepoint/dev/spfx/roadmap`): This is where you'll see every published version of SPFx and be able to determine whether you are using the latest one. For each release note, you'll often find special instructions so that you can update your solution. Depending on the version, *the steps to upgrade your code may vary* (breaking changes, new APIs, new Node.js version, etc.).

The two options mentioned here require you to check different channels regularly and dig into version details to find out what's new. To stay ahead of the curve, we also strongly recommend following the **Pattern & Practices (PnP)** initiative, either on social media (via **X**: @ms365pnp) or through their community, *Microsoft 365 & Power Platform Community Calls*. Since they are managed by Microsoft, this is likely your source of truth for all SPFx-related updates.

> **PnP Microsoft 365 & Power Platform Community Calls**
>
> Community calls are recurrent Teams meetings that are held by Microsoft and the community to communicate about Microsoft 365-related news, showcase community content (`https://pnp.github.io/#events`), or deep dive into a product-specific feature. Among other topics, they also have a dedicated call for Viva Connections and SPFx. The Microsoft SPFx product team often makes announcements and provides demos here, so it is a good place to get the latest news. It is free, and anyone can attend; there's no need to register. Just join the call on Teams with the link provided.

Technically speaking, you don't need to update. As we mentioned earlier, if you are using an outdated version of SPFx, your solution will keep functioning since Microsoft is responsible for this. However, upgrading is a normal process to follow when using a software solution. As a developer, you should regularly check for new updates and features, especially ones related to security and bug fixes, to avoid putting your company or clients at risk.

In this section, we only explained how to check whether a new version of SPFx is available. However, once we've identified one, we still need to update the files and packages in the solution to do the upgrade. In the next section, we will learn how to upgrade an SPFx solution using the CLI for Microsoft 365 tool.

Upgrading your SPFx solution

Unfortunately, regarding SPFx, there is no automatic process that allows you to upgrade your solution. This process is manual and can be done by implementing two different techniques: fully manual or assisted via the CLI for Microsoft 365 tool.

Upgrading your solution manually

When updating an SPFx solution, the default practice consists of updating the Yeoman SharePoint Generator to the latest version by running the following command:

```
> npm install @microsoft/generator-sharepoint@latest -g
```

Then, you must create a new empty SPFx solution using it. Here, you must use the same options you used initially, if possible, such as the JavaScript template (e.g., React) and SharePoint targeted version (e.g., SharePoint Online):

```
> yo @microsoft/sharepoint
```

This will give you the latest configuration for packages and files for the latest SPFx version. At this point, you can compare this new project structure and package versions with your existing ones.

Usually, the following files are involved during an upgrade:

- `tsconfig.json`
- `package.json`
- `yo-rc.json`

To help you spot the differences between the two solutions, you can leverage the Git compare functionality that's typically offered by some Git clients (such as SourceTree). To do so, follow these steps:

1. Copy and replace the aforementioned files in your existing project.

2. In a Git client, inspect differences in the modified files:

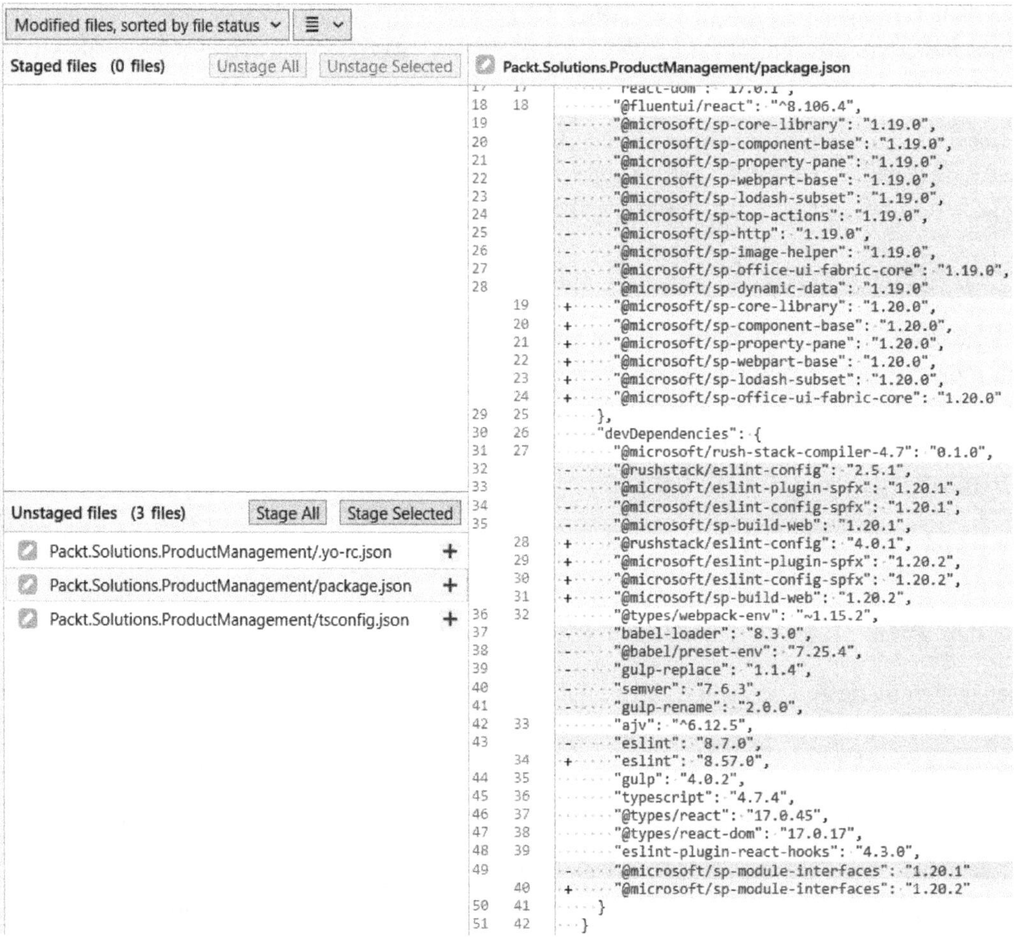

Figure 20.2 – Using the Git compare functionality

Be careful – *do not commit these files*; they are just here for reference! Discard them once you've identified any updates you must perform.

To install new package versions, update the `package.json` file and run the following command from the root folder of your project:

```
> npm i
```

Upgrading SPFx is not about just bumping the version number of the `@microsoft/sp-*` packages in your `package.json` file. These packages have coupled dependencies that must be updated as well, such as those for FluentUI, React, or TypeScript versions. Omitting to upgrade these packages may result in unexcepted behaviors or errors!

Depending on whether the upgrade is minor or major, some new versions might require extra updates, such as installing a new Node.js version or adapting your code due to some breaking changes or new APIs. Therefore, it's crucial to consult the official Microsoft SPFx release notes and/or community updates to determine whether any additional steps must be taken.

As you've seen, upgrading an SPFx solution manually is an error-prone process. Once again, the open source community offers the CLI for Microsoft 365 tool to help streamline the process and allow you to upgrade your solution with confidence.

Upgrading your solution using the CLI for Microsoft 365

The recommended way to update your SPFx solution and avoid any mistakes while doing so is to use the CLI for Microsoft 365 tool. It provides a special command that analyzes your SPFx project and generates a report of the parts you need to upgrade according to the target SPFx version you're using. *The tool does not make any modifications to your solution.* To use it, follow these steps:

1. Install the CLI globally on your machine by running the following command (from any directory):

   ```
   > npm i -g @pnp/cli-microsoft365
   ```

2. In the root folder of your SPFx project folder, run the following command:

   ```
   > m365 spfx project upgrade --toVersion 1.20.0
   ```

This command will produce a report on the files you need to update to upgrade the specified target version. The --toVersion parameter is the version number you want to upgrade to. By default, it outputs the results directly on the console in JSON format:

```
PS C:\                                        > m365 spfx project upgrade -v 1.20.0
[
  {
    "description": "Upgrade SharePoint Framework dependency package @microsoft/sp-core-library",
    "id": "FN001001",
    "file": "./package.json",
    "position": {
      "line": 19,
      "character": 5
    },
    "resolution": "npm i -SE @microsoft/sp-core-library@1.20.0",
    "resolutionType": "cmd",
    "severity": "Required",
    "title": "@microsoft/sp-core-library"
  },
  {
```

Figure 20.3 – CLI for Microsoft 365 SPFx upgrade report

For better readability, you can use the --outputFile and --output parameters to generate a report in Markdown format:

```
> m365 spfx project upgrade --toVersion 1.5.0 --output md >
"upgrade-report.md"
```

This will produce a pretty report in Markdown that contains the steps you need to follow to do the upgrade. The report contains three distinct parts:

- **Findings**: This section shows what pieces you need to update one by one and gives you the commands you need to run to update a particular package:

Upgrade project packt-solutions-product-management-client-side-solution to v1.20.0

Date: 2025-01-29

Findings

Following is the list of steps required to upgrade your project to SharePoint Framework version 1.20.0. Summary of the modifications is included at the end of the report.

FN001001 @microsoft/sp-core-library | Required

Upgrade SharePoint Framework dependency package @microsoft/sp-core-library

Execute the following command:

```
npm i -SE @microsoft/sp-core-library@1.20.0
```

Figure 20.4 – CLI for Microsoft 365 Findings report

- **Summary**: This section provides a command that you can execute directly to update all the packages at once:

Summary

Execute script

```
npm i -SE @microsoft/sp-core-library@1.20.0 @microsoft/sp-lodash-
subset@1.20.0 @microsoft/sp-office-ui-fabric-core@1.20.0
@microsoft/sp-webpart-base@1.20.0 @microsoft/sp-property-pane@1.20.0
@microsoft/sp-component-base@1.20.0 @microsoft/sp-dynamic-data@1.20.0
@microsoft/sp-http@1.20.0 @microsoft/sp-adaptive-card-extension-
base@1.20.0
npm i -DE @microsoft/sp-build-web@1.20.2 @microsoft/sp-module-
interfaces@1.20.2 @rushstack/eslint-config@4.0.1 eslint@8.57.0
@microsoft/eslint-plugin-spfx@1.20.2 @microsoft/eslint-config-
spfx@1.20.2
npm dedupe
```

Figure 20.5 – CLI for Microsoft 365 Summary report

- **Modify files:** This section displays the files you need to update manually in the solution if needed:

  ### Modify files

  ./.yo-rc.json

  Update version in .yo-rc.json:

  ```
  {
    "@microsoft/generator-sharepoint": {
      "version": "1.20.0"
    }
  }
  ```

  Update @microsoft/teams-js SDK version in .yo-rc.json:

  ```
  {
    "@microsoft/generator-sharepoint": {
      "sdkVersions": {
        "@microsoft/teams-js": "2.24.0"
  ```

Figure 20.6 – CLI for Microsoft 365 showing a list of required code updates

After running these commands and applying the listed modifications, your solution will be upgraded to the desired version.

The CLI for Microsoft 365 tool is a must-have tool for every SPFx developer and greatly facilitates the update process. However, it does not prevent you from checking the official SPFx release notes for additional steps! You'll still have to verify whether any other updates are needed.

Summary

In this chapter, we learned how to upgrade an SPFx solution to the latest version.

We began by emphasizing that while the update process is not mandatory, it is essential for the proper maintenance of SPFx solutions to prevent security breaches, as well as to take advantage of new features and performance improvements.

Then, we explained that the SPFx upgrade process must be done manually, requiring developers to stay updated on new versions by checking the official Microsoft documentation or following community news. We also detailed the fully manual update process, as well as using the CLI for Microsoft 365 to reduce the risk of errors.

Finally, we emphasized the necessity for developers to always check the official SPFx release notes, regardless of the update method, to ensure any additional steps beyond simple package updates are carried out. In the next chapter, we'll learn how to leverage tools and libraries from the open-source community to speed up development and build even more advanced solutions.

Get This Book's PDF Version and Exclusive Extras

UNLOCK NOW

Scan the QR code (or go to packtpub.com/unlock). Search for this book by name, confirm the edition, and then follow the steps on the page.

Note: Keep your invoice handy. Purchases made directly from Packt don't require an invoice.

21

Leveraging Community Tools and Libraries

Microsoft 365 and SharePoint are two of the most active open source communities in the world. As an SPFx developer, it means you can benefit from many tools and libraries to speed up your development and learn from others.

In this chapter, we'll present the following major tools and libraries we think you should look into to help you build your solutions:

- The PnPjs library
- PnP React and property pane controls
- PnP Modern Search
- Microsoft Dev Proxy
- SPFx Fast Serve

Please note that we only list tools or libraries we think you should know as a priority for your SPFx projects. With the community being very active, there are a lot more initiatives you can use, and they are not limited to those listed here.

Technical requirements

This chapter relies on the GitHub solution accessible here: `https://github.com/PacktPublishing/Mastering-SharePoint-Development-with-the-SharePoint-Framework-`. You need to first clone the repository locally on your machine to be able to follow the steps.

The following Git branch is used for the entire chapter: `https://github.com/PacktPublishing/Mastering-SharePoint-Development-with-the-SharePoint-Framework-/tree/chapter21/leveraging-community-tools-and-libraries`.

You must check out this branch before using either the Git command line or a Git client such as GitHub Desktop or Sourcetree, which you will use in this chapter.

> **Code snippets**
>
> For brevity and readability considerations, only the relevant parts of the code are detailed in the provided snippets in this chapter. For these reasons, ad hoc code, such as dependency imports and updates to certain files, may be omitted. We recommend having the GitHub solution open alongside the book to get the full working version of the code and review the provided steps.

Exploring Microsoft 365 & Power Platform Community initiatives

As we stated in *Chapter 1*, the **Microsoft 365 & Power Platform Community** (aka **PnP**) focuses on Microsoft 365 and Power Platform, offering a wealth of resources such as articles, videos, samples, tools, and solutions to help you maximize the platform's potential. It's a joint effort by Microsoft and community members, making it one of the most extensive and active technical communities globally.

For SPFx developers, it's a must-visit resource to keep up with the latest developments. The website, `https://pnp.github.io`, is the place to start as it provides reusable code, samples, and blog posts relating to SPFx. In the next sections, we detail the main initiatives under the PnP roof.

Using the PnPjs library

We've seen in *Chapter 18*, *Consuming APIs*, that you can consume different APIs, such as the SharePoint REST API or the Microsoft Graph API, through clients provided by SPFx (for example, `SPHttpClient` or `MSGraphClientV3`). However, such clients still require you to know API-specific endpoints and how to use them (for instance, referring to the API reference to know how to retrieve items from a SharePoint list). What if you could avoid knowing these endpoints' specificities and rely on regular JavaScript objects and methods mimicking the API instead? This is exactly the purpose of the PnPjs library.

PnPjs (`https://pnp.github.io/pnpjs`) is a suite of open source, *fluent* libraries designed for consuming SharePoint, Microsoft Graph, and Microsoft 365 REST APIs in a type-safe manner. It can be utilized within SPFx, Node.js, or any JavaScript project. As a developer, it greatly simplifies the usage of such APIs thanks to a fluent interface syntax, highlighting the API's capabilities dynamically without requiring you to deeply dig into the API reference.

> **Fluent interface**
>
> A fluent interface in software programming is a design pattern that aims to create more readable and intuitive code. This is typically achieved by designing APIs in such a way that they allow method chaining. In other words, you can call multiple methods in a single statement, creating a flow that resembles natural language.

For example, let's consider the following request to retrieve items from a SharePoint list using the SharePoint REST API: `https://tenant.sharepoint.com/sites/mysite/_api/web/lists/GetByTitle("My List")/items?$select=Title,Description&$orderBy=Modifier&$top=5`.

The equivalent using PnPjs would be the following:

```
const items = await sp.web.lists.getByTitle("My List").items.
select("Title", "Description").top(5).orderBy("Modified", true)();
```

Properties and methods are logically organized by name and follow the API specifications (the `sp` property for general SharePoint settings, the `web` property to manipulate websites, `lists` to manipulate lists, etc.). This way, you benefit from the IntelliSense feature of Visual Studio Code allowing you to explore and use API capabilities more easily.

PnPjs is not specific to SPFx. However, the library provides a straightforward integration. To use it within your SPFx solution, you must do the following:

1. Add the required package dependencies to the `package.json` file and install them with `npm i`:

    ```
    "dependencies": {
        . . .
        "@pnp/sp": "^4.0.1"
    },
    ```

> **Package dependencies**
>
> PnPjs provides separate packages for each API you need to use. For instance, to use the SharePoint REST API, you must add the `@pnp/sp` package. However, for the Microsoft Graph API, it will be `@pnp/graph`. It also provides other utility packages to meet different requirements (for example, `@pnp/logging`, `@pnp/queryable`). Refer to the official documentation for detailed usage (`https://pnp.github.io/pnpjs/packages`).

2. Next, initialize an `sp` object (or `graph` in the case of the Microsoft Graph API) using the SPFx Web Part or extension context. This is usually done in the `onInit()` method:

    ```
    import { ISPFXContext, spfi, SPFx as spSPFx } from "@pnp/sp";
    . . .

    protected async onInit(): Promise<void> {

        const sp = spfi().using(spSPFx(this.context as
    ISPFXContext));
        . . .
    }
    ```

3. Use the sp object to consume the required endpoint from the API using the PnPjs fluent syntax:

```
import "@pnp/sp/webs";
import "@pnp/sp/lists";
import "@pnp/sp/items";

...

let items: any[] = await sp.web.lists
getByTitle(listName).items                          .select(...
fields).top(10)();
```

Don't forget to import additional dependencies according to the used properties. For instance, to use web methods, you will need to import the @pnp/sp/web dependency explicitly. That's it!

The PnPjs library can greatly speed up your development by simplifying API usage and abstracting implementation complexity. *However, this is not a reason to become a lazy developer!*

The technical complexity being hidden and managed for you by the library doesn't prevent you from understanding the "raw" API and its basic usage. PnPjs can't be used in all situations you'll encounter, and having a basic knowledge of how this works behind the scenes will help you to build better and more reliable solutions.

In our opinion, you should always consume APIs first using SPFx clients to get to know the APIs and their usage. PnPjs is just an extra on top of that to speed up the development once you already have this basic knowledge.

Under the PnP roof, we also find other useful libraries that provide prebuilt UI components. Let's take a look at them next.

Using the PnP React and property pane controls libraries

The @pnp/spfx-property-controls (https://pnp.github.io/sp-dev-fx-property-controls/) and @pnp/spfx-controls-react (https://pnp.github.io/sp-dev-fx-controls-react/) libraries offer prebuilt React controls and SPFx property controls to be used directly in your SPFx solutions.

These controls are meant to be as generic as possible so they can be reused in many ways. Most of these controls use the Fluent UI styles to fit with the default Microsoft 365 experience. This means using them does not require you to customize any styles. In the next sections, we'll detail how to use them in your SPFx solution.

Utilizing property pane controls

Using property controls is straightforward. You must first add the package dependency in the package.json file and run the npm i command to install it:

```
"dependencies": {
    ...
```

```
      "@pnp/spfx-property-controls": "3.19.0"
},
```

Then, the usage is the same as any other property pane control, as we detailed in *Chapter 6, Working with the Property Pane*. For instance, considering our product catalog scenario, we could have replaced the built-in `PropertyPaneSlider` property pane control for the `itemsCount` property used by `PackProductCatalogWebPart` with a spinner control from the `@pnp/spfx-property-controls` library with just a few lines of code:

```
import { PropertyFieldSpinButton } from '@pnp/spfx-property-controls/
lib/PropertyFieldSpinButton';

...

protected getPropertyPaneConfiguration(): IPropertyPaneConfiguration {

const groupFields: IPropertyPaneField<any>[] = [

  /* Property field coming from the @pnp/spfx-property-controls
library */
  PropertyFieldSpinButton('itemsCount', {
    label: strings.PropertyPane.ItemsCountFieldLabel,
    initialValue: this.properties.itemsCount,
    onPropertyChange: this.onPropertyPaneFieldChanged,
    properties: this.properties,
    disabled: false,
    min: 0,
    max: 5,
    step: 1,
    decimalPlaces: 0,
    incrementIconName: 'CalculatorAddition',
    decrementIconName: 'CalculatorSubtract',
    key: 'spinButtonFieldId'
  }),
  // Other fields
  ...
```

The custom control is then displayed in the property pane like any other control:

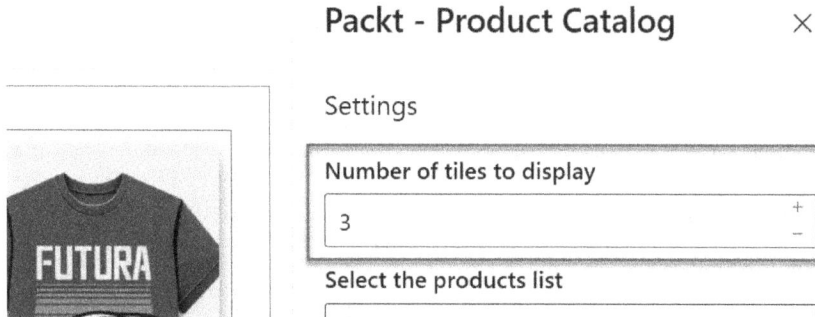

Packt - Product Catalog   ×

Settings

Number of tiles to display

3

Select the products list

Figure 21.1 – Example of a property control from the @pnp/spfx-property-controls library

Because they are open source and made by the community, the implementation and usage can differ between controls. Refer to the official documentation to see how to use each control: https://pnp. github.io/sp-dev-fx-property-controls/controls/PropertyFieldButton.

PnP property controls can greatly improve the development time, especially for complex properties in the property pane. In such cases, before implementing your own control, you should always check whether something similar is already available. The chances of finding something that fits your requirements are quite high. If not, you can still start from an existing control and adapt the code to your needs.

Utilizing React controls

Using React controls is usually the same as using property controls. Most of the time, property controls are just wrappers over them.

Again, to use these controls, you must first add the package dependency to the package.json file and run the npm i command to install it:

```
"dependencies": {
    ...
    "@pnp/spfx-controls-react": "3.19.0"
},
```

Considering the previous product catalog scenario example, we can now replace the basic product tiles display in the PackProductCatalog.tsx file with the more advanced GridLayout control (https://pnp.github.io/sp-dev-fx-controls-react/controls/GridLayout/) from the @pnp/spfx-controls-react library:

```
private _onRenderGridItem = (item: IProductCatalogItem, finalSize:
ISize, isCompact: boolean): JSX.Element => {
```

```
    const previewProps: IDocumentCardPreviewProps = {
      previewImages: [
        {
          previewImageSrc: item.itemPicture,
          imageFit: ImageFit.cover,
          height: 130
        }
      ]
    };

    return <div
      data-is-focusable={true}
      role="listitem"
      aria-label={item.modelName}
    >
      <DocumentCard
        type={isCompact ? DocumentCardType.compact : DocumentCardType.
normal}
      >
        <DocumentCardPreview {...previewProps} />
        {!isCompact && <DocumentCardLocation location={item.
productReference} />}
        <DocumentCardDetails>
          <DocumentCardTitle
            title={item.modelName}
            shouldTruncate={true}
          />
        </DocumentCardDetails>
      </DocumentCard>
    </div>;
}


public render(): React.ReactElement<IPackProductCatalogProps> {

return   <GridLayout
          ariaLabel="List of content, use right and left arrow keys to
navigate, arrow down to access details."
          items={this.state.productItems}
          onRenderGridItem={(item: any, finalSize: ISize, isCompact:
boolean) => this._onRenderGridItem(item, finalSize, isCompact)}
        />
}
```

With a few lines of code, we now have content displayed as cards and adapting to the layout automatically according to the page width. Isn't it awesome?

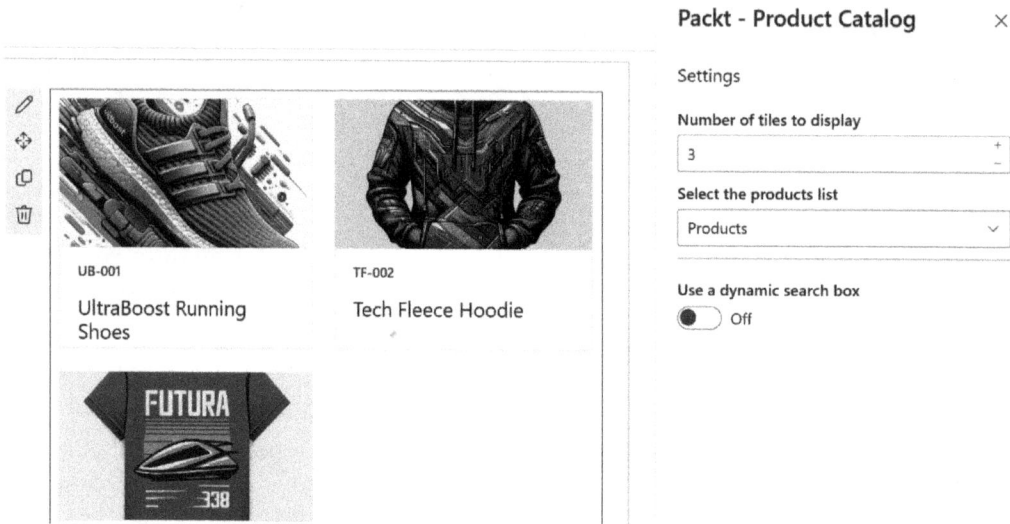

Figure 21.2 – Example of React control integration from the @pnp/spfx-controls-react library

As we've seen, both PnP React controls and PnP property controls can save you a lot of time in your development. However, you shouldn't abuse their usage. The more you rely on open source components, the less control you have over the code and its behaviors. For instance, if something goes wrong or you get an issue once your components are deployed to production that impacts several users, you will likely be one user among others waiting for a fix to be made by the maintainers. Because it is an open source initiative and not created by Microsoft, the maintainers or authors don't have any obligation to provide a fix. You can still fix the error yourself by either cloning the repository and working with your local copy or making a pull request. In such cases, the process is still quite cumbersome.

Last but not least, we will cover, in the next section, a very popular open source solution under the PnP initiative.

Using the PnP Modern Search solution

PnP Modern Search (https://microsoft-search.github.io/pnp-modern-search/) is an open source solution that provides a set of highly customizable and flexible building blocks to create search-based experiences within SharePoint Online. To do so, it offers the following reusable Web Parts:

- A *search results* Web Part to retrieve data from a data source (SharePoint Search or Microsoft Search) and render it in a specific layout (tiles, list, carousel, etc.)

- A *search filters* Web Part to filter and refine data displayed in search results Web Parts

- A *search verticals* Web Part to browse data as silos (i.e. tabs) from multiple data sources

- A *search box* Web Part to let users enter free-text queries sent to search results Web Parts

All of them can be configured and connected on the same page to build a complete business solution. This solution was initially implemented in 2017 and evolved through the years to become one of the most popular open source solutions in the community, and is currently used by thousands of organizations around the world!

Some of the key features of the PnP Modern Search solution, and the reasons why it is so widely used, are as follows:

- It is a highly configurable search query for both SharePoint Search and Microsoft Search sources

- It has built-in layouts for various needs (list view, tiles, carousel, people view, etc.) with customizable fields

- **Handlebars**, **HTML**, and **CSS**-based templates that allow quick creation of custom designs

- It allows dynamic search queries through tokens (for example, current user location and specific page metadata)

- It has a plugin mechanism that allows you to build your own layout or data source using custom code via **SPFx library components**

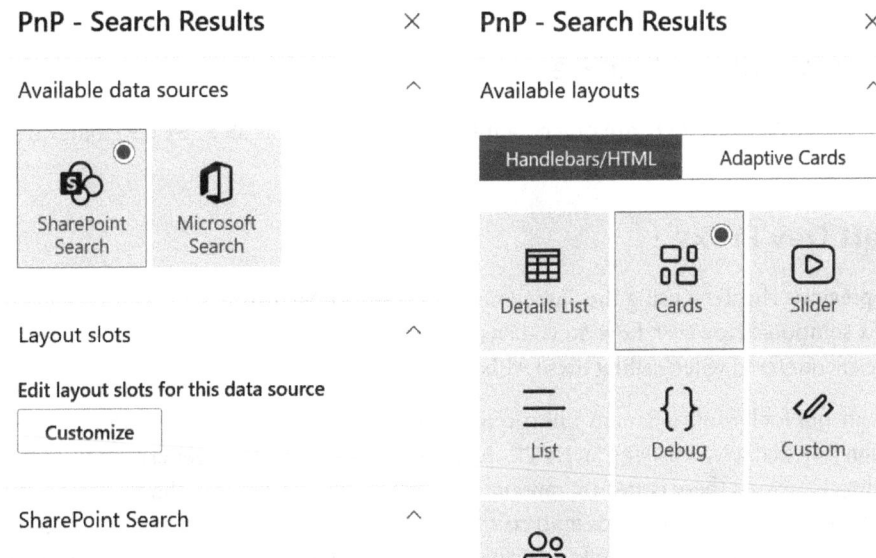

Figure 21.3 – Example of available configurations in PnP Modern Search

PnP Modern Search is not something you will use directly in your SPFx code; it can, however, save you a lot of time by avoiding having to build the same type of solution in the first place.

In fact, before implementing a solution based on search capabilities and reinventing the wheel, you should first see whether your business requirements could be solved with the PnP Modern Search. A solution that could take you several weeks to months to develop can be configured in minutes with the PnP Modern Search Web Parts. This is not something to overlook.

> **PnP Modern Search versus PnP Modern Search Core Components: Don't be confused**
>
> Browsing on the internet, you will probably notice two different PnP Modern Search solutions: **PnP Modern Search** and **PnP Modern Search Core Components**. Let's clarify.
>
> PnP Modern Search is the original solution implemented with SPFx using both the SharePoint Search REST API and the Microsoft Graph Search API with Handlebars templates. This solution *can only be used in SharePoint as Web Parts*.
>
> PnP Modern Search Core Components is a new initiative implemented in 2024 by Franck Cornu and initially extracted from a real company use case (Ubisoft) `https://microsoft-search.github.io/pnp-modern-search-core-components/`. These are reusable web components based on the **Microsoft Graph Toolkit** that rely on the Microsoft Search API *only*. Alongside standalone web components, the solution also provides multiple consumption ways such as using a Microsoft Teams application or SPFx Web Parts. This solution offers the same highly flexible building blocks (search results, search filters, search box, and search verticals) concept as the original solution, but goes beyond the traditional SharePoint Web Parts.

Experimenting with other tools

Beyond the PnP initiatives, there are other useful tools you can use as an SPFx developer to speed up your development.

Microsoft Dev Proxy

As seen in previous chapters, using the SharePoint REST API or Microsoft Graph API is a common task in SPFx solutions. However, how do you ensure your application is resilient and will not break if errors are encountered when calling these APIs?

These APIs are not foolproof, and many unexpected issues can happen after your solution is deployed to production (for example, receiving an HTTP 500 code for an internal server error or HTTP 429 for a throttling issue). As these issues are random, they are, by definition, quite hard to test. The **Dev Proxy** utility tool (`https://learn.microsoft.com/en-us/microsoft-cloud/dev/dev-proxy/overview`) helps you to anticipate them and make your solution more resilient.

Dev Proxy is a command-line tool, created by Microsoft, that acts as a network proxy intercepting requests initiated by applications on the local machine (not specifically SPFx). Therefore, it can change applications behaviors and/or responses to test many different scenarios, normally nearly impossible to test in a real context (for example, how do you force the Microsoft Graph API to fail, like responding with an `HTTP 500` error code? Quick answer: You can't). The tool can be used to simulate multiple types of scenarios:

- **API errors**:
  - Test an application with random errors
  - Simulate errors from OpenAI APIs
  - Simulate errors from Microsoft Graph APIs
  - Change request failure rate

- **API behaviors**:
  - Test that an application handles throttling properly
  - Simulate throttling on Microsoft 365 APIs
  - Simulate rate limit API responses
  - Simulate slow API responses

To use Microsoft Dev Proxy, you must first install it globally using the following command:

```
> winget install Microsoft.DevProxy --silent
```

Certificate installation

The first time you install the tool, you will be prompted to install a certificate on your machine.

Dev Proxy uses a `devproxyrc.json` file for its global configuration. You can open and modify it using the following command:

```
devproxy config
```

The tool uses a plugin architecture to process network requests divided into three categories:

- **Intercepting plugins**, which intercept network requests and responses and can provide insights or modify them. For instance, the `GenericRandomErrorPlugin` plugin will fail a request with a random code and `RetryAfterPlugin` will simulate a throttled request.

  Most of the time, this will be the only type of plugin you need. You can see a list and how to use them directly in the tool documentation (for example, `https://learn.microsoft.com/en-us/microsoft-cloud/dev/dev-proxy/technical-reference/genericrandomerrorplugin`).

- **Reporting plugins**, to record requests and monitor activity.

- **Reporters**, which generate reports based on the data collected by reporting plugins.

These plugins are triggered according to request URL patterns defined in the `urlsToWatch` field. To start watching requests on the local machine, you can simply use the following command:

```
> devproxy
```

Doing this will intercept by default *all outbound requests* from any application on your machine:

```
PS              \Packt.Solutions.ProductManagement> devproxy
 info    GenericRandomErrorPlugin: 1 error responses loaded from
Local\Programs\Dev Proxy\devproxy-errors.json

Got 30 seconds?
Help improve Dev Proxy by answering a 1-question survey: https://aka.ms/devproxy/su

 info    Dev Proxy API listening on http://localhost:8897...
 info    Dev Proxy listening on 127.0.0.1:8000...

Hotkeys: issue (w)eb request, (r)ecord, (s)top recording, (c)lear screen
Press CTRL+C to stop Dev Proxy
```

Figure 21.4 – Dev Proxy default listener

However, in the context of an SPFx solution, you likely want to configure your own URLs to watch, such as the SharePoint REST API or Microsoft Graph API. For this, the Dev Proxy tool can use an arbitrary configuration file that overrides the global one, specific to your solution.

Considering the product catalog Web Part we implemented in previous chapters, we create the `spfx-devproxy.json` configuration file at the root of the `Packt.Solutions.ProductManagement` project folder to intercept a SharePoint REST API request made to retrieve items from the SharePoint list and generate random errors:

```
{
    "$schema": "https://raw.githubusercontent.com/microsoft/dev-proxy/
main/schemas/v0.14.1/rc.schema.json",
    "plugins": [
        {
        "name": "GraphRandomErrorPlugin",
        "enabled": true,
        "pluginPath": "~appFolder/plugins/dev-proxy-plugins.dll",
        "configSection": "graphRandomErrorPlugin",
        "urlsToWatch": [
            "https://*.sharepoint.com/sites/Packt/_api/web/lists/
getByTitle('Products')/items*"
```

```
            ]
        }
    ]
}
```

We can now run the command using this file to start watching network calls:

```
> devproxy --config-file .\spfx-devproxy.json
```

To test the behavior, we can now bundle and serve our Web Part using the `gulp serve` command and browse the hosted workbench page (for example, `https://tenant.sharepoint.com/sites/yoursite/_layouts/15/workbench.aspx`).

At this point, depending on your luck, you will either see no difference at all or get an error in the network tab with nothing displayed in the Web Part. This is because by default, the Dev Proxy tool uses *a failure rate of 50%*, meaning sometimes the original request will be made and sometimes it will throw a random error.

To make sure the API call will fail every time, you set the `--failure-rate` parameter to `100` (`0` means no errors are generated):

```
> devproxy --config-file .\spfx-devproxy.json --failure-rate 100
```

This time, when inspecting the **Network** tab in the browser, you will always get a random error when displaying the Web Part:

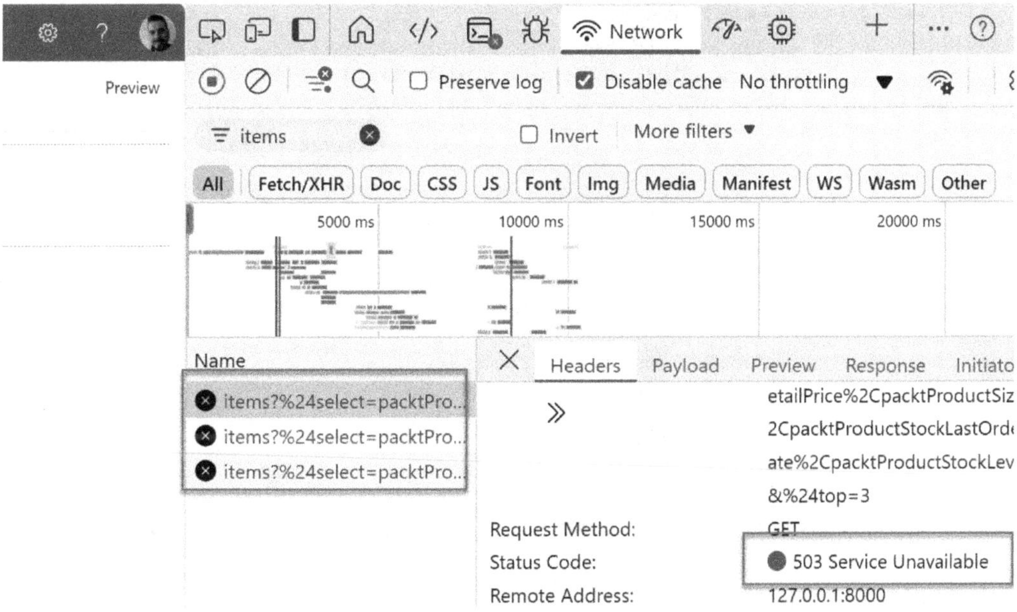

Figure 21.5 – Dev Proxy browser error

The associated error will be generated by Dev Proxy:

```
 req   ┌ GET https://sonbaedev.sharepoint.com/sites/Packt/_api/web/lists/getByTitle
ducts')/items?%24select=packtProductColor%2CpacktProductModelName%2CpacktProductIte
ure%2CpacktProductReference%2CpacktProductRetailPrice%2CpacktProductSize%2CpacktPro
tockLastOrderDate%2CpacktProductStockLevel&%24top=3
 oops  └ GraphRandomErrorPlugin: 503 ServiceUnavailable
```

Figure 21.6 – Dev Proxy-generated error

As you can see, if this type of error is not handled correctly in the code, it can result in a bad user experience (here, an empty display without any information indicating that something failed). Having a way to test this scenario can help us to handle the error properly in the `PackProductCatalog.tsx` component, by adding an error message:

```
public render(): React.ReactElement<IPackProductCatalogProps> {

    return  <>
            { this.state.errorMessage ?
                <MessageBar messageBarType={MessageBarType.error}>{this.
state.errorMessage}</MessageBar>

                :

                <GridLayout
                    ariaLabel="List of content, use right and left arrow
keys to navigate, arrow down to access details."
                    items={this.state.productItems}
                    onRenderGridItem={(item: any, finalSize: ISize,
isCompact: boolean) => this._onRenderGridItem(item, finalSize,
isCompact)}
                />
            }
            </>
}

...

public async componentDidMount(): Promise<void> {
    try {
      await this.getItems();
    } catch (error) {
      this.setState({
        errorMessage: error.toString()
      })
    }
}
```

Now, when an error is raised by the API, the user will see the corresponding error in the UI:

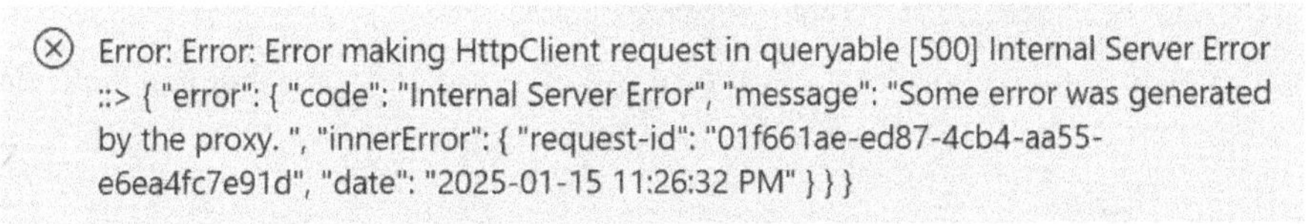

> ⊗ Error: Error: Error making HttpClient request in queryable [500] Internal Server Error
> ::> { "error": { "code": "Internal Server Error", "message": "Some error was generated
> by the proxy. ", "innerError": { "request-id": "01f661ae-ed87-4cb4-aa55-
> e6ea4fc7e91d", "date": "2025-01-15 11:26:32 PM" } } }

Figure 21.7 – API error detailed in the UI

What we demonstrated here is a very basic example of Dev Proxy usage. For more complex scenarios, you could imagine testing specific error codes, testing API throttling of slow performance, mocking API responses, monitoring network activity, and much more!

The open source community even provides a prebuilt configuration preset specifically designed for SPFx: `https://learn.microsoft.com/en-us/microsoft-cloud/dev/dev-proxy/how-to/use-dev-proxy-with-spfx`.

In the next section, we will focus on another community tool that every SPFx developer should use – a tool that will save you a ton of time!

SPFx Fast Serve

By default, in development mode, when you serve an SPFx solution locally via the `gulp serve` command, every update you make to your code will trigger a new bundle generation of the solution with webpack. Even though it can be relatively quick for simple solutions, it can rapidly become an issue for larger ones. As an example, the well-known **PnP Modern Search Web Parts** open source solution, with a lot of code, can take *minutes* to bundle! We'll let you imagine the development time lost for every updated comma…

Luckily, the community provides a solution to drastically reduce this delay thanks to the **SPFx Fast Serve** tool (`https://github.com/s-KaiNet/spfx-fast-serve`). This is a command-line tool aimed to replace the traditional `gulp serve` command by serving the solution and handling updates way faster. Behind the scenes, it uses a completely custom Webpack configuration and Webpack dev server (`https://webpack.js.org/configuration/dev-server`), producing basically the same outputs, but optimized for performance. The tool focuses only on the bundling process, replacing the default SPFx one.

To use it, you first need to install the package globally:

```
npm install spfx-fast-serve -g
```

Then, from the root folder of your solution, use the following command to start the configuration:

```
spfx-fast-serve
```

This will start the configuration. Most of the time, you don't need to configure anything, except confirming the new packages' installation through npm install.

Behind the scenes, the utility updates the package.json file to add some required dependencies and a new npm command, "serve":

```
"scripts": {
    "build": "gulp bundle",
    "clean": "gulp clean",
    "test": "gulp test",
    "serve": "fast-serve"
},
```

It also adds a custom task to the SPFx build rig in gulpfile.js to integrate within the SPFx build rig sequence for the bundling part:

```
/* fast-serve */
const { addFastServe } = require("spfx-fast-serve-helpers");
addFastServe(build);
/* end of fast-serve */
```

If you modified the default SPFx webpack configuration in gulpfile.js, you need to update the Fast Serve webpack config (located in fast-serve/webpack.extend.js) as well with the same configuration. This is because the SPFx Fast Serve tool doesn't use the default SPFx configuration to run.

By default, this file doesn't exist and must be created using the following command:

```
npx fast-serve webpack extend
```

Once created, replicate the changes you made in the build.configureWebpack.mergeConfig file. For instance, take the following configuration made in the gulpfile.js file:

```
build.configureWebpack.mergeConfig({
  additionalConfiguration: (generatedConfiguration) => {
    generatedConfiguration.module.rules.push(
      {
        test: /\.js$/,
        use: {
          loader: 'babel-loader',
          options: {
            presets: [
              ["@babel/preset-env", {"targets": {"ie": "11"}}]
            ]
          }
        }
      }
```

```
    );
    return generatedConfiguration;
  }
});
```

It will be replicated in the `fast-serve/webpack.extend.js` file like this:

```
const webpackConfig = {
  module: {
    rules: [
      {
        test: /\.js$/,
        use: {
          loader: 'babel-loader',
          options: {
            presets: [
              ["@babel/preset-env", {"targets": {"ie": "11"}}]
            ]
          }
        }
      }
    ]
  }
}
```

Once your configuration is ready, you can use the `npm run serve` command (different from `gulp serve`!) to serve your solution locally:

```
PROBLEMS    OUTPUT    DEBUG CONSOLE    TERMINAL    ···    [>] node  + ∨  ▯  🗑  ···  ∧  >

[21:10:08] Finished 'bundle' after 15 s
[21:10:08] ==================[ Finished ]==================
[21:10:09] Project packt-solutions-product-management version:0.0.1
[21:10:09] Build tools version:3.18.1
[21:10:09] Node version:v18.20.4
[21:10:09] Total duration:18 s
[21:10:11] [fast-serve] To load your scripts, use this query string: ?debug=tr
ue&noredir=true&debugManifestsFile=https://localhost:4321/temp/manifests.js
<i> [webpack-dev-server] Project is running at:
<i> [webpack-dev-server] Loopback: https://localhost:4321/, https://[::1]:4321
/
<i> [webpack-dev-server] Content not from webpack is served from 'C:\VS\Packt\
Packt.Solutions.ProductManagement\temp' directory
<i> [webpack-dev-server] 404s will fallback to '/index.html'
```

Figure 21.8 – Example of solution served locally with Fast Serve tool

Now, every time an update is made to your code, the compilation will be done just on updated files, and the overall process will be significantly faster, improving your development times.

Now that we have covered the main tools and libraries you should look at, let's wrap things up and summarize.

Tools and libraries summary

The following table summarizes the main tools and libraries we think you should know as an SPFx developer:

Tool or library	What does it do?	Why should you use it?
PnPjs	JavaScript library to use the SharePoint REST API and the Microsoft Graph API using a fluent syntax.	To facilitate your work with these APIs, especially for complex scenarios such as paging or batching.
PnP React/ Property Controls	Provides reusable React controls and property pane controls.	To save you time for common UI requirements in component interfaces and the property pane.
Microsoft Dev Proxy	Simulates API failures using a command-line tool.	To improve code quality and error-handling scenarios in your components for hard-to-test network and API failures.
SPFx Fast Serve	Improves the bundling time for locally served solutions.	To hugely improve your development time when testing your solution locally.
PnP Modern Search	Provides highly customizable Web Parts to build search experiences in SharePoint	To save you development time and not reinvent the wheel for a use case already solved by this solution.

Table 21.1 – Summary of community tools and libraries for SPFx

Summary

As we've seen in this chapter, the SPFx ecosystem and beyond benefit from a very active community. Through the PnP initiative, a lot of tools, libraries, and samples are already out there to help you build awesome solutions in various areas.

You can also benefit from ad hoc tools such as Dev Proxy and SPFx Fast Serve to improve your development experience and increase the overall quality of your solutions.

In the next and last chapter of this book, we'll cover alternative approaches to set up your environment to build SPFx solutions leveraging tools such as Docker and GitHub Codespaces.

Get This Book's PDF Version and Exclusive Extras

UNLOCK NOW

Scan the QR code (or go to packtpub.com/unlock). Search for this book by name, confirm the edition, and then follow the steps on the page.

Note: Keep your invoice handy. Purchases made directly from Packt don't require an invoice.

22
Development Platforms

In the previous chapter, we saw how we can take advantage of the tools and libraries provided by the open source community and how we can use them in our SPFx projects.

In this chapter, we will switch our theme slightly and understand what platforms can be used for developing SPFx solutions, apart from creating and running them from our local machine directly. Specifically, we will look at the following options:

- **Docker**
- **GitHub Codespaces**
- **Windows Subsystem for Linux (WSL)**
- **Azure virtual machines**

Through the course of this chapter, we will understand the following:

- Why using virtualization is an option for SPFx development
- What some of the virtualization options are

> **Disclaimer**
>
> This is more of a supporting chapter as it covers information that is additional to SPFx development. The concepts explained in this chapter can be applied to non-SPFx projects as well. Since this is an optional chapter, we have added links to external resources that provide detailed information where necessary.

Understanding the need for virtualization

While developing solutions (be it SPFx or non-SPFx), we might think of developing/running our code in a different environment rather than directly on our local machine. This might be because of several reasons. A couple of them are listed here:

- We do not want to have a single version of Node.js on our local machine, as different projects might need different versions.

- The dependencies that are needed for one project might vary from other projects, and there might be a clash of the versions of dependencies. This might be problematic as the versions need to keep changing every time we switch the project we are working on.

- If we want multiple people working on a project, we want them to get set up quickly for the project so that they can start coding right away and not spend time installing all the dependencies from scratch.

For these reasons, having a separate isolated place to develop solutions would make sense, as these isolated places are independent of each other and can have their own dependencies installed without clashing with other isolated places.

A few years back, creating such an isolated environment would have needed a lot of effort. However, that is not the case anymore.

How does virtualization work for SPFx?

When we want to create an SPFx solution on our local machine, we install several dependencies, run several commands, and finally, get the solution working by running the `gulp serve` command, which then exposes port `4321` on our machine. This means that our local machine becomes a server and hosts the code on port `4321`, which is accessed in the workbench page for checking and debugging the code.

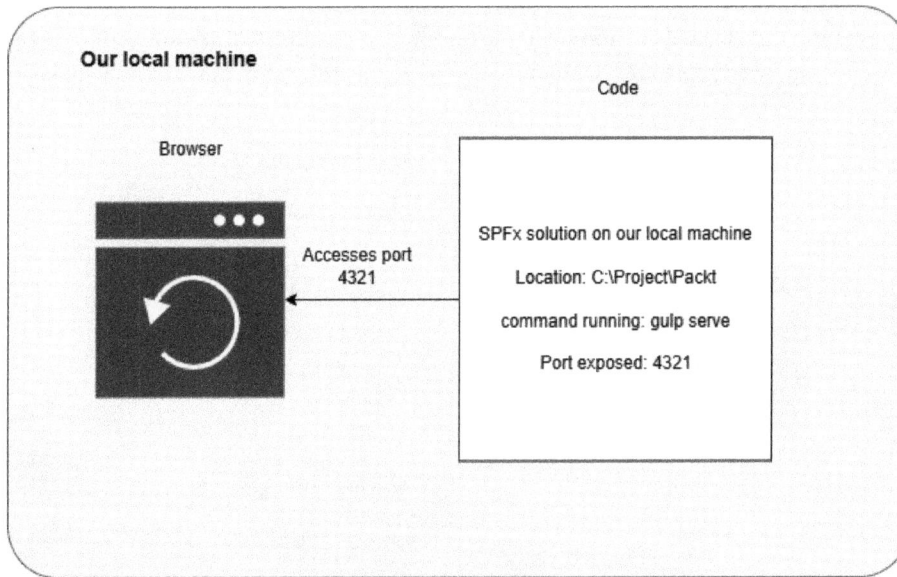

Figure 22.1 – SPFx on our local machine

With virtualization, the code is running in an isolated environment. This isolated environment can be either on our local machine (as a separate part, with its own operating system) or the isolated environment can be a machine in the cloud.

We then access the isolated environment using a code editor (e.g., VS Code).

There are a couple of ways in which this isolated environment can be set up:

- This isolated environment can be blank, and we install the SPFx dependencies
- Or, we can use an isolated environment, which will have the instructions on what dependencies are needed, and those dependencies get installed when we spin up the isolated environment

After that, we run the `gulp serve` command on this isolated environment, with which the isolated environment becomes the server, and the code will be hosted on port 4321 of the isolated environment. We can then use a concept called *port forwarding*, with which port 4321 is forwarded to our local machine, and we use that in the browser of our local machine to check and debug the SPFx code.

So, the code runs in this isolated environment, the resources of the isolated environment are used for hosting the code, and we simply access that hosted code in the browser of our local machine.

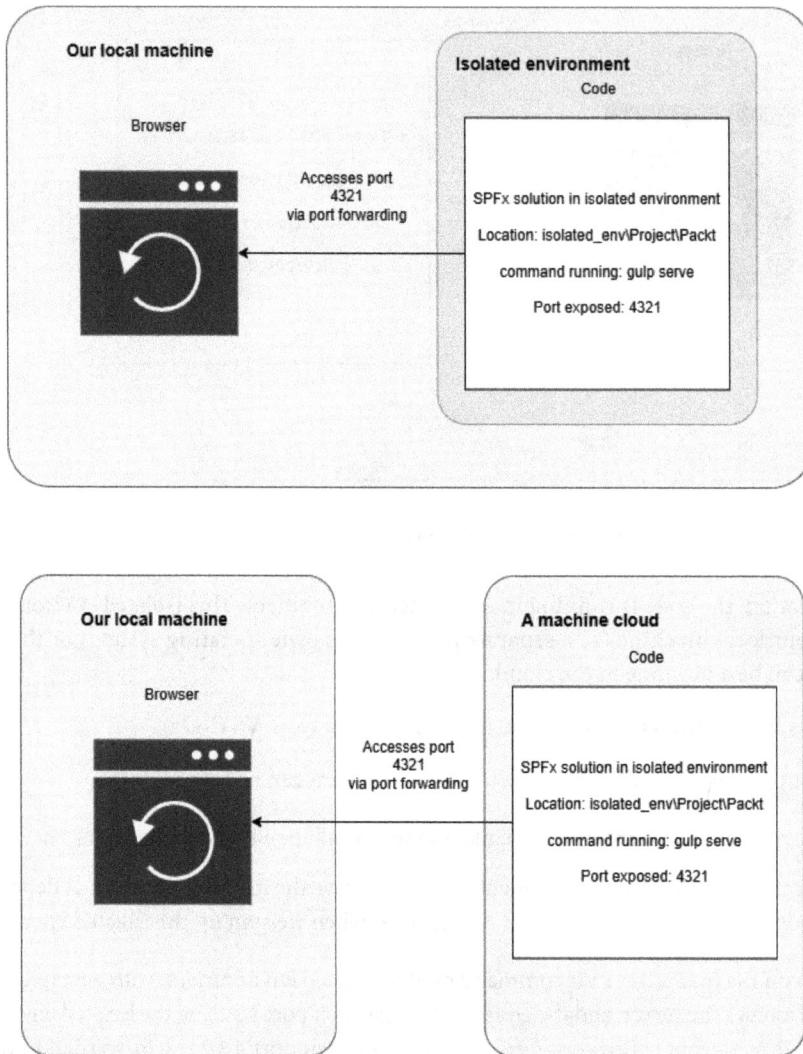

Figure 22.2 – SPFx code virtualization

As shown in the previous figure, our local machine is not responsible for hosting the code, running it, and having the dependencies installed. That is all taken care of by the isolated environment. Our local machine simply accesses the code running in the isolated environment.

By using editors such as VS code, we can easily access the code from an isolated environment and edit the code easily. In that way, the experience is such that we work on the code as if we have the code on our local machine directly. So, as developers, we won't feel the difference in development.

Now that we have an idea about virtualization for SPFx, let's take a look at the options available for virtualization.

Docker

Docker is one of the most popular virtualization solutions. It can be thought of as a virtual machine that runs code isolated from the main operating system of the local machine.

> **Note**
>
> Before delving further, please go through this documentation: `https://docs.docker.com/`.

Most Docker images are Linux-based. However, there are Windows-based ones as well. Docker images have required dependencies installed based on the type of project they are needed for. For SPFx projects, there is also a Docker image available, which is maintained by the open source community. There are images for different SPFx versions, and they can be found at `https://github.com/pnp/docker-spfx`.

The instructions at that link clearly explain how to get started with SPFx development using Docker. After setting up Docker and following those instructions, you will not find any differences in the experience of developing locally, despite the fact that there are no dependencies on the host machine and everything is running in an isolated container on your machine.

We can then share the code along with the Docker file in a repository (DevOps, GitHub, or any other). Our colleagues who want to work on the project can set up Docker on their machines and start working on the SPFx code from the repository. All the dependencies will be present in the Docker container.

GitHub Codespaces

Another option for virtualization is GitHub Codespaces. As mentioned in the official documentation (`https://docs.github.com/en/codespaces/about-codespaces/what-are-codespaces`), codespaces provide *"development environments that are hosted in the cloud."* With this option, all the code is hosted in the cloud and not on our local machine. The code also runs in the cloud by using the resources (compute and disk) in the cloud. All we do on our local machine is access codespaces using an editor such as VS Code.

> **Note**
>
> Before proceeding further, it is recommended to read this guide, which explains GitHub Codespaces and VS Code: `https://code.visualstudio.com/docs/remote/codespaces`.

In order to work with codespaces, we need a GitHub repository. The process is as follows:

1. Start with an empty GitHub repository.
2. Create a codespace in that repository.

These codespaces are usually Linux-based. We can start with an empty codespace and set up SPFx by running the required commands: `https://learn.microsoft.com/en-us/sharepoint/dev/spfx/set-up-your-development-environment`.

The other option is, in the GitHub repository, we can create a folder called `.devcontainer`, and this folder can have files that will be responsible for setting SPFx as soon as the codespace starts for the very first time.

> **The .devcontainer folder**
>
> The files in the `.devcontainer` folder have instructions on what to run when a container starts. This container can either be a Docker container or a codespace.
>
> More information on dev containers can be found here: `https://docs.github.com/en/codespaces/setting-up-your-project-for-codespaces/adding-a-dev-container-configuration/introduction-to-dev-containers`.
>
> For SPFx projects, a sample `.devcontainer` folder can be found here: `https://github.com/pnp/sp-dev-fx-webparts/tree/main/samples/react-at-a-glance/.devcontainer`. It is recommended to understand the files present in that folder.
>
> The `devcontainer.json` file specifies the configuration for the codespace; in this case, it says which base image to use, and that image, in this particular case, is an SPFx Docker image. In the `devcontainer.json` folder, there is an instruction to run the `spfx-startup.sh` file. This file has commands to install npm dependencies and copy the certificate and trust it.

So, the `devcontainer.json` file sets up the codespace and then asks the codespace to run the `spfx-startup.sh` file.

This is one of the many ways of setting up the `devcontainer` folder. More information on this setup can be found by visiting this link: `https://aka.ms/spfx-devcontainer`. We can have a different setup as well (if needed), to suit our requirements.

Once the codespace is set up, we can access it from an editor such as VS Code from our local machine, create a new SPFx solution in that codespace, and run `gulp serve`.

The code runs in the codespace, and port 4321 from that codespace is forwarded to our local machine, after which we follow the normal process of working with the code.

Once done, the code can be committed back to the GitHub repository. If our colleagues want to work on the SPFx solution, then they can use the same GitHub repository, creating a codespace under their GitHub account for this repository. It will take a couple of minutes for the codespace to be set up, so they can start working on the code quickly.

WSL

WSL, as the name suggests, means running Linux on a Windows machine. It is a feature in Windows that lets us run a Linux environment on a Windows machine, alongside a regular Windows desktop and applications, without needing a virtual machine or dual booting. More information on WSL and how to set it up can be found here: `https://learn.microsoft.com/en-us/windows/wsl/about`.

The idea of using WSL for SPFx development is such that we set up SPFx on WSL by following the instructions at `https://learn.microsoft.com/en-us/sharepoint/dev/spfx/set-up-your-development-environment`. After which, we can start the SPFx development, like we have been doing in this book. In this way, WSL becomes the isolated container where the SPFx code runs.

The other option is installing Docker on WSL and using Docker containers within WSL to develop SPFx projects.

With these two ways, SPFx code runs in an isolated environment on our local machine. The resources dedicated to that isolated environment are used for running the code. After running the SPFx code, port 4321 is forwarded from that environment to the host (i.e., our local machine).

A code editor such as VS Code can be used to access the code running on WSL.

Note that WSL is applicable only when our local machine is running the Windows operating system.

Azure virtual machines

Another option for virtualization is using **virtual machines** (**VMs**) in the cloud. Azure is one such cloud provider. We can create virtual machines in Azure and use them for SPFx development. This option needs to be used cautiously as Azure machines might have higher costs based on the configuration. More details on Azure VMs can be found by visiting this link: `https://azure.microsoft.com/en-us/products/virtual-machines`.

One of the ways of using Azure VMs for SPFx development is as follows:

1. Create a Linux-based VM and connect to the VM using **Secure Shell** (**SSH**) by following the instructions provided by Microsoft: `https://code.visualstudio.com/docs/remote/ssh-tutorial`.

2. Set up SPFx on the VM. This can be done by using the instructions provided here: `https://learn.microsoft.com/en-us/sharepoint/dev/spfx/set-up-your-development-environment`.

3. Once done, the SPFx code will be running on the VM, and we will access the code with an editor such as VS Code.

With this, we will not access the interface of the VM; we will only access a folder on the VM via a code editor using SSH. (The folder will have the SPFx code.)

Port `4321` from the VM is forwarded to our local machine, and we can access the SPFx components in the browser on our local machine.

All the resources and compute of the VM are used for running the code. Only the editor from our local machine is used to access the code.

This concludes the options for the virtualization of developing SPFx solutions.

Summary

In this short chapter, we saw how we can use virtualization to develop SPFx solutions. SPFx code can run in an isolated container, and we saw four options for such isolated containers: Docker, GitHub Codespaces, WSL, and Azure VMs. It is not mandatory to use virtualization for SPFx development; however, based on the advantages of virtualization, it can be considered for development.

This brings us to the end of our journey on mastering SharePoint development with SPFx. We have made it. There was a lot of information to cover, and we (Franck and Anoop) have tried to provide the essential information that you need to get started with SPFx development. We hope that you have enjoyed the SharePoint development journey.

Thank you once again for taking the time to read this book, and we wish you all the best in your SharePoint development journey.

Thank you also for your commitment to delivering high-quality software. May your testing endeavors be successful, fulfilling, and rewarding.

Get This Book's PDF Version and Exclusive Extras

UNLOCK NOW

Scan the QR code (or go to packtpub.com/unlock). Search for this book by name, confirm the edition, and then follow the steps on the page.

Note: Keep your invoice handy. Purchases made directly from Packt don't require an invoice.

23
Unlock Your Exclusive Benefits

Your copy of this book includes the following exclusive benefit:

- ⌂ Next-gen Packt Reader
- 📄 DRM-free PDF/ePub downloads

Follow the guide below to unlock them. The process takes only a few minutes and needs to be completed once.

Unlock this Book's Free Benefits in 3 Easy Steps

Step 1

Keep your purchase invoice ready for *Step 3*. If you have a physical copy, scan it using your phone and save it as a PDF, JPG, or PNG.

For more help on finding your invoice, visit `https://www.packtpub.com/unlock-benefits/help`.

> **Note**
> If you bought this book directly from Packt, no invoice is required. After *Step 2*, you can access your exclusive content right away.

Step 2

Scan the QR code or go to `packtpub.com/unlock`.

On the page that opens (similar to *Figure 23.1* on desktop), search for this book by name and select the correct edition.

Figure 23.1: Packt unlock landing page on desktop

Step 3

After selecting your book, sign in to your Packt account or create one for free. Then upload your invoice (PDF, PNG, or JPG, up to 10 MB). Follow the on-screen instructions to finish the process.

Need help?

If you get stuck and need help, visit
`https://www.packtpub.com/unlock-benefits/help`
for a detailed FAQ on how to find your invoices and more. This QR code will take you to the help page.

> **Note**
>
> If you are still facing issues, reach out to `customercare@packt.com`.

Index

‹packt›

packtpub.com

Subscribe to our online digital library for full access to over 7,000 books and videos, as well as industry leading tools to help you plan your personal development and advance your career. For more information, please visit our website.

Why subscribe?

- Spend less time learning and more time coding with practical eBooks and Videos from over 4,000 industry professionals
- Improve your learning with Skill Plans built especially for you
- Get a free eBook or video every month
- Fully searchable for easy access to vital information
- Copy and paste, print, and bookmark content

Did you know that Packt offers eBook versions of every book published, with PDF and ePub files available? You can upgrade to the eBook version at packtpub.com and as a print book customer, you are entitled to a discount on the eBook copy. Get in touch with us at customercare@packtpub.com for more details.

At www.packtpub.com, you can also read a collection of free technical articles, sign up for a range of free newsletters, and receive exclusive discounts and offers on Packt books and eBooks.

Other Books You May Enjoy

If you enjoyed this book, you may be interested in these other books by Packt:

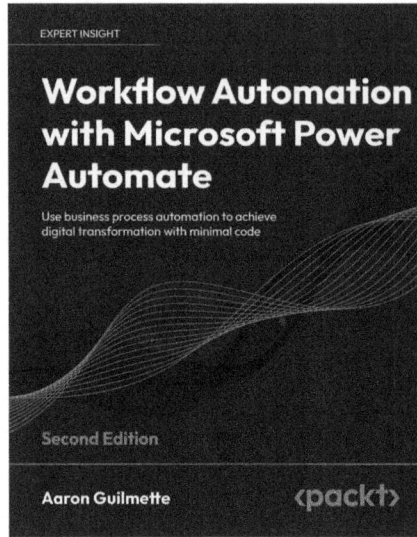

Workflow Automation with Microsoft Power Automate, Second edition

Aaron Guilmette

ISBN: 978-1-80323-767-1

- Learn the basic building blocks of Power Automate capabilities
- Explore connectors in Power Automate to automate email workflows
- Discover how to make a flow for copying files between cloud services
- Configure Power Automate Desktop flows for your business needs
- Build on examples to create complex database and approval flows
- Connect common business applications like Outlook, Forms, and Teams
- Learn the introductory concepts for robotic process automation
- Discover how to use AI sentiment analysis

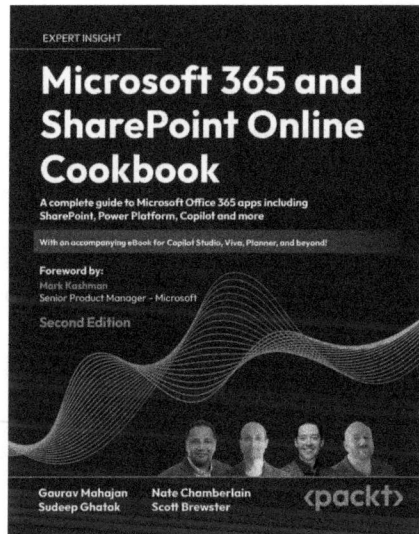

Microsoft 365 and SharePoint Online Cookbook

Mahajan, Sudeep Ghatak, Nate Chamberlain, Scott Brewster

ISBN: 978-1-80324-317-7

- Collaborate effectively with SharePoint, Teams, OneDrive, Delve, Search, and Viva

- Boost creativity and productivity with Microsoft Copilot

- Develop and deploy custom applications using Power Apps

- Create custom bots using Power Virtual Agents (Copilot Studio)

- Integrate with other apps, automate workflows and repetitive processes with Power Automate/ Desktop (RPA)

- Design reports and engaging dashboards with Power BI

- Utilize Planner, To Do, and gather feedback with polls and surveys in Microsoft Forms

- Experience seamless integration in the mobile platform

Packt is searching for authors like you

If you're interested in becoming an author for Packt, please visit `authors.packtpub.com` and apply today. We have worked with thousands of developers and tech professionals, just like you, to help them share their insight with the global tech community. You can make a general application, apply for a specific hot topic that we are recruiting an author for, or submit your own idea.

Share Your Thoughts

Now you've finished *Practical SharePoint Framework (SPFx) Development*, we'd love to hear your thoughts! Scan the QR code below to go straight to the Amazon review page for this book and share your feedback or leave a review on the site that you purchased it from.

https://packt.link/r/1-835-46678-8

Your review is important to us and the tech community and will help us make sure we're delivering excellent quality content.